FIELDWORK EXPERIENCE Qualitative Approaches to Social Research

FIELDWORK EXPERIENCE
Qualitative Approaches to Social Research

Edited by

WILLIAM B. SHAFFIR *McMaster University*
ROBERT A. STEBBINS *University of Calgary*
ALLAN TUROWETZ *Dawson College*

ST. MARTIN'S PRESS *New York*

Library of Congress Catalog Card Number: 80-50015.
Copyright © 1980 by St. Martin's Press, Inc.
All Rights Reserved.
Manufactured in the United States of America.
43210
fedcba

For information, write St. Martin's Press, Inc.,
175 Fifth Avenue, New York, N.Y. 10010

cloth ISBN 0-312-28844-1
paper ISBN: 0-312-28845-x

Acknowledgments:
P. 292: Peter Letkemann, CRIME AS WORK, © 1973. Adapted by permission of
Prentice-Hall, Inc., Englewood Cliffs, New Jersey.

10-21-87

w co

to Rivka, Yael, and Elichai
Karin
Gail, Esther, Carol, and Manfred

Preface

Reports about field research usually describe the methods and techniques of the research. Less often do they tell of the researcher's social and emotional experiences: anxiety and frustration, as well as exhilaration and pride in achievement. These topics are more often discussed in personal conversations between field researchers than written about in the literature. But in fieldwork the social and emotional side of the research is more problematic than in any other form of inquiry. Frequently the formal rules and canons of research must be bent or twisted to accommodate the demands of the specific fieldwork situation and the personal characteristics of the investigator.

Learning about the research experiences of others is essential for students because it enables them to anticipate more accurately the trials and rewards of their own research efforts. In this book field researchers discuss both the methodological decisions and the personal experiences and choices behind their studies of society.

The book is organized into four parts that correspond to the chronology of field research: getting in, learning the ropes, maintaining relations, and leaving the field. The general introduction describes the nature of fieldwork and presents a discussion of its history and the main issues researchers have to confront: validity and reliability, ethics, and the problem of dealing with unfamiliar situations. The introduction to each part further describes the different stages of fieldwork and considers the recent literature.

Each of the contributions in this book is original, specially solicited for publication here. We believe these selections demonstrate a healthy and productive approach to social research, one that will benefit the student as well as the instructor teaching field research methods.

Between early drafts of the manuscript and publication, several revisions have been made. We are grateful for the comments and helpful suggestions of John Johnson and Stanford Lyman, as well as those of anonymous reviewers. We appreciate the cooperation and support of St. Martin's Press.

William B. Shaffir
Robert A. Stebbins
Allan Turowetz

Contents

FIELDWORK EXPERIENCE
Qualitative Approaches to Social Research

The person who cannot abide feeling awkward or out of place, who feels crushed whenever he makes a mistake— embarrassing or otherwise—who is psychologically unable to endure being, and being treated like, a fool not only for a day or week but for months on end, ought to think twice before he decides to become a participant observer.

Rosalie Wax, *Doing Field Work*

Introduction

Fieldwork must certainly rank with the more disagreeable activities that humanity has fashioned for itself. It is usually inconvenient, to say the least, sometimes physically uncomfortable, frequently embarrassing, and, to a degree, always tense. Sociologists and anthropologists, among others in the social sciences, have voluntarily immersed themselves for the sake of research in situations that all but a tiny minority of humanity goes to great lengths to avoid. For instance, James Jacobs (1974) spent the better part of four months doing on-the-spot observation of prisoners and staff in an institution rife with rumor, suspicion, factionalism, and open conflict, which occasionally engulfed even him. Jean Briggs (1970) gained intimate knowledge of an isolated Eskimo band by living with them through thick and thin for over a year and a half. It was months before she knew their language well enough even to ask simple questions and understand the answers. By taking a job as a taxi driver, James Henslin (1968) was able to conduct a firsthand study of the trust relationship that exists between many drivers who are in highly vulnerable positions, and their fares, who include drunks, criminals, and hostile members of other races and ethnic groups.

For most researchers the day-to-day demands of fieldwork are regularly fraught with feelings of uncertainty and anxiety. The process of becoming immersed over an extended period of time in a way of life that is often both novel and strange exposes the researcher to situations and experiences that are usually accompanied by an intense concern with whether the research is conducted and managed properly. Researchers' fieldwork accounts typically deal with such matters as how the hurdles blocking entry were successfully overcome and the emergent relationships cultivated and maintained during the course of the research; the emo-

3

tional pains of this work are rarely mentioned. In discussing anthropologists' fieldwork accounts, Freilich writes:

> Rarely mentioned are anthropologists' anxious attempts to act appropriately when they knew little of the native culture, the emotional pressures to act in terms of the culture of orientation, when reason and training dictated that they act in terms of the native culture, the depressing times when the project seemed destined to fail, the loneliness when communication with the natives was at a low point, and the craving for familiar sights, sounds, and faces (1970:27).

Despite the paucity of accounts describing the less happy moments of fieldwork, such moments are likely present in most, if not all, field research adventures. This is suggested both by the discussion of such problems in the literature (Gans, 1968; Hammond, 1964; Vidich, Bensman, and Stein 1964) and by the frequency with which they become topics of conversation among field researchers. The intensity of the fieldwork process is typically accompanied by a psychological anxiety resulting in a continuous presentation and management of self when in the presence of those studied:

> Especially at the end of the three-year period we . . . were longing for a release from sets of roles which had become stale. . . . For us . . . the change was articulated in terms of being able to return to our "real" or "preferred" selves. It meant a release from repeated clarifications and justifications, for one of the heaviest burdens of our role was that it was never self-explanatory. After three years, repeated efforts to validate our identities became tiresome, and the "song-and-dance act," as we termed it, assumed the weary, glassy-eyed, frozen smile delivery of a well-ingrained vaudeville routine. It meant freedom from the pains of walking the thin line between students and faculty, of pushing ourselves into situations where we felt we did not belong, or worse, were not wanted. We would be released from the necessities of being always jolly, always interested, always concerned, always available. We could again avoid individuals, we could tune out. We could separate ourselves from the continual psychological anxiety of being prepared to "suck everything in," of retaining in our minds sequences of events, verbatim quotes, until we could commit them to our notebooks in the safety of a secluded corner, or the greater privacy of a toilet (Olesen and Whittaker, 1968:46).

Nonetheless, after hearing field researchers discuss their work, one has to conclude that there are exceptional payoffs that justify the attendant hardships. And for these scientists, the payoffs go beyond the lengthy research reports that present sets of inductive generalizations based on direct contact with another way of life. Fieldwork, its rigors notwithstanding, offers many rewarding personal experiences. Among them are the often warm relations to be had with subjects, the challenges of understanding a new culture, and the anxieties to overcome. In short, entering the research setting, learning the ropes once in, maintaining working relations with the subjects, and making a smooth exit are difficult to achieve and a source of pride when done well.

From another perspective, the desire to do fieldwork is founded on motives that drive few other kinds of scientific investigation. To be sure, field researchers share with other scientists the goal of collecting valid, impartial data about some natural phenomenon. In addition, however, they gain satisfaction—perhaps better stated as a sense of accomplishment—from successfully managing the social side of their projects, which are more problematic than in any other form of inquiry. Though they raise questions of validity (Johnson, 1975:161), gratifying relations between observer and subjects frequently emerge in the field (Olesen and Whittaker, 1968; Stebbins, 1972). At the same time, being accepted by subjects as a group is crucial for conduct of the study (Cicourel, 1964:42). Observers must be able to convince their subjects (and sometimes their professional colleagues) that they can satisfactorily do the research and that their interests are of enough importance to offset the frequent inconvenience, embarrassment, annoyance, and exposure that necessarily accompany unbiased scientific scrutiny of any group. It is in attempting to solve this basic problem, which recurs throughout every study, that many of the unforgettable experiences of fieldwork occur.

Completion of a fieldwork project is also an accomplishment because the "situation of social scientists" (Lofland, 1976:13–18) discourages it so. Lofland notes that many social scientists are temperamentally unsuited for the stressful activity of such an undertaking, since they are rather asocial, reclusive, and sometimes even abrasive. Furthermore, all university-based research must be molded to the demands of the university as a large-scale organization. Getting acquainted with an essentially foreign way of life is further complicated when one is intermittently pursued after classes, before committee meetings, between deadlines, and elsewhere (e.g., Shaffir, Marshall, and Haas, 1979). To this is added the lack of procedural clarity that characterizes field research; there are few useful rules (as in other forms of social research) available for transforming chaotic sets of observations into systematic generalizations about a way of life. Then there is the preference of funding agencies for quantitative investigations, which pushes the fieldworker yet another step in the direction of marginality. Finally, the very style of reporting social scientific findings, abstruse and arcane as it tends to be, contrasts badly with the down-to-earth routines of the people under study. Finding it next to impossible to see themselves in the reports of projects in which they have participated, they are rendered ineffective as critics of the accuracy of the research.

Fieldwork is carried on by immersing oneself in a collective way of life for the purpose of gaining firsthand knowledge about some facet of it. As Blumer (1969:37) puts it, field research on another way of life consists of:

> Getting close to the people involved in it, seeing it in a variety of situations they meet, noting their problems and observing how they handle them, being party to their conversations and watching their way of life as it flows along.

Adopting mainly the methodology of participant observation—described as ". . . research characterized by a period of intense social interaction between the researcher and the subjects, in the milieu of the latter" (Bogdan and Taylor, 1975:5)—the researcher attempts to record the ongoing experiences of those observed in their symbolic world. This research strategy commits the observer to learning to define the world from the perspective of those studied and requires that he or she gain as intimate an understanding as possible about their way of perceiving life. To achieve this aim, the field researcher typically supplements participant observation with additional methodological techniques in field research, often including informal interviews, life histories, document analysis, and various nonreactive measures (Webb et al., 1966).

Most fieldwork procedures, at least initially, are unstructured and flexible. In other words, there are few, if any, preestablished categories into which the original data are cast. Needless to say, researchers approach reality with a perspective that will enable them to observe relevant data. In contrast to other research strategies that are principally intended to verify previously completed research, the fieldwork approach is most amenable to what Glaser and Strauss (1967) have termed "the discovery of grounded theory." In field research, data collection is shaped and influenced by emergent hypotheses and themes that develop in the course of the investigation. In other words, field research consists of the simultaneous tasks of data collection, coding, and analysis.

The other forms of social scientific research, all of which are more structured or controlled than fieldwork, are less adequately suited for gaining an intimate understanding of the routine of a group of people. Experiments, surveys, secondary data analyses, and the like are used to avoid the personal stress and validity and reliability problems that plague field investigation or to confirm more precisely generalizations that emerge from it. Unless extensive fieldwork has preceded these controlled studies, students of a particular collectivity or behavior pattern may build their detailed knowledge on a foundation of blissful ignorance of the most fundamental attitudes and actions of the people concerned.

While descriptions and analyses of the various dimensions of the field research experience have recently become more plentiful, it is unfortunate that the social aspects both underlying and shaping this experience have not received more critical attention. These social aspects, involving feelings of self-doubt, uncertainty, and frustration, are both inherent in field research and also the basic stuff of which this methodology consists. One purpose of this volume is to remedy this deficiency by highlighting a central feature of the field research process that has, to date, been neglected.

Field research is accompanied by a set of experiences that are, for the most part, unavailable through other forms of social scientific research. These experiences are bound together with satisfactions, embarrassments, challenges, pains, triumphs, ambiguities, and agonies, all of which blend into what has been described as the field research adventure (Glazer, 1972). It is difficult to imagine a field research project that does not include at least some of these features, however skilled and experienced the researcher. Anyone undertaking field research for the first time—usually an undergraduate or a graduate student—encounters a mix of these feelings but, unlike the seasoned investigator, locates the problem within the self as arising from inadequate preparation and experience. The second purpose of this volume, then, is to help students realize that what they are feeling is a natural part of the experience rather than an outcome of their bumbling and lack of expertise.

In attempting to follow what appears to be a natural history of field research, we have delineated four stages around which field experiences may be coordinated: entering the field setting; learning how to play one's role while there, whether it be that of researcher or someone else; maintaining and surviving the several kinds of relations involved; and leaving the setting. Though analytically separable, these stages merge and interweave at various points of the research since the investigator is required to perform different tasks associated with each of these stages concurrently.

This volume is organized around these four stages in the hope that it will provide the student with an accurate description of the sequence of steps involved in the fieldwork process. This manner of organization also presents a useful vehicle for underscoring the social dimensions of the fieldwork experience. We have asked the contributors to accentuate the personal and social aspects pertaining to their research activity while focusing their account as much as possible around a particular research stage. While some of the selections fail to deal exclusively with one stage, and instead relate and refer to others, this should not be judged as failure but rather as a reflection of the holistic nature of the fieldwork enterprise.

In short, our representative stages are not meant to trace the process by which field research is done. They are intended, however, to offer a convenient foothold for writing about what we judge is a neglected but relevant component of fieldwork methodology—the important influences of the social dimension.

HISTORY OF FIELDWORK

The history of fieldwork as a set of research techniques, an approach to data collection, can be related, in good measure, to the issues of validity and reliability, ethics, and study of the unfamiliar. In grappling with them, fieldwork procedure has gained in distinctiveness and respectability, and its place in the scientific process has been clarified.

Rosalie Wax (1971: Chapter 3), who has written one of the most extensive histories of fieldwork, points out that descriptive reporting of the customs, inclinations, and accomplishments of other societies dates back almost to the origin of writing. From the Roman period on, travelers have been so fascinated with the cultural differences they witnessed that they have recorded their observations as a matter of interest to themselves and their countrymen. And as world passage became easier in the late nineteenth century, so the accounts of "backward" peoples multiplied. Some of these "amateur" reports, as contemporary anthropologists refer to them, are accurate enough to be of scientific value.

While the travelers busied themselves writing biased accounts of foreigners, educated men, and sometimes women (e.g., lawyers, physicians, physical scientists, administrative officials), were gathering firsthand information on certain sections of their own society with which they were originally unacquainted. Charles Booth (1902), for example, combined statistical data with extensive interviewing and participant observation to complete a vast study of the working people of London. In fact, several investigations were conducted in the late nineteenth and early twentieth centuries in England, France, and Germany that used participant observation and interviews (sometimes supplemented by questionnaires) to produce data.

Bronislaw Malinowski (1922) was perhaps the first social scientist to live in a preliterate community for an extended period and to record objectively what he saw. His intimate involvement in the daily lives of his subjects is regarded as a turning point in the history of fieldwork procedure. He even wrote detailed descriptions of how he gathered his data.

Several decades later, former journalist and sociologist Robert Park and anthropologist Robert Redfield turned the University of Chicago into a center for participant observer-based fieldwork that was without parallel anywhere in the world. The first generation of sociologists here concentrated on subjects such as the hobo (Anderson, 1923), the ghetto (Wirth, 1928), the neighborhood (MacKenzie, 1923), and the gang (Thrasher, 1927). Succeeding generations of students and faculty examined, among others, French Canada (Hughes, 1943), an Italian slum (Whyte, 1943), and juvenile delinquents (Shaw and McKay, 1942); and still later, governmental agencies (Blau, 1955), a mental hospital (Goffman, 1961), and medical students (Becker et al., 1961). Unlike Malinowski, however, those who came under the influence of Park and Redfield at Chicago were expected to integrate their field data with the ideas of Weber, Simmel, Dewey, and other prominent social theorists of the day. Furthermore, the fieldwork of this period maintained its pristine state of pure scientific objectivity, which started with the colonial period and the dominance of natural science methods in world intellectual circles. As Barnes (1963:120) puts it:

> The ethnographer took for granted that the observations and records he made did not significantly disturb the behavior of the people studied. In the classical mechanics of the nineteenth century it was assumed that physical observations could be made without affecting the objects observed and in much the same way ethnographers assumed that in their researches there was no direct feed-back from them to their informants.

Barnes goes on to state that times have changed. Modern field research is apt to deal with literate people who can read the researcher's reports, write letters to influential authorities, perhaps sue. In response to this threat and others, ethics committees have emerged in many universities, where they assess proposed social research for its possible unfavorable impact on subjects. And modern field research frequently centers on topics within the investigator's society. Thus the possibility must be faced that some subjects, when in the researcher's presence, will not be candid in their behavior and conversations for fear that their actions and statements, which may be unacceptable to certain people, will become available to them. "There may still be an exotic focus of study, but the group or institution being studied is now seen to be embedded in a network of social relations of which the observer is an integral if reluctant part" (Barnes, 1963:121).

Meanwhile, certain trends have forced fieldworkers to clarify their position in the scientific process. The use of questionnaires was gaining widespread acceptance through the rising popularity of public opinion polling and its close association with the ideas of Paul Lazarsfeld and

Robert Merton (Wax, 1971:40). Rigorous research designs, quantitative data, statistical techniques, and mechanical information processing were becoming hallmarks of social scientific procedure, while fieldwork was being regarded more and more as an old-fashioned and "softheaded" approach.

In other words, while one of the widely acknowledged strengths of fieldwork has been its potential for generating seminal ideas, its capacity for effectively testing these ideas has been increasingly questioned. Field researchers helped to confuse its role by claiming Znaniecki's (1934) method of "analytic induction" as a model of their procedure. In analytic induction, hypotheses are not only generated from raw data but also tested by them. A lively debate sprang up some time later over the logical possibility of conducting both operations simultaneously (based on the same data) and over the general utility of analytic induction (see Robinson, 1951; Turner, 1953).

More than thirty years elapsed after the publication of Znaniecki's book before social scientists sorted out the place of inductive hypothesis-generating procedure in the broader scientific process. Glaser and Strauss (1967) have now firmly established that no procedure can concurrently generate and test propositions. The first requires flexibility, unstructured research techniques, intuition, and detailed description; the second uses control, structured techniques, precision, and logical movement from premises to conclusions. The "constant comparative method," as Glaser and Strauss refer to their approach, is most effective as a means of generating hypotheses and "grounded theory."

We have finally learned that fieldwork occurs at the beginning of the scientific process in any area of empirical inquiry. It constitutes exploratory research. As our knowledge about that area grows—as hypotheses grounded in direct field study begin to coalesce into a theory about it—fieldwork and its less structured techniques fade into the background. At the same time, more controlled techniques come forward. Today, some social science fields are largely or significantly exploratory in their procedural orientation, among them symbolic interactionism, anthropology, community psychology, and classroom studies. Others, such as small group research and family sociology, generally appear to have passed beyond this stage.

Though this has been the chief role of qualitative research, we are not claiming that, in its exploratory mission, it is always "preliminary" in its import. Exploratory studies have been so effective as to become classics—for example, Whyte's (1955) *Street Corner Society* or Goffman's (1959) *Presentation of Self in Everyday Life*. In these instances and others, social science has subsequently learned, through more controlled study, that the initial observations were empirically sound and theoretically significant.

Glaser and Strauss (1967:234–235) advance three reasons why exploratory investigations often turn out to be the final research on a particular topic. First, the qualitative findings are taken by social scientists to be final. Second, interest wanes in conducting further research on the phenomenon. Third, before reserachers can mount more rigorous studies of it, it has changed considerably.

A parallel history of growing self-consciousness about the special status of fieldwork is evident in the progression of its literature. Junker (1960:160) notes that in the first two decades of this century, the publications of field researchers contained little about their problems and experiences. He traces the tendency to discuss these matters in the final report, however briefly, to Robert and Helen Lynd's study of Middletown. But it was not until after 1940 that theoretical treatments of fieldwork issues and experiences began to occur with regularity. Even in 1960 Junker could write that "full accounts are still rare, considering the large number of field studies published and still coming off the presses" (1960:160–161). Since then, however, candid descriptions of fieldwork, which frequently touch on the issues of validity and ethics, have become routine in monographic reports. Several texts devoted exclusively or partially to this method have also been produced (e.g., Bogdan and Taylor, 1975; Douglas, 1976; Johnson, 1975; McCall and Simmons, 1969; Schatzman and Strauss, 1973), at least one of which urges researchers to present detailed accounts of their social relations and private feelings while in the field (Lofland, 1971:131). This book is a further expression of the present awareness among field researchers of their singular approach to social scientific data collection.

ISSUES IN FIELDWORK

Besides acquainting unseasoned field researchers with the nature of the experiences that await them, there are three reasons why a collection of accounts, such as contained in this volume, is valuable. Three issues traditionally considered in methodological discussions of the field approach are also affected by the nature of the researcher's experiences while gathering data: validity and reliability, questions of ethics, and study of the unfamiliar. Since field researchers are virtually part of the data collection process, rather than its external directors, their experiences there become critical.

Validity and Reliability

The problem of validity in field research concerns the difficulty of gaining an accurate or true impression of the phenomenon under study. The companion problem of reliability centers on the replicability of observations. It rests on the question of whether another researcher with similar methodological training, understanding of the field setting, and rapport with the subjects can make the same observations. In field research these two problems fall into the following categories:

> (1) reactive effects of the observer's presence or activities on the phenomena being observed; (2) distorting effects of selective perception and interpretation on the observer's part; and (3) limitations on the observer's ability to witness all relevant aspects of the phenomena in question (McCall and Simmons, 1969:78).

The experiences of the researcher bear on all three.

Reactive effects are the special behavioral responses subjects make because the observer is in the setting, responses that are atypical for the occasion. Webb and his colleagues (1966:13-21) treat four reactive effects that frequently invalidate social science data, two of which—"the guinea pig effect" and "role selection"—are germane here. In the first, subjects are aware of being observed and react by putting their best foot forward; they strive to make a good impression. In the second, which is closely related, they choose to emphasize one of several selves that they sense is most appropriate given the observer's presence.

Special reactive effects may take place when a researcher's rational appearances fail (Johnson, 1975:155-160). Observers are human, too. At times, they get angry, become sympathetic, grow despondent, and are unable to hide these sentiments. Jean Briggs' (1970:284-291) indignation at the Kapluna (white) fisherman who damaged a canoe owned by the Eskimos she was studying resulted in subtle ostracism that lasted three months. The validity of one's data is certainly jeopardized, in some measure, by such outbursts. Perhaps, too, maintaining rationality when emotion is conventionally expected produces the image of a researcher who is calloused or lifeless and to be treated accordingly.

Another condition under which reactive effects could blemish the quality of one's data is the disintegration of trust between observer and one or more subjects. Once the researcher has found or been placed in a role in the group being studied, whether that of observer or something more familiar to its members, a certain degree of trust develops whereby that role incumbent is allowed to participate in affairs expected of such people. Events and observer behavior that contradict the belief that the observer belongs in that position may break the bond of trust. Still more unfortunate, it may suddenly come to light that the observer is just that, an observer, rather than someone else—one of the chief hazards in operating as a concealed researcher. Though Jacobs (1974:231-232) operated openly, the trust he painstakingly established with the white inmates while observing at a maximum security penitentiary was shattered when they began to suspect him of aiding their rivals, the blacks. Thereafter, no useful data could be gathered from the whites.

Observers may also selectively perceive and interpret data in different ways, which ultimately biases their investigations. The most celebrated of these is "going native," or so thoroughly embracing the customs and beliefs of the focal group that the scientist becomes incapable of objective work. Certain other problems bear mention as well. Johnson (1975:151–155) points out how the apprehension that commonly attends entry to the field can slant the perception of events during one's early days there. Moreover, one's commonsense assumptions about life are disturbed during these initial weeks, causing one to see things that other people, with different presuppositions about everyday affairs, would miss.

Special orientations toward subjects, whether love, hate, friendship, admiration, respect, or dislike, also influence our views of these people and their behavior. One wonders what consequences the close bond between Doc and William F. Whyte (1955) or Tally and Elliot Liebow (1967) had for the observers' perceptions of these informants and the informants' social involvements. Undoubtedly there were both advantages and disadvantages to these arrangements. Of equal importance are the field researcher's relations with professional colleagues (Lofland, 1971:132–133). The personal and theoretical views of mentors and other significant scholars can imperceptibly channel our research vision.

The third category of validity and reliability problems deals with limitations on the observer's ability to witness all that is relevant to the study. For example, anthropologist John Barnes (1963:122) points out how the unavoidable involvement with the authorities who grant access to the field setting, who are often viewed in a special light by the subjects, can become the basis for exclusion from certain group affairs. The researcher suffers from a sort of guilt by association. More generally, close connections with any subject or agency may affect access because of what the subject or agency represents to the larger group.

Bogdan and Taylor (1975:50–51) discuss a related fieldwork predicament that can cut off researchers from events of great importance to them. Observers, having become established as individuals who are knowledgeable about the local scene, may be called upon to mediate conflict or advise on how to solve a problem. Those who follow this lead and try to help may find themselves alienated from members of the group whose lives were exposed by or who were opposed to the suggested solution.

The status of the researcher may engender still another type of observational limitation. One thorny status problem, prevalent in anthropology and sociology, is the exclusiveness of sex. Being male, for instance, tends to bar one from direct observation of female activities, as Shaffir

(1974:43) discovered while studying the Lubavitcher Chassidim of Montreal. He was forced to accept different orders of data for males and
females in that community. Rosalie Wax (1971:46) describes the exclusiveness of certain age and sex categories she encountered as a woman
scientist who has worked in several different groups.

All research is subject to the problems of reliability and validity.
Although they are common to the experiment and the survey, they are
also found in fieldwork. This general lack of confidence in the analysis of
and conclusions drawn from field data stems from the commonly held
view that the undisciplined procedures of fieldwork enable researchers, to
a greater degree than practitioners of other methodologies, to influence
the very situations they are studying, thereby flagrantly violating the
canons of scientific objectivity.

A common feature of all social science research is the subjects'
response to the "demand characteristics" of the investigation (Orne, 1962;
Rosenthal, 1970; Sherman, 1967).

> Researchers in the social sciences are faced with a unique methodo-
> logical problem: the very conditions of their research constitute an
> important complex variable for what passes as the findings of their
> investigations. . . . The activities of the investigator play a crucial
> role in the data obtained (Cicourel, 1964:39).

In the case of fieldwork, researchers' very attempts to establish rapport
with the people they are studying may be achieved at the expense of a
degree of accuracy as to how they normally behave or present themselves
in the situations being observed. Indeed, Jack Douglas (1976) argues, for
these reasons and others, that traditional methods of field research must be
discarded in favor of more penetrating or "investigative" procedures that
permit access to these private spheres of life. As Becker (1970:39-62) so
persuasively argues, however, in contrast to the more controlled methods
of laboratory experiment and survey interview, fieldwork is least likely to
permit researchers to bias results to correspond with their expectations.

> First, the people the field worker observes are ordinarily constrained
> to act as they would have in his absence, by the very social constraints
> whose effects interest him; he therefore has little chance, compared to
> practitioners of other methods, to influence what they do, for more
> potent forces are operating. Second, the field worker inevitably, by his
> continuous presence, gathers much more data and . . . makes and can
> make many more tests of his hypotheses than researchers who use
> more formal methods (Becker, 1970:43-44).

One way to attack the validity problem is to play back one's
observations to one's subjects either in verbal or in written form. From the
perspective of the experience of fieldwork, this practice tends to enhance

rapport with subjects (assuming the observations are of interest to them and of little threat) by casting them in the roles of local expert and helpful participant in the research project. "Member validation" is one of several contributions that informants often make.

Ethical Issues

Only part of the seemingly endless list of ethical issues that plague social scientists is germane to the social experience of fieldwork. These issues are of three kinds: ethics of concealment, changes in research interests, and violations of the researcher's moral code. The oft discussed questions of what to write about the group one has studied, how to protect confidentiality against legal proceedings, and the like are of greatest concern after leaving the field. They appear to play no significant role in the actual collection of data.

Of the three kinds, the ethics of concealment has been the most thoroughly examined in the professional literature. It has several facets, one being the issue of the covert observer, or social scientific investigator whose professional aims are unknown to the subjects. They take the individual for someone else, usually one of them. The majority of writers on this topic oppose concealment (e.g., Davis, 1961; Erikson, 1965; Gold, 1958:221–222), though some scholars argue the contrary (e.g., Douglas, 1976). One way in which this issue can affect the actual experience of fieldwork is recounted by Wallis (1977b:155), who secretly observed a Scientology group:

> At the Scientology lodging house the problem was equally difficult. The other residents with whom I dined and breakfasted were committed Scientologists and in a friendly way sought to draw me into their conservations. I found it difficult to participate without suggesting a commitment similar to their own, which I did not feel. Returning to the course material, I found as I progressed that I would shortly have to convey—either aloud or by my continued presence—assent to claims made by Ron Hubbard, the movement's founder, with which I could not agree and of which I could sometimes make little sense.

Even where the observer's true role is known, ethical considerations still arise when there is concealment of certain aspects of the project. Occasionally, its very aims are kept secret (cf. Janes, 1961:450). Or concealment may be more subtle, but no less questionable in the eyes of some scientists, when data are gathered by means of a hidden tape recorder, inadvertently overheard remarks, or intentional eavesdropping. These clandestine methods add tension to the conduct of fieldwork, since there is always the risk that what is hidden will somehow be uncovered. Finally, individual researchers may question the propriety of concealing opinions that are diametrically opposed to those held by their subjects. Howard Newby (1977:118), for example, suffered pangs of conscience of this sort when as a liberal university student he interviewed conservative farm workers about their political attitudes. On a related theme, Yablonsky (1965:72) sees the researcher's failure to moralize, when accompanied by an intense interest in deviant life styles, as de facto encouragement of the subject's aberrant behavior.

Changes in research interests are inevitable in field study, where one of the central aims is to discover data capable of generating original theory. Johnson (1975:58) notes how investigators may gain entry to a field setting by stating a particular set of interests, only to find themselves in a moral dilemma because their observations have spawned new interests, ones that the sponsors had no opportunity to consider. To make things worse, these new interests may touch on sensitive matters, where formal permission for observation or interviewing might never be granted.

Barnes (1963), among others, has written about the ethical conflict suffered by fieldworkers who feel compelled to engage in, or at least witness, illegal activities. Should such activities be reported? The agency whose permission has made the research possible may expect this will be done. Should researchers try to maintain or strengthen rapport with their subjects by participating in unlawful events when invited to do so? Polsky (1969:127), who has systematically observed criminals in their natural habitat, says that this is up to the individual investigator, but that, in the study of criminals anyway, one should make it clear what one is prepared to do and see and not to do and see. William Whyte (1955:313–317) got caught in the ethical dilemma of whether to vote in place of another man in a local mayoralty election.

While all field researchers are faced with ethical decisions in the course of their work, a review of the fieldwork literature reveals that there is no shared consensus concerning the researcher's duties and responsibilities either to those studied or to the discipline itself. As Roth has so aptly argued, the controversy between "secret research" and "non-secret research" is largely misguided. For all research is secret in some way. A more profitable line of investigation is to focus on ". . . how much secrecy shall there be with which people in which circumstances" (Roth, 1960:283). Most field researchers hold that some measure of responsibility is owed the people under study, though the extent of this conviction and its application are left to each researcher's conscience.

Studying the Unfamiliar

Dealing with the unfamiliar is bound to produce at least some formative experiences, whether in the course of doing research or something else. In field investigations the use of unstructured procedures, the pursuit of new propositions, and the participation in strange (for the scientist) activities are the stuff of which memorable involvements are made.

Unlike controlled studies, such as surveys and experiments, field studies avoid prejudgment of the nature of the problem and hence the use of rigid data-gathering devices and hypotheses based upon a priori beliefs or hunches concerning the research setting and its participants. Rather, their mission is typically the discovery of new propositions that must be more rigorously tested in subsequent research specially designed for this purpose (Glaser and Strauss, 1967). Hence, field researchers always live, to some extent, with the disquieting notion that they are gathering the wrong data (e.g., Gans, 1968:312), that they should be observing or asking questions about another event or practice instead of the present one. Or they are bewildered by the complexity of the field setting and therefore unable to identify significant dimensions and categories that can serve to channel their observing and questioning. These feelings of uncertainty that accompany unstructured investigation tend, however, to diminish as the investigator grows more familiar with the group under study and those of its activities that bear on the research focus.

Blanche Geer (1964:327) describes the confusion of her first days in the field as she set out to examine the different perspectives on academic work held by a sample of undergraduates:

> Our proposal seems forgotten. Of course, there were not enough premedical students at the previews (summer orientation for fresh-men) for me to concentrate on them. To limit myself to our broader objective, the liberal-arts college student, was difficult. The preview-ers did not group themselves according to the school or college of the University they planned to enter. Out of ordinary politeness ... I found myself talking to prefreshmen planning careers in engineer-ing, pharmacy, business, and fine arts, as well as the liberal arts. Per-haps it is impossible to stick to a narrow objective in the field. If, as will always be the case, there are unanticipated data at hand, the field worker will broaden his operations to get them. Perhaps he includes such data because they will help him to understand his planned objectives, but he may very well go after them simply because, like the mountain, they are there.

The requirement that one discover something only increases the anxiety of fieldwork. Nowhere does originality come easily. The field experience does offer a kaleidoscope of contrasts between the observer's routine world and that of the subjects. New patterns of behavior and thought flash before the observer's eyes. But the question is always: Are these of any importance for science? Researchers note these contrasts and often virtually everything else they perceive. Nevertheless, the ultimate goal is conceptual. One strives to organize these novel perceptions into some sort of grounded or inductive theory, which is done to some extent while still in the field. Some of the generalizations that constitute the emerging theory are born from on-the-spot flashes of insight. Herein lies the art of science. And these insightful moments can be among the most exciting of the fieldwork experience, while their absence can be exasperating, if not discouraging.

As if unstructured research procedure and obligatory discovery were not enough, field investigators must also be ready to cope with unfamiliar events. Furthermore, they need to learn new ways of behaving and possibly new skills, the mastery of which is crucial for success in their projects. Powdermaker (1968:419) describes this problem for the field anthropologist:

> During the first month or so the field worker proceeds very slowly, making use of all his sensory impressions and intuitions. He walks warily and attempts to learn as quickly as possible the most important forms of native etiquette and taboos. When in doubt he falls back on his own sense of politeness and sensitivity to the feelings of others. He likewise has to cope with his own emotional problems, for he often experiences anxieties in a strange situation. He may be overwhelmed by the difficulties of really getting "inside" an alien culture and of learning an unrecorded or other strange language. He may wonder whether he should intrude into the privacy of people's lives by asking them questions. Field workers vary in their degree of shyness, but most people of any sensitivity experience some feelings of this type when they first enter a new field situation.

MARGINALITY

If there is one especially well-suited adjective that describes the social experiences of fieldwork, it is "marginality." Field researchers and their activities are marginal in several ways.

For one, field research, because of its emphasis on direct human contact, subjective understanding of others' motives and wants, and broad participation in their daily affairs, is closer to the humanities than most forms of social scientific research. While structured data collection is now the most traveled methodological route in nearly every social science, fieldworkers are riding off in a different direction. For this they are scorned by many positivists, who see field research as weak science. From the humanists' perspective, however, it is still too scientific, owing to its concern with validity, testable hypotheses, replicability, and the like. The public, who might be expected to take a neutral stand in this intellectual debate, sometimes appears to have embraced the position that good social science is characterized by methodological rigor. Thus, it occasionally happens that field researchers also have to convince even their subjects and sponsors that theirs is a legitimate approach for the problem at hand.

Yet, the fieldworker who is identified as an atypical social scientist has an advantage. For here is a researcher who is viewed by group members as interested enough in them and their activities to maintain extensive direct contact instead of relying solely or chiefly on such substitutes as questionnaires and measurement scales. Many subjects appreciate this special effort. They seem to know that their lives are too complicated to be accurately and adequately studied by structured means alone. By the same token, it is to be expected that fieldworkers will make some subjects uneasy by their ability to plumb the group's dark secrets.

Field researchers are also marginal in their own professions (except in anthropology). Recall Lofland's (1976:13) observation that many social scientists are unsuited for engaging in field study. Being rather asocial, reclusive, and occasionally abrasive, they would fail to gain entrance to the setting to be examined, or, if they somehow succeeded, they would fail to maintain the level of rapport upon which good field research depends. Social scientists who have the requisite interpersonal skills to do fieldwork are in a minority; providing they discover their talents, they find occupational fulfillment in ways most of their colleagues see as strange or exotic.

Once in the field, all participant observers, if they are known as such to their subjects, are more or less marginal to their subjects' world. The former never quite belong—especially while the research is getting underway—a fact that is made amply clear time and again. As Hughes (1960: ix) argues, even though the sociologist might report observations made as a member of the group under study, ". . . the member becomes something of a stranger in the very act of objectifying and reporting his experiences." In a similar vein, Freilich, writing about anthropologists, cautions against the common desire among researchers to become a native:

> Irrespective of what role he assumes, the anthropologist remains a *marginal man* in the community, an outsider. No matter how skilled he is in the native tongue, how nimble in handling strange social relationships, how artistic in performing social and religious rituals, and how attached he is to local beliefs, goals, and values, the anthropologist rarely deludes himself into thinking that many community members really regard him as one of them (1970:2).

From the researcher's standpoint there are humbling experiences inherent in this kind of marginality. Lofland (1976:14) points out that one must admit to laymen that one is ignorant, though willing to learn. Such an admission is incongruent with the self-image of savant, dignified university professor, or learned Ph.D. As a field researcher, one is a mere student in need of particular instruction or general socialization.

What is worse, subjects have been known to take advantage of this situation and put on or mislead the observer about aspects of their lives of interest to the study (e.g., Wallace, 1965:198–199). Field researchers must be alert to such deception but be prepared to take it in good stride. Nonetheless, being the object of a put-on, while it adds zest to the subjects' routine, is frequently embarrassing to the "mark" (Stebbins, 1975).

And fieldwork, even when conducted in the researcher's own community, has been known to become all-absorbing, leaving time only for absolutely mandatory family and work activities. Marginality is the best characterization of the committed social scientist, who spends practically every waking minute riding with police or observing a juvenile gang, as did some of the contributors to this collection. As with professionals in any occupation, the line between work and leisure is sometimes erased for fieldworkers, which casts them in a strange light when viewed from the perspective of a leisure-oriented society.

On balance, marginality, despite its drawbacks, seems to breed a peculiar strain of motivation among committed field researchers. Being atypical in one's profession, to the extent that such a condition is free of stigma, has the potential appeal of salutary visibility, of being commendably different. Field researchers have stories to tell about their data collection exploits that enchant students and colleagues, most of whom have no such accounts to swap. Field researchers have "been around" in a way seldom matched by the run-of-the-mill social scientist. They have gained in personal sophistication through contact with other cultures and life styles and through solving thorny interpersonal problems in the course of completing their projects.

It is no wonder, then, that the fieldworkers whose social experiences are recounted in this book enjoyed their assignments so much. They are writing about events in their lives that are significant for themselves as well as for science. Some are also writing about an engrossing way of life that they have found in their occupation.

CONCLUSION

Social science textbooks on methodology usually provide an idealized conceptualization of how social research ought to be designed and executed. Only infrequently, however, do sociologists, and field researchers in particular, report on how their research was actually done. As most field researchers would admit, the so-called rules and canons of fieldwork are frequently bent and twisted to accommodate the particular demands and requirements of the fieldwork situation and the personal characteristics of the fieldworker. The following observations reflect this view clearly and accurately:

> As every researcher knows, there is more to doing research than is dreamt of in philosophies of science, and texts in methodology offer answers to only a fraction of the problems one encounters. The best laid research plans run up against unforeseen contingencies in the collection and analysis of data; the data one collects may prove to have little to do with the hypotheses one sets out to test; unexpected findings inspire new ideas. No matter how carefully one plans in advance, research is designed in the course of its execution. The finished monograph is the result of hundreds of decisions, large and small, made while the research is under way and our standard texts do not give us procedures and techniques for making these decisions. . . . I must take issue with one point . . . that social research being what it is, we can never escape the necessity to improvise, the surprise of the unexpected, our dependence on inspiration. . . . It is possible, after all, to reflect on one's difficulties and inspirations and see how they could be handled more rationally the next time around. In short, one can be methodical about matters that earlier had been left to chance and improvisation and thus cut down the area of guesswork (Becker, 1965:602–603).

> My discussions of theory, measurement, instrumentation, sampling strategies, resolution of validity issues, and the generation of valid causal propositions by various methods proceed on the assumption that once the proper rules were learned, adequate theory would be forthcoming. Unfortunately, of course, this is seldom the case. Each theorist or methodologist takes rules of method and inference and molds them to fit his particular problem—and personality. Concepts do not automatically generate operational definitions, and theories do not fall into place once all the data are in. Rather, theoretical formulations arise from strange sources—often out of personal experiences, haphazard conversations with friends and colleagues. And many times these formulations bear only a distant relationship to data (Denzin, 1970:315).

The following selections hardly constitute a recipe for doing field research. Because of the ever-changing social and political contexts in which research is undertaken, the ingredients for such a recipe can, at best, only be suggested. Instead of demonstrating how field research ought to be done, the selections point to some of the dynamics involved in doing it. We have conceptualized the social experience of the field research process in terms of four stages—getting in, learning the ropes, maintaining relations, and leaving the field—fully realizing their arbitrary nature. The stages are not necessarily sequential or distinct but, more likely, blend together, at times involving the researcher in matters pertaining to each simultaneously. That these stages are, in fact, complementary and interwoven in the actual execution of fieldwork is reflected in the difficulty encountered by some of the authors in organizing their material around a distinctive focal concern. We are inclined to believe that this difficulty stems from our somewhat arbitrary designation of research stages.

Our interest in this volume is to focus on the social dimension of field research. A shortcoming of our effort may be our failure to consider the relationship of this dimension to other aspects of the methodology. Fieldwork consists of a multitude of tasks, each bearing a relationship, at some point, to social and political considerations impinging upon the researcher. For instance, the processes of coding and analyzing field data, and the subsequent generation of theory, cannot be divorced from the range of social contingencies confronting the researcher. As indicated earlier, our modest aim is to direct attention to an insufficiently stressed component of fieldwork methodology and to stress that the problems and challenges posed by this approach are most accurately viewed as inherent in the doing of the methodology rather than attributable to the failings and shortcomings of the observer. It is here that we hope to have made a contribution.

1

Getting In

The 1960s and 1970s witnessed a renewed use of field research methods. Most of the literature on this subject focuses on discovering the research setting and establishing and maintaining good relations with subjects. For example, how adequately have sociologists analyzed the process of getting permission to conduct a study? Johnson (1975) claims that since entry must be gained before a study can begin, researchers' reports describe the seemingly unlimited range of possible problems. On the other hand, Schatzman and Strauss (1973) contend that since researchers become preoccupied with the flow of data upon gaining entry, little is known about the tactics employed to secure it.

A problem shared by all field researchers is getting in: securing permission to do the study, gaining access to people you wish to observe and talk to. This first phase of the research process accompanies another research requirement: developing rapport and thereby gaining initial acceptance from informants and respondents.

Upon entering the field, the researcher often faces different forms of resistance and suspicion. Regardless of the setting, efforts at getting in and developing rapport are matched by the wariness of prospective respondents, who raise questions and concerns about the fieldworker's presence and the purpose and outcome of the research project (Lofland, 1976). The way researchers identify themselves and their work is crucial in reducing these barriers. In the following discussion we will outline some of the highlights of the process of getting in, including the preresearch phase of the investigation, whether the research is overt or covert, whether it is viewed as beneficial by those granting permission, the nature of the research bargain, and the characteristics of the research setting.

Accounts describing gaining entry, or getting in, vary with the fieldworker and the situation. Researchers are cautioned about the variability of field settings and warned against inflexibility in gaining access. To date, fieldwork accounts have offered a general set of guidelines about this stage of the research process. While E.C. Hughes claims that the basic problems of field research are the same in all situations, he also maintains that ". . . the situations and circumstances in which field observation of human behavior is done are so various that no manual of detailed rules would serve" (1960:x). Although sociologists and anthropologists have attempted to outline these basic problems, researchers must still "play it by ear."

Successful entry is affected by the researcher's preparations. These include taking on both the general and specific characteristics of the people and setting to be studied and making certain decisions concerning procedures. Schatzman and Strauss claim that during this stage, which they call "casing and approaching," researchers examine the suitability of the setting—that is, whether the site meets their requirements—and consider the feasibility of the project—whether the size and complexity of the setting match their academic and personal resources. They must also decide on the most suitable tactics to learn about the place and people prior to negotiating entry (1973:19). Johnson (1975:56), too, pays special attention to these preparations and stresses that successful entry is not the beginning of the research but follows a preresearch phase. Familiarity with the routines, realities of factionalism, and the social structure of the proposed setting may facilitate the negotiations that follow. Fieldworkers must consider the options available to them during this period, for failure to do so will hamper the research effort.

Casing the research setting may result in defocusing the research— the methodological tactic of casting a wide net in an attempt to broaden the range of subjects and settings that might prove relevant to the research problem. Kotarba's, West's, and Lopata's contributions emphasize the utility of this approach. Unsure of the parameters shaping the population of chronic pain sufferers, Kotarba's data, derived from three types of resources—the community, the university, and personal contacts— provided a wealth of information on the utilization of medical and non-medical health care services, the relation of chronic pain to work and play, and the effects of chronic pain on self-image. In a discussion of access problems in studying deviant youth, West emphasizes the advantage of allowing the research problem and organizing concepts to "emerge" rather than seeking them from the outset. Such flexibility not only maximizes the chances for unanticipated discovery but, as important, allows for the development of topics and themes after access has been gained. Along these lines, Lopata informs us that before beginning her survey on widows she devoted considerable time to becoming sensitive to the forms of social interaction related to widowhood, including kinds of role involvements and modifications, social networks, types of loneliness and methods for coping with them, and emotional support systems.

Among the contributions of Spector's exploration of the application and modification of qualitative methodology for the study of elites and social controversies is his attention to the range of backstage preparation that the researcher must do before even meeting the informants. Library, documentary, and bibliographic research are critical elements of such work: they shape the researcher's sampling procedures and preparations for interviewing. The importance of preparatory research is also highlighted in West's discussion of how entry was initially achieved in his "drifting clusters," "greasers, freaks, and straights" and "thieves" research projects. Using his experience as a streetworker, he was able to recognize the characters and contours of the research setting and define the specific problems of his investigation.

The problems of getting in are also influenced by the decision to engage either in overt or covert research. This is largely a moral dilemma confronting all researchers. However, the discussion seems especially directed at field researchers.

Although the distinctions between these approaches are unclear and at times slight (Roth, 1962), overt research involves publicly identifying the fieldworker's research intentions; in the covert approach, the researcher's interests and goals are hidden or disguised. Arguments for and against both approaches have been addressed in detail (Davis, 1961; Erikson, 1967; Lofland, 1961).

The covert approach has two justifications. First, it is claimed that access to certain research settings would probably be denied if the researcher's intentions were known to the subjects. Second, it is argued that if the subjects are aware of the purpose of the research, they might wittingly or unwittingly manipulate and alter their daily routines. Proponents of overt research stress morality and question the appropriateness of investigating people without their consent.

The covert research approach eliminates the need to explain and justify the research. By posing as a potential convert, one can penetrate the group without negotiating entry. This advantage may, however, be soon offset by certain difficulties. A false pose often limits the range of expected and suitable questions and probes, thereby potentially limiting both the range and depth of the data collected. Our point here, however, is that the approach selected will probably facilitate or aggravate the initial attempts to gain access and develop rapport.

The chances of getting permission are increased when the researcher's interests are seen to coincide with those of the subjects. Gatekeepers of formal organizations may believe that the research will report favorably on an issue they wish publicized. Thus, the investigator's proposal must make sense to both gatekeepers and subjects. The researcher's theoretical problem is a practical matter for the group. As Wax (1952:34–37) claims, the group wishes to know not only what the researcher is up to but also what they stand to gain by cooperating. For potential assistants, the theoretical sophistication of the research design or the relevance and significance of the problem are probably unimportant. Rejection and opposition are most likely to occur when the people we approach do not understand what we are doing and what we wish to know (Glaser, 1972).

Successful entry is also shaped by the bargain struck between researcher and subjects. Ideally, the researcher wishes to complete the work without interference. Securing a free hand is not easy. Research accounts have shown that the nature of the bargain may constrain maneuverability within the setting, sometimes undermining the research or even terminating the project (Diamond, 1964; Haas and Shaffir, 1978, Habenstein, 1970).

The formal bargain is likely to differ from the day-to-day reciprocities between researcher and group (Habenstein, 1970:5). As fieldworkers have sometimes painfully discovered, completing a successful bargain with the gatekeepers is no guarantee of full cooperation from the group members or even the gatekeepers themselves. Typically described as a set of mutual obligations concluded at the outset of the research, the bargain is conceptualized more accurately as a continuing process of negotiation that does not end until the research is published (Geer, 1970:85) and as an agreement in which promises between the various parties may shift and change over time. While the formal requirements are usually negotiated at the outset, getting in involves a continuous effort to establish, maintain, and cement relations. These relations may furnish complete access to the group's activities; they may, however, cast the researcher in one of many "crippling roles" (Wax, 1957) that limit observation.

The research bargain may be viewed as an exchange relationship between the researcher and those studied. In return for providing the researcher with information, respondents are usually guaranteed confidentiality and anonymity, which encourage honest answers to questions. Spector's analysis of the problems involved in studying elites and social controversies suggests that it may sometimes be necessary to modify this research bargain: sociological analyses of elites and social controversies would be incomplete if the identities of the individuals and organizations were suppressed.

The organization of the research setting may also influence the effort to secure access. In formal settings such as public bureaucracies or business corporations, permission is typically granted by those with authority and power. The researcher must usually contact such persons in order to get in. In contrast, less organized settings, such as ethnic communities and deviant subcultures, usually lack such authoritative positions. Thus, the researcher may informally penetrate the community. This point is related to Karp's claim that urban public places, with their distinctive normative structures, pose unique access problems for which the available field research literature offers little help. The author describes the access problems he faced while trying to learn about the behavior of Times Square pornographic bookstore and movie theater patrons. The well-elaborated privacy norms in these contexts constitute useful cases for highlighting the types of problems researchers can expect to face in a variety of public settings.

Whatever else may be involved, gaining successful access requires that the researcher find subjects who are willing to cooperate. A technique for successfully locating respondents used in the following selections is that of "snowballing," whereby the sample of respondents is generated by respondents themselves, who provide the researcher with names of others who might be contacted. West requested that subjects introduce him to other deviants; as part of his defocused attempts to locate pain-related phenomena, Kotarba mentioned his work to friends and acquaintances and successfully established valuable contacts; Hoffmann asked board members she knew to refer her to others; and Lopata relied upon a very heterogeneous social network to locate widows for interviewing. As West suggests, the snowball effect can also indicate the major social boundaries of respondents' worlds.

To reduce the uncertainties, field researchers have attempted to delineate the general considerations and tactics of getting in. Such attempts are meant to show that successful entry depends largely on sound fieldwork practices. In contrast, other field researchers argue that entry hinges on the personal judgments made of the researcher; the conventional wisdom of the field research literature is deemphasized. Wax's (1971:365) summary of the significance of personal attributes is to the point:

> In the long run, his hosts will judge and trust him, not because of what he says about himself or about his research, but by the style in which he lives anf acts, and by the way in which he treats them. In the somewhat shorter run, they will accept or tolerate him because some relative, friend, or person they respect, has recommended him to them.

This emphasis suggests that entering the field and cultivating rich relationships are due mainly to the researcher's personal attributes and to others' judgments of him or her as a human being.

The relationship between one's entry and the kind and amount of information one can collect is exemplified in Hoffman's study of hospital boards of directors and their elite membership. Her use of personal social ties provided access both to persons and qualitatively more insightful data than had been available before she marshaled her family connections. The analytical significance of Hoffman's selection lies in demonstrating that how the researcher is socially defined by members of the setting bears directly on the validity of the data subsequently collected. Identified by her respondents as a social peer, she enjoyed a trust relationship that ensured her successful penetration of the "old guard" membership's views concerning the reorganization of hospital boards of directors.

As suggested above, sociologists have paid scant attention to the personal dimensions of their research. Upon reading fieldwork accounts, the novice researcher may gain the mistaken impression that feelings of unease and anxiety, particularly in getting in, are due largely to inexperience. When focusing on the personal and social dimensions, however, one discovers that various aspects of field research are regarded as stressful and anxiety-laden (Schwartz and Schwartz, 1955).

Experienced researchers provide convincing evidence that feelings of uncertainty and self-doubt, particularly in getting in, are common. Hughes, for example, admits: "I have usually been hesitant in entering the field myself and have perhaps walked around the block getting up my courage to knock at doors more often than almost any of my students . . ." (1960: iv). In discussing the personal aspects of his research activity, Gans writes:

> Despite my success in gaining entry, the process is for me one of great anxiety. . . . Until I feel that I have been accepted, the research process is nerve-wracking; I lack the personal security to banish rejection or anxieties, to feel free to observe fully, and to take in as much data as possible (1968:310–311).

Finally, Wax (1971:20) draws attention to the anxieties and feelings of incompetence and stupidity experienced by the fieldworker, suggesting a circular and cumulative relationship between anxiety and competence. As the fieldworker becomes less anxious, the work improves, and this awareness of doing better work leads to less anxiety.

The influence of gaining entry on subsequent field experiences may vary sharply across research settings. Official permission may introduce the researcher to a highly suspicious group that is overly cautious and skeptical about cooperating. Alternately, successful entry can result in a solid relationship based on trust and cooperation, providing access to all group members and their activities. The many factors influencing the pace of entry suggest that this process may be speedy in some cases and very slow in others.

In describing field research, we have attempted to sketch some of the factors involved in getting in. Successful entry and researcher requests are influenced both by the nature of the research setting and how the researcher is defined by others. This phase of the research process occurs at the beginning, which often obscures its connection to later phases, especially the establishment of trust and rapport. As Schatzman and Strauss have written: ". . . how one gets in and manages to stay in will shape, if not determine, what one gets out of the site and its host" (1973:22). Glazer (1972:13) suggests that a fuller understanding of how the researcher gains initial acceptance is related to three components of the research relationship: (1) the appropriateness of the research project to the setting; (2) the researcher's personal makeup and his or her ability to enlist the support of others; and (3) the way respondents, given their personal needs and perspectives, view the project and the researcher.

Detailed exploration of the process of getting in may not only clarify the fieldworker's many and varied research roles but should eventually help delineate appropriate means of getting in. At this point, however, there is no simple formula that will guarantee successful entry. We hope that the following selections will provide some general advice. It will become clear that conditions affecting and determining access vary broadly across research settings.

Access to Adolescent Deviants and Deviance

W. GORDON WEST   *University of Guelph*

All social research involves the marshaling of data or empirical evidence which has relevance to the general claims (theories or propositions) being advanced or examined. Data gathering necessitates gaining access to the phenomena under study, either directly or by proxy through secondary analysis of previously gathered records (such as census material). Access is a particularly crucial aspect of participant observation research; this method attains its unique open-endedness and flexibility through the unusually wide and deep degree of access attained by the researcher. Whereas the typical experimenter or survey researcher asks for only a few minutes of the subjects' time to perform a simple task or answer a few questions, the participant observer asks subjects to share a considerable portion of their lives, setting only vague limits on demands.

Although participant observation of all social phenomena involves this basic problem of access, it is perhaps most central in research on deviance, which by its very nature is socially stigmatized and often illegal (Becker, 1970a). Deviants wish to hide their status from some members of society. Experiences in gaining access to deviant populations should therefore be instructive as a limiting or extreme case of gaining access to other populations.

Since the participant observer attempts, to some degree, to blend in with subjects, access problems are also exaggerated when certain of the researcher's ascribed characteristics differ markedly from those of subjects. In the research reported here, the marked age difference between child and adolescent subjects and myself as the adult researcher is such a barrier.

Although these difficulties in research may initially appear threateningly prohibitive, further reflection suggests some possible avenues of access. Almost all deviants have some relationships with nondeviants who come to know them. Most deviants commit deviant acts only part of the time and are quite normal otherwise (for instance, in their recreational activities). Since all of us have some secrets which we protect from others (Simmel, 1950), the problems of access are better seen as extreme in the study of deviants rather than unique.

Barriers of ascribed status are equally overcome. Without transcending such boundaries, mothers could not communicate with their children or guards with prisoners. Awareness of how we cross such boundaries should give us hope as well as clues for managing research. It should also make us realize that full participation and understanding are ideals rarely if ever achieved; nonetheless, our less-than-perfect knowledge is frequently pragmatically adequate.

In the following account of gaining access to deviant children and adolescents, the analytical problems mentioned above are illuminated with case study reports of research. Although I will refer to experiences related to me in fieldwork classes and thesis supervision by some one hundred student researchers, most of the following is heavily based on my own research experiences with preadolescent nongang delinquents in Toronto (West, 1968); "greasers," "freaks," and "straights" in Chicago (West, 1971; 1977a; 1977b; forthcoming); youthful Toronto thieves (West, 1974; 1978a; 1978b; 1978c); and misbehavers in Toronto classrooms (West, 1975). As indicated in the research reports cited, the subjects included both deviants and nondeviants and ranged in age from six to twenty-four, although most were involved in delinquency or crime and concentrated in the ten-to-twenty-year period. Fuller discussions of the research methodologies employed in these studies are available in the reports themselves and in West (1977c). Only brief reference will be made to more analytical literature available elsewhere (e.g., Becker, 1970a, 1970b; Berk and Adams, 1970; Irwin, 1972; McCall and Simmons, 1968; Schatzman and Strauss, 1973).

TOPIC AND ACCESS

Participant observers infrequently follow the traditional research sequence of first selecting a topic, then defining research questions and instruments, and finally encountering subjects and gathering data. Although topics are sometimes first selected on orthodox grounds (e.g., theoretical import, practical relevance to public issues and funding agencies, or personal interest), they are just as often chosen because access has become available to the researcher, who later incorporates other justifications. My initial interest in deviant adolescents was aroused by personal and practical social work concerns at summer camps and settlement houses, and in the drifting clusters research on predelinquents and the Toronto thefts, I initially utilized contacts already established.

Even when the researcher first chooses a general topic (as I did in investigating the Chicago teenagers), there is a considerable advantage to adopting specific foci as topics "emerge"; concepts should be chosen pragmatically to organize what one knows. Such flexibility maximizes the chances for unanticipated discovery, an advantage of participant observation. Not infrequently, projects formulated around one topic will generate information relevant to others. Many students have incorporated my interest in adolescent deviance into their own research (often as a subsidiary topic). In reviewing their papers and theses on schools, I realized that we had collectively gathered considerable material on classroom deviance in this rather unorthodox manner and wrote a report on social order.

The Kingston research on the Frontenac Juvenile Court Diversion Program is also complicated. Since this was fundamentally a contracted evaluation of a demonstration project, many of the questions and the main topics in the proposal were derived from their theoretical and policy relevance. An experimental design with observation and in-depth interviews, the gathering of court records, and a large-scale survey have served to answer most of these preformulated questions. The participant observation, on the other hand, has been most useful in uncovering and understanding unanticipated events, such as the reluctance of half the experimental subjects to avail themselves of the noncourt diversion option or the resistance of officials to the program they publicly supported. Again, in my experience, participant observation has had its greatest strength in allowing the development of topics *after* access has been gained.

ENTRY

Becker (1970a) and others have outlined the main analytical possibilities for gaining entry in doing research on deviants. These range from being a natural member of the group, through contacting officially processed persons, random sampling, advertising for volunteers, offering a desired service to deviants, to frequenting hangouts. Word-of mouth referrals and snowball sampling are suggested adjuncts (Irwin, 1972). In addition, other people, records, and published sources often provide indirect contact. My own work has used various combinations of these techniques.

The drifting clusters and thieves projects both relied initially upon contacts established as a street worker, a form of natural semimembership. But street work itself is not unlike participant observation research in that access is a crucial problem and obtained through similar methods. I was initially introduced to some delinquents by previous workers. Others were suggested to me by officials (police or settlement house workers, school attendance counselors, etc.).

I met both these referred delinquents and others by frequenting their hangouts, such as stores, pool halls, restaurants, and alleys, and by trying to strike up casual acquaintanceship over bottles of pop, by joining games, chatting amiably, and other methods. Some boldness and a tough-skinned attitude to occasional personal rejection were helpful, in addition to skills in repartee, sports, empathy, and sensitivity. I recall few incidents of outright rebuff. I generally made frequent "rounds" of a chosen neighborhood, perhaps twice daily at the beginning, stopping at a corner, walking down frequented streets, dropping into stores, playing a game of pool, watching baseball games, or drinking pop at a restaurant. After leaving each location, I surreptitiously jotted down names or descriptions of teenagers met or noticed, then proceeded on. After a few visits or perhaps a couple of weeks, I became recognized as something of a regular, and usually had managed to strike up conversations with a few young-sters.

Gaining entry as a street worker was good practice for later research work, and I used the same basic tactics in the drifting clusters; greaser, freaks, and straights; and thieves projects. As a street worker, I had been able to attract teenagers by providing obvious social work services (such as recreation, job and legal referral, and personal counseling), and they would bring their friends along or tell others about me. Although I had fewer and less recognized resources to exchange when doing research, I remained conscious of sharing a bag of chips, contributing to conversa-tions, offering advice I considered helpful when requested, taking a few adolescents to the beach when I wanted to go anyway, and so on. In general, most adolescents seemed to find a somewhat strange sociological researcher at least as interesting as each other. I suspect this is a largely unrecognized resource for research on frequently bored populations such as teenagers, bus drivers, or old people.

Though I utilized social agencies, police, and schools for contacts and suggestions, I was not restricted to populations known by any single formal organization in the earlier projects. Through such contact with as many multiple entries as possible, I believe I was informed more accu-rately of the specific populations I sought.

I did not initiate research on vague and amorphous "social move-ments" of teenagers by going through formal hierarchical channels of access and requesting permission or cooperation from groups such as parents, schools, or politicians who might claim authority over the youth contacted. Since teenagers command little private space and hence frequent public ones, I could usually maintain contact in public places where I was not particularly responsible for the youths' behavior, and I felt no obligation to obtain formal permission for conversation or observation. I can recall events where I felt I was imposing, only to be later told that I was not at all, especially compared with some "undesirables" who were naturally present. The subjects saw me, then, as a natural part of the scene. In cases where my involvement was more profound and potentially legally hazardous (such as taking juveniles to the beach), I sought verbal parental permission. Since many teenagers consider authorities hostile to their interests, and since I felt morally inclined to recognize such youthful autonomy, I tired to avoid contacts which might engender role conflicts for me.[1]

I was nonetheless frank with youngsters, parents, and organizations on the subject of my research aims (in the two projects growing out of street work, these became established only later). Fundamentally, this consisted of developing a straightforward, simple explanation of my interest which could be used with all parties. I usually supplemented this with interests of particular concern to the parties immediately present and was prepared to elaborate if desired. I stated who paid me, my university connection, and my intention to write about my findings. A few youths I've observed casually probably never realized I was doing research, as the occasion for such explanation never arose. Others forgot my research role in the ongoing rush of planning capers, fighting, or chasing girls. At these times, I was in effect a disguised unobtrusive observer.

In the classroom order and juvenile court projects, I contacted youngsters after going through official channels. Although neither of these projects could have been executed without official permission from the appropriate social organization, I am convinced that such access routes almost always retard—or in some cases prevent—the establishment of rapport with delinquents. Not only is permission required from more parties (the officials and the juvenile subjects), but it becomes subtly difficult to avoid the priority of obligations to officials and time-consuming to detach oneself from association with them. The requirement of multiple permission, of course, increases the likelihood of rejection for each subject. Such organizational research, however, does add a different dimension to our knowledge of deviant youth.

Given all the above tactical suggestions, in gaining entry nothing seems as important as a genuine appreciative interest in the subjects. When people know that someone likes them, they probably feel similarly and certainly are more willing to trust.

In general, I have found that even the most elaborate credentials will open only physical doors, and that genuine rapport is established when subjects accept the researcher for personal qualities rather than formal status. Once again, research duplicates everyday life.

BARGAINING FOR A ROLE

There are a number of issues surrounding the adoption of a role which have been extensively discussed in the literature on participant observation (e.g., Filstead, 1970). Generally, one must attempt to structure one's role in such a way as to collect the type of information sought. Since the researcher often doesn't know exactly what data to seek, an immediate dilemma arises which is typically handled by being quietly unobtrusive until the topic emerges.

Nonetheless, some issues cannot be ignored until a topic is selected.

1. Almost invariably, one must identify oneself shortly after arriving on the scene, unless one is a natural member of the group.

2. Probably the best identification is to state that one is a social researcher, which carries enough legitimacy to allow one to stay but enough vagueness so that the role can be more fully shaped later as one gains personal acceptance. Even with such an "honesty is the best policy" orientation, however, researchers usually find themselves hiding their most objectionable personal traits and adopting the subjects' style to be more inconspicuous.

3. As long as such minor deceptive tactics are basically of everyday life, serious ethical problems do not usually arise. When they threaten to become more contrived, honesty is still desirable solely on practical grounds of providing the best access in the long run. In a few cases, moral considerations alone are relevant.

4. In establishing role relations with subjects and teaching them how to be sociological subjects, the researcher strikes implicit bargains. These may be such tangible payoffs as monetary payments for interviews; providing data or completed reports to sponsors and hosts; or agreements by subjects to tell their side of the story; or the researchers agreement to act as a confessor or simple participant who contributes certain resources (such as a car) to the group. At the very least, the researcher must tacitly agree to respect and accept the subjects in order not to threaten them.

5. Yet one must studiously avoid being coopted in such a way as to preclude accomplishing the major task of research.

6. As the study progresses, the researcher's role will change. Learning how he or she is perceived, one can, within ethical limits, consciously make alterations in order to get better data.

7. In every good in-depth study, the researcher becomes assimilated, becomes "a regular," and adopts the viewpoint of the subjects. Periodic withdrawal for theoretical reflection may become necessary in order to avoid "going native" entirely. If the researcher has been wise enough to take extensive notes on the self during the project, he or she will realize that the various stages of the role allow different kinds of data to be collected. The neophyte, for instance, can and should ask different questions than the regular, who is also different from the "withdrawing old-timer."

8. Throughout this process, researchers must ask what behaviors and presentations of self will get the job done while allowing them to remain faithful to their obligations. Just as one is never completely "in" in everyday life, and doesn't need to be to continue living successfully, one is never completely "in" while doing research, and doesn't need to be. Sometimes less rapport gives adequate data more efficiently.

9. Dilemmas arise as to how active or passive one need be, as to when one is justified in intruding (often for very human reasons of friendship) or in intervening intentionally to measure effects.

10. How much subtle coercion is justified in encouraging resistant subjects to talk?

11. How much access can authoritative sponsors provide?

12. How does one move successfully between conflicting role expectations held by different subjects, such as police and delinquents? How can one remain both a "stranger and friend" (Powdermaker, 1966)?

In the drifting clusters project, I was conscious of bargaining for a social work role, offering services to kids, and promising confidentiality while disapproving of most illegalities. Though I regularly sided with the youngsters and established a certain trustworthiness over a couple of years, only when I later explicitly and publicly shed my social work role and adopted a research role did it become apparent to me how much I had cut myself off from much information on illegal behavior. As I made it obvious by my behavior in the greasers, freaks, and straights project and the theft research that I was not a policeman, newspaper reporter, homosexual, drug pusher, or social worker, the teenagers became more accepting and gingerly tested me. My nonintervention to prevent minor illegalities (such as smoking marijuana), acceptance of bottles of beer offered to me by juveniles in parks, participation in baseball games and talks, and other actions all served to confirm my identity claims.

Over time, this role was explained by the teenagers to each other, so that a personal reputation preceded me. As I conducted most of the street research during my early and mid-twenties and deliberately adopted youthful dress (jeans, boots or running shoes, old shirts and sweaters, longish hair), I fitted unobtrusively enough into streetcorner gatherings that casual strangers failed to notice me. On a few occasions, even police did not distinguish me, and took me to the station for "cooling off" and questioning about public disturbances involving others. (On such occasions I professed to "know nothing," the standard practice of my subjects, and was released with them.)

Subjects gradually became secure enough about our relationship to joke about it. Discussion of my work sometimes occupied dull afternoons or evenings. I indicated my desire not to participate actively in the relatively risk-prone crimes with victims (e.g., theft, assault), explaining how such behavior was not worth the risk to me or was personally repugnant; I turned down invitations for "cuts in jobs." Although the few occasions when I was accidentally present at the commission of such victim crimes presented invaluable data, my wishes were generally respected, and my obvious discomfort resulted in subjects warning me on subsequent occasions. My participation in relatively safe victimless offenses which I commit privately anyway (e.g., being drunk in a public place, buying a "hot" wallet or shirt, gambling) established sufficient credibility that my very rare requests for "real life" demonstrations of criminal techniques were readily met. Most of my data, however, have been collected in casual conversations and interviews before and after the fact, and I now doubt that my relatively high involvement was really necessary or worth the risk (Irwin, 1972).

Conducting formal interviews (especially with a tape recorder or in an office) seemed to solidify my research role in most subjects' minds (although the taping was also inhibiting). Living in the neighborhood, sharing in street parties, being a victim of some crimes, working together on projects, and offering special assistance (e.g., tutoring) widened my access and further confirmed my trustworthiness. In "hanging out" less on the corner and acting more like an adult, I "settled down" simultaneously with some of my subjects and could better explore relationships between adolescent delinquents and adult criminals.

Having to live in the field meant that I too had to operate in the subjects' world (Glaser and Strauss, 1970). In order to do so, on many occasions I had to adopt their way of perceiving and acting; I "tested" some hypotheses by my own behavior (e.g., in buying hot goods). When subjects acted or talked in a natural field setting, they had to meet everyday exigencies and could not simply "play" to me (Becker, 1970b, *passim*).

The classroom order and juvenile court diversion projects required different roles. Many of the students doing the classroom order research were natural members (teachers, supply teachers, lay assistants), and others agreed to assist teachers as part of their entry bargains. Some nonetheless managed to escape being authority figures and gained pupils' trust regarding minor deviance. In a similar way, the court research has necessitated entry through formal channels, with the implicit assumption that we researchers act as responsible (i.e., law-abiding) adults, at least when around the juveniles. Breaking minor laws (such as drinking) with adults, however, has proven as effective in establishing rapport with them as it did with youngsters in the previous projects. Shared secrets definitely seem to establish social bonds (Simmel, 1950). In the juvenile court research, however, our informal participant observation has been more established and effective with adults than with youngsters.

GATHERING DATA

The particular kind of data one gathers obviously depends on access and the questions asked. In addition, one's philosophy of science determines what one chooses to regard as the proper subject matter of sociology. Participant observers generally hold to some variety of the "social action" tradition, which maintains that human perceptions and meanings are important to understand since they shape behavior into purposive action. Much attention must therefore be given to subjects' definitions and concepts, upon which analytic concepts are based.

To this end, one advantage of participant observation is its flexibility in assessing various data sources. Observations, verbal reports, and written records, whether offered in groups or by individuals, whether revealed naturally or upon request, are all considered potential sources of information. Since multiple methods are used, validity becomes more assured. McCall and Simmons (1968), among others, offer a good discussion of the pros and cons of different sources, but naturalistic unrequested group discussion and observation remains a unique strength of participant observation (see Becker, Geer, Hughes and Strauss, 1961).

It nonetheless remains true that the bulk of participant observation data is probably gathered through informal interviews and supplemented by observation. Standard interviewing techniques are useful but can be adjusted with more informal, less standardized variations as the researcher seeks jigsawlike configurational answers rather than frequency distributions. Neophyte status allows the researcher to play dumb and assimilation allows one to stretch one's feeling to match those of the subjects later, followed by detached recording and analysis; alternatively, acceptance allows friendly challenges which demand elaborated explanations.

Data collection in my own work has followed these fairly typical patterns. Although I attempted to gain some observational data on the major aspects of my subjects' lives, interviews and requested demonstrations became more predominant as the projects progressed. Only a very few interview requests have been refused, by those subjects least known; most teenagers apparently enjoy the attention of being interviewed.

Subjects with whom I became friends, and who were socially perceptive members of their groups—often leaders or retired old hands—became key informants. These people were invaluable in reading drafts of working papers and correcting misimpressions.

In the formal organizational projects on classroom disorder and juvenile court diversion, records were made available and permission for interviews was implicitly granted at the time of granting entry. Access was also granted for observation of *in camera* meetings, hearings, and classroom sessions. Yet individuals retained the right and power to be more or less cooperative in what they themselves would volunteer. And in some cases—for instance, interviewing deviant pupils or convicted juveniles— such cooperation required clearly distinguishing the research from the "oppressing" teacher or judge. What seemed like a more firm offer of data, then, often proved illusory, as entangling role obligations to such officials sometimes prevented such a clear symbolic separation. Only extensive and concerted role definition seemed able to overcome these problems, and contact with individual youngsters in the juvenile court project was too short for that.

In requesting that subjects introduce me to other deviants, I experienced a methodological problem which could be transformed into substantive information. My snowball sampling stopped at certain levels (freaks would not introduce me to heroin addicts or big dealers, serious thieves would not introduce me to professionals or fences, etc.). Although such occasions initially seemed to frustrate my research aims, I came to realize that they indicated major social boundaries where deviants did not know each other well enough to make word-of-mouth referrals possible. Once more, methodological flexibility resulted in unanticipated knowledge.

MAPPING THE SOCIAL ORGANIZATION

The more information one has early in the research, the better one is able to choose appropriate sites for certain topics and to structure one's role. Schatzman and Strauss (1973) recommend "casing" organizations as much as possible before the initial approach, and much information can be gained from records, local histories, and knowledgeable informants.

Hughes (1971) has suggested a useful basic framework for investigating social organization. He recommends looking at the members, the cast of characters, their roles and hierarchical relations, both formal and informal. The setting should be examined in terms of its effect on the normal procedures of conduct, deviance, and trouble. Decisions can be examined and purposes described. To this set of rather static interests should be added aspects of process, such as socialization and career sequences, as well as institutional changes.

Participant observers perhaps best deal with bias by focusing on serendipitous, unanticipated discoveries and consciously seeking evidence which negates emerging hypotheses (see Becker, 1970a; Glaser and Strauss, 1967; Robinson, 1951; Turner, 1953). Berk (1974) and Becker, Geer, Hughes and Strauss (1961) suggest how careful sampling can assist in determining relationships using much the same basic logic as in survey or experimental research.

In discussing entry, I indicated the construction of overview social maps by making daily rounds, placing subjects in geographical locations, and establishing basic demographic categories (regarding age, sex, social class, etc.), legal statuses, formal organizational memberships (in families or clubs), and friendship groupings. I could then select the best groups or individuals to provide me with the knowledge I wanted (e.g., about freaks, or car stealing) and begin to spend more time with them. By forcing myself to describe the subjects in interim working papers, I began to make claims (e.g., that freaks smoked an unusual amount of marijuana) which I could then check by comparing with other subjects (e.g., greasers). As such descriptions became elaborated, categories became more clearly defined (e.g., "stoner greasers" smoked as much as freaks but did not share their "peace" ideology or dress), and the search for exceptions narrowed (e.g., to finding a stoner greaser who was into a "peace" ideology).

Such sampling had a number of potential biases. More obvious street teenagers could be overselected; I had to refer to more "retreatist" recreation center or school-oriented youth for balance. As in any participant observation study, the price of good rapport and "rich" data is the bias of self-selection; my samples have been overloaded with subjects with whom I was friendly.

Research on the young involves recognition of their status within the wider social hierarchy. I discussed above how their generally subordinate position vis-à-vis adults led me to avoid approaching them through adult authorities to whom they were unlikely to reveal their deviance. Without many resources (in terms of money, private spaces, etc.) teen groups tend toward loose social movements, especially for deviant activities— temporarily commanding public spaces (such as alleys or stores) to meet their own needs, then fading away like guerrilla bands when confrontations develop. As a result, their life styles are somewhat chaotic, requiring flexibility in terms of time to which graduate student life is perhaps more suited than a professor's (see Gaffield and West, 1978; Snider and West, 1979).

Thus, it seems no accident that since taking regular university appointments I have found it easier to conduct research on adolescent deviants by relying on the time structure provided by schools or courts. Formal organizations usually have clear lists of members, rules and relationships, a geographical location, and so on. After officials have granted entry on examining one's credentials, they often cooperate by providing offices, coffee breaks, and other amenities. As it becomes a little easier, though, I wonder if it isn't a bit less fun!

CONCLUSION

As these various projects have progressed, I have been repeatedly amazed at how easily access has been granted across major ascriptive and legal boundaries. Children, teenagers, and adults have let me into their worlds, even when open revelation could prove potentially seriously damaging to them. I have come to realize that such trust is a fundamental aspect of social order, although it probably attains unique qualities among deviants. It seemed most easily extended when it was clear that I would gain from maintaining the relationship; when I was open to sanctions (e.g., personal violence); when the relationship existed in a community context where participants relied on the good opinion of third parties; and when it was ideologically supported (see West, 1974).

The resulting relationships have been as demanding and as pleasurable as those in the rest of my life. Subjects who opened themselves most to me have naturally insisted upon some reciprocity (Irwin, 1972); those who have given me most have received most in return. I believe this is what Hughes (1971) refers to when he describes fieldwork as a process of personal growth and self-awareness.

Notes

1. Although I have dealt more extensively elsewhere (West, 1974) with the obvious ethical considerations, some comment is in order regarding this point and later ones. Fundamentally I regarded my direct personal obligation to subjects as superceding legal niceties concerning the age of consent, behavior "contributing to delinquency," or unlawful activities. The personal betrayal (entailed in violating the numerous tacit agreements a deviance researcher makes to overlook illegalities) supercedes one's political misdeeds in the eyes of the state.

This does not mean that such illegality is to be committed lightly, especially in regard to sociology's need for organizational legitimacy. For me, however, the question of whether participant observation entails an ultimate betrayal of one's friends by publicly exposing them, however individually disguised, in eventual published reports is a more serious and profound issue.

References

BECKER, H.S. "Practitioners of Vice and Crime." In R. Habenstein, ed., *Pathways to Data*. Chicago: Aldine, 1970a.

BECKER, H.S. *Sociological Work: Method and Substance*. Chicago: Aldine, 1970b.

BECKER, H.S., B. GEER, E.C. HUGHES, and A.L. STRAUSS. *Boys in White*. Chicago: University of Chicago Press, 1961.

BERK, R. "Re: Qualitative Methodology," Unpublished manuscript. Evanston, Ill.: Dept. of Sociology, Northwestern University.

BERK, R.A., and J. ADAMS. "Establishing Rapport with Deviant Groups." *Social Problems* 18 (1970), 102–117.

CAMERON, M.O. *The Booster and the Snitch*. Toronto: Collier-Macmillan, 1964.

FILSTEAD, W.J. *Qualitative Methodology*. Chicago: Markham, 1970.

GAFFIELD, G., and W.G. WEST. "Introduction." In H. Berkeley, C. Gaffield, and W. G. West, eds., *Childrens' Rights in Canada: Educational and Legal Issues*. Toronto: OISE Publications, 1978.

GLASER, B., and A. STRAUSS. *The Discovery of Grounded Theory*. Chicago: Aldine, 1967.

GLASER, B., and A. STRAUSS. "The Discovery of Substantive Theory." In W. Filstead, ed., *Qualitative Methodology*. Chicago: Markham, 1970.

HANNERZ, U. *Soulside*. New York: Columbia University Press, 1969.

HUGHES, E.C. *The Sociological Eye*. Chicago: Aldine, 1971.

IRWIN, J. "Participant Observation of Criminals." In J.D. Douglas, ed., *Research on Deviance*. New York: Random House, 1972.

LIEBOW, E. *Tally's Corner*. Boston: Little, Brown, 1967.

MATZA, D. *Delinquency and Drift*. New York: Wiley, 1964.

McCall, G., and J.L. SIMMONS. *Issues in Participant Observation*. Reading, Mass: Addison-Wesley, 1969.

MORTON, M.E., and W.G. WEST. *An Evaluation of the Frontenac Juvenile Diversion Program*. Ottawa: Ministry of the Solicitor General, 1978.

POWDERMAKER, H. *Strangers and Friends: The Way of an Anthropologist*. New York: Norton, 1966.

ROBINSON, W.S. "A Logical Structure of Analytic Induction." *American Sociological Review* 16 (1951), 812–818.

SCHATZMAN L., and A. STRAUSS. *Field Research*. Englewood Cliffs, N.J.: Prentice-Hall, 1973.

SIMMEL, G. "The Secret." In *The Sociology of George Simmel*, ed. K.H. Wolff. New York: Free Press, 1950.

SNIDER, L., and W.G. WEST. "Crime and Conflict in Canada." In R.J. Ossenberg, ed., *Canadian Society: Conflict and Change*. Toronto: McClelland and Stewart, 1979.

44   W. GORDON WEST

SUTHERLAND, E., and C. CONWELL. *The Professional Thief.* Chicago: University of Chicago Press, 1937.

TURNER, R.H. "The Quest for Universals in Sociological Research." *American Sociological Review* 18, (1953), 604–611.

WERTHMAN, C. "Delinquency and Moral Character." In D. Cressey and D. Ward, eds., *Delinquency, Crime, and Social Process.* New York: Harper & Row, 1969.

WEST, W.G. *Drifting Clusters: A Study of Non-Gang Delinquency,* B.A. thesis, Toronto: York University, Dept. of Sociology, 1968.

WEST, W.G. "Adolescent Perspective: On Being a Greaser, Freak or Straight." Presented at the Annual Meetings of the Canadian Sociology and Anthropology Association, Edmonton, Canada, 1975.

WEST, W.G. *Serious Thieves: Lower-Class Adolescent Males in a Short-Term Deviant Occupation,* Ph.D. dissertation, Evanston, Ill.: Northwestern University, Dept. of Sociology, 1974.

WEST, W.G. "Participant Observation Research on the Social Construction of Everyday Classroom Order." *Interchange* 6 (1975), 35–43.

WEST, W.G. "Adolescent Perspectives and Delinquency: A Corroboration of Control Theory." Kingston, Ont.: Queen's Univeristy, Dept. of Sociology, 1977a.

WEST, W.G. "Adolescent Territoriality." Kingston, Ont.: Queen's University, Dept. of Sociology, 1977b.

WEST, W.G. "Participant Observation in Canadian Classrooms: The Need, Rationale, Technique and Development Implications." *Canadian Journal of Education* 2 (1977c), 55–74.

WEST, W.G. "The Short-Term Careers of Serious Thieves." *Canadian Journal of Criminology,* 20 (1978a), 169–190.

WEST, W.G. "Serious Theft as an Occupation." Paper presented to the Annual Meetings of the Society for the Study of Social Problems, San Francisco, 1978b.

WEST, W.G. "Serious Thieves: Lower-Class Adolescent Males in a Short-Term Deviant Occupation." In E. Vaz and N.A. Lodhi, eds., *Crime and Delinquency: The Canadian Case.* Toronto: Prentice-Hall, 1978c.

WEST, W.G. "Adolescent Perspectives and Identity Changes." *Adolescence* (in press).

Problems of Access in the Study of Social Elites and Boards of Directors

JOAN EAKIN HOFFMANN   *McGill University*

The problem of access is basic to all field research. How do social scientists obtain entry to organizations to observe, interview, or otherwise collect data? How do they persuade individuals to let themselves be visited or interviewed? The problem of access, moreover, is not resolved upon entry into a social setting or upon securing an interview. Researchers then have to acquire and maintain access to the activities, beliefs, and experiences of their informants. How do they get "behind the scenes"—that is, beneath personal and institutional public fronts? How do they penetrate the inside workings of organizations and the private perceptions of individuals? This selection examines some of these problems of access, drawing on my research experience in a study of hospital boards of directors and their upper-class members.

English-speaking hospitals in the province of Quebec were originally founded by groups of socially prominent, wealthy citizens who contributed land and money for their construction and then conducted regular fund-raising campaigns among themselves and in the community to support their subsequent operation. These hospitals were administered by boards of directors made up of these same citizens or their appointees. Over the years, the provincial government came to assume the entire operating budget of these hospitals, but the institutions remained under the administrative direction of the community elite. In 1973 the government ended this private administration and broadened the membership of hospital boards of directors to include individuals representing such new constituencies as patients, nonprofessional hospital employees, nurses, community organizations, and so on. About one-third of the new board positions, however, were retained by the "old guard" membership. My research attempted to assess the social consequences of this reorganization. A major focus, of course, was on the social organization of the former board system, which meant the study of how the old elite boards operated and the nature of the participation of the top-level executives and professionals who comprised their memberships.

The relative scarcity of literature on society's higher social strata and on such organizational settings as boards of directors is doubtless related to difficulties of access. Board meetings are typically closed to nonmembers and proceedings are kept confidential, like other high-level decision-making processes, they are conducted more outside the boardroom than within it. Moreover, directors and other members of the community's financial and professional elite are often extremely busy, fast-paced individuals who have very little time to spare and who give low priority to being studied by social scientists. Business executives and senior professionals, furthermore, are protected by secretaries or junior personnel, who divert, discourage, or refuse those requests on their employer's time that they deem illegitimate or irrelevant. In other words, researchers cannot just attend a board meeting, note pad in hand, and expect to observe what boards do. Nor can they reach a company president by simply calling and requesting an interview.

My initial approach to the field research illustrates these difficulties. Introducing myself as a sociology graduate student, I had very limited success in getting by the gatekeepers of the executive world. Telephone follow-ups to letters sent requesting an interview repeatedly found Mr. X "tied up" or "in conference." When I did manage to get my foot in the door, interviews rarely exceeded a half hour, were continuously interrupted by telephone calls (for "important" conferences, secretaries are usually asked to take calls), and elicited only "front work" (Goffman, 1961), the public version of what hospital boards were all about.

My access problem was thus twofold: obtaining an interview in the first instance, then penetrating beyond what anyone could have read in the hospital's annual report.

ACCESS AND SOCIAL IDENTITY

By chance during one interview, my respondent discovered that he knew a member of my family. "Why didn't you say so?" The rest of the interview was dramatically different than all my previous data. I was presented with a very different picture of the nature of board work. I learned, for example, how board members used to be recruited, how the executive committee kept control over the rest of the board, how business was conducted and of what it consisted, and many other aspects of the informal social organization of board work.

The sudden richness of this data, once my informant discovered that he "knew" me, signaled the importance of the researcher's *identity* in field research. Who I was or was perceived to be influenced the information to which I would be given access. The management of my identity thus became an important aspect of my research strategy.

Sampling Based on Social Ties

Abandoning my original intention of interviewing a representative sample from different institutions, I began to choose my subjects on the basis of social ties, seeking interviews with all those board members who personally knew me or a member of my family. I usually wrote a letter first, outlining my interests in a formal, businesslike fashion consistent with the customary approach to executives. Most of these people must cope with large volumes of correspondence, much of which is nonbusiness in nature, soliciting time, money, cooperation, information, or whatever. Unless something attracts their attention as they skim through the daily mail, executives are quick to refer correspondence to the waste basket or to a subordinate to handle. In order to catch attention or to compete with other requests, I included personal references in my letter (such as, "I hoped you might have the time between fishing trips . . . ," where I knew the board member often went fishing with a member of my family) and made certain my surname was written largely and legibly for them to recognize. In the letter, I usually stated that I would telephone to make an appointment. (Without such a preceding letter, a telephone call rarely reached its destination, because my name meant nothing to the secretary. The letter, however, could be marked "personal" and be assured of being opened by the board member.)

Having exhausted these direct personal contacts, I asked those board members I *did* know to refer me to others whom they felt could help me. Sometimes they would call a colleague directly on my behalf. In other cases, I found that "Mr. X suggested I come to you" obtained for me an interview; if I delayed a few days before the interview, I generally found that my new informant had made inquiries about me in the interim and established my identity.

The methodological use of personal social ties yielded substantially more informative and insightful data. Referral interviews were less productive than those drawing on direct social contacts, but they remained superior to those where I was an unknown sociologist encumbered by the variety of stereotypes associated with such a label (such as radical, or socialist, or someone likely to disapprove of the traditional elite board system). The following examples from my field notes illustrate the nature of the data obtained under these different identities:

Response to an Unknown
    Sociologist   *Response to a Known Individual*

BOARD MEMBER A   BOARD MEMBER B

*Q. How do you feel in general about how
the board has been reorganized?*

I think the basic idea of participation is good. We need better communication with the various groups. And I think they probably have a lot to offer.

This whole business is unworkable. It's all very nice and well to have these people on the board, they might be able to tell us something here and there, or, describe a situation, but you're not going to run a hospital on that!

*Q. How is the new membership working out?
Do they participate? Any problems?*

. . . oh yes, Mr. X [orderly] participates. He asked something today, now what was it? Sometimes they lack skill and experience, but they catch on. There is no problem with them. We get along very well.

Mr. X [orderly] hasn't opened his mouth except for a sandwich. But what *can* he contribute? . . .
You could rely on the old type of board member . . . you knew you could count on him to support you. You didn't have to check up all the time. But these new people, how do you know how they will react? Will they stick behind you? And there is the problem of confidentiality. Everything you say you know will be all over the hospital ten minutes after the meeting. You can't say the same things anymore. You have to be careful in case someone interprets you as being condescending or hoity-toity.

Q. On the subject of administrator-board relationships

The board never does anything without first going through the administrator.

I met X [board member at another hospital] at the club once and broached the subject with him. Once I got a general agreement I approached Y [the administrator].

The contrast is marked. Replies from board member A are heavily "front" work, a bland commentary reflecting what the board member thought he ought to say or what I wanted to hear, and revealed little of the complexity of the social situation. Board member B's answers were franker, less self-conscious, and exposed some of the more subtle aspects of the board's social organization. The differences are not just due to a difference in the opinions of my respondents. In a second interview with member A, this time under a "known" identity, I established that "backstage" he shared most of member B's views.

Another indication of my improved access was the off-the-record comments in which informants told me things with the caution "You don't need to write this down, but . . . ," a gesture of confidence absent in earlier interviews.

I am suggesting, then, that the use of social ties as a research tool improved my access to hard-to-reach persons and their experiences. Why?

Friendship and Membership Factors in Access

Friendship norms were factors in my new-found access. In general, the closer the friendship tie with members of my family, the less frequently informants postponed or canceled interviews and the more inside information they allowed me. Two aspects of friendship may have elicited this receptiveness: obligation and trust. Undoubtedly, certain of my respondents felt unable to refuse me because of their personal acquaintance with my family. This sense of obligation was sometimes reinforced by other social commitments, such as returning favors (a close relative had once found a job for a board member's son) or ongoing business situations (one board member was in the midst of a business deal with a member of my family). A second element, trust, also helped explain the influence of friendship ties. Douglas (1976) suggests that suspicion and conflict of itnerest are inherent in all research situations and that people do not spontaneously bare themselves to anyone who asks. Clearly, if respondents are to reveal backstage information about themselves, they need to be confident that it will not be used against them in any way. Friendship ties reduced the perceived risk associated with confiding in me by acting as a form of security that information would not be misused or that boards would not be portrayed in an unfavorable light.

A second factor in my improved access was my quasi-membership status in the social group I was studying. Instead of a clearly delimited occupational or organizational group, such as schoolteachers or workers on an assembly line, the relevant social unit here is, I suggest, social class. Although the question of class consciousness has been debated and members of upper social strata have been observed to deny class issues (Domhoff, 1971), most of the elites in my study did perceive their board work and reorganization in class terms, although not always explicitly. (For example, consider the evidence of group consciousness in the pronouns of this board member's comment: "It is very different now [after democratization]. *We* just don't speak the same language as *they* do)." I grew up in the same social environment as most of the board members; my parents were part of the same social circuits, having gone to the same schools, or grown up in the same neighborhood, or belonged to the same clubs, or attended the same parties, or done business together, or even sat together on other boards. Although I myself was not a board member, or a businessman, or even of the same generation as my respondents, I reaped some of the benefits of insider status by virtue of belonging to their social class—an attribute the data indicated was central to their role and function as board members. As with friendship, common class membership increased the level of trust in our relationship over any that I could create as an unknown interviewer. I do not say, of course, that I had their *entire* confidence, only that my inferred class background lowered the perceived risk of information being misused. Because I came from a known social milieu. I was more predictable to them; board members felt more able to anticipate how I would feel about certain issues and react to certain confidences. Common social class membership also increased the likelihood that I would "understand" their perspective and would present their points of view "fairly."

Membership as a Research Strategy

Neutrality and the elimination of bias are basic methodological concepts in sociology, a discipline striving for scientific legitimacy. Membership and the application of one's own cultural experience and understanding to research problems are often frowned upon as too "subjective" or "slanted." Some very penetrating social analysis, however, has been carried out by researchers who were members of the organizations or social groups they studied. For example, Roth (1963) was himself a patient in the tuberculosis sanitorium he studied; Dalton (1959) was a manager in the organization whose leadership he studied. It is also perhaps noteworthy that, among the few who have studied the upper classes, two of the most valuable contributors I know of came from an upper-class background (Baltzell, 1964; Ross, 1954). In my study, I felt that the advantages of inside status outweighed the risk of bias. I did, however, make a special effort to remain constantly aware of the possible influence of such a status on my data and my analysis.

My most fundamental research strategy, then, was the management of my social identity in order to maximize the benefits of social ties with my respondents. A number of other tactics, however, complemented this strategy and further increased my access to backstage action and belief.

ACCESS AND INTERVIEW TECHNIQUE

A major objective of my research strategy was the suppression of "front work." One tactic, as I have just discussed, was the use of friendship and social class ties to foster trust. The nature of the interaction at the interview itself, however, also influenced the kind of information I received. Here, careful management of cues, impressions, leads, innuendo, and other means of communication encouraged respondents to share inside information. Two tactics were particularly useful: deflection and tracking.

Deflection

It sometimes proved useful to camouflage the real research questions, to "deflect" informants' attention from the main targets of study. Because it reduced self-consciousness and perceived threat, deflection was a useful technique for subjects who were anxious about personal exposure. Many of my respondents became reticent when they perceived themselves to be the object of study—that is, when I told them that I was interested in how the old elite board system worked. I found, however, that they were prepared to offer their views more freely on "external" topics, such as reorganization policy or problems of the new membership. With respondents who appeared defensive about the old system ("I'm not saying the old way was perfect, but . . .") or who countered direct questions with front work, I presented myself as being interested in the consequences of reorganization or organizational problems rather than in the board as a social group or in board work as an elite social institution. Ostensible concern for the new board structure deflected attention away from the elite system per se and made my respondents feel more at ease. At the same time, however, I was still able to elicit the kind of data I sought since it was impossible to discuss the consequences of reorganization without constant comparison with the past. Discussion of the new board structure proved an excellent cover for investigating the former system. Indeed, many aspects of the "old guard" boards were never explicitly recognized until reorganization disrupted taken-for-granted patterns of behavior. One example was the issue of the confidentiality of board proceedings. Because the former socially homogenous boards had closed ranks, it was only when newcomers began to "leak" information that the implicit norms governing board behavior became manifest. In my research, then, deflection reduced the self-conscious and at times defensive posture sometimes evoked by a more direct approach and provided a *reflected image* of the real research target. Chosen thoughtfully, the "dummy" interview issues may even, as in my case, provide access to information unobtainable through direct questioning.

Another way in which I deflected attention away from the main unit of analysis was to avoid displaying too much interest in information that was "juicy" from the perspective of my analysis. Rather than raising my eyebrows and risk having respondents think they had been indiscreet, or that there was something unusual or bizarre about their behavior, I tried to create the impression that the information was neither surprising nor of *intrinsic* interest to me.

A final technique for deflecting attention from the main research target was through the judicious use of note taking. I never wrote continuously during interviews, recording only key words and phrases to jog my memory later.[1] Occasional note taking, however, made the movement more conspicuous and appeared to signal information of value. Thus, I worked so as not to indicate the importance of certain data by immediately recording it.

Tracking

While I sometimes found it useful to obscure what I was most interested in, it was sometimes more constructive to do the opposite. "Tracking" consisted of putting informants *on* rather than *off* the track; it attempted to elicit desired information by using cues that clarified rather than concealed the research objectives.

Tracking did not mean, however, outright disclosure of working hypotheses. Rather, it referred to the communication of selected information about the research that suggested to informants the *kinds of things* I was looking for. The most direct tracking device, of course, was explicit questioning. However, particularly in semistructured or unstructured interviewing, where the researcher follows only a rough question schedule, too many questions were sometimes disruptive, and less conspicuous tracking mechanisms were needed. Positive feedback was one such tactic. Expression of interest, such as nods, appreciative comments, note taking, and so on reinforced desired topics or directions and had the effect of gradually aligning my informants' inputs with my analytic categories.

I also tracked by using previously learned inside information. By incorporating bits of fact, or a name or incident into my questions or comments, I communicated a number of messages to my respondents. First of all, respondents learned what I already knew and were less inclined to waste time going over familiar points. (I used inside information in this way only when the relevant analytic categories were "saturated" [Glaser and Strauss, 1967]—that is, when I no longer *needed* repetition.)

Secondly, dropping inside information made my informants better able to appreciate my level of analysis and hence to make more appropriate responses. For example, most board members were businessmen, lawyers, or financial men who were not accustomed to providing the kind of information I sought. They presumed that facts and figures were wanted and tended to perceive their own ideas and experiences, as well as many backstage details, as either irrelevant or too trivial to bother mentioning.

In contrast to the strategy of deflection, where subjects were seen as suspicious and reluctant to reveal backstage information, this tracking method assumed that informants were basically willing to talk and that this cooperativeness could be fostered by proper guidance. The strategic use of inside information was also effective when respondents felt ambivalent about talking too freely. First, respondents learned that I was "in the know," that I had penetrated through the public veneer to the underlying social reality. Front work was discouraged because they knew that I could distinguish it from backstage information and because it might look as if they were covering something up. Second, the use of insider details possibly acted to reassure reticent informants. I often had the impression that respondents felt relieved by the knowledge that they were not the only persons to make such disclosures, that initial responsibility lay with someone else, and that this person must have had reason to trust me in the first place.

An example of the use of inside information to get backstage data was the following interview question about membership criteria in the elite boards:

Tell me a bit about how the old board chose its members. I have been told, for example, that you try to get people with specific skills, or that sometimes members of families who have contributed a lot to the hospital are invited to join. What other considerations might there have been?

This approach used a bit of inside knowledge to (1) reduce repetition (by eliminating the need to elaborate the official recruitment policy of "skills and experience"); (2) illustrate the nature of the information I sought (the informal bases of recruitment); (3) discourage front work (by indicating my awareness of another level of reality); (4) and imply that others had been telling me such things, so why not they too?

The use of inside knowledge in this way, however, did have limitations. First, when I had assured my respondents that what they told me was confidential, the display of too much inside information might have caused them to doubt my sincerity. Consequently, I took care never to use sensitive details or those that could be identified too readily as coming from particular individuals. Second, while my appearing "in the know" reassured some people, others felt less threatened when I appeared to be rather naive and harmless.

Choice of Strategy

Deflection and tracking, then, were two techniques that improved my access to backstage information in elite hospital boards. The former tried to divert attention away from my basic unit of analysis, the latter to highlight it. Both attempted to control front work and reduce the extent to which respondents felt threatened or distrustful. The tactics of each, however, had their pros and cons. The use of "dummy" research targets may have alleviated self-consciousness and allowed reflected images of otherwise inaccessible phenomena, but it sometimes precluded the advantages of direct questioning or of such tactics as the manipulation of insider knowledge. The use of inside information, in turn, generated trust but at times also eroded it. Playing the boob may have reduced suspicion, but it also encouraged front work. I found I had to remain constantly on the alert to avoid wasting the techniques' potential (using deflection with an uninhibited, cooperative subject); employing them in inappropriate places (displaying inside knowledge in conflict situations); allowing them to undermine each other (revealing inside information while playing the boob); or pushing them to the point of diminishing returns (deflecting attention so far from the unit of analysis that the data became irrelevant).

Few specific rules govern the application of these and other interview techniques. It is primarily a question of judgment and experience; the researcher learns instinctively which tactic might be effective in drawing out an informant.

At the beginning of every interview, I spent time chatting on a very general level with my informant, starting perhaps with "Tell me a bit about your involvement with this hospital." The question was relatively innocuous but, because it centered on the person, it allowed me to get a "feel" for his personality, the nature of his involvement, and his probable response to various approaches. I never commenced the interview in earnest until this was established, preferring to "waste" time on peripheral matters than risk choosing the wrong approach.

Interview strategy, however, must constantly evolve. Throughout the session, the researcher must always be prepared to test tactics, alter approaches, patch mistakes, jump at sudden opportunities. After the interview, it is essential to go through the field notes and to review the event in its entirety in order to assess what went right or wrong and why. With each subsequent interview, researchers find that their instincts become more accurate, which maximizes the effectiveness of their tactics and improves their access to the desired level of social experience.

Douglas (1976) has criticized classical field research for assuming that informants will be essentially open and cooperative in imparting information and sharing their experiences. He proposes an "investigative" paradigm based on the assumption that " . . . profound conflict of interests, values feelings and actions pervade social life. . . . Instead of trusting people and expecting trust in return, one suspects others and expects others to suspect him." (p. 55).

Essentially, I agree with him. In my research, the act of board reorganization itself implied that something was lacking and undemocratic about the old system. This implicit accusation naturally put many of the "old guard" board members on the defensive. Failure to appreciate such inherent conflict would have prevented me from achieving the trust and frankness essential to the study. For example, some of the details that interested me the most—such as informal decision-making processes and the significance of social homogeneity for how the former boards worked—were those which my informants were the least disposed to reveal. Recognition of this conflict of interest meant a more appropriate choice of interview strategy.

At the same time, however, I think Douglas goes too far in rejecting the notion of cooperation. To assume that certain individuals want to keep their beliefs or behaviors private is to make just as many a priori judgments as to assume that they will willingly expose themselves. For example, one reason boards of directors have not been widely studied may be that researchers *assume* their activities are private and that board members will be tight-lipped. I found, however, that much of what went on at the board level was "private" only because no one on the outside ever expressed any interest in it. Similarly, as I have already mentioned, many board members talked in general, noncommital terms not because they were trying to conceal what was going on but because they simply had no idea what kind of information I wanted. To assume conflict of interest in this case would have led to the use of deflection tactics where tracking techniques, which assume a cooperative posture, might have been more productive.

In other words, the researcher must be cautious about making a priori assessments of what "ought" to constitute a conflict-suspicion research situation. The will to cooperate cannot be taken for granted, but its absence may be due to factors other than conflict of interest or fear of exposure. Moreover, individuals are not *either* trusting *or* suspicious. They may be frank and open in one instance, evasive and deceptive in another. Researchers should not prejudge what areas of their respondents' knowledge or experience is private or public. This information must be established empirically through trial and error or important data may be sacrificed.

SUMMARY

This selection concerns the problem of access in field research. Drawing on my fieldwork experience in a study of hospital boards of directors and their elite membership, I secured interviews with high-ranking community leaders and enhanced my access to backstage data through the use of social ties and membership status and through such interview strategies as tracking and deflection. These strategies were based on the recognition that interviews are *social encounters* in which respondents are influenced by how they perceive their interviewer and the nature of the research.

References

BALTZELL, E.D. *The Protestant Establishment.* New York: Random House, 1964.
DALTON, M. *Men Who Manage.* New York: Wiley, 1959.
DOMHOFF, G.W. *The Higher Circles.* Toronto: Random House, 1971.
DOUGLAS, J.D. *Investigative Social Research.* Beverly Hills, Calif.: Sage Publications, 1976.
GLASER, B., and A. STRAUSS. *The Discovery of Grounded Theory.* Chicago: Aldine, 1967.
GOFFMAN, E. *The Presentation of Self in Everyday Life.* New York: Doubleday, 1959.
ROSS, A. "Philantropic Activity and the Business Career." *Social Forces,* 32 (1954), 257–280.
ROTH, J. *Timetables.* New York: Bobbs-Merrill, 1963.

Discovering Amorphous Social Experience: The Case of Chronic Pain

JOSEPH A. KOTARBA   *University of California, San Diego*

Amorphous social experiences are those facets of everyday life that are unique to individuals and not specific kinds of settings. The sociological study of these existential experiences of self, rich in their social forms and implications, requires innovative strategies for "getting in," since the researcher cannot expect to locate them (or representative examples of them) in any one setting, as would be possible in the examination of bureaucratic or organizational behavior. Whereas the entry into a single setting can be accomplished through a one-time effort of locating the appropriate setting, negotiating and selling the project to the hosts, and so on, the researcher of amorphous social experience must be prepared to encounter numerous and various entry situations, especially if the experience in question transcends age, sex, occupation, ethnic, and status categories. The experience of health and illness is a good example of an amorphous phenomenon that is more fully understood sociologically if the researcher is not restricted to the constraints of a single setting.

Traditionally, sociologists of health and illness have located their subject matter within normal medical settings. This "sociology in medicine" approach (Straus, 1957:203) denotes a situation in which "the basic concepts utilized by a researcher as well as the primary research problems are taken from authorized professional or organizational officials" (Kotarba, 1975:150). In effect, general explanations of health and illness experiences are implicitly grounded in only one facet of the experiences—namely, the situational involvement with official medical interventions. Little attention is paid to coping mechanisms in operation during the vast majority of time not spent in the doctor's office or hospital.

My own research on the chronic pain experience has clearly demon-

57

strated the shortcomings of this "management bias" (Roth, 1962:47–50)
approach. My goal was a comprehensive understanding of the total pain
experience, including the ways it affects familial and occupational
relations and the means used to seek help from lay and professional
others. Doctor-patient interactions thus formed only one although important, aspect of my study, for I was also interested in learning about the
alternative modes of health care utilized to fight chronic pain (e.g.,
chiropractic and acupuncture). Furthermore, my early research on acupuncture indicated, as we will see, that the population of chronic pain
persons is unexpectedly large and amorphous, and is not realistically
represented by those patients seeking help solely in the doctor's office or
clinic.

Since I was unsure of the parameters shaping the population of
chronic pain persons, I decided to defocus my search for various experiences and be open to discoveries in all walks of life and all segments of the
community. Douglas (1976:195) refers to this methodological strategy as
"casting a wide net"; the researcher talks to all kinds of people and
investigates all kinds of settings, seeking contact with those who either
experience the phenomenon in question directly or know of others who
do. The most effective way of approaching this task is to submerge oneself
in the everyday social world as a competent member and to keep in tune
with that world, for as Douglas has indicated: "The first thing a social
researcher must do is be able to *do* social life" (1976:116). My own
initiation into the social world of chronic pain came quite easily because I
have had the experience myself.

THE BACKGROUND: DIRECT EXPERIENCE

My involvement with research on chronic pain began in 1974, when I was
a graduate student at Arizona State University. At the urging of my
roommate, I decided to undergo acupuncture treatments for a nagging
backache I had had for several years following surgery for a slipped disc.
Like many others, I learned of the burgeoning practice of acupuncture
through the glowing media reports of its effectiveness emanating from the
Nixon trip to mainland China in 1973. In any event, I felt I had nothing
to lose by trying this apparently nonreactive therapy.

I located my acupuncturist by means of a feature article in a Phoenix
newspaper describing its practice there. He turned out to be a kindly
person whose specialty was general family medicine, but who had learned
acupuncture during a summer-long sabbatical in Hong Kong. For the
first several treatments, while he was probing my back and legs with
numerous three-inch needles, we talked openly about possible explana-

tions for acupuncture's effectiveness with pain, dietary, and hearing problems. He was also a knowledgeable and open-minded man who attributed plausibility to non-Western accounts of illness etiology, mind-body fusion, ying-yang energy flows, and other topics. My fascination with the topic grew until, one day, I asked the doctor if he would be willing to let me use his practice as the setting for a sociological study of acupuncture. When he tentatively agreed, I proceeded to write a detailed research proposal that guaranteed noninterference with the functioning of his practice in return for access to him, his staff, and those patients who would agree to be interviewed. My request was successful, I believe, because our close and trusting doctor-patient relationship was easily transposed to one of subject-researcher. I thus began a five-month field research project that was to culminate in an M.A. thesis (Kotarba, 1975).

During the course of the research, I simply tried to blend in unobtrusively with the day-to-day operation of the office. I spent many hours in the office even when there were no patients present just to make my presence as routine as possible. My membership in the office "coffee clatch" left me party to many informal discussions of patient idiosyncracies. For example, I learned which patients were considered hypochondriacs or malingerers, as well as those perceived as being truly in constant pain. I was also able to learn some of the background medical and biographical information on patients that was, in some cases, unobtainable in the course of relatively short interviews with them. Again, good relations with the bookkeeping and billing staff led to an awareness of the economic facets of chronic pain, such as trying to convince insurance carriers to cover a new and experimental mode of treatment like acupuncture.

I attribute much of my success in developing rapport with the physician and his staff to what I call the "good boy" approach. (Johnson similarly refers to this strategy as "using charm in developing trust" [1975:110].) When studying a specific setting, the field researcher is to a large degree at the mercy of his or her contacts. Any perceived mistake or breach of trust can result in expulsion from the setting (Johnson, 1975: Chapter 5) if access is dependent simply on the good graces of the person in charge. I have found it valuable in my research experiences not only to take precautions against making gross mistakes (e.g., interrupting doctor-patient consultations) but to become a *positive* influence in the setting. For example, I made a habit of bringing coffee and doughnuts to the office at least once a week. I occasionally helped move patients from wheelchairs to treatment tables, backed by an open offer to be available whenever needed. I never placed myself above involvement with office gossip or idle talk. In other words, I tried my best to be liked by everyone in the office. There are essentially two reasons for this strategy. First, all members of a setting are potential sources of data, especially in an exploratory study like mine. I realized this fact when the nurses' assistant, a quiet, elderly woman, once remarked how some patients confided their past to her—and sometimes current—consultations with chiropractors, information that the patients would never feel free to tell the doctor or regular nurses. Second, I soon realized that the doctor, who was often too busy to pay much attention to me, would occasionally ask his staff members "how the kid was doing." They always gave glowing evaluations that were more personal than professional, such as, "He's really nice and always tries to be helpful." Of course, this strategy of constant deference meant that occasionally I had to swallow my pride and smile at someone I personally disliked. However, the importance of maintaining open access to a crucial field setting helped me to hide my existential self, when necessary, and project my pragmatic research self. This approach was quite valuable in dealing with patients too.

As Johnson (1975:118–123) has noted, developing trust in the setting is not only necessary for purposes of entry, but must constantly be worked at in order to ensure the successful completion of the project. In dealing with the physician-acupuncturist, I translated this notion into an "honesty is the best policy" strategy. Every time I wrote up parts of my research, whether they were sections of my thesis or simply transcriptions of patient interviews, I would show them to the doctor and discuss them with him later. This served several functions of trust maintenance. First, the physician appreciated my concern for his opinions on the project. Second, he was able to correct obvious mistakes and fill in missing data. Third, he provided an alternative medical interpretation for many of my sociological analyses. Fourth, and perhaps most important, I made it very clear early in the research that I was critical of certain aspects of the practice of acupuncture. For example, I wrote that the use of acupuncture as a means of weight loss was, to many middle-class housewives, a fad that corresponded to the flood of miracle diets (Kotarba, 1975:163–165). At first, the doctor took offense at this statement, maintaining that acupuncture helps *some* people who have failed to lose weight using conventional methods. By calmly discussing this point of contention, I was able to further clarify my view that many of the patients I interviewed were placing unrealistic expectations on the power of acupuncture, partially as a result of the glowing accounts of it given by the popular press. We both learned something from this talk, although we never really came to full agreement. Nevertheless, the physician came to understand that he didn't have to worry about seeing a final report on my research that would be either shockingly biased, libelous, or misleading. By being kept up to date on my research, he came to appreciate more the distinctive perspective on health and illness we call sociology and the fact that it is not necessarily opposed to medicine.

After five months of intensive study in the acupuncturist's office, I had completed the research necessary for my masters thesis but had expanded the scope of my interest in chronic pain. I was fascinated by the vast majority of acupuncture patients who sought the relief of pain unmitigated by analgesic drugs and surgery, medicine's traditional means of treating pain. I had also witnessed several cases of analgesic drug abuse. I had also learned that chronic pain patients consult a wide range of potential healers in the search for a cure, including chiropractors, naturopaths, faith healers, and hypnotists. Of special interest were the accounts of how the pain affected other facets of their lives, such as family and occupation. Through the original physician and several of his patients, I made contact with other pain patients and healers in the area, and gained entry to a pain treatment center that was just beginning its operation. This additional research provided sufficient insight and data for a second work dealing specifically with the chronic pain experience (Kotarba, 1977).

BEGINNING ANEW IN SAN DIEGO

When I returned to graduate school at the University of California at San Diego in 1976 to complete a doctorate on the chronic pain experience, I was able to put the idea of "casting a wide net" to good use. Being new to the area, I had little idea of what health interventions were available to chronic pain patients but surmised that they were extensive since Southern California is a hotbed of marginal and holistic healing practices. I also wanted to explore further everyday pain experiences, which lessened even more my dependency on any one health care setting. My defocused attempts to locate pain-related phenomena led to my use of three general types of resources: the community, the university, and personal contacts. I will now describe these three types of encounters in detail.

COMMUNITY RESOURCES

The most obvious starting point for a search of communitywide health care facilities is the local hospital. A quick look through the telephone directory indicated that San Diego was blessed with numerous hospitals and outpatient facilities, including several operated by the U.S. Navy. Noting that one hospital listed its rehabilitation unit, I called the director to set up an appointment. Through her, I learned of all the special hospital services in the county available to chronic pain patients.

The local press was most helpful in locating individual pain practitioners. The major "alternative" weekly newspaper regularly carries advertisements by marginal healers (e.g., chiropractors and naturopaths) which describe in some detail the types of problems they serve. Through one of these ads, for example, I was able to make contact with an enormously successful chiropractor who allowed me entry to his classes in self-hypnosis. The local newspapers also run occasional feature stories on topics such as "What's New for Bad Backs." One such story told of a special back exercise program run by the local YMCA. Through personal contact with the director of the program, I was able to interview six class participants, including people who had already run the gamut of ineffective medical interventions.

Another feature article described an interview with the director of a newly founded pain center in which certain innovative techniques such as transactional analysis were discussed. This "catch" turned out to be a "flounder," for the director refused to even see me. I later learned that he had bad experiences with academic persons who entered his clinic and either disrupted the setting or left with harshly critical evaluations of the program. I was later able, however, to learn the basic features of the program by attending a seminar delivered by the director to an audience of professional health workers.

ACADEMIC RESOURCES

As a member of the academic community, I soon learned that I was surrounded by a wealth of pain-related resources. In fact, my participation in a weekend extension class on Siddha Yoga meditation marked the beginning of a whole network of contacts that ultimately provided me with some of my most important data. As is common in adult education today, the University Extension Service provides numerous classes in self-actualization (e.g., meditation, self-help health care, assertiveness training). In spring 1977, I enrolled in a two-day seminar on Siddha Yoga meditation. I was not only personally interested in learning this relaxation skill but was open to the possibility of there encountering people with chronic pain, for my earlier research in Arizona produced examples of several individuals who obtained relief this way. During lunch and break times, I made a point of joining as many informal groups as possible in order to hear casual evaluations of the class as well as personal anecdotes of pain experiences. To my amazement, I learned that nearly a third of the class was there to explore yet another way of coping with pain. My best contact in this regard was a middle-aged woman who had suffered chronic postoperative pain for nearly five years. According to her account, she was always on the lookout for university extension classes related to health care and, in a later interview, mentioned how she enjoyed meeting other chronic pain sufferers and learning about the latest "cures."

My participation in the meditation seminar did not end with five extensive interviews. During the second day of the seminar, I had lunch with a younger woman who had an academic nursing background. She had published several articles on patient care, and we enjoyed swapping stories on common interests. During our conversation, she mentioned that her husband was the public information officer for the university. My eyes immediately lit up, for it seemed that with his extensive contact with the media and the entire university community, he could be a valuable resource. Not knowing where this contact would lead me, I nevertheless made arrangements to meet this publicist for lunch the following week. As we talked about my research interests, he asked if I was doing any work with athletes and their injuries. I said that I had never thought about the possible implications of chronic pain for athletic performance. To my surprise, he remarked that he was a good friend of the public relations director of the local major league baseball team, who might grant me access to the players. He agreed to call his friend and use his influence to set up an appointment for me.

Before actually meeting the team's public relations director, I carefully planned my approach. I had to be extremely careful not to present my work as an expose of any kind. The previous year, the local professional football team had received much adverse publicity as a result of media coverage of a drug abuse problem among the players. In light of this, I prepared a detailed resume that made my academic qualifications quite clear.

I mentioned this sports contact to a friend who was also interested in research among athletes, and he accompanied me on my first appointment. I explained that I was prepared to abide by any rules set up for my research; the audiences for my work were strictly academic; I would take all precautions necessary not to interfere with the operation of the ball club; I would eliminate all questions dealing with drugs; and copies of all my written work on the research would be sent to the publicist. The publicist agreed to give me a two-game press pass. This allowed me access to the press box, the field before the games, and the clubhouse, where I could talk to the players before and after the game. If I received no critical evaluations from either players or coaches, he would extend my pass for the remainder of the season. During my two-day tryout, I again applied my "good boy" strategy to the maximum. I talked only to the three players who were college graduates, for I guessed that they would be most interested in and sympathetic to academic research in sports. During the games, I sat close to the public relations director in the press box, making sure that he saw I was busy taking notes throughout the game and using my press pass to work and not simply to enjoy free games. Above all, I tried to stay out of the way of the regular press corps, who I was afraid might object to my invasion of their territory.

I called the public relations director the next afternoon to see if I had passed my test. He assured me that the players I had talked to enjoyed the interviews and that he believed I was earnest in my work. He then extended my pass for the remainder of the season. I was eventually able to interview approximately thirty-five players and numerous coaches from several teams, six members of the local press corps, the team trainer, and various auxiliary personnel. My extension of the "net" to the world of sports did not stop there, however. In August of that year, I returned to my home town of Chicago for the national sociological meetings. Knowing that Chicago has two major league baseball beams, I felt that access to them would help triangulate and expand the data I received in San Diego. Before leaving San Diego, I asked the public relations director to write two letters of introduction to his counterparts in Chicago. Through these letters, I was able to spend six days interviewing approximately twelve players on both Chicago teams. I now felt quite secure in knowing that my study of ball players and pain was fairly comprehensive.

My research with professional baseball players provided an understanding of how chronic pain can affect career mobility, relations at home, and the meaning of the expression "play in pain, talk about injuries." Fruitful as this line of research turned out to be, it did create two related problems. First, gaining entry to the ball park was only my first obstacle. I also had to convince the players that I was not a member of the regular press corps—a difficult task, since I was always carrying a tape recorder and note pad and constantly "hawking" interviews. This imposed identity precluded access to those players who always refused interviews with the press in light of perceived past exploitation. Again, I had to convince these players that my purposes were strictly academic and that all interviews would be kept anonymous. Even then, I failed to convince several players of my sincerity. Second, I had to overcome the players' previous experience with interviews once they agreed to talk to me. For the most part, they were used to answering short questions about their play and the day's game with standard answers laden with baseball jargon (e.g., Q: "How did you guys manage to win today's game?" A: "We've got a good attitude, we're playing well together, and things are going our way for a change"). Since my questions dealt with some usually unexplored facets of the players' personal lives and their deepest physical and emotional feelings, they were unsure at first of how to respond. Only through extensive, patient probing was I able to give the players a meaningful sense of the depth I was seeking. In all, some of my most productive interviews took place away from the ball park, when I would meet a few players for dinner or a drink and project more easily my social science researcher identity.

The university public information officer helped me in another way to locate chronic pain experiences. Soon after we met, he asked if I would be interested in having a press release made of my research on pain. At first I was hesitant, having heard horror stories of the ways the media discover university news releases and proceed to write misleading and often erroneous copy on them. Before agreeing, then, I required assurance that I would have final approval, when possible, on where follow-up stories would appear. The unexpected benefit of media coverage was the personal response I received from both professional and lay people who were interested in my work and offered to recount their own experiences with chronic pain. The most fruitful of these contacts was an elderly woman who had received acupuncture in Taiwan in 1955 for nagging neck pain. It was interesting to learn how she had encountered acupuncture many years before it became widely publicized in the United States.

Finally, my involvement with the university indirectly led to the discovery of the importance of alcohol use for pain relief among regular tavern clientele (Kotarba, 1978). During the 1977–1978 school year, as a research assistant I explored all facets of the drinking/driving phenomenon. A large part of my work consisted of ethnographic analysis of drinking/driving talk occurring in the bar. While listening to discussions of lawyers, judges, police, and angry wives, I was struck by the large proportion of talk devoted to personal health problems, including chronic pain conditions. A bar drinker with pain not only sought sympathy for his suffering but consulted his peers for information on effective health care practitioners, ways of successfully presenting oneself to these healers, and ways of dealing with occupational adjuncts such as disability compensation claims. Most importantly, I observed how many tavern drinkers either consciously or unconsciously use alcohol as an analgesic for chronic pain as an alternative to debilitating narcotics or fear-evoking surgery. I not only recorded notes on this naturally emerging bar talk on pain but was able to schedule interviews in locations outside of the noisy atmosphere of the bar. These interviews helped to minimize interference with the primary purposes of the research project.

PERSONAL RESOURCES

While conducting this open-ended research, I took care to mention my interests to as many friends and acquaintances as possible. Ever since my original research in Arizona, I realized that most people know of others who suffer chronic pain. By simply mentioning my work, I received an incredible number of responses such as the following: "Oh, you should talk to my brother-in-law. He's had a bad back for years." Friends and acquaintances have proven to be excellent resources in the search for common, everyday life experiences. In casual conversation, or at the beginning of a class in which one is lecturing, people seem most interested in research topics, especially if they can respond with relevant personal experiences or the experience of their contemporaries.

Two such informal contacts have proven quite valuable. The first was made through the secretary of our drinking/driving project. We were talking about my pain research one day when I mentioned that I was on the lookout for unusual pain experiences. She then told me that her sister-in-law had had spinal problems since birth and was now contemplating spinal fusion surgery as a last resort. Probing further, I learned that this woman had been an advocate of natural health and holistic healing for many years and had tried meditation asnd biofeedback for her problem long before consulting physicians for help. Through the secretary, I made an appointment to interview her, for her experience was decidedly different from the usual pain career in which the individual seeks alternative modes of healing *after* medicine fails. Even more so, I had the rare opportunity to interview this pain person (in a nonclinical setting) immediately before and after corrective surgery and to check for changes in her attitude (if any) toward medicine.

The second informal contact occurred at a wedding reception. A close friend had married a woman who was previously married to a professional football player. I told her of my findings from earlier research with athletes and she concurred from her own experience. She agreed, for example, that her ex-husband would rarely come home after a game and complain about injuries or pain. She attributed this behavior to his "machismo," but I saw it as just another example of the complex ways that occupational contingencies enter into familial interactions at home. In any event, we later sat for several hours and discussed the experience of living with a person whose occupation normally risks injury and premature physical aging. I had successfully made contact with someone who was willing to be open regarding her most personal family problems, which had been something of a stumbling block up to that point.

The search for informal contact with chronic pain experiences has its drawbacks, however. I was being swamped with personal stories, most of which involved experiences quite redundant and ordinary at this late stage of my research. I was careful to immediately probe my initial resource to find out if further contact would be rewarding. This strategy involved a balance between showing great initial interest in the experience in order to find out about it and the possibility of having to admit to the resource that the contact was "not exactly what I'm looking for." The only rule governing this strategy was the constant use of tact and the realization that all chronic pain experiences were not equally valuable to my project.

CONCLUDING REMARKS

The defocused search for topical social experiences can be effectively applied to any phenomenon which is located in a specific setting. In medical sociology, this approach is especially relevant to the study of chronic or minor illness behavior that is only *occasionally* shaped and defined through interaction with medicine in a clinical setting. The strategies discussed in this selection (i.e., the use of community, university, and personal resources) are useful in obtaining a comprehensive understanding of any experience that permeates one's everyday social life. These methods should be considered when the researcher is unsure of the parameters of the population in question.

The objection could be raised that the widespread search for relevant phenomena might lead to an unmanageable "explosion" of data and subsequent distraction from primary research objectives. The researcher can minimize this unlikely risk by carefully evaluating each potential contact to see whether it adds to his or her developing theoretical model or simply provides interesting yet irrelevant data. In the long run, the field researcher benefits by risking close involvement with the social world.

References

DOUGLAS, J.D. *Investigative Social Research.* Beverly Hills, Calif.: Sage Publications, 1976.

JOHNSON, J.M. *Doing Field Research.* New York: Free Press, 1975.

KOTARBA, J.A. "American Acupuncturists: The New Entrepreneurs of Hope." *Urban Life,* 4 (1975), 149-77.

KOTARBA, J.A. "The Chronic Pain Experience." In J.D. Douglas and J.M. Johnson, (eds.), *Existential Sociology.* New York: Cambridge University Press, 1977.

KOTARBA, J.A. "Alcohol Use and the Interstitial Management of Chronic Pain." Paper presented at the annual meeting of the Society for the Study of Symbolic Interaction. San Francisco, September 7, 1978.

ROTH, J. "Management Bias in Social Science Study of Medical Treatment." *Human Organization,* 21 (1962), 47-50.

STRAUS, R. "The Nature and Status of Medical Sociology." *American Sociological Review,* 22 (1957), 203-213.

Interviewing American Widows

HELENA ZNANIECKI LOPATA *Loyola University of Chicago*

"Getting in" to do field research, defined as making contact with people or groups to be studied, is not the first problem facing sociological researchers. Several stages and problems precede this one, especially if the subject matter is previously underexplored and in any way stigmatized or at least not currently in vogue. Above all, the researcher has to become conscious of a sociological problem, to select it as worthy of three, four, or five years of focus and as researchable through available or potential resources. There are so many scientific problems which can be investigated, which are sufficiently important to any researcher to direct him or her into this commitment, that the selection process is indeed a major screening device.

My selection of the study of role modifications and support systems of American urban widows grew out of one area of my interests: American women as members of this unique, highly urbanized, and industrialized society. This interest undoubtedly came from my having been socialized in a different society, Poland, and from having come to this country during World War II. As a budding sociologist, I became fascinated by the gap between the image American women had of themselves and others had of them, on the one hand, and the competence and creativity with which they performed their roles, on the other hand (Lopata, 1971). I then studied American urban women in the "full-house plateau" stage of their life course, with a husband and at least one pre-high-school child in the household (see *Occupation: Housewife*, 1971), before deciding to find out what happened to these roles and support systems once the husband had died and the children developed more independent lives. The sociologically relevant decision to study widows, however, was followed by repercussions complicating the process of "getting in" to fieldwork. In the

68

first place, this decision to apply the social role and, later, the support system frameworks to the study of widows immediately drew negative reactions from my social circles both inside and outside of the academic world. The subject matter was judged as depressing and as unworthy of serious sociological research while "more important" scientific problems remained unstudied. Although funding became available, even the funding agency had some qualms over my entrance into the field; thus, it suggested that I not interview women widowed less than six months.

I attributed all these negative personal and official reactions to my new research area to sexism, and to the Anglo-Saxon fear of certain emotions defined by Gorer (1965), as "the pornography of death." I did not realize how strongly I had been affected by similar biases until I caught myself spending extended, though comfortable, weeks in libraries, picking up bits and pieces of knowledge on this understudied topic. It finally dawned upon me that I was thus delaying doing what sociologists are supposed to do—go into the field, talk to and observe the people about whom the theoretical formulations and future interview "operationalizations (!)" were to be made.

This hesitancy over getting into the field and pulling together a team willing to commit several years of study to widowhood forced me to examine the undercurrent of biases inherent in American and possibly other societies concerning widows. Felix Berardo (1967), who studied widows and widowers in the State of Washington, pointed out as late as 1968 that this was a "neglected aspect of the family life-cycle."[1] My examination of why I was not as yet in the field, although I had planned the study since 1965 and was funded in 1966, began in 1967.

There were many culturally and personally relevant reasons for my hesitation and for the neglect of research on various aspects of widowhood by other social scientists.[2] The processes of dying and death have only very recently become sociologically popular, if not yet professionally proper. The terminally ill, as well as the survivors, have been relatively invisible, societally as well as sociologically. Widows form a social minority in several different ways, in spite of their numbers, which now total more than 10 million (Lopata, 1971, 1979). Studies of their situation offer opportunities to test many social scientific theories of social change, role modification following crises, the relation of societal members to communities and other social networks, and so on. However, widows are women, which establishes them as being of lower status than men in the society and in sociology; the latter has considered subjects such as complex organizations of much greater significance. Second, they are women deprived of the major roles assigned this sex in this society: that of wife and, for most of them, that of active mother. These roles of women still attract the greatest amount of attention in America, as indicated not only by *The Total Woman* (Morgan, 1973) literature but also by the struggles over the Equal Rights Amendment. Third, they are husbandless women in a society devoted to couple companionate activities, so that they are treated, or feel that they are treated, as a "fifth wheel" in social situations (Lopata, 1973; Treas and Morgan, 1978). In addition, these women not only lack a male escort and companion but are also deprived of the husband's social status, since wives traditionally depend on vicarious sources of prestige (Lipman-Blumen, 1973). Fifth, many widows are old, and old people let alone old women, do not have a positive image in this society (Troll, Israel, and Israel, 1977). The sixth factor contributing to the social invisibility of widows in all but the recent past is that so many are poor, members of minority groups in other ways, undereducated and unorganized. Finally, the whole specter of widowhood raises the possibility of outbursts of grief, of emotional upset with all its symptoms, shocking the social network's emphasis on pleasurable interaction.

It is not surprising that even a sociologist trained in objective research could hesitate over talking with widows, even after having selected the subject "role modifications following the death of a husband" as a major focus of research. Fortunately for me, in the late 1960s Robert Fulton had organized a conference on death and dying at the University of Minnesota. I attended this meeting and had the unexpected opportunity of talking with the originator of research on grief, Dr. Eric Lindemann (1944), whose work with sufferers and survivors of the Coconut Grove Fire established the first theoretical framework for the understanding of the process of grief (see also Glick, Weiss, and Parkes, 1974, *The First Year of Bereavement*). Lindemann gave a speech, and I later asked for a few minutes of his time to explain my research problems, mainly my hesitancy over intruding on the privacy of a grieving person and the concern of many of my associates and governmental personnel over my planned fieldwork with widows. Dr. Lindemann's reaction was instantaneous and definite—encouraging me in this subject of research for years to come:

> But that is the main problem of the bereaved—the fact that people will not allow them to talk about their feelings, do not ask them questions as to what happened, how the person so important to most of them died and how they are managing their lives at the present time!! No one wants to hear about their problems. Go and interview widows of all ages and all stages of widowhood; it will give them a chance to accomplish some more of their grief work and to feel that they are making a contribution to other widows.

This fifteen-minute conversation released me of many (though not all) of the culturally acquired inhibitions preventing a sociological in-depth study of American urban widows. The next step proved even more helpful. Equipped with an awkward Wollensack tape recorder, I started to interview widows whom I contacted through a wide range of sources available from Roosevelt University and other associates, fortunately a very heterogeneous social network. My clumsiness with the tape recorder in the exploratory stages of the research proved to be a boon, preventing me from making some of the mistakes of new researchers not really familiar with the world of their subjects. I knew what I wanted to ask these women; all my reading, friends, relatives, and sociological colleagues had filled me with questions and anticipated responses. The mechanical problems of using the recorder, and the accompanying nondirected interaction with prospective interviewees, finally forced me to listen to what the widows wanted to talk about before I had a chance to ask questions. Their monologues often focused on subjects very different from what I had assumed to be important to them. For example, one widow, a mother of three young adult sons, kept talking at a rapid pace while I introduced myself (she knew of my coming at that time), tried to locate an electric outlet, plugged in the Wollensack, put on the tape, and tried to get the whole thing going (it was a very cold Chicago day, and it refused to warm up immediately). I was frankly irritated with her constant chatter, because she would not wait for the tape recorder to start and because she was not talking about the death of her husband and being a widow but about the new wife and the fiancee of two of her sons. By the time the tape recorder was working and I was ready to start asking questions, I realized that she had actually been talking about her grief work because it was just now beginning. Her husband, a very busy professional focused on his career, had died many years ago, but she had lived vicariously before and after that event through the sons, running her home as a social center for them and their friends. Now one son was married and gone, the second was engaged to "not a very nice girl" who kept him away from home a great deal of the time, and the third was frantically resisting her increased attempts to depend on him. This woman was in a panic. The interview contributed to my increasing awareness that role modifications and support systems of widows contain a variety of realities which my lack of familiarity with the lives of widows had not anticipated, partially because of the stereotypical effect of the subject matter.

Let me warn the reader that this is not the end of the trials and tribulations of interviewing widows as a means of gaining sociologically and societally relevant knowledge. I have always given myself a full year of exploratory research, using as many social science techniques as relevant, in order to broaden my understanding of the social world of the subjects before entering the restricted world of survey research. The simple insights described above do not lead automatically to such understanding or the ability to convert it into interviews and communicate the results to others.[3] There are many forms of role involvements and modifications, social networks, types of loneliness and methods of coping with them, emotional support systems, forms of social interaction, and so on available to adults in a complex urban center in a society as huge and complicated as that of America. We sociologists must select a few aspects of social reality and use a limited number of tools in the research process. As an example, before even beginning to formulate the role modification interview, I did the following:

1. A content analysis of two sets of letters directed to me in response to a television program and after the announcement of the study appeared in the newspapers.

2. Interviews of one to two hours with ten of the letter authors selected from among seventy-four based on the largest range of socioeconomic factors.

3. A reexamination of the literature on aging, grief, divorce, single status, ethnic family construction, and other factors that I had neglected before because I had not realized how deeply these aspects of life affect widowhood.

4. Reinterviews with some former contacts and thirty-five additional open-ended and taped interviews, mainly with widows alone, but also in situations involving relatives. Again, attempts were made to cover all combinations of living situations under which role modifications can occur. For example, I interviewed Greek women, whose culture prescribes that they live with a married daughter and who were either able or unable to follow the norm. I interviewed Polish widows who do not even understand the language of the society in which they are living. Black members of the research team interviewed black women. We tried experiments with interviewers, varying them by age and sex to test interviewer influence.

5. Interviews with groups of women, or those affiliated through residential proximity, in order to learn more about the effects of situational factors (see Rosow, 1967). For example, I met several times with the members of the La Grange Senior Citizens club (in a suburb of Chicago), or the racially and ethnically integrated residents of Chicago Housing Authority buildings, and later interviewed members individually.

6. Interviews with dyads of mother and daughter, or other kin members, which provided insights regarding relational strains. Daughters, sons, and, in some cases, even granddaughters tended to maintain a protective bubble around the widow, deflecting questions they considered threatening either by answering themselves or by shifting the conversation, with varying levels of sophistication.

7. Attendance at meetings of organizations especially for widows or single people, establishing contacts, supplemented by an analysis of their publications.

8. Attendance at meetings of groups which by their very nature attract widows, although they are not focused on helping people through widowhood, such as women's church groups, ethnic clubs, branches of the YWCA, and so forth.

9. Attendance at meetings, tours of facilities, interviews, and publications analyses of such agencies as the Mayor's Commission on Senior Citizens, the Chicago Housing Authority, and Home Delivered Meals in order to determine their perception of widows and the problems of widowhood.

10. Collections and analysis of diaries and histories of events and daily problems, as well as their solutions by widows in a variety of living situations, by size of community, type of residence, household composition, race, age, and so on.

11. Interviews with friends and relatives of widows, based on the hypothesis that relations within the network can become strained at times, to determine how such strains are explained by the associates and the process by which some people remain close to the widow while others withdraw from her. I was particaularly interested in the process by which one child, almost inevitably a daughter, becomes selected to carry the basic responsibility for the mother.

INTERVIEW FORMULATION

The reader must imagine the task of combining the theoretical framework with which any researcher must start and the mass of data collected from all these sources and converting all of it into a single interview. Next, please imagine that the initially open-ended interview, during which the interviewer asks general questions and records the answers verbatim, must become with each pretest more and more structured so that alternative answers are precoded and respondents must choose among these alternatives. All of us have had to answer tests limited to multiple-choice questions which appeared meaningless in our own situation so that the "other (specify_____)" answer was the only one with which we felt comfortable. Unfortunately, precoded formats are necessary for most large surveys, not just because of the costs of coding idiosyncratic and thus divergent answers into a simplified system for statistical manipulation but mainly because such dependence on coders offers too many opportunities for error.

Case studies or a few in-depth interviews do not require such strict precoding of alternative answers and make their own contribution to the understanding of a social phenomenon in depth. Survey research is needed whenever we wish to determine how frequently and among which categories of people a given behavior, definition of a situation, or belief appears and which variables affect their occurrence. Survey research is thus highly dependent upon the quality of the interview schedule and its applicability to the sample population. Sociologists always know that they developed a good interview when reading a completed one gives them an "aha" picture of the person, or at least those aspects of the person's internal and external world with which they are concerned.

FINDING THE FIELD: LOCATING THE RESPONDENTS

Even when the stages of selecting the sociological problem, committing oneself and a staff to its study, and developing the best possible interview for survey research are completed, the remaining problems are not insignificant. In the first place, one has to find the respondents. Although there are more than ten million widows in the United States, finding them, or a sample of them, in a geographical area such as metropolitan Chicago is not easy. There is no automatically available means of obtaining a list of widows and selecting a sample from them which would ensure that each widow would have the same opportunity as any other widow of being interviewed. I used the sampling experts of the National Opinion Research Center of the University of Chicago to locate the areas in which its interviewers would find a sample of the 300 widows, aged fifty to sixty-four or sixty-five and over, which I and the Administration on Aging finally settled upon to study. We trained experienced, middle-aged women for this study, trying to match the interviewer with the probable racial and ethnic characteristics of the respondents by assigning blocks by known composition of the population. The study proved very expensive because of the problems of locating eligible widows. We had much less difficulty in actually interviewing widows once they were located, in spite of dire predictions of high refusal rates. As Eric Lindemann predicted, the women were usually eager to be interviewed, unless the presence of another adult in the home complicated the contact situation.

Once the role modification study[4] of older widows had been completed, I was asked by the U.S. Social Security Administration (SSA) if there were any scientific questions still unanswered and which could provide data of interest to its policy planners. As of that time (early 1970s) there was still little knowledge about the living patterns of widows, and the SSA was concerned with all five categories of women influenced by its policies. We were also interested in expanding into comparative research wherever local social scientists wished to use the same instrument. I was particularly interested in approaching the subjects through an alternative theoretical framework, splitting role relations into support systems. Extensive discussions with the statisticians of the SSA, which funded the second, support systems, study,[5] led to the conclusion that the prior method of locating widows through a modified area sample had been too expensive for a larger sample containing a greater variety of widows. I was then under contract with the SSA, and so, we could use its lists of widows of all ages who were or had been beneficiaries of the Social Security system. Samples of five categories of widows were pulled from the SSA files: beneficiaries who were mothers of dependent father orphans; older widows of entitled workers; women eligible for only the "lump sum" payment to help defray funeral costs; former beneficiaries who had remarried; and former beneficiaries whose children were beyond the eligibility age but who themselves were not old enough to qualify on their own. The SSA staff was able to draw samples of these five categories of women but our use of these lists met with many problems, some anticipated and unavoidable, some simply not anticipated. It took all of our Chicago-based teams, this time including the Survey Research Laboratory of the University of Illinois as the data collection agency, almost a year to pretest from subsamples, discover the problems of locating many of the women, and interview them. Some of the addresses of former recipients were quite old; many widows had moved from their former residence, some even out of the metropolitan area. The remarried women were especially likely to have moved, and their name change complicated location problems even more. In spite of valiant and often very imaginative efforts by the interviewers, including five callbacks after the widow was located but not home at varied hours, we ended up with a 25 percent of the sample uncontacted and 11 percent found ineligible, mainly because they had died or moved out of the area (Heinemann, 1977).

An additional problem appeared in this second study of widows because of our procedures. The role modification research team interviewed women right after they were found within the designated geographical areas. Therefore, they had no time to formulate rigid expectations as to the topics the interview would cover or to discuss the potential of such an interview with significant others. The support system project sent out letters informing the recipient that an interviewer would contact her concerning her widowhood experiences. This mailing occurred at a time when the whole subject of confidentiality had become an issue in American society. Our contact letter naturally stated the measures we would take to ensure such confidentiality, but the warning itself tended to worry many women. They turned to friends or relatives for advice; these people then became their "protectors," preventing "invasion of privacy." Occasionally we would receive an indignant phone call from a relative insisting that the widow not be interviewed, to be followed later by a phone call from the woman herself, very interested in having the interviewer come and talk with her. The negative reaction of some relatives, especially adult children, following the initial letter is itself very interesting. It may have been a consequence of the stigmatizing of widowhood (Treas and Morgan, 1978). However, there is also the possibility that relatives had tried to dissuade the widows from being interviewed. Our refusal rate of 24 percent came mainly from the older widows, as well as those about whom we had too little information to estimate age. Younger widows who failed to be interviewed were mainly impossible to locate.

The fact that the study was funded by the Social Security Administration made some potential respondents fearful of answering certain questions because of the possibility that they might lose benefits by divulging other sources of income. Survey research has become increasingly affected by urban Americans' suspicion of strangers claiming to be interviewers. This is a result of the misuse of this identification by salespeople and even criminals, and by the actions of people such as Senator William Proxmire, who has made fun of social science research.

There was an additional, unexpected effect of our introductory letter to the widows. The receivers who were located and willing to be interviewed (49 percent of the eligible sample) went through a process of "psyching up" for the encounter, expecting us to focus immediately upon the circumstances of the husband's death and surrounding problems. We had not realized the potency of such an anticipatory rehearsal. We had organized the interview in a rather traditional manner, beginning with needed background data and then following historically the main events of their lives in order to establish possible resources in their support systems. During the pretests, we rapidly learned that many widows became increasingly irritated as the interview progressed. Several debriefing sessions with the experienced interviewers finally made us realize that these women had anticipated our immediate concern with the "heroic" aspects of their widowhood. They did not want to be asked first about other events, their childhood, education, marriage, the contributions of the late husband to their emotional support systems, residence, and so forth. A simple rearrangement of the order of the questions solved this problem easily. We thus asked only those basic questions which would enable us to determine which segments of the interview were important and then led immediately to the subject the widow had primed herself to discuss. Once the husband's death was covered, with the help of some open-ended questions, the women were perfectly willing to talk about resources, past and current support systems, and other subjects of interest to us. The questions focusing on the events leading to the widowhood proved to have significance for us beyond the cathartic one for the respondent, since they provided invaluable depth of detail and differentiated how widows are able to reconstruct these traumatic events in their memories.

The pretests pointed up other problems with the interview, especially in terms of flow and language. The factor of interview flow is very important, because people vary in the ways in which they anchor past, present, or even future reality. For example, although we considered it logical to ask women about their support systems (economic, service, social, and emotional; see Lopata, 1979) for the time before the husband's death and then to repeat the questions for the present time, many of the respondents did not follow this line of reasoning and became irritated over what they considered to be repetitious questions. When we changed the format to compare the two time periods within the same support, they responded with ease. For example, we asked, "Who was closest to you in 1964?" (or whatever year the respondent named as preceding the death-related events) and then asked "Who is closest to you now?" and the respondents followed the order with no problem.

We also changed the interview during the prefinal phase because of governmental concerns with the subject of death and widowhood. Two troublesome subjects emerged which were highly indicative of the American attitudes toward widows. Obviously, one of the solutions to the problems of widowhood is finding a new husband. The subject of remarriage made some reviewers uncomfortable, but the precoded question as to what activities the woman shared with a "close male associate" really put fear in the hearts of Washington officials concerned with Proxmire-like reactions. During the open-ended pretesting, we actually asked what women did with such associates (the widows often called such people "boyfriends" and spoke of dates), and some of the responses included "make love," "have sex," and "sleep together" or even "live together." We had to eliminate the precoded alternatives using any such language and rephrase them as open-ended questions. This decreased the probability of finding out what the relation involves, since many more women are willing to check a precoded answer than to give answers with sexual connotations to open-ended questions. The second subject which bothered governmental reviewers pertained to the consequences of the death of the father upon the children. The question passed review in the open-ended stage, but the alternatives bothered some people because they included, as given by the women themselves, "not at all" or even "they were relieved." As stated before, our society finds many aspects of death and its consequences very uncomfortable.

GETTING OUT: CONSEQUENCES OF INTERVIEW INTERACTION

During the actual interviews (Kuhn, 1962), we usually found the widows not only willing but even eager to talk about their experiences and support systems, often mentioning a lack of opportunity of doing so with close associates. However, the interview situation sometimes presented special problems to the interviewer and the rest of our staff, leading to interviewer attrition and much internal discussion (Heinemann, 1977). Over and over, we found the respondents expecting some sort of direct help as a result of the interview, a solution of problems and even a complete change in life. They assumed that the interviewer, or at least the university staff, has the power to bring societal resources to them or to change the attitudes or behavior of significant others toward them. It is difficult to be faced by a respondent, caller, or letter writer who is so obviously in pain or need and whom we are not trained to help. Our staff at Loyola University of Chicago, to whom calls or letters were referred, tried to learn more about the resources of the community and were occasionally able to serve as intermediaries, establishing a link between the widow in need and these resources. Often the attempts ended in total frustration when an indifferent agency representative could not be bothered with the problem or was unable to direct us to the right resource. Through these efforts, we learned some of the helplessness felt by these women, many of whom could not even explain their situations as lucidly as did the staff members. Even community groups or personnel supposedly in the "helping professions" or announcing themselves as the mainstay of community life were not only absent from the support systems of these widows, as documented in the interviews, but were unable to change their policies, procedures, or eligibility requirements to assist us in helping widows reaching out for support. At the time of the study, very few groups existed to help people going through grief work, or else their membership was inappropriate to a specific kind of widow, one of a different race or lacking skills in the English language.

WHAT NOW?: RESEARCH UTILIZATION

The final problem with the study of widows in America, one common to other research products, is the underutilization of the results. Many members of our society are well aware of the gap between what researchers produce and what people in governmental agencies or in the field, who actually plan or apply programs designed to help Americans in trouble, learn of this research or can do to change existing procedures accordingly. Many a research report sits on desks or in file cabinets without reaching agencies or community groups who could benefit from the findings. Researchers are often blamed for putting these results into language or statistical tables unintelligible to the applied staff or the layman. This situation occurs partly because funding agencies require reports to be documented in a precise and complex statistical format. The situation is also partly a result of the researcher's training and vocabulary, which made the research possible since they are needed to plan a project, delineate it clearly, and conduct it. Sociologists are not trained to be popularizers; and it becomes expensive to do so because it pulls them away from their basic job of doing research, sharing results with others, and training new researchers.

Yet, the problem remains. Those funding agencies that contain trained scientific personnel with the skills to interpret survey research reports are also too busy to serve as knowledgeable disseminators. Actually, there are few agencies with enough personnel to do this; people involved in funding, research, and evaluation assume that someone else will do the job. It will probably take a few more years before people trained as knowledge translators and disseminators are hired by funding agencies so that research findings are not wasted.

During and after the research projects on widows, I tried to disseminate the results; there seemed to be a great demand for this knowledge in view of the lack of other research. I went to colleges, mental health associations, and groups organized for the "spares" or "parents without partners" and made innumerable speeches all over the United States, Canada, and even in Kiev, Jerusalem, and Tokyo. There have been some very rewarding consequences of such attempts at dissemination, in addition to the personal pleasure derived from travel and contacts with a variety of people. The main reward has been that people are now talking about widowhood, widows are no longer the invisible millions, and research into aspects of their social systems is expanding. The few of us working on related subjects, such as some of the Harvard Medical School group, consisting of Robert Weiss, David Maddison, or Phyllis Silverman (see Glick, Weiss, and Parkes, 1974) have met on several occasions and exchanged ideas; these are extremely satisfying meetings for researchers who, after all, do their major work alone. In addition, several teams of social scientists have become interested in reproducing all, or at least some, of the research. As of now, the study is in the field or in planning stages in Teheran, Iran, under the direction of Dr. Jacqueline Touba, and in Cairo, Egypt, under the guidance of Dr. Nawal Nadim; it may also spread to Japan, Canada, and India. My only hope is that the effort spent in disseminating the knowledge to so many groups within the United

States will provide greater resources for people in periods of transition so that many problems facing widows and others are met through more knowledge-based community programs. Meanwhile, I must return to research.

NOTES

1. The fact that Nye and Berardo (1975:591–620) devote a whole chapter to "Death and the Widowed Family" is probably influenced by Berardo's (1970) prior research.

2. Britain was a bit ahead in initiating such research, although not necessarily following through later. Peter Marris published *Widows and their Families* in 1958, Peter Townsend's 1957 *Family Life of Old People* makes reference to widowhood, and Jeremy Tunstall's 1966 *Old and Alone* is of obvious relevance.

3. There is a vast and growing literature on problems connected with interviewing people in all sociological texts on methodology. One of the earliest was Manford H. Kuhn's (1962) "The Interview and the Professional Relationship." Although focusing on the social worker's role in the "social act" of interviewing, rather than on the researcher's, his chapter in the Rose book provides many insights and leads for those of us who talk to people in order to expand sociological knowledge and can influence their lives only indirectly.

4. The research of role modification in the lives of American urban women who have been widowed was financed by a grant from the Administration on Aging, Department of Health, Education and Welfare (Grant AA-4-67-030-01A1), with the cooperation of Roosevelt University. Special thanks go to the members of the Midwest Council for Social Research on Aging and Ethel Shanas, Bernice Neugarten, and Robert Winch for their help in designing the basic interview schedule, and to the staff of the National Opinion Research Center for their cooperation at the different stages of work.

5. The support systems study was funded through a contract with the Social Security Administration (#SSA 71–3411), with the cooperation of Loyola University of Chicago. The interviews were conducted in 1974. I wish to thank Drs. Ethel Shanas, Bernice Neugarten, and Robert Winch, who served as consultants, and Drs. Henry Brehm, Chief of the Research Grants and Contract Staff of the Social Security Administration, Nada Smolic Krkovic of the Institute of Social Work in Zagreb, Yugoslavia, and Adam Kurzynowski of the Szkola Glowna Planowania i Statystyki, Warsaw, Poland, for help with interview construction. Gloria Heinemann and other members of the University of Illinois Survey Research Laboratory conducted the interviewing and data reduction. The members of the Center for the Comparative Study of Social Roles of Loyola University of Chicago deserve special thanks, especially Deb Burdeno, Monica Velasco, Sue Meyering, Terry Bauman, Gertrud Kim, and Frank Steinhart.

References

BERARDO, F. M. "Social Adaptation to Widowhood among a Rural-Urban Aged Population." Washington State University, College of Agriculture, Experiment Station Bulletin 689 (December).

———. "Survivorship and Social Isolation: The Case of the Aged Widower." *The Family Coordinator*, 1 (1970), 11–25.

FRIEDSON, E. *The Profession of Medicine.* New York: Dodd Mead, 1970.

GLICK, I., R. WEISS, and C.M. PARKES. *The First Years of Bereavement.* New York: Wiley, 1974.

GORER, G. *Death, Grief and Mourning.* Garden City, N.Y.: Anchor Books, 1965.

HEINEMANN, G. "Methodology." Appendix A3 in *Support Systems Involving Widows in a Metropolitan Area of the United States* by Helena Z. Lopata. Washington, D.C.: Social Security Administration, 1977.

KUHN, M.H. "The Interview and the Professional Relationship." In *Human Behavior and Social Processes,* ed. Árnold M. Rose. Boston: Houghton Mifflin, 1962, pp. 193–206.

LINDEMANN, E. "Symptomatology and Management of Acute Grief," *American Journal of Psychiatry,* 101 (1944), 141–148.

LIPMAN-BLUMEN, J. "The Vicarious Achievement Ethic and Non-Traditional Roles for Women." Paper presented at the annual meeting of the Eastern Sociological Society, New York: 1973.

LOPATA, H.Z. *Occupaton: Housewife.* New York: Oxford University Press, 1971.

———. *Widowhood in an American City.* Cambridge, Mass.: Schenkman, 1973.

———. *Women as Widows: Support Systems.* New York: Elsevier, 1979.

MARRIS, P. *Widows and Their Families.* London: Routledge & Kegan Paul, 1958.

MORGAN, M. *The Total Woman.* Old Tappan, N.J.: Revell, 1973.

NYE, I.F., and F.M. BERARDO. *The Family.* New York: Macmillan, 1973.

ROSOW, I. *The Social Integration of the Aged.* New York: Free Press, 1967.

TOWNSEND, P. *The Family Life of Old People.* London: Routledge & Kegan Paul, 1957.

TREAS, J.K., and L.A. MORGAN. "Widowhood Stigma: Pitfall to Intervening and Advocacy." Paper presented in the Widowhood and Middle Age session of the XIth International Congress of Gerontology. Tokyo, Japan: 1978.

TROLL, L., J. ISRAEL, and K. ISRAEL (eds.). *Looking Ahead: A Woman's Guide to the Problems and Joys of Growing Older.* Englewood Cliffs, N.J.: Prentice-Hall, 1977.

TUNSTALL, J. *Old and Alone.* London: Routledge & Kegan Paul, 1966.

Observing Behavior in Public Places: Problems and Strategies

DAVID A. KARP *Boston College*

Discussion in the sociological literature concerning problems of "getting into" the situation one wishes to study refers nearly exclusively to organizational or community settings. This writing (e.g., Bogdan, 1972; McCall and Simmons, 1969; Schatzman and Strauss, 1973) describes the problems researchers are likely to encounter in gaining access to clearly bounded situations with stable and organized populations. Perhaps this methodological emphasis is explained by the fact that so much important participant observation fieldwork has been conducted within particular institutional or community settings.[1] The access problem literature offers important practical advice concerning relations with research subjects, strategies for dealing with persons in power, ways to manage political disputes internal to a bureaucracy, and the like. However, these treatments of the entry problem offer little direct help to researchers studying behavior in public places.

On first consideration, studies in public places seem not to pose problems of access. After all, public places *are* public. With the exception of those who study organizations of which they are already members, investigators appearing suddenly in, say, the offices of a law firm, on the wards of a hospital, or in the production area of a factory will shortly have to account for their presence. But presumably anyone can use a public park, go shopping in a store, be in waiting areas such as bus depots, or go drinking at a neighborhood tavern. Alas, the matter is not so simple: sociologists spending any substantial time in such public places will also eventually find it necessary to explain themselves and their activities. Although public places may not have perfectly clear boundaries or formally prescribed authority structures, they too are highly coordinated, ordered, and controlled.

Public places are guided by social norms or "background expectancies" (Garfinkel, 1967) that make persons' behaviors predictable and meaningful. These places "work" because we hold common assumptions about the proper behaviors required in them. In addition, researchers will find that public places, like organizations, have their gatekeepers who may deny some persons access to the spaces they control. Public parks, as one example, are often organized spatially along class, ethnic, racial, or age lines. Old persons, teenagers, or members of any other group who define certain territories as their own will often make intruders unwelcome enough to recognize that they are in the wrong place. Even in the most anonymous urban public settings, therefore, researchers may find their activities questioned and sometimes restricted.

The central goal of this selection is to describe the access problems I experienced while spending nearly two years (between February 1969 and September 1970) trying to learn about the public sexual scene in the Times Square area of New York City. During this period, I observed persons' behaviors primarily in pornographic bookstores and movie theaters. In such contexts persons engage in activities that are defined, at the least, as unconventional. Given the general social value placed on their behaviors, I was initially interested in how bookstore and movie patrons managed their personal identities, fostered anonymity, and controlled information about themselves. Persons engaging in deviant or stigmatized behaviors will normally seek to minimize the costs and risks of such behaviors. Through ethnographic accounts of regularities in bookstore and theater behavior, I hoped to better understand the meaning of these settings to the participants and, therefore, the quality of their experiences.

Following the several writings of Erving Goffman, I was interested in how persons orient themselves to social audiences in order to create favorable impressions of themselves. I thought this would be an especially difficult problem for those frequenting pornographic bookstores and theaters. I also began my study with the belief that I could discover in the Times Square context some important features of anonymous city life and the organization of public places. In his book *Behavior in Public Places*, Goffman argues:

> Although this area [the study of behavior in public and semipublic places] has not been recognized as a special domain for sociological inquiry, it perhaps should be, for the rules of conduct in streets, parks, restaurants, theatres, shops, dance floors, meeting halls, and other gathering places of any community tell us a great deal about its most diffuse forms of social organization (1963:3–4).

Like any fieldworker, then, I entered the field with some sensitizing ideas about the kinds of things I might find and their potential significance. As already intimated, however, there were several data-gathering problems that I did not envision at the outset of my study. In the following pages, I will focus less on the empirical and theoretical findings of my investigation than on the kinds of obstacles researchers might expect to face when studying behaviors in urban public places. To begin, I will briefly describe the research setting.

TIMES SQUARE: THE RESEARCH SETTING

One novelist, John Rechy, in his book *City of Night* (1963:24, 26, 34), describes Times Square in the following way:

> Times Square, New York is an electric island floating on a larger island of lonesome parks and lonesome apartment houses and knifepointed buildings stretching up. . . . Times Square is the magnet for all the lonesome exiles jammed into this city. . . . I stand on 42nd Street and Broadway looking at the sign flashing the news from the Times Tower like a scoreboard. . . . Along this street I see young masculine men milling idly. Sometimes they walk up to older men and stand talking in soft tones . . . going off together, or if not, moving to talk to someone else. . . . From the thundering underground . . . the maze of New York subways . . . the world pours into Times Square. Like lost souls emerging from the purgatory of the trains, the New York faces push into the air: spilling into 42nd Street and Broadway . . . a scattered defeated army. And the world of that street bursts like a rocket into a shattered phosphorescent world. Giant signs . . . Bigger . . . Than . . . Life . . . blink off and on. And a great hungry sign groping luridly as the darkness screams
>
> F*A*S*C*I*N*A*T*I*O*N

Times Square is buildings and businesses of nearly every shape and variety. There are fleabag hotels on nearly every street, catering to prostitutes and those down on their luck. There are theaters showing the latest movies, both of the Hollywood and pornographic variety. There are theaters where for ninety-nine cents you can spend the afternoon sleeping in air-conditioned comfort, legs draped over two or three seats. There are numerous small shops selling novelty items to tourists. Here you can buy a variety of items, ranging from postcards to garish ties, to plastic replicas of the Statue of Liberty, to glasses that will drip their contents on the lap of the unsuspecting victim of a practical joke. There are "Playlands" where for a quarter you can get pictures of yourself in six different poses and test your skills at a variety of games. There are bookstores where persons satisfy their taste for every imaginable kind of erotic literature. There are "peepshow" places where for a quarter customers view a "XXX" movie, in full color and sound and in the privacy of a separate booth. There are cheap restaurants and numerous bars, some with a cover of three dollars and nude dancers and others badly run down, frequented mostly by local alcoholics.

But Times Square is not a static place. Its flavor, its motif, its tenor change at different times of the day. By 9 A.M. the streets are bustling with persons on their way to work, entering the various office buildings in the area. By 10:30 A.M. some "regulars" have already appeared and are lounging especially near the subway stop at Forty-second Street and Seventh Avenue. By now, also, the movies have all opened, and here and there a few persons enter, perhaps to kill a couple of hours or to sleep off the events of the previous night. By this time one is likely to be accosted by someone needing a quarter, or someone secretively displaying "an expensive diamond-studded watch" for a "terrific bargain." A quotation from field notes illustrates my general impression of Times Square at this time of day:

> Times Square gets real active early—by 10:30 there are lots of things happening around me. A young boy (18 or 19) walks up beside me and talking more to himself than to me says "I'd better watch out or I'll get another sore mouth." (His mouth is all cut up and lots of blood spots are on his shirt); a young Negro boy is in business selling tokens at the subway entrance; an older man walks up to a group of young boys and begins to joke with them. Abruptly he lifts up the shirt of one and rubs his stomach. They all laugh. He walks off with one of the boys. The crowd builds up and rushes by. A very effeminate looking man makes a telephone call. Shortly thereafter he is met by a badly dressed, gaunt, unshaven man. They talk with one another as if making plans. The second man guardedly shows the first a new watch in its case. They walk off together. An older man talks with a young boy in the middle of the sidewalk. They laugh and joke. The boy walks off. The man seems bewildered. He stands for a few minutes in place as if deciding what to do now. He disappears into the subway. These are the kinds of things one can see in a short time and in a limited space. The same kinds of things, however, are happening all along the street.

By noon, the business offices have begun to expel their workers for lunch, and again the streets around Forty-second teem with activity. Remarkably, as if guided by radar, hundreds of persons pass each other without colliding. A kind of controlled chaos describes the flow of sidewalk traffic. On Eighth Avenue there are a surprisingly large number of prostitutes casually strolling the street. The streets remain relatively quiet during the afternoon. Between five and six, as the workers leave the area, the street traffic seems especially chaotic. By 7 P.M. the Times Square nightlife is underway. Most of the men and women who work in the area during the day have gone, and the pace has lessened. Persons appear in no particular hurry as they casually walk down the street, taking in the store windows and bright lights. Tourists, cameras around their necks, talk animatedly. They are also identified by the presence of their children and by their clothes. Tourists are much more conservatively dressed than the habitués of the area.

Early in the evening, groups of young men begin to stand around, some obviously homosexual, holding hands and whispering intimately. The "queens" are in "high drag," wearing carefully done hairdos, tight multicolored slacks, and high-heeled shoes. The regulars constantly cruise up and down Forty-second Street to bump into friends, to find out "what's up," and to make plans for the evening. Periodically, however, a bargain is struck. The encounter is generally brief and straightforward:

> Right near me I saw a well dressed man about 40-years old. After a short time, a young black man stands beside him along a store-front. The older man initiates the conversation with a simple "Hi." They talk for some time (I could not hear). . . . Intermittently the man looks at his watch. Finally I see him nod his head and the men leave together. . . .

On Eighth Avenue, between Forty-fourth and Forty-ninth Streets, and on Broadway in the vicinity of Forty-sixth Street, prostitutes have begun work by 8:30 or 9 P.M. As the night wears on, they must periodically get off the streets as the police go by either on foot or in cars. By 11:00 the movie theaters have released hundreds of persons onto the street. At this time the streets appear more crowded than at any time during the day. Now Forty-second Street is populated by large numbers of men and women holding hands as they slowly amble along, absorbing the street's excitement.

As the night wears on, the number of moviegoers, tourists, and passersby begins to diminish, and by 2 A.M. the streets take on a different tone altogether—a sinister tone. As the tourists depart, only the denizens of the area remain. On Forty-fourth and Forty-fifth Streets, between Broadway and Sixth Avenue, the prostitutes appear in large numbers, hanging together in groups of three or four all along the street, much more overtly propositioning men than earlier in the evening. In contrast to the incessant activity earlier, the streets seem silent and forbidding.

EARLY RESEARCH STRATEGIES
AND PROBLEMS

During the early stages of my work, I tried to become as well acquainted with the Times Square area as I could and self-consciously remained as flexible as possible in the accumulation of data. Generally speaking, my days and nights in the field were spent observing a variety of behaviors. At this point my strategy was to record everything that was even vaguely interesting or relevant since I did not know whether it might be useful later on as my problem developed and my focus narrowed. A "liberal," detailed recording of events is necessary especially during the early stages of an observational study. As my study became more focused later in its development, there proved to be considerable data the use of which I could not have readily foreseen during the initial stages of the study.

I carried a small pocket-sized notebook and tried to record my observations or conversations with persons as soon as possible after they occurred. This often necessitated moving off to a "private" or "semiprivate" place (doorways, coffee shops) where I could unobtrusively make notes. Whenever possible, I transcribed these brief notes in detail the same day or night that they were made. I found it helpful at times to dictate my notes and descriptions into a tape recorder before trying to put them down on paper.

Although I considered a number of alternative methods, I soon came to believe that observation was the most feasible means of data collection given the deviant nature of the context that I was studying. Even if I knew exactly what I was after, it would have been impossible to question systematically a sample of persons. At first I saw my inability to talk with customers as a critical problem. My notes at the time expressed this concern.

> There is the problem of being unable to use techniques other than pure observation. It would seem extremely doubtful that I could talk to customers in either a structured or a nonstructured way. The inability to interact in any way with customers in the bookstores or theaters may be a crucial flaw in the study of behavior in this context.

My training in traditional survey research techniques caused me to feel that talk was the sociologist's stock in trade. Not being able to talk to a systematic sample of persons so disturbed me that initially I began to think of schemes for talking to customers in some structured way. For example, I thought about the possibility of working with an ally. Together we could work out a system whereby we would stop persons on the street whom we knew had been frequenting the bookstores or theaters. We would than ask them to respond to a questionnaire on some contrived topic, such as "the uses of the city." We could begin with a few innocuous questions and then ask these persons whether they had ever been inside a pornographic bookstore, how they would feel if someone they knew saw them in such a store, and so forth. I finally dismissed this plan on two grounds. First, in practical terms, it was very difficult to put into operation. Second, and more important, I began to feel that such a procedure was unethical. I decided that such a plan was just too devious.

Related to restrictions in data-gathering techniques, I soon realized a variety of additional problems. Questions of the following sort began to appear in my field notes:

> How long can I stand outside the bookstores in the cold weather? What is the best way to record my observations? Should I start out with preconceived categories? . . . The problems of observation inside the bookstore seem especially difficult. . . . How can I stand around the bookstores for any length of time without getting kicked out?

Shortly after beginning the study, I had these thoughts:

> Clearly the study of deviant behavior poses special problems. Perhaps the biggest problem is the problem of access. Given the fact that I would like to observe what must be considered deviant behavior, by at least some involved, I may not be welcome in the stores by owners to observe for any length of time. Given the type of business I might be considered a threat. Am I really a member of the police department, Better Business Bureau, local civic association or whatever? So, how do I present myself to owners? How do you explain the nature of the study especially when you are far from sure yourself? How am I to convince them that I am not a spy, that I am morally neutral?

Plainly, there is no logical progression of events that uniformly occurs in participant observation. The choice of behaviors for observation is particularly arbitrary at the beginning of the research, although even then researchers are necessarily curious about certain behaviors or events and may have some a priori and vaguely formulated hypotheses which they will want to verify or discard in a loose way. As the research progresses, however, and researchers begin to accumulate more detailed information, hypotheses begin to present themselves more systematically and the choice of events and persons for observation becomes increasingly focused. From an early period, though, I began to appreciate the problems of access existing for even the researcher studying public places.

Problems of Access

Although the context of my own work was a public one and I could freely enter bookstores or theaters, there were still difficult problems of access. A few examples will illustrate just how tricky the problem of access can be. My field notes describe first attempts to gain entry to bookstores.

> I tried to gain access to a couple of bookstores today. I got up the guts to tell the managers in two places that, in essence, I would like to hang around and observe behavior for a few hours. I say it took guts because I had absolutely no idea of what their reactions might be. I began to feel, though, that were I flatly refused or thrown out that it could mean the end of the study.
>
> In the first place that I went, I sought out the manager and told him, by way of legitimizing myself, that I was a professor at Queens College [I was actually an instructor, but that didn't sound as good as professor]. I told him that all I wanted was permission to stay in the store for a few hours and that I simply wanted to watch the people and nothing more. I told him that I was interested in how people behaved in the Times Square Area and stores like his own were natural places to watch people. I assured him that neither he nor his store would in any way be identified in anything that might eventually be written. During all this time he smiled broadly, almost suppressing a laugh as if there were something funny about me and my observing behavior there. He seemed to think about it for a few seconds and then told me that he didn't "think it was practical." I assured him that I would in no way jeopardize his business, but for the time being his mind seemed made up. I did not persist. I thanked him and left.

Several times I had similar experiences in stores as I told my story. Although I did finally obtain access to several of the stores, I was puzzled by my early failures. I was particularly puzzled, however, by the grin that covered the faces of the managers and workers, puzzled by the suppressed laughter that I kept getting from these men as I delivered my opening remarks. These early attempts at access were frustrating and may have been much easier had I realized what I was doing wrong. My initial attempt at access provides a useful example to show how researchers make mistakes that cannot be anticipated prior to entering the field.

When I discussed the access problem with colleagues, they pointed out where the mistake in my opening approach might have been. The clue was the suppressed laughter itself. They suggested that the mistake was in introducing myself as a professor at Queens College. The store managers had probably not heard of Queens College, which is part of the New York City University system. Rather, they understood the word "queen" in its slang form, meaning "effeminate homosexual." My colleagues suggested that I was introducing myself as a kind of "super queer" or "super freak," and the combination of "queen" with "professor"—"a professor of queens"—was more humorous still. Quite unwittingly, therefore, an attempt to legitimate myself had exactly the opposite effect.

Later, I found that in certain instances the explanation "I am writing a book about Times Square" proved quite enough. In other cases, persons required a much more detailed explanation. In still other cases, potential informants refused to be bothered with me at all. I was always trying to make contact with useful informants. To that end, I frequently tried to strike up conversations with persons on the street, bookstore personnel, and so on. The norm against speaking to customers in bookstores was so strong, however, that I could never bring myself to break it.

When striking up conversations on the street, my tactic frequently was to act naive. For example:

Are the movies around here any good?

What do you mean?

You know, the "dirty movies." Are they worth seeing?

Well, if you want to see a good movie don't pay anything less than three dollars.

You mean the ones for less than three dollars are no good?

Right.

What makes a movie a good one? What's the difference between the cheap ones and the more expensive ones?

I don't know.

This procedure had some merit, but I felt disinclined to continue the naive stance when persons on the street began to recognize my face and question my presence. The regulars on the street looked askance after seeing me on the street, sometimes for hours at a time. They wanted to know whether I was hustling, whether I was a potential "mark," or whether I was a cop. I frequently got "what-are-you-up-to" looks from them and was directly approached more than once. The following was typical of such encounters:

You from [New] Jersey?

No, why do you ask?

Oh, I saw you hanging around on the other corner.

Ya, I'm just hanging around.

Did you skip work today?

No, I'm outta work right now. (I don't know why I told this lie exactly. It just seemed like the appropriate thing to do at the time.)

You hustling by any chance?

No, I'm straight.

Well, that's life man.

In one instance, a whole day of observation was nearly ruined because of a similar problem.

My determination not to lose potentially interesting informants led to a problem later on in the day. I decided to stop and eat lunch. I went into *Childs* restaurant at the corner of 42nd and 8th. Sitting beside me at the counter was a young kid (I later learned that he was 20 years old), singing along with the juke box music. He began to engage me in conversation. He told me that he had just come here from Ohio, that he had lived on a farm and that he was an unemployed truck driver. He elaborated on each of these facts. I encouraged him by listening and nodding my head. He asked me what I did and seeing my opening I told him that I was studying pornography in the Times Square area. I thought that perhaps he had spent time in the bookstores and that he would then talk about it. It turned out that he was terribly inarticulate and there were often long pauses during which he sought out the proper word. He did begin to tell me about his views on sex and love. Typical of his conversation were statements like "Sex is beautiful. Some people think that sex is dirty and that's why the world is so fucked up." He continued in this vein for some time. He laughed, rubbed his crotch and told me, "I haven't had anything for two weeks." I asked him where he got it when he wanted it. He told me that he never had to pay for it and said, "sometimes when I can't get a girl I look around for a nice looking guy." He laughed as he said it. He began to ask me about my own sexual experiences. I was very noncommital [sic] and simply said I was married. We ended up paying our bills at the same time and I began to walk down 8th Avenue. I found him beside me continuing the conversation. I tried to act uninterested at this point, but he seemed oblivious to my silence. Most of his discussion centered about his sexual exploits. At this point I said, "I'm going home" and headed up toward 42nd. Again he was at my elbow as I began to walk away. I finally said, "Well, maybe I'll see you around." This incident nearly ruined the day because I did not want to run into him after I said that I was going home. I did, however, circle around the block back to 46th Street to observe the theaters.

Attempts to establish relationships with prostitutes in the Times Square area proved especially difficult. On several occasions, I tried to get a picture of the typical working day of a prostitute. I wanted to observe the women just as an occupational sociologist might want to observe workers on, say, an assembly line. I wanted to know, for example, when they started work, when they took their breaks, how much territory they covered, how many "tricks" they "turned" during their working hours. I wanted to stand around and record their behaviors all day, if possible. However, this plan was continually frustrated when the women became aware that I was standing around for a longer period of time than they deemed normal. They no doubt thought I was a plainclothes policeman, many of whom, like me, dress casually and have beards. Consequently, I could not obtain the kind of detailed information on the behavior of prostitutes that I wanted.

I was able to have short conversations with some women but did not normally identify myself as a researcher. I had a few extended interviews which proved uninformative and cost me ten to twenty dollars. My zeal to talk to some of the women created potentially dangerous situations for me. For example, I had this confrontation:

About halfway down 47th Street between 6th and 7th Avenues I spotted five women working. I decided to try to strike up a deal; to talk to one of the women. All the women were white.

As I leaned up against a car one woman came up and said to me, "Do you want to go out?" I said, "Look, I'll level with you. I'm doing a study of the Times Square Area. I'm not interested in sex but I am interested in information. I'll pay you for it. How much will it cost me?" She asked, "How long?" . . . "A half hour." . . . "Twenty five." . . . "That's a little bit too steep." She walked away from me but I continued to lean against the car. At that point a new woman came and was greeted by the others. One of them said, "Here's the girl in white." This woman was very tall and wore an all white pants suit. Then the woman that I first talked to made a general announcement to all of the others. She said, "He's making a survey. Do you want to go with him? He'll pay." The new arrival, the "girl in white," turned to me and said, "I won't talk to you, you'll bring me in." I replied, "No, I'm straight." Finally, she did walk over to me and said, "What are you doing?" . . . "I'm interested in prostitution. I'd like to talk to you." . . . "How much?" . . . "Ten dollars." . . . Then she said something like "Are you kidding? The best way to find out is to go out with me." I said, "No." She then said, "Then get the hell out of here. Get the hell off the street. I'll call a cop. You better believe it. Get the fuck out of here. Fuck, bastard, go write that I said fuck in your fucking survey. . . ."

In the last few pages, I have tried to convey some of the access difficulties likely to arise in studies of public contexts, especially those in which persons have reason to conceal their activities. We would do well, however, not to overstate these access problems. Field researchers who are flexible in the research roles and methods they adopt can collect the data necessary for rendering a valid picture of the public settings they study.

GETTING THE DATA

Those who do public place ethnographies must learn to piece together data culled from a number of sources: observation alone, personal introspection, deliberate intervention in a situation, and casual conversation. I will briefly discuss these data sources.

The character of public places is significantly shaped by clear norms of noninvolvement (Stone and Yoels, 1977; Milgram, 1970). These norms, ensuring "public privacy" for persons, are especially well elaborated in those public contexts in which persons engage in unconventional behaviors. Customers in pornographic bookstores and theaters make no physical or verbal contact with each other. The normative structure of the stores requires silence among customers. Indeed, store clerks will eject anyone interfering with another customer's privacy. Under conditions like these, researchers will normally be obliged to rely on observation as their primary means of data collection.

Reliance on pure observation is not as much a limitation as it might first appear. Researchers who develop an eye for detail in observing settings can collect an enormous wealth of data. Close, careful observation allows the discovery of important aspects of behavior and social structure in any setting. Using only observation, I was able to collect data on a wide range of activities occurring in the Times Square area. Without talking to anyone, I could learn such things as the way persons enter and leave bookstores and theaters, space rules governing behavior in bookstores, the way persons browse at pornographic magazines, the purchasing techniques of customers, the manner of choosing seats in pornographic movies, how bargains are struck between prostitutes and clients, conflict between prostitutes and the police, and rules of territoriality established by prostitutes (particularly along racial lines) on the street.

Sometimes researchers studying public places will want to adopt a more active stance. To test the operation of norms, they may intervene in a situation; they may purposely break a presumed norm, predicting in advance persons' responses. I did attempt such strategies as sitting next to persons in movie theaters when I believed that behavior was improper. Persons indicated their discomfort by screwing up their faces, sighing loudly, shifting their bodies away from me, and the like. In nearly all cases, those whose space I invaded eventually moved to a more isolated seat.

Researchers should also consider as data their own feelings and behaviors. Because personal introspection is unavoidable, researchers' own experiences will significantly shape their ideas and hypotheses, and so the course of future data collection. Data of the following sort informed my own research activity:

> I can on the basis of my own experience substantiate, at least in part, the reality of impression-management problems for persons involved in the Times Square sexual scene. I have been frequenting porno- graphic bookstores and movie theaters for some nine months. Despite my relatively long experience I have not been able to overcome my uneasiness during activity in these contexts. I feel, for example, nervous at the prospect of entering a theater. This nervousness expresses itself in increased heartbeat. I consciously wait until few people are in the vicinity before entering; I take my money out well in advance of entering; I feel reticent to engage the female ticket seller in even the briefest eye contact.

Of course, whenever the opportunity arises, researchers will have casual conversations with persons in the setting. These conversations, however brief, can serve to validate earlier observations and to open up new and sometimes unexpected areas for inquiry. Once I became familiar to bookstore personnel as a "regular" (which took some time), I could engage them in brief conversations, and in some cases we became friendly enough to have more extended conversations. These conversations pro- vided valuable data on various aspects of bookstore behavior. In one case, for example, I discovered a category used by store clerks in typing customers:

> There's an interesting type. There's a little humor here. We call them the "moochers." These are the guys that browse aimlessly. There's no buying potential here. This guy uses a lot of gimmicks. Generally, he picks up a magazine, looks through it, but then doesn't put it down

again. He holds the magazine in his hands trying to give the impression that he is going to buy it. He keeps collecting magazines this way. Finally, on his way out he puts each magazine back in place. There are others too. Instead of piling books up in his hand, he keeps the money out in his hand. These must feel that you will believe the money; that you won't believe his just piling up books in his hand.

As I began to collect substantial data from casual conversations, I was able to check on the validity of information provided by one clerk by asking questions of others. In one case a store clerk described some of his customers as "weirdoes" [sic]. Because I was interested in how store personnel thought about and evaluated their customers, this description of customers became a standard part of my conversation with the several clerks I had come to know.

I once heard someone in another store describe some of their customers as "weirdoes." What does that mean to you?

Well, maybe forty percent of the people who come into the store are straight, the others all have some kind of hangup.

How can you tell the "weirdoes?"

I don't know. After a while you can tell just by looking at them. You know, by the way they walk, by the way they talk, the look in their eyes. . . . Well, what do you have to think when a guy buys a book on teenage lesbianism. You've got to think there is something wrong with the guy. He's got to have some interest in the subject matter and must at least fantasize about it. Same thing with the sado-masochism stuff. I mean, that's not normal.

With the foregoing examples, I have tried to describe the kinds of data it is possible to collect in those public situations in which norms governing interaction between strangers prohibit extensive conversation. Data of the sort I collected enabled me to analyze the structure of urban anonymity and the social organization of everyday city life. Before concluding, however, I should mention the kinds of data that I was never able to collect, data that might have produced a quite different line of analysis from the one I took.

Every researcher finds that he or she must make personal decisions concerning aspects of the studied situation to be left untouched. My data were limited primarily to the interactions of persons in the public places I observed. Although I did participate in both movie and bookstore behaviors, there were certain areas of the sexual scene that I never learned much about. Although interested in the relations of prostitutes and clients, I never became a total participant in this aspect of sexual activity. In another instance, I considered trying to learn about the more private worlds of pimps and prostitutes. This meant hanging around the bars where the pimps congregated (see Milner and Milner, 1972). Feeling thoroughly out of place in these bars and concerned with personal safety, I eliminated this area of data collection. As a last example, I note that my data do not illuminate how the pornography industry is structured and organized. I was never able to find out who owned the stores and theaters, their possible links to organized crime, and so on. The collection of these data would no doubt have changed the overall direction of my research.

CONCLUSION

Because Times Square epitomizes the anonymous urban public place, it is useful in highlighting the kinds of problems researchers may confront in a variety of public settings. The reader should recognize, of course, that the difficulty in talking with persons in pornographic bookstores and theaters is especially severe. Nevertheless, the data presented in this selection indicate that access problems in public places are related to the way public life, in contrast to life within organizations, is managed.

City persons are faced with public situations in which the number of potential encounters with strangers is enormous. Given the volume of possible contacts, persons adapt by structuring their public lives in ways designed to minimize the chances of unpleasant or unwanted encounters. Most important, persons construct *norms of noninvolvement* that insulate them from unnecessary contact with strangers. Persons rarely implicate themselves in each others' public lives. Strangers in public settings largely avoid each other. In most public settings we close ourselves off from interaction with others. We try to maximize "public privacy" as we travel on buses, sit in waiting rooms, stand in lines, or simply walk along the street. The researcher is no different. Those who study conduct in public places will, like everyone else, be constrained by the rules that inhibit unnecessary verbal interaction. These restrictions, however, do not prevent the collection of significant data.

The experiences related in this selection suggest that researchers who set out to investigate behaviors in public places should expect to collect most of their data through pure observation. Contexts such as Times Square force researchers to rely on their eyes and ears in ways less necessary when they have unlimited access to respondents' talk. At the same time, resourceful investigators can complement observational data with personal introspection, casual conversation, and, on occasion, deliberate intervention. These data sources powerfully combine, allowing researchers to comprehend the meanings persons give to the public settings in which they act.

Notes

1. A few examples of such research, spanning several decades, include: Robert Lynd and Helen Lynd, *Middletown* (1929); Lloyd W. Warner and Paul S. Lunt, *The Social Life of a Modern Community* (1941); Alvin Gouldner, *Patterns of Industrial Bureaucracy* (1954); William F. Whyte, *Street Corner Society* (1955); Erving Goffman, *Asylums* (1961); Herbert Gans, *The Urban Villagers* (1962); Gerald Suttles, *The Social Order of the Slum* (1968); Stephen Pfohl, *Predicting Dangerousness* (1978).

References

BOGDAN, R. *Participant Observation in Organizational Settings.* New York: Syracuse University Press, 1972.

GANS, H. *The Urban Villagers.* New York: Free Press, 1962.

GARFINKEL, H. *Studies in Ethnomethodology.* Englewood Cliffs, N.J.: Prentice-Hall, 1967.

GLASER, B. and A. STRAUSS. *The Discovery of Grounded Theory.* Chicago: Aldine, 1967.

GOFFMAN, E. *Asylums.* New York: Doubleday, 1961.

———. *Behavior in Public Places.* Glencoe, Ill.: Free Press, 1963.

GOULDNER, A. *Patterns of Industrial Bureaucracy.* New York: Free Press, 1954.

KARP, D., G. STONE, and W. YOELS. *Being Urban: A Social Psychological View of City Life.* Lexington, Mass.: Heath, 1977.

LYND, R., and H. LYND. *Middletown.* New York: Harcourt, Brace, 1929.

McCALL, G., and J.L. SIMMONS. *Issues in Participant Observation.* Reading, Mass.: Addison-Wesley, 1969.

MILGRAM, S. "The Experience of Living in Cities." *Science,* 167, (1970) 1461–1468.

MILNER, C., and R. MILNER. *Black Players: The Secret World of Black Players.* Boston, Mass.: Little, Brown, 1972.

PFOHL, S. *Predicting Dangerousness.* Lexington, Mass.: Heath, 1978.

RECHY, J. *City of Night.* New York: Grove Press, 1963.

SCHATZMAN, L., and A. STRAUSS. *Field Research: Strategies for a Natural Sociology.* Englewood Cliffs, N.J.: Prentice-Hall, 1973.

SUTTLES, G. *The Social Order of the Slum.* Chicago: University of Chicago Press, 1968.

WARNER, L., and P. LUNT. *The Social Life of a Modern Community.* New Haven: Yale University Press, 1941.

WHYTE, W. *Street Corner Society.* Chicago: University of Chicago Press, 1955.

Learning to Study Public Figures

MALCOLM SPECTOR *McGill University*

In recent years, there has been increasing attention to problems of studying elite groups and powerful segments of society. Both theoretical and methodological considerations may be responsible for a previous lack of studies of such groups. For those working in the tradition of participant observation and qualitative methodology, practical problems, such as access to such groups, may have been as important as putative failings of the interactionist perspective to deal with concepts like power or social structure. The question remains: Will the research techniques we have developed in qualitative methodology serve us well in studies of elite groups? A general answer to that question is beyond the scope of this selection. But I would like to describe some methodological problems I encountered in two studies of social controversies; here some of the research subjects were well-known public figures and might in some sense be considered elite or powerful people.[1] The general question I would like to consider is: How will our research be affected by the fact that the people we are studying are prominent, well-known public figures?

My experience is based on two studies of social controversies involving psychiatry. One study involved conflicts of interest inherent in the psychiatric role (Spector and Kitsuse, 1977:97–128). The other was a controversy over whether homosexuality should be considered a mental disorder or a life style in official psychiatric nosology (Spector, 1977). Perhaps studies of social controversies are a biased sample to use in generalizing or even speculating about problems of studying elites. While controversies often appear in social research, there is no well-established model or procedure for making them the units of sociological analysis. Controversies frequently do not have definite beginning points or conclusions. They often are not confined to one organization or institution. The focal point or center of debate may shift; there may be changes in personnel, with new parties entering and others dropping out or taking their complaints elsewhere. The arena of conflict may change or the controversy may be spread over several different areas.

Certain parties to social controversies are, or temporarily become, public figures. Controversies draw the attention of the media, and leaders of different groups or factions may become known to the general public or any number of smaller, more specialized publics. Some may be genuinely powerful in the larger society; others may be leaders and local elites within their communities, organizations, or professions. This notoriety differs from the typical fieldwork situation in which the research subjects are not chosen because of their public stature and typically have no special claims to fame, at least for the purpose of the study. I would like to discuss three ways in which field research techniques are altered when research subjects are persons with public reputations:

1. The fact that these research subjects are in the news means that there are important sources of data in public documents that are not available or relevant in most other field studies.

2. Sociological interviews and observations fall into the category of elite interviews and observation. The sampling procedure and the preparation for interviewing are quite different than in field studies where informants are not public figures.

3. It may be impossible or foolish to write analyses without using the actual names of the participants. We may want to avoid guaranteeing anonymity and confidentiality and make sure we can use the names of informants and their organizations.

SOURCES OF DATA ON PUBLIC FIGURES

When the people we want to interview are public figures, much background work and preparation are required before the researcher can approach them. Sociologists who feel that this work is not real research will no doubt grow quite impatient with the long involvement with documents that is required in projects of this kind. As Glaser and Strauss observe:

> For many, if not most, researchers, qualitative data is virtually synonymous with fieldwork and interviews, combined with whatever "background" documents may be necessary for putting the research in context. . . . The emphasis on using fieldwork and interviews may [also] rest on a feeling of wanting to see the concrete situation and informants in person. . . . The well-trained sociologist may brave the

rigors of the field or confront the most recalcitrant interviewees, but quail before the library. But sociologists need to be as skilled and ingenious in using documentary materials as in doing fieldwork. Various procedures, or tactics, available to the field worker for gathering data have their analogues in library research (1967:162–164).

This documentary research should be clearly distinguished from the "review of the literature." The researcher should open a file on each public figure who participates in the controversy. Then, using tools such as biographical dictionaries, membership directories of professional associations, and *American Men and Women of Science*, the researcher should identify these people—what positions they hold, what offices or honors they have received, what areas they work in or are noted for.

The fact that one is studying, and will eventually interview, well-known individuals does change the spirit of the review of the literature. Scholarly articles, exchanges, or symposia in scientific publications may also constitute important data. When adversaries in a conflict are scientists, they frequently fight part of their battle in print; this may involve a long list of publications. Suppose we discover that in the midst of the controversy over homosexuality, an article appeared by Judd Marmor stating that homosexuality is best viewed as a life style and that imputations of disease only serve to increase the suffering of homosexuals, many of whom do not feel disturbed by their sexual preference. The researcher must ask: Who is Judd Marmor? Why is he writing on this subject now? Why should anyone care what he thinks? It is a good hypothesis that parties to a controversy will write about it and that anyone writing on a controversial subject is probably a participant in the conflict. The researcher should expect that well-known or powerful people in public positions will express their views in scholarly publications, journals of opinion, or popular magazines and newspapers. There is, of course, some counterpart to these documents in the more typical field study. Field-workers habitually collect copies of local publications, put out by members of organizations they study. Also, they generally try to obtain copies of anything printed by their research subjects, from phone lists and organization tables to petitions and contentious letters. These have their counterpart in research on public figures, in which press releases, reprints of articles, and position statements may be made available to anyone making inquiries.

The fact that research subjects are public figures means more than the opportunity to do some background work before the interview. Well-known people tend to expect this work—and, in fact, a mastery of what is in the public record. They may grow impatient with questions that could be easily answered by a look at public documents or their writings, or they may not take an uninformed researcher seriously. Fear of this rejection, carried to an extreme, may lead researchers to feel that they are never completely ready to proceed to the interviews. This tendency must also be resisted, for after all, all interviews contain some element of discovery and reveal new aspects of the activity under study.

THE INTERVIEWS

The interviews, then, come late in the research process. Mine were quite unstructured but rarely exploratory. Searching the documents had been the exploratory stage; the interviews permitted me to raise specific questions. Interviews supplemented data gathered from published and archival sources. The bulk of the data came from documents. The interviews—if and when the researcher decides they are necessary—test hypotheses, fill in blank spots in the facts already assembled, and seek interpretations or clarifications unlikely to appear in published accounts.

After completing my documentary research, I knew who were the central figures in each controversy. I wrote to them, identifying myself as a researcher, requesting an interview, and saying that I would call in several weeks. I encountered little difficulty and soon had a schedule of appointments. I was never told that I must get permission before an interview could be conducted. None of the psychiatrists occupying official positions in the American Psychiatric Association wished me to ask the organization for approval. The same was true of representatives of the gay liberation groups and members of the judiciary. Nor was I ever refused an interview. However, several people who lived in distant parts of the country were eliminated because I had very limited research funds to subsidize my travel.

The more interviews I did, the less original materials I collected in each succeeding interview. Some of the events we discussed had occurred as much as two years earlier, and several informants had rather vague and inaccurate memories of them. Even taking into account the value of cross checking several accounts of the same activity, I was able to recognize the point of diminishing returns. Often I knew when my informants were factually incorrect—when, for example, they had confused two sets of meetings or put them in the wrong sequence. I would normally point this out, and they would correct themselves. The ability to do this is an important resource in making these interviews go well. Such errors were almost always lapses of memory and not, I think, attempts to mislead. However, the better prepared the researcher, the more seriously the informant will treat the project.

These interviews may be called elite interviews for several reasons.

Dexter has defined the elite interviewee as anyone who is given "nonstandardized" treatment:

> But nonstandardized treatment I mean 1. stressing the interviewee's definition of the situation. 2. encouraging the interviewee to structure the account of the situation. 3. letting the interviewee introduce to a considerable extent his notions of what he regards as relevant, instead of relying upon the investigator's notions of relevance (1970:5).

This definition could cover a great variety of interviews. Using it, in fact, almost all unstructured interviews could be considered elite. While it is always a good idea to try to understand the point of view of the subject, it would not be very good advice to let the informant have such wide control over the interview. Sometimes informants don't know how well informed the researcher is and, with the best of intentions, may cover familiar ground. A person reluctant to be interviewed, but not wishing to refuse contact with the researcher, may try to stay on such subjects in order to avoid making any new relevations. Since time is scarce in such interviews, a cagy informant can fill up the time alloted to an unprepared or naive researcher with banal background. For example, one subject tried to begin our interview with a long, inaccurate history of the controversy. I interrupted and said I had several questions to ask, if I might. Did he have any idea why a certain meeting of the board of trustees had not been tape-recorded, as was its usual practice? Had he had any contact with a particular person who had been put in charge of the project after a certain date? I would have wasted a valuable resource in allowing this person to dwell on general background easily available in published documents.

I consider these interviews elite for three reasons. First, my informants were usually powerful and successful members of prestigious professions, representatives and officers of large organizations, well-educated members of society who had every resource to refuse contact with the researcher if they so chose. Second, some were already public figures. Their names had been in the newspapers; they had led movements, made public statements, held press conferences, and been praised and attacked in print. Third, they occupied unique positions in the activities I wished to describe.

My informants were pleased to participate in the research. Like many research subjects, some were flattered that their activities were considered worthy of attention. Psychiatrists, in particular, are a much criticized and beleaguered group. More than once I was commended for actually seeking out the psychiatrists' view of things before criticizing or ridiculing them. Many of my informants asked where I stood on the controversies in question. Since the topics were in the news and many people have definite opinions about them, it was expected that I would also have an opinion. Some of my informants thought they knew where a sociologist must stand on such subjects as conflicts of interest and homosexuality. I made no attempt to hide my personal beliefs, but I also insisted that my interest was in the process and dynamics of controversy; these cases were, for me, simply examples of that larger class. The most important demonstration of my goodwill or objectivity was my stated intention to interview people on all sides of the controversy. I was always asked, "Who else are you going to interview?" I was able to name the major individuals on all sides of the issue. This, and the relatively factual orientation of my questions, contributed to whatever rapport and trust developed. With one exception, I conducted only one interview with each person and thus had no opportunity to establish a real relationship. Many of these people had been interviewed before on the subject and treated me as just another journalist, writer, or researcher. I offered to send my informants a copy of any article I eventually published; the response was sometimes a shrug of boredom and the statement that since they had so much to read, they couldn't guarantee more than a glance at it.

In other ways, my informants were involved in the interviews and willing to give me as much help as they could. Many had extensive files. They often said during or after an interview, "Here is my file on this matter. Why don't you sit over there and see if there is anything that interests you." There were many letters, memos, minutes of meetings, early drafts of documents, clippings, and notes. I was able to take notes from these materials and, in some cases, to make photocopies of them for myself. These were an important supplement to the published documents and interview data. I found it striking that I was so frequently given the entire folder to take away and photocopy, and trusted to return it promptly.

USING NAMES IN THE ANALYSIS

A third issue arising out of studying well-known people is whether they may be cited by name. Are their statements made in confidence or are they on the record? This question is particularly troublesome because sociologists almost always regard this as an ethical consideration and consider it their obligation to protect the identity of informants and research subjects. The practice of ensuring anonymity and confidentiality is usually related to the possible harm that informants may suffer if they are publicly identified. It is generally believed that sociologists have no right to subject their research subjects to harm or gratuitous embarrassment. Some authors have suggested that the scientific value of publication must be weighed against possible harm and suffering to research subjects. Becker (1964) has suggested a variety of ways that researchers in some settings can work with their subjects to lessen the blow and avoid misunderstanding.

It is sometimes claimed that public officials have less claim to our sympathies than private individuals. Rainwater and Pittman claim that when sociologists study "publically accountable behavior," they have both the right and the obligation to withhold confidentiality in order to "further public accountability in a society whose complexity makes it easier for people to avoid their responsibilities" (1967:366). Here, presumably, harm to the subjects would not be a major consideration. Sagarin (1973) seems to agree when the research subjects are large, powerful organizations with the resources to refuse or repel the researcher. But he feels that weak and powerless groups should have not only the right to confidentiality but the right not to be researched at all. These issues become increasingly difficult to discuss. Is there any value to scientific publishing that could balance harm done to an individual? Should sociologists try to make public officials fulfill their responsibilities? Must we side with weak and powerless groups? These questions, all relating to anonymity and confidentiality, avoid another question: Can a given sociological analysis be made sensibly without identifying the persons and organizations involved?

A variety of sociological practices and habits confuse this basic issue. There is a tendency to think that the use of names implies an individualistic, personalistic, or reductionist level of analysis. Sociological readers may have little interest or patience with such details and may feel that writings that contain them are not sociology (perhaps journalism) and treat only the actions of specific individuals. In many studies the names of individuals, organizations, cities, or regions play no role in the analysis. None of the names involved may be newsworthy. No one would recognize the names and they would add nothing to the analysis, because the additional resource of information from the public record is negligible.

However, there are a great many research reports in which the reader cannot evaluate the possible relevance of the identities of the subjects and where the researcher cannot consider using information from the public record. This occurs because many sociologists ritually guarantee anonymity to their subjects at the beginning of the project without considering whether it will be possible to present the analysis adequately without using the names of individuals and organizations. This question may never arise in surveys or in research projects where the investigator may choose a sample from a very large population. But whenever the research subjects are chosen because of their uniqueness or some exceptional or innovative characteristic, the researcher should consider alternatives. Rainwater and Pittman have commented:

There are some situations for which the offer of confidentiality may be both unnecessary and technically a bad choice. . . . It may be impossible to communicate the findings once the informants have been told that what we see and hear will be kept confidential. It seems to us that we should rethink our automatic assumption that we offer to maintain the privacy of our informants. The question of whether or not to make such an offer demands a conscious and thoughtful decision that is made in the light of needs and goals of a particular research (1967:364–365).

Without such planning, confidentiality of sources arises most frequently in the form of questions over publication rights. Some researchers who have guaranteed anonymity to their subjects later conclude that it would be desirable from a scientific point of view to identify organizations or individuals. Very late in the project, they may seek to renegotiate the original research bargain. Colvard has commented on his own efforts to gain publication rights.

It was only after this first serious fieldwork of my own was over that I began to realize that the custom of withholding names was a professional and political norm rather than one supporting scientific ideals. Any such procedure is actually a form of censorship. . . . The ideal of scientific documentation is that of full disclosure of evidence essential to critical interpretation, and ultimately replication. The burden of proof that names are not essential to social science field reports should be on the investigator. And whether made in advance, or after permission has been sought and rejected, a decision to withhold names forecloses that obligation (1967:343–344).

While researchers have often not thought through these issues, informants who are public figures are very sensitive to them. Some wanted to know at the beginning of the interview whether they would be quoted. Some were quite seasoned and accustomed to being in the public eye; they spoke with an obvious awareness that they might be identified with their statements. Others, who were less used to being public figures and who had only recently and occasionally been subject to public attention, were concerned with this issue but were less adept at handling the situation. They used the popular jargon of investigative journalism, but uncomfortably and without knowing exactly what it meant. For example, one person told me that our interview was on "deep background." I said fine, but what was the difference between deep background and background? Neither of us knew.

None of these questions arise with persons who are not in the public eye, nor did they occur to me while I was preparing for my interviews. During the work with documents, I had not considered how much factual detail would be necessary to the analysis. My informants, however, were extremely aware of the problem and quickly taught me that they did not presume or seek the "normal" custom of anonymity.

I learned this in my first interview, when an officer of the APA paused in mid-sentence, whirled around, and said, "That's off the record. If you quote me on that, I'll deny I said it." With that understanding, he continued to discuss the subject while I attempted to recover my wits and figure out what was happening. That statement implied that this person expected my account to identify the participants and their positions. He expected to be quoted, and he would hold me responsible for quoting him accurately. Finally, if I used some of the information he was giving me, he would call me a liar in public. Many other people I interviewed also assumed that they would be named and identified with their statements. Only one informant to whom I had sent a draft of an article complained of being quoted "so often" and asked me to edit a few sentences.

My informants assumed what I came to conclude: that the analysis of these controversies would have been quite incomplete if the identities of the organizations or individuals had to be suppressed. Many statements derive their significance from the fact that they are said by public figures whose previous statements are a matter of record. If the source is not given, there is no way of knowing whether the statements are of interest. Identifying sources also provides a check on the researcher, because sources can then deny the statement or attempt to dissociate themselves from it. It also makes possible replication by other scholars in a way that is not possible if identities are concealed. The practice of granting anonymity, said to protect the research subject, also shields the researcher from criticism and refutation both by the informants and by other scholars.

Speaking on the record has an important effect on motivating the informant to participate in the research. Since most controversies have several sides and can be presented in a number of lights, most informants want the researcher to know the story from their point of view, hoping that in the final version, their actions will not be described only through the testimony of their adversaries and enemies. At the same time that the informants may serve the needs of the researcher, the researcher may fit into the agenda of the informants. Rainwater and Pittman have observed:

> Since publically accountable individuals often recognize their accountability and the useful purposes that might be served by sociologists studying them, one can often gain a good deal of cooperation without the promise of confidentiality (1967:366).

This statement implies that public figures would prefer anonymity if they could secure it. However, in some cases informants want to speak on the record in the hope that when the researcher writes a report, they will be portrayed in a favorable light, as heroes, and not as villains or fools. They may hope to be quoted in certain ways. Researchers who guarantee anonymity cannot motivate informants in this way. The following excerpt from an interview with a psychiatrist who supported the illness view of homosexuality shows such an attempt to manipulate the researcher:

> I've been in the forefront of the fight for homosexual rights, just as I've been in the forefront of the fight for sexual liberation. (I'd like to hear more about that.) During World War II, I was in the army as a psychiatrist. The military police would pick them up and send them to a psychiatric ward essentially for disposition under Section 8, discharge without honor. I never 8ed a homosexual. If they could do their work I sent them back to their unit. . . . (Could you describe some other things you were doing?) In the thirties I used to lecture parents' groups on masturbation, not to interfere. I've been doing this since I was a young man. Do you know (X)? a spokesman for the gay lib? I wrote a letter for him once that there should be no discrimination against him. I've been saying these things for years, long before the gay lib people were born, literally. (Look, suppose someone says, "You say you've been in the forefront, but what have you done? Where did you do it?" I need the details.) Well I told you, the army, wrote letters for people. I supported Bill 21 in the city council (Did you testify?) I wasn't asked to testify. (A person can ask to testify.) Well, since World War II I have stayed away from medical legal work because it breaks up my practice.

This informant finally realized he would not be able to document the kinds of activities that would permit me to agree with and therefore quote his opening statement. But he had tried.

SUMMARY AND CONCLUSION

This selection has discussed some general issues that confront researchers who try to study public events, persons and organizations. A different mix of skills is required for such research than those traditionally used by field researchers. These include greater attention to documents and library research, elite interviewing techniques, and a bargain with the research subjects that permits the use of names and reference to current events.

Several important questions related to these issues are not dealt with here. One is the ability of the researcher to protect the confidentiality of research data from, for example, courts or prosecutors. Although re-

searchers have tried to establish a privileged relationship in which they
have the right to guard data gained under the guarantee of confidentiality, in general they have not succeeded in having this right recognized.
Such a claim would be even more difficult to sustain for information
obtained on the record. However, it should be clear that the later
relationship should not oblige researchers to identify sources unless they
decided it is crucial to the analysis. (See Nejelski and Finsterbusch, 1973,
for a discussion of the researcher's right to maintain confidence.)

A related question I have not discussed is how to quote from and cite
the large variety of documents that informants make available. I accumulated a large file of revealing documents that I wished to use, but it was
never clear to me which were in the public domain and which required
permission. Documents such as summaries of meetings are a case in
point. So are early drafts of documents, including marginal notations and
editing suggestions. There were a number of letters that became semi-
public documents when the recipient made numerous photocopies and
sent them to many people. I was not able to find satisfactory guidelines on
this problem, but in the long run, researchers who amass such documents
must find a way of deciding what may and may not be used.

It has become commonplace to criticize much sociology for being
ahistorical. This criticism usually refers to the lack of a macrosociologi-
cal orientation in the theoretical framework, a failure of the perspective to
cast the net wide enough to see the larger contexts in which a smaller-
scale social drama takes place. Another pressure toward the ahistorical is a
squeamishness to make research bargains in which people and organization located on the East Coast" necessarily forgo the possibility of citing
accuracy of dates and documentation must square with the public record.
Research reports on "Central City" on "a large multinational corpora-
tion located on the East Coast" necessarily forego the possibility of citing
and using studies done by local historians or company annual reports. We
have long assumed that great advantages accrue to us by protecting the
confidentiality of our sources. We may also examine the advantages of
reversing those assumptions.

Notes

1. Howard S. Becker and Robert Faulkner criticized an earlier draft of this paper.
I feel that it is critical to maintain eye contact during interviews and not to miss facial
expressions and other nonverbal cues. Tape recording would eliminate the need for note
taking, but in my view, it inhibits most in-depth interviewing.

References

BECKER, H.S. "Problems in the Publication of Field Studies." In A.J. Vivich, J. Bensman, and M.R. Stein, eds., *Reflections on Community Studies.* New York: Wiley, 1964, pp. 267–284.

COLVARD, R. "Interaction and Identification in Reporting Field Research: A Critical Reconsideration of Protective Procedures." In G. Sjoberg, ed., *Ethics, Politics, and Social Research.* Cambridge, Mass.: Schenkman, 1967.

GLASER, B., and A. STRAUSS. *The Discovery of Grounded Theory.* Chicago: Aldine, 1967.

NEJELSKI, P., and K. FINSTERBUSCH. "The Prosecutor and the Researcher: Present Prospective Variations in the Supreme Court's *Bransburg* Decision." *Social Problems*, 21 (1973), 3–21.

RAINWATER, L., and D.J. PITTMAN. "Ethical Problems in Studying a Politically Sensitive and Deviant Community." *Social Problems*, 14 (1967), 357–366.

SAGARIN, E. "The Research Setting and the Right Not to be Researched." *Social Problems*, 21 (1973), 52–65.

SPECTOR, M. "Legitimizing Homosexuality." *Society*, July/August 1977, 52–56.

SPECTOR, M., and J.I. KITSUSE. *Constructing Social Problems.* Menlo Park, Calif.: Cummings, 1977.

2

Learning the Ropes

Descriptions of field research focus on the skills that were discovered to be useful. Though emphasizing a particular problem or set of problems encountered, the authors typically speculate about the generalizability of their situation to other research sites. Thus, the warnings and advice about fieldwork practice identify the most salient "dos" and "don'ts" of field research. In short, these accounts allow the reader to learn the ropes (Geer et al., 1966).

In analyzing field research, we can separate this second phase from the earlier one of getting in. Whereas getting in is designed to secure access to the setting and its participants and lays the groundwork for achieving trust and rapport, learning the ropes involves attaining an "intimate familiarity" (Lofland, 1976:8) with a sector of social life. The boundary between these two phases becomes blurred in the actual doing of field research. Learning the ropes begins as soon as the researcher sets out to learn about the people and their activities in the research setting and continues until he or she exits from the field.

Much like getting in, learning the ropes is affected by the characteristics of the research setting, the personality of the investigator, and the group members' feelings and responses to the researcher and the project. The ropes to be learned and the timing involved are as varied as the settings selected. Although the cardinal rule for field research—". . . initially, keep your eyes and ears open *but keep your mouth shut*" (Polsky, 1969:121)—seems like reasonable advice, specific recommendations for learning the ropes in all settings should be cautiously considered. Nonetheless, based on available fieldwork literature, it is possible to provide some general advice—both warnings against certain approaches and suggestions regarding the use of others.

First, however, it is important to examine why field researchers emphasize the need to learn the ropes of the research setting. The symbolic interactionist perspective states that peoples' attitudes and behavior derive from their perceptions and understanding of their social world. A group's social life is based on shared definitions of particular situations which are shared through language and symbols. It is precisely this feature of social interaction that makes human behavior so unique. The sociologist's principal task is to analyze and capture this interpretive process, which is the basis of human behavior. Blumer summarizes this position:

> Insofar as sociologists . . . are concerned with the behavior of acting units . . . the student [is required] to catch the process of interpretation through which they construct their activities. . . . To catch the process, the student must take the role of the acting unit whose behavior he is studying. Since the interpretation is being made by the acting unit in terms of objects designated and appraised, meanings acquired, and decisions made, the process has to be seen from the standpoint of the acting unit (1969:188).

Responding to criticisms of the subjective nature of field research—the data may be based on the perceptions, whims, and fancies of the fieldworker—Blumer adds:

> To try to catch the interpretative process by remaining aloof as a so-called "objective" observer and refusing to take the role of the acting unit is to risk the worst kind of subjectivism—the objective observer is likely to fill in the process of interpretation with his own surmises in place of catching the process as it occurs in the experience of the acting unit which uses it (1969:188).

Little can be gained by ignoring the personal states of the subjects and stressing model building. Field research requires an understanding of the interpretive process that shapes and guides human behavior (Wax, 1971:3). Fieldworkers believe that since ". . . to understand a people's thought one has to be able to think in their symbols" (Evans-Pritchard, 1974:79), data must be collected "within the mediums, symbols, and experiential worlds which have meanings to [their] respondents" (Vidich, 1955:354). Data collection preferably involves ". . . [participation] in the daily life of the people under study, . . . observing things that happen, listening to what is said, and questioning people, over some length of time" (Becker and Geer, 1957:28).

Fieldworkers' efforts to capture the subjects' perspectives have yielded a variety of fieldwork roles by which data are collected. Ideally, the role(s) adopted blend with the demands of the research setting, requiring the observer to learn the subtle mix of norms and expectations of the group.

In other words, the researcher must learn the ropes of the research setting. And although, as we have said, there is no foolproof method, to adopt one particular approach is futile. Such rigidity is usually seen in inexperienced fieldworkers.

While there are no magic formulas for learning the ropes, the researcher must begin by participating in the subjects' daily life—talking to them, observing what they do, and listening sympathetically to what they say. As the accounts of seasoned field researchers attest, it is a process loosely described as "hanging around" and is an absolute requirement (Becker et al., 1961; Gans, 1962; Glaser and Strauss, 1967; Liebow, 1967; Olesen and Whittaker, 1968; Suttles, 1967; Whyte, 1955). Researchers soon realizes that many different research roles can be assumed in the field (Gold, 1958; Junker, 1960). As the research progresses, the roles shift; the particular roles they claim, and/or to which they are assigned, are among the most important for learning the ropes.

Themes uniting the contributions in this section include the relation between the role selected by the researcher and the researcher's subsequent ability to gain acceptance in the group; the concept that research roles are not static but undergo continuous change as rapport is gained; and the recognition that owing to the kinds of information we seek from respondents, learning the ropes of the research setting typically accompanies feelings of discomfort and uncertainty. It is suggested that success at learning the ropes in the research setting is shaped and channelled by the researcher's self-presentation.

Fine's article explores the process of learning the ropes in his studies of preadolescent male Little League baseball players. Four possible participant observation roles are described—supervisor, leader, observer, and friend—and the implications of learning the ropes for each role are discussed. As Fine suggests, whatever technique is used to explain the research to the subjects, it is necessary that the observer's role be structured to create a climate of trust in which reciprocal sharing of information is possible. Although a wide range of researcher roles is possible, the continuous negotiation of relationships and the nature of the trust developed influence the observer's presentation of self.

Pointing to parallels between the activities of professional hustlers and field researchers, Prus draws attention to a variety of researcher roles, each of which is related to different phases of the research. As learning the ropes is an ongoing set of activities, the nature of the researcher's role will shift and alter as familiarity with the participants' activity patterns increases. Sanders's contribution analyzes the research roles he assumed in a variety of field projects and the advantages and limitations of his various self-presentations.

Assuming a particular research role to learn the ropes may reflect the researcher's deep sense of unfamiliarity with the social world under investigation. The researcher must adopt role options to become knowledgeable about the group and to collect specific information about its members and activities.

A research role may, however, reflect our impressions about the group to be studied. By anticipating the kinds of behavior we consider characteristic of a group, we select a manner of self-presentation. Kleinman informs us that her use of a bland and polite style of conversation was based on her initial estimate of seminary students as overly committed individuals engulfed by their collective calling. Her role modifications derived both from learning an alternative manner of self-presentation from the students themselves and by sharing (and withholding) personal experiences to encourage her respondents to accept her.

Adopting reserach roles and organizing presentations of self typically result in a sense of edginess or uncertainty. Feelings of discomfort and anxiety are present, in varying degrees, especially during data collection. Sanders draws attention to three sources of researcher discomfort: an uneasiness about prying into peoples' private lives, the risk of being rejected, and intense self-consciousness. Other contributors in this section suggest that feelings of uncertainty about fitting in with the people studied are best seen as routine features of the field research adventure. Our discomfort usually derives more from imagined than from actual difficulties but, as Kleinman suggests, recognizing these imagined problems will not help us overcome our insecurities about project organization and research findings.

The range of research roles is theoretically unlimited. In practice, however, as revealed by the contributions in this section, role alternatives available to the researcher are circumscribed by the nature of the research setting and its participants as well as by the personal characteristics of the observer. Although McCall and Kleinman were able to participate fully in a wide range of activities with their respondents and became recognized as regular participants of their groups, the deviance-related nature of Prus's and Sanders's research required that they carefully establish strict professional boundaries. Fine's adulthood obviously restricted the extent to which he could become a participant in Little League baseball groups: he adopted the "friend" role.

In anticipation of being rebuffed, field researchers often mistakenly strive to become completely immersed in the world they are studying, hoping to gain immediate and total acceptance. They believe that learning the ropes is an inevitable by-product of the effort to enhance rapport with the group. Hoping to win early acceptance, researchers delude themselves into believing that their presence in and involvement with the group members is tantamount to being one of them (Wax,

1971:47). This potentially serious error has been emphasized in fieldworkers' reflections on their research tactics and strategies.

Recalling his study of Boston's North End, Whyte states that early in his research, in an attempt to enter into the spirit of his friends' small talk, he blurted out a string of obscenities and profanities. His friends stopped to look at him in surprise. Doc, shaking his head, said: "Bill, you're not supposed to talk like that. That doesn't sound like you." Recounts Whyte, "I tried to explain that I was only using terms that were common on the street corner. Doc insisted, however, that I was different and that they wanted me to be that way" (1955:304). Whyte realized that ". . . people did not expect me to be just like them; in fact, they were interested and pleased to find me different . . ." (1955:304). The importance of maintaining an outsider's status was impressed on one author in his study of an orthodox Jewish community. Hoping to impress Chasidic Jews by his involvement in their activities, he made suggestions about organizing a community event. He was later counseled against such participation. This involvement, he was advised, might easily lead others to seriously question his ultimate intentions in the community.

These examples suggest, as Wax wisely advises, that the fieldworker should aim " . . . to maintain a consciousness and respect for *what he is* and a consciousness and respect for *what his hosts are*" (1971:48). Inattention to such advice may lead to a situation of "overrapport" (Miller, 1952) or going native, with the attendant dangers and disadvantages.

The researcher who works painstakingly, who shows a respect for those studied and a willingness to consider their views and claims seriously realizes that the subjects are prepared to teach the ropes. As many fieldworkers have observed, the process of learning the ropes is not usually explicitly defined. It is a task requiring the assistance and cooperation of the group. As the researcher becomes increasingly familiar with the subjects, he or she develops an intimate appreciation for their life style, one that cannot be comparably achieved by any other research method.

The ropes to be learned are dictated by the group studied. The study of deviant subcultures—for instance, prostitutes or motorcycle clubs— entails exposure to different experiences, situations, and value codes than does the study of voluntary associations such as church groups or ladies' auxiliary societies. But however different the social groups may be, common to each is a native language—an argot—consisting of expressions and phrases that help members to assess their experiences and organize their lives. Familiarity with this argot is crucial in learning the ropes (Becker and Geer, 1957; Bruyn, 1966; Cicourel and Kitsuse, 1963; Polsky, 1967; Szasz, 1970; Wallace, 1965). The special vocabulary provides significant clues about the group's basic assumptions about themselves and how outsiders are defined. Familiarity with it provides a solid, rich basis for becoming attuned to the group's life style. McCall discusses her discovery of an artist' terminology that helped to explain the organization of their social world. Her categories—"professionals" and "amateurs"— were not terms in the artists' vocabularies and were replaced by designations used by the artists themselves—"serious" and "dedicated."

Learning the ropes involves more than achieving a certain intimacy with the group's way of life. For instance, wittingly or unwittingly, the researcher may act out an old or a new bias toward the group, selectively perceiving information to support the biased view. The researcher may also react personally to a situation inherent in the setting, thus losing a scientifically neutral stance. In both cases, the fieldworker's personal considerations influence the degree of involvement with the group.

Although our examination of learning the ropes is limited to the process of assimilating the group's attitudes and behavior, clearly one must also examine one's fieldwork practices and continuously assess how to best organize the research. Unanticipated developments may lead to discoveries and research problems that may earlier have seemed peripheral. Learning the ropes, then, requires simultaneous attention to both substantive and theoretical findings and how these relate to the methodology and direction of the research.

Learning the ropes involves assuming research roles that can be modified as new relationships are established and rapport is developed. As the research of each of the contributors in this section shows, learning the ropes is a continuous process, integral to field research and not something done before the "real work" begins.

Cracking Diamonds: Observer Role in Little League Baseball Settings and the Acquisition of Social Competence

GARY ALAN FINE   *University of Minnesota*

It is an axiom of sociological methodology that the form of data collection one employs will affect the data that one is able to collect. Research is thus dependent upon the constraints imposed by one's methodological choices. This is well attested to in general discussions of methodologies, but less notice has been given to this point when examining strategic approaches within a methodology. In the case of participant observation, which presupposes that the observer will interact intensely with those being studied, this argument is worth making explicitly. The role one chooses to adopt in dealing with research subjects will influence the speed and adequacy with which the researcher is able to "learn the ropes" in the situation under observation, and this will influence the type of information which will be collected. Further, the explanation of that role to the group being examined will provide assistance and constraints in learning the mechanisms by which the group operates. Participant observation assumes that the researcher can, with time, learn the ropes of the group under examination and, as a result, can become part of the group's interaction system. Thus, it seems of particular importance to examine the interrelationship among the observer's role (as seen by members), the explanation of that role, and the behavior of members as a result of that explanation and their observation of the observer. This will allow us to understand how the observer becomes adjusted to the chosen field setting.

Although sociologists are generally knowledgeable of the national culture in which their research is embedded, this does not imply that they examine their own subgroups; in fact, this reflexive orientation toward one's membership groups has not often been attempted. The sociologist's modus operandi is to choose a relatively underexplored group of theoreti-

117

cal or descriptive interest and detail its social processes, traditions, and behavior patterns. Thus, the sociologist assumes an outsider's position in regard to the group, and learning appropriate modes of behavior typically is problematic.

Research with children's groups, the focus of this selection, poses interesting issues in this regard. Central is the biological fact that all adults have once been children. Children's cultures do vary across time, through space, and through environmental and demographic differences; still, children's cultures tend to be rather conservative, and their content changes slowly (Newell, 1963; Opie and Opie, 1959). Thus, one might suppose that adults could recall the dimensions of children's culture and would readily feel comfortable dealing with children on the children's own terms. However, by the end of adolescence, adults have become blissfully unaware of what passes in the more secret realms of preadolescent society. What was once central has been discarded as childish and not of practical utility for accomplishing "adult" tasks.

That childlore has been forgotten poses no difficulty for the average adult, except perhaps in disciplining offspring, and adult ignorance may actually provide children with needed room to grow. However, for the participant observer this lack of knowledge poses a frustrating barrier to research rapport and understanding. Because adults believe that they are familiar with children's behavior and talk, despite all they have forgotten, this difficulty may surprise the neophyte participant observer, who expects immediate understanding and acceptance and finds instead a feeling of awkwardness in the early stages of research.

The process by which the researcher acquires competence in dealing with children is tied to the role adopted. As noted above, this assertion is applicable to all participant observation environments, although we shall focus only on the relationship between role and social competence in regard to children's societies, and shall use this example to an understanding of how the researcher comes to learn the ropes in a semifamiliar situation.

This study is based on three summers of intensive data collection in five Little League baseball "major leagues" in Massachusetts, Rhode Island, and Minnesota.[1] The primary methodological technique employed was participant observation; the author (and, in one league, a research assistant) interacted with the players and coaches over the course of the Little League season (see Fine and Glassner, 1979 for further details). Two teams in each of these leagues were observed in detail. During practices and games, the participant observer stayed with the team in the dugout or on the field and attempted to maintain as much contact as possible with the players in nongame situations. While the original intent was to examine the processes and content of interaction in the

Little League setting, the research focus was expanded to include an examination of how children act when adult supervisors are not present. Particularly in the final year of research, efforts were made to learn about that side of children's life hidden from adults. This emphasis produced special obstacles for the participant observer which would not have been present if only "public behavior" were to be examined.

The five communities which were examined represent distinct social environments: (1) Beanville,[2] an upper-middle-class professional suburb of Boston, Massachusetts, (2) Hopewell, an exurban township outside of the Providence, Rhode Island, metropolitan area—consisting of small towns, oceanfront resorts, farms, and a campus of the state university, (3) Bolton Park, an upper-middle-class professional suburb of St. Paul, Minnesota, similar to Beanville except for geographical location, (4) Sanford Heights, a middle-to lower-middle-class suburb of Minneapolis, consisting primarily of developers' tract homes, and (5) Maple Bluff, an upper-middle-class neighborhood within the city limits of St. Paul, examined by Harold Pontiff. These five communities are not intended to represent a random sample of locations in which preadolescents live and congregate; however, they do cover a substantial range of environments, and they guard against making generalizations on the basis of a single idiosyncratic community.

CULTURE AND ROLES

Adult researchers can choose from a number of roles when conducting observation among children. Roles for research of this type include supervisor, leader, observer, and friend (Fine and Glassner, 1979). The role that the adult researcher adopts will have implications for gaining acceptance and for discovering the rules of appropriate behavior in children's groups.

Supervisor

The supervisor is a researcher who has direct authority over the child and yet lacks any direct, positive contact. Such figures include authoritarian teachers, camp supervisors, and religious instructors. Generally, this role provides access to a relatively restricted range of preadolescent behavior. The preadolescent attempts to follow the dictates of the authority when under observation; thus, there may be a marked difference in behavior between situations in which the supervisor is present and those in which the supervisor is absent. The children are thus managing the impressions the adult gains of them, with the intent of avoiding negative sanctions.

The behavior that is being observed may be natural, but it will not constitute the range of behaviors that preadolescents engage in. Within the context of this research role, it is unlikely that the barriers between adults and children can be eliminated. Adults will find it impossible to feel comfortable in collecting private information from children, although they may feel secure in the position of authority this role implies.

Leader

The leader can be differentiated from the supervisor by the presence of positive contact, although legitimate authority remains. Were the social researcher to become a Little League coach, the role that would be adopted would necessarily be that of the leader. Many professionals who regularly deal with children adopt this role—teachers, camp counselors, or coaches. A wider range of behaviors is legitimate here, and even if preadolescents overstep the line, some tolerance will be shown by the adult; however, the normative frame of reference will be that of the adult. Preadolescents may even feel constrained to act "properly" in order not to embarrass their adult leader. Preadolescents' affection for and affiliation with their adult leader may prevent their revealing their private behavior—which may be contrary to their desired presentation of self (Goffman, 1959). Their respect may, in effect, serve as a research barrier for the adult who wishes to acquire social competence. While the adult leader will have free access to a wide range of children's activities, the line between adult behavior and children's behavior remains strong, and the adult must behave in accord with adult prescriptions rather than those of children.

Observer

The observer role is the inverse of the leader role. The observer is an adult without formal authority and affective relationships. While preadolescents do not consciously behave in a particular fashion to obtain approval, neither do they admit the observer into their confidential circle. This is unlike the situation of the leader, in which preadolescents conspire to protect the adult role. Preadolescents have no motivation to allow the observer to learn of the social contingencies by which their group operates. By preadolescence, children are well socialized in the nuances of impression management and realize that some of the activities in which they regularly engage are frowned upon by adults. Thus, preadolescent groups will sometimes post a lookout for adults and will quickly change the subject when an adult is present. The pure observer has little more right to witness preadolescent behavior than any member of the general public, although this may vary according to the way in which the observer presents the research role. Further, because of the lack of positive affect and intense relationships, questioning about private and sensitive topics becomes problematic. The observer may witness behavior, but its meanings and motivations may not be self-evident and may remain hidden or be explicated only through the observer's knowledge as a former preadolescent and a current member of adult society. Thus, the observer, through a combination of choice and role, remains an outsider, destined not to acquire the competence to behave as a preadolescent.

Friend

The fourth major type of participant observation role, and the one emphasized in this research, is to become a friend to one's subjects and interact with them on as intimate a level as possible. One can never fully achieve the position of a peer, because of demographically based social requirements. There is value in being able to differentiate oneself from one's subjects—a feature which allows for a wider range of behaviors by the researcher than might be legitimate otherwise, such as asking "ignorant" questions. However, the adult who is able to transcend or bracket most of the status-based role requirements of adulthood may acquire greater social competence, leading to access to the recesses of children's culture. The friend role is conducive to the development of trust, although this trust must be cultivated by the researcher. Preadolescents may be willing to suspend their usual manner of dealing with adults, but this extraordinary relationship will take a substantial period of time to develop. Often special note is taken of the relationship—to signify its differences from other adult-child relationships. This was impressed upon me at one point in my research experience when one preadolescent labeled me an "honorary kid," to signal to a friend of his, with whom I did not have a relationship, that it was appropriate to talk freely in my presence. While that felicitous phrasing occured only once, many similar messages were conveyed by my preadolescent friends to their friends that I was an acceptable participant in their sexual and aggressive discussions. The key to this role is its explicit expression of positive affect combined with a relative lack of authority and a lack of sanctioning of preadolescent behavior. In turn, adopting the friend role suggests that the participant observer has the desire to acquire preadolescent social competency. The observer's acceptance will depend partly on the extent to which his or her behavior is congruent (though not identical) with that of preadolescents. Thus, there is a need for the adult to learn the ropes early in the research process—a process in which one's newly acquired preadolescent friends will provide sympathetic support.

DEVELOPMENT OF THE FRIEND ROLE

In any research endeavor, one must obtain access to the scene one wishes to examine. In gaining permission, it becomes necessary to present a rationale of why one wishes to be present. This is not only a feature of participant observation but applies to any long-term relationship. One needs some justification or "cover" to explain one's actions. In nonresearch situations, one may be able to cite the sponsorship of an acquaintance or the existence of some biographical interest that would immediately legitimate one's presence—an explanation that makes sense in terms of the structure of the setting. These natural explanations are routinized and conventionalized and are not problematic; further, in natural interaction the explanation that the participant gives will be the one that he or she explicitly accepts—the real reason for the person's presence. From this, two issues emerge that relate to the acceptance and acceptability of any explanation of presence: (1) its acceptance by the others in the situation and (2) its acceptance by the participant. In participant observation these two features may become problematic, and in settings where one deals with several distinct groups of participants, each with its own criteria for acceptance and its own level of understanding, this issue becomes especially difficult—as the researcher may be forced to take sides in an explanation of presence.

One of three basic approaches is typical in explaining the participant observer's presence (we are assuming, for simplicity's sake, that the subjects may be taken as a single group). First, the participant observer may provide the research subjects with a rather complete and detailed explanation of the purposes and hypotheses of the research; this we shall term "explicit cover." Second, the researcher may explain that research is being conducted, but be vague or not completely candid about its goals; this we shall term "shallow cover." Finally, the researcher may deliberately hide the researcher role from the subjects—a situation we shall term, with apologies to our intelligence apparatus, "deep cover." The explicitness of explanation may relate to any of the research roles described above. Since our Little League research involved the use of the friend role, it is this that we will deal with in the subsequent discussion.

Explicit Cover

While this approach may seem at first to be the most ethically responsible, it creates methodological problems. The observer presents the research role as objectively as possible, but this may not provide an adequate explanation for the research subjects, who lack experience with sociological investigations. There is danger in telling subjects too much about one's research goals, and this danger consists of more than the expectancy effect by which knowledgeable subjects attempt to confirm or deny the researcher's hypotheses through their timely actions. The explanation given may, if sufficiently explicit, prove limiting to the subjects, who may feel compelled to reveal only that behavior under study and may exclude the researcher from areas outside of this range of interest. Further, by presenting the research endeavor as more formal than it is (considering the flexible nature of grounded research), the effect may be to make intimate friendships less likely. The relationships which do develop under such a circumstance are likely to be utilitarian ones, based on the formal research bargain. Because of this, the researcher may find it difficult to become comfortable investigating topics outside of the stated research bargain.

Shallow Cover

The approach adopted for my Little League research was shallow cover and involved the "sin" of omission. While it was explicitly mentioned and reaffirmed that the author was a social psychologist interested in observing the behavior of preadolescents, this was not expanded upon in detail. The researcher claimed that he wished to discover what children said and did, and that he would spend as much time with them as possible. This vague bargain permitted informal bargains to be struck with many individuals—explanations which at times differed substantially from each other. This allowed some players to treat the researcher as an intimate, sharing their dirty stories and vile exploits with him; allowed other boys to use the researcher as a protector against the bullying of their peers; provided isolates with someone to talk to about their baseball concerns; and gave parents and coaches an opportunity to describe their frustrations in raising children.

Shallow cover makes explicit one's structural role, and as such, the researcher's credibility as a role inhabitant cannot be undermined. However, since the research interests are not specified, individuals may feel deceived when they learn that the researcher's presumed interests at the beginning of the research were not the "real" topics. No matter how vague the researcher attempts to be, subjects develop ideas about what is being tested—ideas that can be cruelly or benignly disconfirmed and that will affect the researcher's access to the sudjects. Shallow cover is perhaps the most frequent approach and may account for the fact that occasionally after a research account is published (Gallagher, 1964; Vidich and Bensman, 1964), subjects will feel betrayed by the researcher when the ambiguous cover is made explicit. The sociologist is still seen as a researcher, and in that the subjects were not defrauded, but the topics of study were not what subjects defined them to be. In such a situation, some subjects may feel deceived, while others may not—either because their expectations were not similar or because the explanations given to them differed materially.

In shallow cover, one has sufficient flexibility to create a research bargain that will allow a wide range of situations and behaviors to be examined. Since the researcher may initially be interested in a wide range of topics or unsure of a precise set of interests, the research problem can be narrowed or changed while still maintaining the research bargain. Because of the nature of the research explanation, expanding my focus from what occurs in Little League fields and dugouts to what preadolescents do in their leisure time was not problematic because of the initial explanation. Once the final report of my research findings is made available to the subjects, we will have the opportunity to determine how well they believe the research bargain has been upheld.

Deep Cover

In research studies in which subjects are not aware that they are under investigation, the position of the researcher is structurally equivalent to that of the undercover intelligence agent, although presumably there is a different set of motives. In that situation the researcher may witness a wide variety of behaviors, but simultaneously may find it difficult to inquire about any of these behaviors without the cover being suspect. A cover that is blown in such a situation—when subjects discover that their new member is actually a professional observer—may have profound implications. This uncovering discredits not only the research (as is true when one's shallow cover is blown) but the researcher as well, and perhaps the entire scientific enterprise.

In the case of research with preadolescents, deep cover is impossible to maintain since adults cannot "pass" as prepubescent (although this has been attempted with adolescents (Tornabene, 1967). However, one can live a false existence if one pretends to portray a role other than a researcher while surreptitiously taking notes about preadolescents (e.g., Sherif's position as a camp custodian in his summer camp studies: Sherif and Sherif, 1953; Sherif et al. 1961). This deception, while generally innocuous, can be sustained only for a short period of time for two reasons: (1) the frustrations that affect the role performer and (2) the limitations that are built into the role in terms of lack of access to the meanings that events have for the participants. The researcher learns about the operation of the group through a process of induction, generalizing from behavior to what these behaviors must mean for the group. Thus, while legitimate group members may believe that the researcher knows as much about the rules of the game as they do, actually the researcher knows less and finds no easy way of discovery.

The research announcement that the participant observer chooses to make affects the observer's ability to feel comfortable within the field setting. In this regard, deep cover is the most problematic, since the research is in danger of being unmasked at any point. In addition to learning the exigencies of proper social interaction, the researcher must be careful that discrediting information is hidden. This uncovering can occur with dramatic and potentially devastating suddenness, and in at least some accounts the problematic feature of deep cover has led the researcher to terminate participation in difficult situations (Wallis, 1977). While explicit cover promotes personal comfort in the field—since there is little discrepancy between public and private roles and questioning can be done openly—if the researcher decides to change the focus of the investigation, a feeling of anxiety may develop as the research bargain is altered and the observer must acquire new social competencies (such as the ability to talk about preadolescent sexual behavior as well as baseball). It is the third approach which seems most conducive to acquiring situational competencies. Shallow cover avoids possible discrediting, and because of the open focus on the researcher's role, it allows for questioning of the norms and appropriate behaviors of the group, both in public and in private. Generally, the more congruent the observer's desired social role is with the role as seen by informants, the more rapidly will the observer feel comfortable in the chosen setting; this consideration is important in choosing a research bargain.

DEVELOPING TRUST

Despite the explanations that are given as justification for the observer's presence (we shall focus on shallow cover), individual participants may attempt to use the researcher for their own purposes (Johnson, 1975). This manipulation will influence the research arrangements and may facilitate or hinder the collection of data. Thus, while the adult with children will *always* be treated as some kind of adult by children (and the concept of *"honorary kid"* implicitly acknowledges this), there are services which the researcher-friend can provide in exchange for information. The observer may provide rewards for the preadolescents; may be used to satisfy some psychological needs (such as being able to tell their story); or may be dealt with as a friend—and in this case, the rewards are supplied by the mere presence of the researcher. In turn, the researcher looks for interactional rewards: status and information, fulfillment of the research-

er's psychological needs, and enjoyable and emotionally satisfying friendships with the subjects. The development of social exchange patterns
between researcher and subject allows for successful participant observation.

The behavioral content of preadolescent society varies in the extent to
which it may normatively be revealed in the presence of adults. Some
behaviors, such as playing baseball, are performed unhesitatingly in the
presence of adults. This public behavior is easily observed and readily
explicable with the aid of informants. The fact that preadolescents have
little trouble spending time with adults indicates that there is a wide
range of public behavior options available, and some parents believe that
their offspring have no clandestine behavior.

The traditional adult concept of preadolescent socialization suggests
that preadolescents strive to master the adult culture and that deviations
imply the incompleteness of this learning. However, as Speier (1973) has
pointed out, children can be profitably described as maintaining a culture
of their own, separate and distinct from that of adults. He extends the
argument to suggest that adult-child contact can be seen as an example of
culture contact. On the basis of my research, I agree with Speier that this
separate culture is a sizeable part of children's interaction, although
preadolescents are competent to deal with adults using the adult-
sanctioned culture. This concept of dual cultures is not unique to
children but applies also to adults who are members of one or several
subcultures. The culture of childhood may be seen as one of the numerous
subcultures in contemporary heterogeneous society.

The research question involves *obtaining access* to this secretive
culture—a process which is time-consuming and demands the development of trust. Preadolescent culture is akin to a deviant subculture in that
its participants strive to keep the content hidden from their adult
guardians. They do this for two pragmatic reasons. First, there is a desire
to maintain a morally proper "face" in front of adults—that is, to manage
the impressions their parents have of them. Second, the rough edges of
children's culture must be hidden if the child is to avoid punishment. For
example, one boy in Sanford Heights was grounded for a week when his
mother heard from his sitter that he told a peer (in a phrase that
psychoanalysts would find delightfully symptomatic) that "my cock has
teeth." It is pragmatically necessary that adults be kept ill informed about
the sexual and aggressive content of this culture.

The observer of children, like the researcher who studies deviant
groups, finds that trust is essential. Polsky (1967) argues that the researcher who seeks acceptance by a criminal group must: (1) become
willing to break some laws (if only as an accessory to crimes and not

reporting information to the authorities), (2) make his or her contacts believe these intentions, and (3) prove that these acts are consistent with relevant beliefs. In the case of preadolescents, the issues are structurally similar. The participant observer may be, as I was, tested. This testing appears to be a precondition for acceptance in the private settings of the group. One key area in which this testing by preadolescents occurred was in determining my reaction to rowdiness (see also Glassner, 1976). This constellation of behaviors included shouting, shoving, fighting, insulting, and arguing. Repressing my adult desires to intervene at the slightest provocation led to my being allowed to observe other occasions, as an adult who knew how to behave around children.

On one occasion, I was in a Sanford Heights park with a group of preadolescent boys who, over a period of about five weeks, had begun to trust me. Suddenly, these boys spotted a group of girls they did not know, seated around a park bench near a thermos of water. One of my companions felt that it would be great sport to bother them (and simultaneously pay attention to them). He and his friends plotted to rush them, steal their thermos, and pour out the contents, disrupting their gathering. After a short period of insults between boys and girls (mostly about their physical attractiveness), the plan was put into effect—with the expected screaming and squealing on the part of the girls. At one point, several of the girls turned to me (busily taking notes and appearing, I assume, furtively guilty) and asked me, as the adult presumably in charge, why I didn't stop them. This reasonable question placed me in a difficult situation as a participant observer. Since no serious harm seemed to be occurring, and since I felt from various cues (such as the boys not looking at me) and prior actions that the behavior was natural and not being done for my benefit, I decided not to intervene, and said only that I was not in charge and had no control over their behavior. The boys were gleeful at hearing this, and shortly, with their mission completed (and the beginning of cross-sex contact begun), left the scene of battle. In retrospect, that occasion seems a significant step in my acceptance as an honorary preadolescent and indicated to the boys that I would not restrain them excessively—that I knew "my place" in the group. After that time I began to hear more detailed accounts of "making out"; one boy even used my recorder to tape a mutual masturbation session, and then returned the tape to me without commenting on what was taped.

Total acceptance is impossible, and I was fortunate to have been accepted by a handful of boys in the leagues who felt they could trust me (which never really occurred in Bolton Park or Maple Bluff). After I had won the trust of several boys in Beanville, they would tell me how they had just mooned[3] at passing traffic on a nearby street. The first time this occurred, I felt exhilarated for having been trusted sufficiently to be told about this example of preadolescent deviance, and yet somewhat frustrated for not having seen it in its natural context. When a similar revelation occurred several times without warning, I came to realize that this was an important part of the relationship; it was necessary that I not witness the actual mooning in order to protect both parties from embarrassment. Similar events happened in the other locations. In Hopewell, I heard about egging houses (throwing eggs at homes), but never witnessed it. In Sanford Heights many pranks and sexual acitivites were discussed in my presence, but despite attempts to go with the boys when they played pranks or to attend boy-girl parties, this never seemed possible. The barriers between adult and child are too powerful to be totally erased, although I was privy to a lot of dirty talk and verbal reconstructions of sexual and aggressive events. Adults can never really be treated as children, despite the behavioral competencies which they feel they might have reacquired. Indeed, the adult will not feel comfortable behaving as a child, despite the possible benefits such a total role enactment would bring. Although sociologists can learn what constitutes proper behavior of the subjects, a very different set of behaviors may be expected of researchers.

THE KEY INFORMANT

Crucial to learning the ropes and acceptance by a preadolescent group is the sponsorship of a "key informant." This individual is frequently cited in the sociological literature as the "hero" of the research—the person without whom the research could never have been conducted, or at least, not in its present form. In the course of this research, I gained the assistance of several boys who can properly be termed key informants. In Beanville, for example, without the assistance and sponsorship of a twelve-year-old named Rich Janelli, who suggested techniques of gaining rapport with his friends, I might have given up in frustration early in the research. These key informants expended their time, energy, and prestige to help me—although they gained prestige among their peers for having access to the observer. Within any population there may be several potential key informants. One criterion for this position is that the individual has a central position in the social structure of the group, which implies access to persons and knowledge. One can distinguish between two components of the key informant role: that of *sponsor* and *source*. Needless to say, these two components need not be embodied in the same individual. In the course of this research, many adult coaches and parents acted as sponsors, allowing me to gain access to their charges, but were unable, despite their best intentions, to provide much information about the nature of children's culture. Some low-status preadolescents provided a wealth of information, but little aid in gaining entry to the group of which they are nominally a part. It is the convergence of ability and willingness to supply the researcher with information and entry that is the mark of the key informant. In reviewing my research, it is difficult to determine why those individuals who became important to the research behaved as they did. One element which seems to characterize these boys is a sense of security in their social positions. Like Doc in Whyte's (1955) research, Rich, Justin, Whitney, Tom, and Frank in my own research were leaders in their groups, and they recognized this. They were socially self-confident, and this self-confidence allowed them to bridge the gap between adult and child and caused them to feel secure in their social authority and competence over a friendly, yet ignorant, adult. They were preadolescent teachers, willing to suggest ways I should act or react (i.e., don't be shocked; don't be too pushy; don't ignore the middle-status group members). This point is important in research with children, in that it represents something of an inversion of the normal relation between adult and child. It also represents placing trust in an adult, when normally, because of the topics being considered, that trust would be misplaced.

Thus, this research is in the debt of Rich Janelli from Beanville, who invited me to one of his private parties as "one of the boys," and to Tom Jordan, who was willing to assure his Sanford Heights peers that they could talk about girls in my presence, and in fact, on one of these occasions explained to his peers the proper techniques of "frenching." These individuals also gained from our relationship. Justin, Whitney, and two of their friends were taken from Hopewell to see a Boston Red Sox game; Frank and Tom were taken to see *Star Wars* in Sanford Heights; and neither group was rebuked for most of their antics in the process. Over the course of the research I came to be very good friends with these boys. We developed relationships of exchange which were balanced, even though different commodities were involved (including their desire to be immortalized through my writings and my desire to relearn how to be a preadolescent).

The role that I adopted with these boys was complex. Friend is certainly a part, as is big brother, student, journalist, and protector. However, with each boy my role had to be somewhat different. This factor is at the core of participant observation research. The basic interactionist perspective is not that of a single, simple, immutable role but a continual shaping to fit an ongoing relationship. This affected the way in which my knowledge of preadolescent culture was acquired.

SUMMARY

There is a relationship between the role that researchers choose to employ and their ability to gain acceptance and rapport in the group. In every research setting this relationship will take a somewhat different form, owing to the nature of the research roles that can be adopted and the modes of behavior that group acceptance requires.

The position that researchers must adopt in regard to preadolescent subjects can be seen in this light. Because of physical appearance, social knowledge, and status, researchers are forced to operate within the role boundaries which constrict adults. Although the researchers may know how preadolescents do behave, other standards are applicable to their own behavior. While these behavior constraints are not grossly restricting, the range of permissable behaviors is narrowed by the researcher's self-image, the subjects' image of the researcher, and the normative expectations of other adult onlookers. Similar constraints on participant observers operate in all cases in which the researcher's own membership group is not being examined.

These research roles are not reified constellations of behavior. Rather, they are guides which channel action. As researchers learn the expectations of the group under study, behavioral options undergo continuous change as rapport is gained, relationships are negotiated, and new situations are encountered. The behavioral options available to researchers who study children are altered during the research, although this change does not necessarily imply an increase or decrease in the absolute number of options. At the outset, before researchers have acquired a behavioral competence in dealing with the group, a wide range of researcher roles are available. Researchers choose among these possibilities, thus affecting the manner in which the group will be known and how the group will react. For example, once positive relationships have developed, a researcher cannot easily retreat to the role of uninvolved observer. However, as research roles are developed, these roles allow for considerable flexibility and a feeling of comfort in the research setting.

The basic argument is that behavioral interaction acquired through participant observation is learned in ways similar to those of natural interaction. These social understandings are transmitted as a function of the social relationships which have developed between participant observer and subject—and these relationships, in turn, depend on the researcher's understanding of situational proprieties.

Obviously we are not dealing with a simple cause-and-effect relationship; the observer's social competence in the group affects the treatment by the group, and this treatment, in turn, expands and refines the observer's social competence. Learning the ropes in a group different from one's own is a continuous process, affected by the situated motives of both researcher and subject. However, by carefully considering the choice of role announcement, the researcher's acquisition of social competence can be supported by subjects' perceptions of the research goals.

Notes

1. Since a large majority of our preadolescent subjects were male (approximately 98 percent), we shall use masculine terminology exclusively. Differences between boys and girls were not examined in this research.

2. All names of persons and places are pseudonyms.

3. In this prank, preadolescents quickly pull down their trousers and briefs while facing away from oncoming traffic. See Licht (1974) for a psychiatric analysis.

References

FINE, G.A., and B. GLASSNER. "Participant Observation With Children: Promise and Problems." *Urban Life*, (1979), 153–174.

GALLAGHER, A., JR. "Plainville: The Twice-Studied Town." In A.J. Vidich, J. Bensman, and M.R. Stein, eds., *Reflections on Community Studies*. New York: Harper & Row, 1964, pp. 285–303.

GLASSNER, B. "Kid Society." *Urban Education*, 11 (1976), 5–22.

GOFFMAN, E. *The Presentation of Self in Everyday Life*. New York: Doubleday, 1959.

JOHNSON, J.M., *Doing Field Research*. New York: Free Press, 1975.

LICHT, M. "Some Automotive Play Activities of Suburban Teenagers." *New York Folklore Quarterly*, 30 (1974), 44–65.

NEWELL, W.W. *Games and Songs of American Children*. New York: Dover, 1963. (Orig. 1883.)

OPIE, I. and P. OPIE. *Lore and Language of School Children*. London: Oxford University Press, 1959.

POLSKY, N. *Hustlers, Beats, and Others*. Garden City, N.Y.: Doubleday, 1969.

RYNKIEWICH, M.A., and J.F. SPRADLEY. "The Nacerima: A Neglected Culture." In J.F. Spradley and M.A. Rynkiewich, eds. *The Nacirema*. Boston: Little, Brown, 1975, pp. 1–5.

SHERIF, M., and C.W. SHERIF. *Groups in Harmony and Tension*. New York: Harper & Row, 1953.

SHERIF, M., O.J. HARVEY, B.J. WHITE, W.R. HOOD, and C.W. SHERIF. *Intergroup Conflict and Cooperation: The Robbers Cave Experiment*. Norman, Okla.: University of Oklahoma Book Exchange, 1961.

SPEIER, M. *How to Observe Face-to-Face Communication*. Pacific Palisades, Calif.: Goodyear, 1973.

TORNABENE, L. *I Passed as a Teenager*. New York: Simon & Schuster, 1967.

VIDICH, A., and J. BENSMAN. "The Springdale Case: Academic Bureaucrats and Sensitive Townspeople." In A.J. Vidich, J. Bensman, and M.R. Stein, eds., *Reflections on Community Studies*. New York: Harper & Row, 1964, 313–349.

WALLIS, R. *The Road to Total Freedom: A Sociological Analysis of Scientology*. New York: Columbia University Press, 1977.

Whyte, W.F. *Street Corner Society*. Chicago: University of Chicago Press, 1955. (Orig. 1943.)

Sociologist as Hustler: The Dynamics of Acquiring Information

ROBERT PRUS   *University of Waterloo*

> *You just can't read a book and say, "Okay, now I'm a hustler."*
> *(C.R.D. Sharper)*

Often, when people envision confidence games, they limit their attention to the "sting," the point at which targets are relieved of their possessions.[1] They generally fail to consider the preparations, the work, or the social aspects of the hustle. Similarly, when people think of field research, they often have the image of someone simply going around observing or talking to people. Here, as well, they tend to overlook the preparations, work, and social aspects of doing fieldwork. In what follows, I would like to indicate some of the critical features of doing fieldwork, using professional hustling as a model. It is suggested that fieldwork may be seen as a "hustle," and that researchers may learn a great deal about doing fieldwork by examining the operations of professional confidence men.

In developing this discussion, I will be drawing mainly on some insights I have gained doing research on (1) card and dice hustlers and (2) the hotel community. Although these settings, by conventional standards, are more "deviant" than some in which persons might be doing research, it seems that many of the insights arising therein have applicability in other contexts. By way of providing a little background material, I might note that professional card and dice hustlers generally work in groups of three to four men and travel about the countryside cheating at card and dice games which they or others initiate. This represents full-time work for these individuals, whose hustle depends much more on their ability to do public relations work (and manage impressions) than on the physical manipulation of game equipment. The hotel research focuses on the social organization of the hotel community and examines the careers, activities, and interrelatedness of an assortment of actors—staff, entertainers, patrons, hookers, and other hustlers—who together constitute the hotel community. Although the latter project is considerably broader in scope, in both instances participant observation and interview materials were utilized in an attempt to learn how people work out aspects of their lives. Space limitations preclude more specific elaboration of these life styles, but interested readers may consult Prus and Sharper (1977) and Prus and Vassilakopoulos (1980).

In what follows, I will endeavor to indicate parallels between successful hustling and the successful acquisition of information on the part of field researchers. Although our objective is to obtain knowledge and understanding of everyday group life, rather than to relieve people of their valuables, researchers can take lessons concerning dedication, planning, flexibility, and public relations from professional hustlers.

GETTING PREPARED

Although it is more difficult for a field researcher to measure success than for the hustler (researchers, for example, cannot simply count pages of notes, as hustlers might count money, to determine how well they have done), it should not be assumed that preparation is any less important. Professional hustlers are very concerned about their game preparations, and the same should be true of researchers. Three aspects of preparation seem particularly noteworthy: "getting the inside track," "getting connected," and "teamwork."

Getting the Inside Track—Knowing Your Game[2]

Regardless of the hustle(s) to be worked, confidence men who are knowledgeable about many hustlers and comfortable with a hustling orientation have significant advantages over other hustlers. Not only are they apt to be more resourceful, but they themselves are much less likely to represent obstacles to the successful realization of their objective(s). Similarly, field researchers well aware of theory and other research situations tend to be closely attuned to the situational contingencies they encounter and adept at maximizing their outcomes. Likewise, persons adapting a "value disinterested" perspective are less likely to impede their own research.

One way of "getting the inside track" is by knowing your theoretical orientation. Thus, it is suggested that researchers be familiar with theory and attempt to ascertain the extent to which theoretical notions are in evidence in the situation. Also suggested is that they review all research pertaining to the theoretical issues they wish to examine, regardless of the particular substantive area to be investigated. A researcher without a theoretical frame and concepts, not unlike a hustler without a "gaff" (game) or "tools" (paraphernalia), is unlikely to get very far.

A second means of "getting an edge" on one's research is by being prepared to fit into the group life to be studied. This is suggested as a general orientation rather than being at ease with particular activities, as ethnographic projects tend to expose researchers to a wide range of contact with those whom they study. Accordingly, researchers who have a capacity to fit into a variety of situations, not as stars or leaders but as one of the group, are more apt to be successful. Persons unable to maintain their "cool" (Lyman and Scott, 1970), who become easily offended, indignant, or flustered, or who feel obligated to educate, improve, or crusade vis-à-vis those they encounter are a definite liability and represent a threat to the delicate balance fieldwork entails. Thus, some chameleon-like qualities seem fundamental to field research. It's not that researchers have to like those whom they study, or to identify with or emulate them. They cannot, however, let their personal likes and dislikes interfere with their research. Just as researchers frequently have to overcome the "subject mystique," it is also important that they help those whom they study overcome the "researcher mystique." Fitting in is a two-way process. Thus, persons more willing to view activities from a variety of perspectives are more likely to help the respondents adjust to them. Most people, I have found, do not wish you to be just like them, but they don't want the differences to threaten them.

Getting Connected—Start Acquiring Information with Your First Contact[3]

Since professional hustlers think of hustling as a long-term activity, they tend to look for hustling opportunities in almost all settings they encounter. Card and dice hustlers, for example, do not particularly care whether the event they are going to work is a community picnic, an undertakers' convention, a turkey shoot, a benefit dinner, or a policemen's retirement party. Much more important is whether they can locate the event and successfully involve the participants in a gambling event. Similarly, researchers interested in recruitment, socialization, or conflict, for example, could examine these aspects of group life among bikers, dating couples, clergymen, and insurance salespeople, as well as within police departments, women's liberation groups, hospitals, and schools. If researchers build their projects around existing contacts, they, like the hustlers, can often expedite the process.

Much of my research has had a fortuitous quality to it. I had no intention of studying road hustlers or the hotel community. In both cases, however, as I became acquainted with people in these situations, I began to envision exciting prospects for research. My contacts did not promote their substantive areas as research sites but rather assumed these to be rather unexceptional. Although different in many ways, C.R.D. Sharper (road hustler) and Steve Vassilakopoulos (hotel community) were both instrumental in influencing the directions of my research. I have also seen similar prospects for research in the backgrounds of others. Sometimes these individuals didn't have the contacts they had implied; at other times, they lost interest in the project or we became geographically separated. On still other occasions, I found that I did not have the time or energy to devote to another project. But through these cases, I have become keenly aware of the potential for research afforded by routine contacts. If you have a fairly consistent theoretical orientation, then you are more likely to be open to a variety of research sites.

In some contexts, one's initial contacts are exceedingly important. Not only can they provide entry to key affiliational networks, but they also help you prepare for field encounters. They can demystify activities and actors, and they can provide a great deal of information about the situations you are likely to encounter, the norms and terminology of the group, and the nature of the players and layout of the field. In exploring the situation with initial contacts, as well as with subsequent ones, it is important to emphasize the "what and how" of research, to state that you are interested in what happens and how, not whether something is good or bad, right or wrong. It is also useful to ask continuously for examples, illustrations, and clarifications ("How's that?", "Do you remember what happened then?", and so forth), thus revealing your interest and your desire for careful descriptive information. You may have to prove yourself reliable, trustworthy, reasonable, and so on, but you also want to know how solid your contact is, because "getting connected" can be a big step.

While your initial contact can save you an immense amount of time and frustration, it is highly advisable to treat all this information tentatively, and, in particular, to avoid drawing conclusions. As far as possible, you should treat this information as representing the views of only one insider. This may seem a little disloyal to your contact, but it is essential that you continue accumulating observations and remain receptive to contradictory evidence.

Teamwork—The Research Crew[4]

Although one can do ethnographic research alone, fieldwork (not unlike other hustling) tends to be facilitated by teamwork. Not only do partners help to sustain interests and perspectives over the length of the project, but they also have other advantages. First, two or more observers can split up to "catch more action" simultaneously and/or compare notes in the same settings. Second, individual researchers may find subjects differentially accessible. Not only have Steve and I, for example, found that we had differential success in approaching particular people in the hotel community, but we also found that female assistants were extremely valuable in locating other persons (male and female) otherwise difficult to reach. Partners can also help establish credibility for one another. Thus, for instance, we found that occasionally it took two of us to convince some persons that we were actually studying the hotel community and that they were not targets of other hustles.

To a large extent, one thinks of partners as being either academics or initial contacts. Although this has been largely the case in my own research, I have also found that various persons in the hotel community have served as team members and have been highly instrumental in introducing (and "qualifying") us to others. These friends in the field took a greater than usual interest in our project and in various ways expedited our research. As with other hustlers, however, field researchers are apt to find that partners or friends in the field who are indiscreet, argumentative, or unreliable can make their work both frustrating and risky.

HUSTLING IS WORK

One of the things I find a little humorous (and occasionally annoying) is the notion that fieldwork is fun. Admittedly, it's often interesting, even exciting at times, but it is work, and serious researchers are not there to enjoy themselves. There is work to be done, and the researcher's task is to gather data on the ways in which the participants work out their activities with one another as thoroughly and systematically as possible.

Patience and Perseverence

Participant observation can be a very time-consuming, wearying experience. While projects vary in the directness with which one can approach persons, ethnographic work assumes that researchers go through routines with those they study. The subjects have activities in which they are engaging, and you have to work around them. Sometimes, so much happens in a period of time that you cannot keep track of it; at other times, you feel yourself desperately waiting for something to happen. Unfortunately, the haphazard elements of group life make it extremely difficult to know when and where something is going to happen. Unlike the office or at home, your choices of time-filling activities may be severely limited in the field. Further, because you don't want to miss anything, you always try to be ready, and you keep looking for people to approach and/or attempting to figure out ways of approaching them.

Fieldwork with hustlers and hotel people has some other drawbacks as well. Their hours run from noon to about 4 A.M., often later. Then, after leaving the scene, we spend another hour or two reviewing the day's events. Further notes are added the following morning, and then it's back to work in the field. After a while, the days start to blend, so that on leaving the field, it takes some time to reorient ourselves to regular hours. However, this is their way of life, and if you want to see how a group of people live, you have to go to their places and keep their hours.

While attempts to obtain data in routine field settings can be trying, it should not be assumed that attempts to structure opportunities to gather information will automatically proceed smoothly. Thus, for example, we found that many hotel people were relatively unreliable in keeping meetings. We would be there on time because we did not want to risk "burning" a contact, but their life styles frequently made planning precarious. A "deal" might suddenly come up, or they might encounter some difficulty with the police or an acquaintance or simply didn't have alarm clocks. Whatever the reason, you may waste valuable time waiting. You may also meet seemingly promising contacts and accompany them as they go about their activities, only to find that because of the "action" they encounter, their drinking, or their animosities with others, it may be difficult to find a block of time to engage in more involved conversation.

Bouncing Around

If your insider has more extensive contacts, or if your field is more limited, you may spend less time "bouncing around," trying to make additional contacts. The hotel research was quite sweeping, and while we had established a series of contacts at a few bars, it was necessary to go out and make new contacts in new bars with a variety of other people. Lacking a "sponsor,"[5] one faces the problems of approaching strangers alone. The situation is much more unstructured, and you are apt to spend much more time trying to obtain information than would otherwise be the case. However, you often need only reach one person initially, and the more time you spend in a setting, the more likely you will be to make a friend in the field. However, lacking advance information on the situation, you run the risk of becoming affiliated with more marginal members of the group. You cannot be too selective in whom you meet, but you may want to avoid becoming closely affiliated with persons until you have a better sense of their "community" standing. The linkages between persons are often much more extensive than they appear on the surface, and so, any contact has some potential and is best accorded genuine, albeit somewhat tempered, recognition.

Looking for Action—"Where It's At"[6]

One of the frustrations in fieldwork is waiting for something to happen. Not unlike other hustlers, researchers may endeavor to (1) situate themselves in high action spots; (2) move about, trying to locate ongoing action; (3) become affiliated with "action people"; and (4) create action. Hustlers generally cannot afford to sit back and wait for action to come their way and thus strive to make their own breaks. Similarly, unless researchers have unlimited time, it would seem to be in their best interests to learn from the hustlers in this respect as well.

The first point, that of situating oneself in strategic locations, seems basic to fruitful participant observation. Many of the hotels we studied were chosen precisely because of the elements of hotel life they represented. Although many of the aspects of hotel life studied occur much more generally, these places offered contrasts and activity levels less evident in other settings. Similarly, we not only sought out a variety of hotel work positions (e.g., Steve has worked as a barboy, waiter, bartender, desk clerk, and doorman) to maximize exposure to action but also endeavored to situate ourselves in specific bar locations conducive to studying group exchanges.

The second option, moving about in search of action, is another course we have used. Besides learning the hours and places where action is most likely to occur, we also checked out common gathering spots. Thus, while a quiet setting might lend itself to certain valuable insights from a casual interview, we noticed the tendency of "action people" to cluster in certain settings at certain times. If one wants to find them, some mobility is necessary. Here again, teamwork enables partners to split up and cover two or more spots. The third route, getting connected with action people, is another valuable strategy. Not only will these people help you find action, but they will also introduce you to other action people.

The fourth method of locating action, creating action, is one we avoided almost entirely. Not only did we have reservations about the naturalness of this strategy (i.e., experimentor effects), but we did not want to get involved in any hustles or action in which we might be seen as taking sides. Something as seemingly innocent as throwing a party could lead to animosities and a variety of legal risks. Furthermore, we wanted to blend into the setting rather than stand out as major players. Persons openly creating action tend to be defined as more noteworthy.

"WORKING THE CON"

In discussing hustling, Prus and Sharper (1977:2) suggest that five steps are fundamental in "conning a mark": (1) locating a target; (2) consolidating oneself with the target; (3) promoting target investments; (4) obtaining possession of target investments; and (5) cooling the target out. Although some important differences exist between sociologists and card and dice hustlers, it nevertheless seems that sociologists doing fieldwork could productively apply aspects of this model to their research.

In contrast to hustlers, researchers do not endeavor to relieve targets of their money. Their objective is to obtain as much reliable data as possible. However, if researchers wish to obtain as much information as they can from as many people as possible, some hustling seems inevitable. Sometimes, sociologists have the funds to buy information. I have never been in that situation, but some people have suggested that I pay them for their information. Usually I suggest, jokingly (but often truthfully), that it would take a lot more money than I have to pay them for all they know. While I don't think in terms of "conning people," I do envision myself as something of a hustler, since I try to get people to help me with my projects. In the following section, I will try to indicate how this works.

Finding Targets—The Hustle Begins

Getting connected can be an important aspect of finding respondents for your research, but it is only the beginning. You will want to locate other persons with whom your contacts are not affiliated, and you may have to "move in" on your respondents. Not only must you try to be open to everyone so that they may approach you, but you should also take the initiative in approaching them, regardless of whether they appear friendly or distant.

When your targets are other hustlers, additional problems are presented. First, when you make yourself accessible to them, they may "put a move on you." Sometimes your inside contact will qualify you for them, defining you as a nonmark. Also, if you have done your homework, you may have an idea of what to expect and from whom. In any event, however, it is important that you not be hustled (i.e., be defined as a "sucker") and that in averting the hustle, you not offend the hustler. Second, in studying hustlers, you must also be careful that your activities do not interfere with their ability to make money. You must not only be sensitive to the timing of your encounters with these people but must also ensure that you do not in any way alert prospective marks to your target's hustle. This can be somewhat frustrating since researchers try to work their quests for information around the activities of their subjects.

Persistence in approaching targets is usually rewarding, so initial disappointments in approaching particular targets should not be allowed to deter field researchers from approaching the same targets at different times. Not all people are equally accessible, nor are they receptive to the same styles of approach.

Consolidating Oneself—"Getting Tight"

Having made the initial contact with a respondent, the next task is to establish a trust relationship with the target. Participation in illegitimate activities is one way of establishing oneself as somewhat trustworthy among hustlers and thieves, but most researchers wish to avoid this. It is important, however, to recognize that just as you try to establish confidence in your respondents, so are they likely to watch and test you, to see if you are "solid."

One way of consolidating oneself with hustlers is to frequent their more casual meeting places. If you are able to do this without offending them, you are apt to find that they feel more comfortable with you. Likewise, having an insider vouch for your credibility can promote trust, although the extent to which this is effective reflects this person's standing in the community.

While these and other means of establishing credibility are effective at a general level, I have found that many hustlers require a more personalized level of trust before opening up to you. There seems no best route in this respect, but I have found it useful to keep in mind the idea that individual hustlers do not trust all other hustlers. If you are able to show that you are reasonably discreet and can maintain the confidences of others, then the persons with whom you interact are more likely to trust you to maintain their confidence. Similarly, it is important that the respondents see you as largely autonomous, someone who functions independently of others in the community. Unless you establish your own integrity apart from your inside contacts, this too may interfere with your ability to obtain information.

Promoting Investments—"I Need All the Help I Can Get"

Ideally, researchers like to take the time to consolidate themselves with respondents before making a pitch for information. However, researchers (and hustlers) often do not have sufficient time. This means that how and when they disclose their research interests can have considerable impact on the degree of trust they establish with respondents and their subsequent ability to acquire information from them. Personally, I have found it best to tell respondents my interests directly and personally at a time when they seem most open to new ideas. For example, if a person has been in an argument or has become excited about something else, I will try to wait until a quieter time, when that person is "cleared for interaction." This problem becomes multiplied when one attempts to explain the research to two or more respondents simultaneously. Not only may these persons distract one another, but the element of trust becomes more problematic, as each may have reservations about the other learning of their cooperation.

I try to explain my projects in relatively simple terms, indicating in general how I think particular persons could help me. I also emphasize that I am not interested in taking sides or in determining what is right or wrong, good or bad, but only in what goes on and how it happens. I try not to overwhelm the respondents, but rather focus on the contributions they could make.

My least favored strategy is the "fast hit." Occasionally, I have found that a potential respondent is due to depart shortly, and I will sometimes try to make contact very quickly. This means briefly explaining the project and then trying to consolidate oneself with the target. Few hustlers like doing this, but they see it as an essential aspect of hustling: "If the money's there, you have to get it."

Obtaining Information—"I was wondering . . ."

Probably my basic operating premise in the field is, "Given the chance, people will help you." This may seem somewhat inconsistent with a hustling model, but I have also found that people enjoy talking about their experiences, especially when they are given a chance to explain the situations in which they have found themselves. In this respect, the first criterion for being a good interviewer is to be a good listener. A good listener is not someone who assumes a wall-like stance but rather one who comes across as interested but nonthreatening. Ideally, one would like the respondents to be as open with the interviewer as they are with themselves, only finding this conversation more stimulating. I try to convey the impression that my respondents are "the stars of the show" (and to me, they are). This doesn't mean that I pursue the dramatic incidents in their lives, for although these often emerge, I emphasize that I am interested in their daily routines. This is not as easy as it may seem. Many people are used to giving others only summary statements and tend to assume that others do not want to hear the details. While I have found that many people appreciate having the opportunity to fully discuss aspects of their lives with others, the idea of doing so may seem a little foreign to them. So, you may have to spend some time helping them adjust to this procedure.

In trying to maximize the amount of information obtained from persons, it is also important to be sensitive to one's own image. In general, I try to tell people what I am doing, with some concern to the timing and form of the explanation. However, regardless of how and what they are told, I have found that a low-profile approach is much more effective than appearing knowledgeable, in either an academic or a field sense.

While naive but interested and nonthreatening persons are apt to have more things fully explained to them, persons assuming this stance should also recognize that respondents may keep information from you or provide you with misinformation (assuming that you wouldn't know the difference). If you're seen as highly knowledgeable, on the other hand, respondents may take for granted the very information you would like to acquire or wonder why you want to know such elementary things. At the same time, if you're seen as really knowledgeable, you may get drawn into more action than you desire, and if you're seen as "too sharp" you may scare respondents away. However, if you seem somewhat aware of field-related events, respondents may open up to you, assuming that you know anyway. Thus, one of the tasks in ethnographic research is striving to achieve the balance of naiveté and knowledge which best elicits information.

This process becomes further complicated when one realizes that each person in the field may view the researcher somewhat differently and that it would be useful for the researcher to be aware of some things and not others in reference to each respondent. Thus, researchers may have to adjust their style somewhat from person to person and across topics. I don't know how well it would work for others, but in general, I prefer to start out with vague questions, ultimately trying to achieve detailed accounts of specific situations. I try to give the impression that "I know a little about something, but I am really not too sure how it works. Perhaps you could explain it to me." From then on, I try to be a good student— interested, thoughtful, inquiring, but always keeping in mind that I am there to learn from the respondent rather than vice versa. There are, however, certain things that I wish to know, so I am concerned about guiding the general direction in which the conversation flows. I will pursue a given issue from a variety of perspectives and at different intervals over a period of time. If someone suggests that I am probably already aware of various aspects of the situation (a statement I try to avoid), I will tell them that different people have different experiences and that I wondered how theirs had turned out. I am concerned about establishing the generality and validity of earlier observations and try to avoid being refused information, however elementary. In any event, it seems desirable to circumvent objections such as these. A useful way of doing this is to get respondents involved in discussing their experiences: "I was wondering how . . ."

Cooling Out Targets—If You Treat People Well, You Can Go Back

Given that researchers are persuading respondents to share their information, rather than depriving them of a limited resource, the problems sociologists face in cooling out targets are apt to be considerably less than those experienced by other hustlers. In part, the researchers' task of "cooling out targets" is accomplished when they outline their research interests. If respondents realize their objectives and accept them fairly early, then this aspect of hustling is apt to be facilitated.

Whether the respondents will like what is written about them is another problem. It also places the researcher in something of a dilemma when writing a report. While names and places may be changed in an attempt to conceal the participants' identities, the researcher may also feel obliged to omit some highly personalizing data. And regardless of what is or is not omitted, the researcher may find that particular respondents may become annoyed about some aspect of the report for any number of reasons.

In addition to cooling out targets, sociologists engaged in fieldwork may also find themselves going native or being drawn more heavily into the action than they had anticipated. When this happens, it may not only interfere with the researcher's ability to obtain certain kinds of data (while possibly facilitating the gathering of other data) but also tends to make disengagement more difficult for all concerned.

A final aspect of cooling out targets should be noted. If researchers have maintained good working relations with the participants, they may find that they have established a set of contacts conducive to research in a variety of related fields. Should they wish to pursue these subsequent contacts, they are likely to again find themselves advantaged. Not only have they had a chance to become somewhat familiar with such people but they should be able to assess these new contacts from a more informed base than would otherwise be possible.

EPILOGUE

In writing this selection, I have endeavored to indicate the kinds of things sociologists engaged in ethnographic research might profitably learn from professional hustlers. Although working toward rather different goals, the *modus operandi* of hustlers suggests invaluable insights for field researchers. Learning the ropes, which I would define as developing a capacity for the thorough, careful, and efficient execution of activities, is of considerable significance to both field researchers and hustlers. It involves preparation, work, and the ability to relate to people. In part, the nature and extent of the learning reflects those with whom one works and one's sense of dedication. I would, however, suggest that learning the ropes is an ongoing activity, and that as researchers we should be sensitive to learning from our contacts, in reference not only to content but also to technique.

Notes

1. In addition to the editors, I would like to thank John Goyder, Steve Vassilakopoulos, and Ed Vaz for comments and suggestions on earlier drafts of this selection. In discussing ethnographic research, I am particularly indebted to C.R.D. Sharper (Road Hustler). I learned more about field research from him than from any academic works on the subject.

2. "Game" is another name for a "hustle," "con," or "gaff." It is in reference to the "game" imagery that hustlers (particularly pimps) will sometimes call themselves "players."

3. "Getting connected" is a critical element affecting one's life chances as a hustler. Persons whose family or friends are established hustlers are greatly advantaged, but successful hustlers value new contacts and the opportunities they represent. Field researchers should adopt this attitude.

4. Among hustlers, the terms "crew," "mob," and "gang" tend to be used interchangeably to refer to the (typically small) groups in which hustles are worked (relatively few hustles are conducted alone, and most professionals work in crews). In general, ethnographers seem less attuned to the value of working in groups than do professional hustlers.

5. Professional hustlers greatly appreciate "sponsors" (insiders introducing them to events and targets). Persons performing adequately in this respect are likely to be given equal partner-sized earnings for the event. "Bird dogs," in contrast, who merely alert hustlers to prospective targets, will typically receive only minor compensation. By and large, sociologists seem to have underestimated the value of their routine (and fortuitous) contacts with respect to sponsors. This may in part reflect the amount of time necessary to complete projects, but it may also be attributable to a tendency to concentrate on substantive specialties rather than to focus on generic aspects of group life.

6. Since they do not get paid for putting in time, hustlers are particularly concerned with finding profitable situations. Professionals thus continually try to create action situations and locate targets receptive to their hustles. Field researchers face similar problems. Much more important than how many months or years are spent in the field is how much one learns from contact with the people there. In part, this means that since they are less free to create action (lest this disrupt ongoing routines), researchers have to work more diligently at acquiring information in other ways if they are to make more productive use of their time.

References

LYMAN, S., and M. SCOTT. *A Sociology of the Absurd.* New York: Appleton-Century-Crofts, 1970.

Prus, R., and C.R.D. Sharper. *Road Hustler: The Career Contingencies of Professional Card and Dice Hustlers.* Lexington, Mass.: Lexington Books, 1977.

Prus, R., and S. Vassilakopoulos. *Hookers, Rounders, and Desk Clerks: The Social Organization of the Hotel Community.* Toronto: Gage, 1980.

Who and Where Are the Artists?

MICHAL McCALL   *Case Western Reserve*
University

I learned how to do participant observation fieldwork while learning about the setting where my fieldwork—a study of female painters, sculptors, and printmakers in St. Louis—was done. I had not taken a fieldwork course, but I read the methodological literature and got regular advice from an experienced participant observation fieldworker.[1] Doing it is the way participant observation should be learned, I think, and it is the way I teach it now. First, students need a chance to practice each of the data-gathering methods used in doing fieldwork: structured and unstructured, respondent and informant interviewing; observation, both structured and unstructured; administering tests and questionnaires; and use of documents (G. McCall, 1975). Any good general methods course provides this practice. Next, students need advice on selecting a site or group of people to study. In general, one is as good as another, but some require larger investments of time and energy. Finally, students can be sent out to do fieldwork with an idea of where to start and an ongoing, structured opportunity to get advice about how to proceed, both from an experienced fieldworker and from one another. The goal in this kind of research is a "comprehensive understanding" of the social life being studied (Becker, 1971:76). The outcome will be an "analytic description" which uses the concepts, propositions, and empirical generalizations of sociology to report what is learned (McCall and Simmons, 1969:3). Fred Davis (1974) has called these frameworks of concepts propositions, and empirical generalizations the "stories of sociology." The experienced fieldworker helps by pointing out what else the student needs to know, suggesting ways of finding out and thinking of sociological stories the data might tell.

Each setting poses different generic problems for the participant observer; at the same time, some problems must be solved in all settings. Learning the "native language" of the group, organization, social movement, community, social world, or situation being studied, and using it to understand the social organization—both structure and process—of that group, community, world, or whatever is a problem every fieldworker must solve. The special problems of the setting I chose were finding *where* it was and *who* was in it.

The people I wanted to study—female artists in St. Louis—were not a group and did not have a site. They were part of several local art worlds whose boundaries it became part of the research to identify. I could not simply go somewhere, watch what happened there, and ask questions about it; first, I had to find the people and determine the shape and locales of their world. As a result, interviewing—both informant and respondent—was the data-gathering method I used first and most. Later, I also observed various events, made use of documents, and asked respondents to do a paper-and-pencil task (rating). An advantage of the setting I chose was that no one controlled access to a site, so that I avoided some problems of getting in.

I was interested in female artists because it seemed to me that the ones I knew faced a common dilemma: how to identify themselves—to themselves and to others—as artists when they weren't employed as artists. hadn't the requisite degrees in art, and in some cases weren't currently making art. Since knowing *who* was an artist was a major conceptual goal of my work, it was not a simple solution to the methodological problem of finding *where* art worlds were. Even so, I began with a snowball sample of female artists, finding people and asking them who and where, as well as what and how.

WHAT AND HOW

I brought a richly varied conceptual framework—symbolic interaction—to the field, thus avoiding the problem of finding or inventing analytic tools. I am not saying that I set out to test a theory and gathered data with which to do so. But I had learned to use the symbolic interaction framework to look at the empirical world. Early in my fieldwork, Howard S. Becker's (1974) article "Art as Collective Action" reminded me of George Herbert Mead's philosophy of acts and objects (1932). The Becker and Mead stories, together with Robert E. Park and Everett C. Hughes' story of the marginal man, shaped my choices of data to be gathered. The data, in turn, modified these stories to produce the idea which became central to my analysis: that art is the social object of ongoing, multisituated social acts we call art worlds and that the changing conventions of art worlds determine *who* is identified as an artist in each world and *how*, and *what* things become social objects called art and *how*.

The following is what I did and how. I did two- or three-hours semistructured interviews with thirty-one female, self-designated artists. By "semistructured" interviews I mean that they followed loosely, as to order of questions and information elicited, an outline of important topics I carried with me to each interview.[2] Early interviews differed somewhat from later ones, since as should happen in participant observation research, my questions changed as I became more knowledgeable. The participant observer can always return to a situation or person and retrieve missing data, and I did that in two cases, but for the most part my interviews changed as I weeded out naive or less fruitful questions. After the first four interviews, I had established the list of topics; then if a topic did not emerge during discussion, I asked questions about it. The list of topics was glued to a piece of red construction paper the size of the notebook I carried; this made it easy for me to find the list and check to make sure I had covered every topic.

I did not tape-record interviews. I carried a 9 × 6 inch spiral notebook for taking notes; it was large enough to be useful, small enough to be unobtrusive, and stayed open easily. Nor did I try to take verbatim notes during interviews. Writing everything down is distracting to those being interviewed, makes listening difficult, and interferes with participation. During interviews, I made notes of dates, names, places, unexpected topics, and hard-to-remember facts; as soon as I left an interview I made additional notes, mostly of ideas and quotations. Then I went home and typed the notes immediately. The list of topics helped organize what I remembered, so my fieldnotes were fairly complete. With experience, I could remember enough to get five to ten pages of single-spaced typed fieldnotes from a two-hour interview. My teacher's advice was: Tell your typewriter first, because every time you tell it you will edit, abstract, and drop details.

Doing a good interview, recording it well, and understanding its relevance to the study require creativity, tremendous concentration, a certain degree of social skill, and time; typing fieldnotes takes approximately twice as long as doing an interview. For all these reasons, I tried never to schedule more than one interview or event per day.

The thirty-one women were *respondents* insofar as comparable data were obtained from each of them. Respondent interviewing is "the collection of information about the personal feelings, attitudes, motives, actions, and habits of the interviewee" (McCall, 1975:6) and is appropriate when variability is assumed and one must interview all or a sample of persons in some category in order to describe the category as a whole

(Zelditch, 1962). I asked the (thirty-one) women about their own careers in art, personal histories, experiences in St. Louis art worlds, and opinions and attitudes. Respondent interviews provided the basic data on female artists.

Informant interviews, observation, and documents provided basic data on the several St. Louis art worlds. The same thirty-one women were informants, or surrogate observers, insofar as I asked them about art world events, divisions of labor, and culture—"norms, concepts, rules, practices, conventions, occasions, shared beliefs, and values" (McCall, 1975:6). Informant interviewing is appropriately used to obtain information about events the observer cannot get access to, institutionalized practices and norms, or specialized information (Zelditch, 1962). A person can be both an informant and a respondent during the same interview, if both kinds of data are gathered.

Other semistructured informant interviews were done with two female artists working in media other than painting, sculpture, or printmaking,[3] and two who belonged to different local art worlds;[4] one female art historian and professor; one male artist; and one female art dealer. Interviews with local informant-artists followed the outline used with female respondents. Other local informants were questioned about St. Louis art worlds and their own occupations in them. I also interviewed three nonlocal female artists; these women were questioned about their own careers, with special attention to problems of working in their own locales and problems they associated with being female artists. I listened to taped interviews conducted by a male art history professor with two St. Louis art dealers (one female and one male), two collectors, and one former curator.

Documents were used in analyzing St. Louis art worlds and for comparison with art worlds in other cities; a collection of invitations to exhibitions, reviews and artists' vitae, donated to the University of Missouri by a former St. Louis Art Museum curator, was used as a record of changes in the St. Louis art market over twenty years. Bimonthly and yearly St. Louis Art Museum reports were used to determine the status of the museum, measured by the number and kinds of exhibitions originating locally and donations and purchase of art works. I recorded the weekly listings of exhibitions in Sunday newspapers and newspaper art critics' reviews. These records were used to determine the proportion of exhibitions and exhibitions reviewed, by male and female artists. Lists of nationally known St. Louis and Chicago dealers, collectors, and artists in *Who's Who in American Art* (Jacques Cattell Press) were used to compare the art worlds in those two cities. Sociological studies of art worlds in other cities, published "insider" accounts, and articles in national art magazines were useful in understanding the shape of St. Louis art worlds, compared to art worlds in other cities.

I joined and participated in the activities of the Community of Women Artists (CWA), a female artists' organization. I attended all but two bimonthly meetings, including business meetings, members' individual presentations of their work to the group, a visit to a local dealer's gallery and the graduate instructional facility of a local university art school, and guest lectures. I attended three lectures by nationally known artists and dealers sponsored by the St. Louis Area Coordinating Council for Art (ACCA), an association of local art faculties and students. At each lecture and meeting, I observed, and later made fieldnotes about, the event and those attending it. On three occasions, at exhibitions and meetings of the ACCA or CWA, I was able to informally interview male artists. I attended three meetings and informal lunches with the women in a drawing group which had met weekly for three years. After each, I made fieldnotes of what was said and done, including spatial positions during work and lunch. On one occasion, at their request, I participated by drawing from a model and having my drawings critiqued. I took a course in female art history from one respondent and attended a regional feminist art conference with her. I went to exhibitions constantly—at least one group or solo exhibit of work by every woman I interviewed and others in schools, museums, galleries, shopping centers, and cinema lobbies. During and after the exhibitions, I made notes on the conventions of presentation being used.

I was in the field for twelve months, from June 1974 through May 1975. I have listed all of the above activities to emphasize the variety of data-gathering methods that can and should be used by fieldworkers. Participant observers are responsible for continually reviewing what they have learned and still need to know, and for seeking opportunities to learn more—past and present—about the people, places, events, situations, and activities under study. To study a diffuse social world, it may be necessary to develop independent sources of information about *what* is going on and *where*. I used documents such as newspapers and magazines, but the newsletter of the organization I joined helped, too. And in interviewing and observing, I always listened to what people said about what was going on in their world. If there was something they thought I should know, I tried to learn. If there was something I thought I should know, I asked for the opportunity.

WHO AND HOW

I began by interviewing a female artist who was a friend. She gave me the membership list of an organization she belonged to (the Community of Women Artists) and let me mention her name to other potential respondents. In the early phases of research, I obtained names of other female artists from every woman I interviewed. At this stage, mine would be called a "snowball sample" because I was using the sample of women I had acquired to pick up more. Later, as I learned the rules being used to decide *who* was an artist, and as I learned about the status of particular women in the several art worlds, I could begin to sample purposively. ("Purposive sample" is a designation used, primarily by sample survey methodologists, to refer to nonprobability samples chosen on the basis of the researcher's interests or purpose.)

Fieldworkers seldom draw random samples. Sometimes it is impossible to enumerate the relevant population in advance. The area probability sampling methods used by survey researchers under the same circumstances are wasteful when the objective of research is *not* to determine the distribution of some variable(s) in a population. Sometimes the fieldworker is attempting to gather data from or about every person or event in some population and is aware that a few omissions will rarely alter the results if a very large proportion of the population is included in the sample, no matter how it is drawn (McCall and Simmons, 1969:239). The student should be aware of the purpose of describing samples. It is done to allow other scientists to judge the adequacy of the sample, in order to evaluate the conclusions based on it. Even though the sample is not a standard variety, the fieldworker is responsible for describing the sample and how it was drawn, so that others can judge and evaluate.

Because my research was concerned with questions of artistic status and identity, I could not define or enumerate the population of female artists in St. Louis when I started. On the other hand, I could not let my early informants define the sample; had I done so, I would not have discovered the several art worlds or understood the differing conventions which separated them.

During the first interview I realized that, whereas I could use the criterion of self-designation—an artist is someone who claims to be an artist—to find informants and respondents, it was not the criterion used by artists themselves. On the other hand, I realized that my informant, who claimed to know or know of all the women artists in St. Louis, did not know the women who belonged to and exhibited with several artists' organizations I had read about in the newspapers. At first I thought this meant that there were several networks of people who were simply unacquainted with one another. I contacted women my informant suggested and others she didn't know. I talked to each of them about their careers and about working in St. Louis and asked them for names of other female artists. In this way, I became aware that there were not simply several different networks but several different worlds of meaning. The members of different art worlds had learned and were using different conventions of art making (size, style, subject matter, media, and so on) and presentation (where exhibited, how framed, labeled, and displayed, and so on) and had, as a result, different definitions of *what* was art and *who* was an artist. I found three visual art worlds in St. Louis: a commercial art world of advertising, layout work, and design; a picture painting world of art fairs, shopping center exhibitions, blue ribbons, and trophies; and the world of high art, in which I was primarily interested.

Within the high art world—the world of museums, New York galleries, university faculty positions, and famous painters—I found six types of females artists: women with Bachelor of Fine Arts degrees who were full-time mothers and part-time artists; women with Master of Fine Arts degrees who had faculty positions and others who did not; women trained as art teachers who had become painters, sculptors, or printmakers; semipicture painters who were trying to join the world of high art but retained ties to the picture-painting world; and "old-timers" who used outdated high art conventions. Because they used different conventions, had different credentials, and presented themselves and their work in different ways, the six types of women were differentially successful in claiming artistic identity for themselves and status as art for their creations in the world of high art.

I became aware of the several types of female artists by noticing differences in their evaluations of local galleries, museums, collectors, and critics, and discrepancies in their evaluations of one another as artists. For example, both nonfaculty MFA's and BFA mothers had trouble getting others to accept their claims of artistic identity. BFA's also had trouble gathering the resources they needed to do art, especially time, materials, and places to work. I first noticed the differences between nonfaculty MFA's and BFA mothers—indeed, I first noticed that they were two different types—because nonfaculty MFA's defended whereas BFA mothers attacked the local art museum. Whenever I noticed patterns of difference such as this, I tried to account for them by sorting the women into categories. I thus became aware of several types of female artists and sought interviews with women of each type, attempting to represent each type in my sample in proportion to their numbers in the population of local female artists. In this way, I finished with the most commonly used sample in participant observation fieldwork: the nonrandom quota sample (McCall and Simmons, 1969:238). Note that the respondent sample of thirty-one women—six BFA mothers, six MFA faculty members, five nonfaculty MFA's, five semipicture painters, four art teachers, two old-timers, and three deviant cases[5]—was defined by the numbers and types of women from whom I gathered comparable data. I interviewed numerous other women but counted them only as informants if they did not make art, worked in different media, were not local artists, or belonged to different art worlds.

When I began, it was difficult for me to ask women for interviews. I was comforted in this by Everett C. Hughes' claim to have spent more time than any of his students ever did, walking around the block, trying to get up nerve to knock on doors and ask for interviews (Hughes, 1971a:497). I used a different solution: Once a week, I forced myself to call enough women to make at least four appointments for the following week. Later, as they heard about my study from other women and recognized me as a regular participant in their world, women were openly interested in being included and the phone calls became less difficult for me to make. No one refused to be interviewed, and one woman asked me to interview her. This is not unusual and should, I think, be done even though the data may be useless; it is humane and good for field relations. This high response rate was partly a result of choosing to study people who did not measure their time in economic terms and who lacked people to talk to about themselves and their work, and partly a result of the content and structure of interviews. I let each woman show me her body of work at the beginning of the interview (most of them presumably associated what I was doing with art history or criticism). I understood from an early informant that refusing to look at their work was equivalent to refusing to take them seriously as artists. In any case, I enjoyed looking at the paintings, sculpture, and prints, so that it put both of us at ease. I structured the interviews around questions about each woman's own career, a topic that did not close off other topics of interest: art worlds and artistic conventions.

WHERE AND HOW

As I have said, art worlds, the form of social organization I wanted to study, do not exist as sites. The collective activity which constitutes an art world—producing, distributing, and evaluating works of art—is structured by a division of labor and organized and mediated by changing conventions of art making and presentation about which members of an art world share knowledge and use. Becker's (1974) article made me aware of art world divisions of labor and conventions. While doing local fieldwork in St. Louis, I read "insider" accounts (especially Burnham, 1973; Gruen, 1972) and sociological studies of other art worlds (especially Christopherson, 1974; Levine, 1972; White and White, 1965) and compared what I found in St. Louis with other worlds of high art.

In the New York City high art world and its satellites in Chicago and Los Angeles, the current division of labor is an art market. Art is sold by dealers, exhibited in commercial dealers' galleries and museums, purchased by museums and collectors, and discussed by critics and art historians in art periodicals and books. In St. Louis there were few dealers, fewer commercial dealers' galleries, and no gallery district; the St. Louis Art Museum seldom exhibited and did not collect local contemporary art; there were few private collectors and fewer who bought local art; there were no local art publications, and St. Louis artists and art activities were not reviewed or discussed in national circulation art magazines. In short, St. Louis was a marginal art market. Art schools and faculties were alternative means of socially constructing artistic value and identities. Noncommercial galleries located on college and university campuses and in private secondary schools took the place of commercial dealers' galleries as places to exhibit high art; and faculty positions took the place of sales, dealers, and gallery and studio districts in providing a living, credentials, and colleagues for local artists and a locale for the local art world (McCall, 1977).

I used informants and documents to find the locales where art world activities took place and observed events at each locale: gallery openings, museum exhibitions, meetings of artists organizations. Different sets of people attended events in the locales of different art worlds; the same people attended various events in the locales of each art world. Informants and respondents knew and talked about events and people in the art worlds they belonged to. Local and published insiders knew and could talk about the conventional division of labor in their worlds: how to find a dealer, what a dealer does, where to show, who collects, what the critics say, and who makes art. In high art worlds, the conventions of art making and presentation are embodied in art history and current art news. I took a course in art history, read the art magazines, and studied published catalogs of museum exhibitions of contemporary art to learn the conventions and the artists who used them successfully. I asked respondents[6] to rate the prestige, using a scale of 1 to 5, of forty-three local galleries, museums, and other places to exhibit, listed in the weekly "arts events" columns of a St. Louis Sunday newspaper. The averaged prestige ratings of each space varied with membership in different art worlds and with artistic status in the world of high art (McCall, 1975).

For students interested in studying other social worlds, I will summarize what I did to discover the several St. Louis art worlds. I determined what the activities of an art world were, found the locales where these activities took place; attended and observed events in those locales; observed who attended events; and talked about events and people to people who attended events and engaged in activities. I also talked to people about events they did not attend, people they did not appear to know, and activities they did not engage in. Mutual knowledge of events, activities, and people defines membership in a social world. Members of a social world also share a culture—knowledge and use of conventions which define the activities, events, and status of people in the social world—and identify themselves as members in and through the shared culture.

Whether or not the fieldwork setting has a physical boundary (a site), the fieldworker gradually discovers and maps the social organization of the setting. All forms of social organization have a shape or division of labor; bonds of commitment, attachment, and investment among members and between members and the form of social organization; a structure—prestige, power, authority, liking, and communication hierarchies; a culture, including boundary rules and a focus (M. McCall, 1970); and all forms exhibit certain social processes, including recruitment, socialization, interaction, logistics, social control, and social change (G. McCall, 1970). And whatever sociological story is chosen to analytically describe the processes, the social boundaries or social organization must also be comprehensively understood. Learning and learning how to use the native language are both crucial to the gradual discovery and mapping fieldworkers must do.

A NOTE ON NATIVE LANGUAGE

Other participant observers have commented on the importance of learning and learning how to use a native language. For example, Becker et al. (1961) described their discovery that the term "crock," used by student doctors to refer to nonpreferred patients, had important meaning in terms of student expectations concerning the purpose of medical education (Becker, 1970:35). Because art world criteria for establishing artistic status were central questions in my own research, I want to describe my discovery of the terminology used to express those criteria.

I began by thinking that there were professional artists and amateurs. I learned in the first interview, and found consistently, that visual artists in high art worlds did not use the term "professional" to refer to themselves. (It seemed to connote "commercial" in art, just as it seems to connote "organized" in crime.) Artists sometimes used the term "amateur," but they were as likely to describe someone as a hobbyist, a suburban housewife, a little old lady, or a Sunday painter. Furthermore, picture painters, who were most likely to be called hobbyists and Sunday painters by members of the high art world, could point to sales of their work in support of their claims to be professional. (In fact, picture painters appeared to be more successful in selling work in St. Louis than artists in the high art world.) Other naive ideas of mine were that art degrees and employment were requisites of professional status, and that talent or skill might be used as criteria by artists. As I listened to men and women in the world of high art talk about one another, St. Louis as a place to work, and what it takes to be an artist, I became aware that they talked about artists and nonartists instead of professionals and amateurs;

that they used two terms—"serious" and "dedicated"—to describe artists; and that seriousness and dedication were unrelated, in usage, to questions of taste (liking) or skill and only indirectly related to questions of education and earning a living. I did not persist in using my (admittedly limited) language to describe their world but set about trying to understand what their language revealed about the way their world worked.

In and through art world divisions of labor, physically real things, such as paintings and trenches in the earth, become valuable social objects called "art." To be art, a thing must look like art; lend itself to being discussed as art; be presented as art by and to persons who regard it as art, and in places where art is presented; and be bought and sold in the way art is, by persons who buy and sell art. In this division of labor, artists are the persons who make art. Not only do artists produce the things that become art; each artist is ultimately responsible for making sure that her things are treated as art. To be an artist, then, the individual must produce a thing that is capable of being treated as art and must protect her art by deciding how and by whom it shall be handled. A serious artist intends to make art, not merely decorative or useful things. The artist signals this intent by making things that look the way art is expected to look and by making sure that they are presented as art—that is, by conforming to current art world conventions of art making and presentation. If it is apparent to others in the art world that the individual makes things to express her unique artistic vision and that she expects them to be treated as art, then she is taken seriously, no matter how bizarre her creations appear to people outside the art world. If this is not apparent, the things are not considered art and she is not taken seriously as an artist. A dedicated artist intends to make art for a living or, failing that, not to let earning a living interfere with making art. Thus, hobbyists and even "suburban housewives"—that is, women who rely on a husband's financial support—are not taken seriously. For women, success in the world of high art depended upon wherther they were serious and dedicated and whether their credentials (degrees and employment), their things, and their decisions about how their things were handled (especially where, how, and by whom exhibited) reflected seriousness and dedication. The status dilemmas of these women (Hughes, 1971b) were based in the fact that women were not expected to be serious or dedicated and so had to convince themselves and others that they were.

CONCLUSION

In any social situation, the person who knows the ropes is comfortable and unself-conscious. Fieldworkers are always nonexperts in the situations they study, but students will be more comfortable if generic fieldwork

156   MICHAL MCCALL

problems are understood and anticipated. For example, there are always problems of getting in, getting started, and carrying on, but students can choose research projects which minimize their own problems. I believe my project was easier for me because I was a woman in the same situation as the women I studied, and because they had not been studied before.

Fieldworkers aim for comprehensive understanding of the situations they study. Students can be comfortable in the realization that this aim makes them flexible about defining problems, prepared for unexpected results, and able to consider the interrelatedness of many observations— even though the aim is never achieved. Students can also take comfort in the knowledge that research questions are often redefined during the fieldwork process. Sometimes other questions will be more important or will need to be answered before the original question can even be asked. For example, I had to study St. Louis art worlds before I could study female artists in them. Sometimes the original question is naive or limiting—e.g., my use of the term "professional artists." Finally, students can be comfortable with what they know and with what they don't know, so long as fieldnotes are reviewed periodically and attention is paid to discrepancies and unexpected findings.

Students needn't be self-conscious because they don't know the ropes of the situations they study. Focusing one's attention on others is a well-known way of combatting self-consciousness. Informants cannot do the participant observer's work; each of us is responsible for making a comprehensive whole from the bits and pieces they give us. We can accomplish this and overcome self-consciousness by learning to use the native language and by taking seriously the people we study and their folkways. As Wiseman put it, "There is nothing that happens or that people tell you that 'doesn't make sense.' It is part of their lives. They think it makes sense. It is up to you to make sociological sense of it" (1974:236).

Notes

1. Following McCall and Simmons (1969), I use the terms "fieldwork" and "participant observation" interchangeably. Both terms refer to a range of research designs and combinations of methods, having in common the fieldworker's actual participation in the social life of the people being studied.

2. The topics were: training, showing, selling, making it, working, artists groups, St. Louis art worlds, keeping up with art, artistic activities, opinions of your work, and who is an artist.

3. I knew several weavers and had intended to include them in the study, along with painters, sculptors, and printmakers. In the first interview, and consistently, I found that painters and others considered weaving not an art but a craft. Therefore, they considered

weavers to be craftsmen, not artists. The movement of various media from the category "craft" to the category "art" is comparable to the movement of occupations into the category "profession" (See Becker, 1978; Christopherson, 1974).

4. Picture painters emphasized execution rather than ideas; they achieved artistic status and identity in and through the art associations they belonged to and exhibited at art fairs; and their pictures were purchased instead of collected.

5. The deviant cases were useful in understanding differences among types of female artists. Each deviant case illustrated the importance of seriousness, dedication, or credentials in the determination of artistic status and identity.

6. I asked twenty-one women to do the rating task; twenty women were able to do so.

References

BECKER, H.S. *Sociological Work.* Chicago: Aldine, 1971.

BECKER, H.S. "Art as Collective Action." *American Sociological Review,* 39 (1974), 767–776.

BECKER, H.S. "Arts and Crafts." *American Journal of Sociology,* 83 (1978), 862–889.

BECKER, H.S., B. GEER, E.C. HUGHES, and A.L. STRAUSS. *Boys in White.* Chicago: University of Chicago Press, 1961.

BURNHAM, S. *The Art Crowd.* New York: David McKay, 1973.

CHRISTOPHERSON, R. "Making Art with Machines: Photography's Institutional Inadequacies." *Urban Life and Culture,* 3 (1974), 3–34.

DAVIS, F. "Stories and Sociology." *Urban Life and Culture,* 3 (1974), 310–316.

GRUEN, J. *The Party's Over Now.* New York: Viking Press, 1972.

HUGHES, E.C. "The Place of Field Work in Social Science." In E.C. Hughes (collected papers), *The Sociological Eye.* Chicago: Aldine, 1971a.

HUGHES, E.C. "Dilemmas and Contradictions of Status." In E.C. Hughes (collected papers), *The Sociological Eye.* Chicago: Aldine, 1971b.

LEVINE, E.M. "Chicago's Art World: The Influence of Status Interests on Its Social and Distribution Systems." *Urban Life and Culture,* 1 (1972), 293–323.

McCALL, G.J. "The Social Organization of Relationships." In G.J. McCall, M.M. McCall, N.K. Denzin, G.D. Suttles, and S.B. Kurth, eds., *Social Relationships.* Chicago: Aldine, 1970.

McCALL, G.J. *Observing the Law.* Rockville, Md.: National Institutes of Mental Health, Crime and Deliquency Issues, 1975.

McCALL, G.J., and J.L. SIMMONS (eds.). *Issues in Participant Observation.* Reading, Mass.: Addison-Wesley, 1969.

McCALL, M.M. "Boundary Rules in Relationships and Encounters." In G.J. McCall, M.M. McCall, N.K. Denzin, G.D. Suttles, and S.B. Kurth eds., *Social Relationships.* Chicago: Aldine, 1970.

McCALL, M.M. "The Sociology of Female Artists: A Study of Female Painters, Sculptors, and Printmakers in St. Louis." Ph.D. Dissertation, Urbana: University of Illinois.

McCALL, M.M. "Art Without a Market: Creating Artistic Value in a Provincial Art World." *Symbolic Interaction,* 1 (1977), 32–43.

MEAD, G.H. *The Philosophy of the Present.* Chicago: Open Court Press, 1932.
WHITE, H., and C. WHITE. *Canvases and Careers.* New York: Wiley, 1965.
Who's Who in American Art, 1973. New York: Jacques Cattell Press, 1973.
WISEMAN, J. "The Research Web." *Urban Life and Culture,* 3 (1974), 317-328.
ZELDITCH, M. JR. "Some Methodological Problems of Field Studies." *American Journal of Sociology,* 67 (1962), 566-576.

Rope Burns: Impediments to the Achievement of Basic Comfort Early in the Field Research Experience

CLINTON R. SANDERS   *University of Connecticut*

Becoming well-socialized members of the groups in which they are interested is both a major research goal and the key source of data for participant observers. Only through the ongoing, consistently problematic process of assuming the perspectives of the actors in the field can qualitative researchers develop a disciplined and descriptively grounded understanding of the social behavior encountered. In this selection, I will use my own participatory experiences in various research settings to focus a discussion of some of the major problems encountered by the fieldworker.[1] I want to deal with three issues which are particularly problematic during the early stages of the research endeavor, when the fieldworker is most overtly and consciously concerned with acquiring a rudimentary understanding of the rules of the social game which is played out in the research setting. While the issues discussed— recognizing and dealing with research fear, identifying and avoiding certain types of inappropriate behaviors, and balancing relationships with various subgroups in the setting—are of central importance, I would caution the reader not to view the following guidelines and observations as definitive or unvarying. Participant observation is an exciting and creative process because of its flexibility and the evolving nature of its techniques. The instructions found in even the most competent guides to field research (e.g., Bogdan and Taylor, 1975; Bruyn, 1966; Douglas, 1976; Junker, 1960; Lofland, 1971) should not be seen as absolute truth. Instead, these guidelines should be adopted, discarded, violated, or adapted according to the characteristics and requirements of the specific setting and the interactants within it.

Another caution: Since participant observation, like any other form of socialization, is an ongoing process, the ideal of acquiring complete comfort in the field is never (or rarely) entirely achieved. Field research requires a focused, analytic attention to objects and activities and an overt consciousness of self-presentation and interaction. Consequently, if we continue to act as researchers in a particular setting, we cannot expect or feel as comfortable and at home as we do in everyday, familiar, nonresearch situations. In fact, acquiring this everyday comfort can act as a significant impediment to the continuing research endeavor. Focusing systematic attention on one's newfound friends tends to make one feel parasitic. This instrumental interaction with those with whom one ostensibly has primary relationships may force the researcher to confront personal feelings of hypocrisy and treachery. While, as Goffman (1959) has amply illustrated, we all engage in a certain level of concealment and subterfuge in even our most intimate interactions, the self-consciousness of the fieldwork experience tends to make us uncomfortably aware of this particular feature of social life.

The participant observer should, then, expect to feel some edginess throughout the course of the data collection process. This is a price we pay for the acquisition of a systematic, grounded, theoretically coherent understanding of human behavior as it is constructed and played out in social situations.

RESEARCH FEAR AS AN IMPEDIMENT

Participant observation is not an approach with which all researchers are equally comfortable. Some people are particularly accomplished fieldworkers because they possess significant social and verbal skills and have an ability to work analytically with qualitative data. While these skills may be learned through experience and instruction, certain aspects of field research often deflect the sociologist from employing this approach. A natural and common experience encountered by all participant observers is the fear which arises from finding oneself to be a stranger in the home territory of a group of actors bound together by common understandings, strategies, and problems. During the early stages of learning the ropes in the field, the researcher must consistently confront the fear of

160   CLINTON R. SANDERS

personal risk, which is a significant barrier to the building of relationships and the assumption of the roles which are the key sources of data.
This fear has its foundation in the salient proscriptions we have learned
concerning the illegitimacy of asking people probing questions about
their personal lives. In violating these rules, we risk personal rejection.
However, as one confronts and controls this fear and gains experience in
the field, a rather remarkable fact becomes clear: Most people are quite
pleased when a sympathetic observer communicates to them that he or she
finds the activities and perspectives which the actors see as routine,
mundane, and commonsensical to be intensely interesting. This honest
show of interest is the major currency with which the participant observer
rewards the interactants.

A few years ago, while engaged in a study of drug enforcement
patterns (Sanders, 1975), I was sitting in a room adjacent to the major
narcotics court in Chicago, trying unobtrusively to record a conflictual
interaction between a narcotics officer and an assistant states attorney.
Having noticed my rather furious scribbling, the officer confronted me
with a demand that I accompany him to the state attorney's office. I was
extremely frightened as I followed him into the private office. I was afraid
that the tenuous access which I had achieved was threatened, and was
(somewhat irrationally) fearful about my personal well-being. Character-
istically, I reacted to this threatening situation with a rapid monologue in
which I presented myself as a (mere) sociology student engaged in a study
of "the problems that police officers have in dealing with drug abuse."
After further selective revelation of myself and the research, the officer,
who had been in conflict with the prosecutor over the lack of concern
shown for overworked officers in the scheduling of cases before the court,
began tentatively to define me as a nonthreatening and sympathetic
listener. Consequently, I emerged from this feal-inducing encounter with
an excellent field interview and the foundation of what proved to be an
invaluable key informant relationship.

Not only does field research appear to violate some deeply held rules
of interaction, it also thrusts the researcher into an intensely self-
conscious situation. This self-consciousness in early field experience is
rather similar to the "paranoia" which novice marijuana smokers commonly report feeling while being high in social situations in which they
wish to conceal their condition from straight associates. Self-
consciousness induced by the pharmacological effects of the drug and the
realization of the problems which may be encountered if one's deviance is
discovered results in a feeling that "everyone is looking at me" and "I am
acting strange and everyone knows I'm stoned" (see Matza, 1969:109–142).
The similar "dis-ease" encountered by novice fieldworkers and inexperienced marijuana users is the result of a critical focusing of attention on
the self. This discomfort eventually dissipates as one gains more experi-

ence and comes to realize that others generally do not evaluate our actions as critically as we ourselves do. The "bizarre" behavior of both novice fieldworkers and drug users (inappropriate staring, asking "stupid" questions, speaking incoherently, etc.) is readily normalized by others in the context of the ongoing flow of social experience.

The sources of research fear presented above—uneasiness about prying into people's private lives, the risk of being rejected, and the intense and novel self-consciousness of the field experience—have their roots in the basic role conflict which confronts all participant observers. This conflict centers on the tension between the investigator-as-person and the investigator-as-researcher. The former role complex is familiar, governed by well-known rules and relatively unproblematic. The latter role activity is unfamiliar and threatening and requires extensive analytic focusing and the apparent violation of various rules of interaction which we have come to accept as given. There are, however, other features of field research which lead the novice observer to experience some aversion and, consequently, to avoid this research approach. The core of participant observation is personal involvement, and since not all of the settings and actors of interest to the investigator are entirely conventional, the research endeavor may lead to situations in which the observer's personal safety and legal standing are threatened. Understandably, this sense of threat can significantly interfere with the building of a feeling of comfort in the field.

As my research into narcotics enforcement patterns progressed and I came to understand more about the motivations and activities of the vice officers who worked in the narcotics section of the Chicago police department, I found myself becoming more and more uneasy. I realized that a number of the activities which I was hearing about and observing were ethically questionable or overtly illegal. In addition, I would occasionally encounter friends and associates who were arrested for narcotics violations and brought before the court I was observing. I began to realize that I possessed secret information which was threatening to the enforcers and that they routinely arrested (and occasionally "set up") recreational drug users who were part of my own social network. As my knowledge (and paranoia) grew, I found myself routinely checking in the rear-view mirror to see if I was being followed, taking circuitous routes home from the various settings in which I was collecting data, and circumspectly questioning my key informant in the narcotics squad about any conversations his fellow narks had concerning me or my research.[2] Although my fears turned out to be unwarranted, this was a situation in which data collection and the building of an intimate familiarity with the activities of the group I was investigating acted to increase my *discomfort* and, therefore, to make my research more difficult.

My point here is that field research is a complex process; various levels of difficulty are commonly encountered and various forms of comfort achieved. The fact that one has learned the ropes and has gained a working familiarity with the norms and structures in the setting does not necessarily mean that the stress of the research activity is entirely alleviated. Knowing the rules of the game and being able to play with confidence does not necessarily mean that one likes the game itself or approves of its outcomes. This general discomfort with the activities of the actors in which the investigator is interested is most problematic when the researcher is "observing up"—that is, when the actors occupy authoritative or powerful roles and therefore have the resources to physically, psychologically, or legally harm the observer.

INAPPROPRIATE RESEARCHER BEHAVIOR AS A HINDRANCE

The fieldworker in the early research stages of reconnoitering the setting—learning the structure, rules, and activities—runs the risk of violating norms which are held dear by the interactants. As (at best) a minimally socialized actor in the setting, the wise researcher will exercise considerable caution in behavior. This means that the early process of learning the ropes generally entails some passivity as participation is kept at a minimum and data collection is focused on mapping the setting and observing the overt behavior of interactants. While not always appropriate in all settings, the passive stance decreases the chances of stepping on toes, becoming identified with a particular clique or individual, asking questions about touchy topics, or otherwise making mistakes which can seriously impede the process of being accepted as a competent interactant in the setting.

Special care should be exercised in employing the terms and linguistic styles routinely used by the actors. Inappropriate use of situated jargon will often be interpreted as indicative of abysmal ignorance or overt ridicule.

A major feature of learning the ropes in the setting has to do with understanding what questions may legitimately be asked. This is a particularly salient issue when one is working with actors who are engaged in activities of questionable legality. Inappropriate questions may be reasonably interpreted as an indication that the researcher is an informer engaged in collecting data for enforcement interests.

A few years ago, I was part of a research team which was working under contract to a suburban public school district in Illinois. I was in charge of the initial fieldwork phase of the research project, which focused on the extent and nature of illegal drug use by high school students.[3]

Soon after entering the field, I discovered a corner of the grounds of one high school where some of the more alienated students would congregate to socialize and smoke. One afternoon I was hanging out in this area with a number of students, making small talk and asking a few tentative questions, when a fascinating subject came up: What drugs are going out of vogue and what drugs are gaining popularity within the local drug-using network? One student observed that in the last few months a number of people he knew had gotten involved in the recreational use of heroin. This was a particularly interesting piece of information for me, since I was at that time also directing a fieldwork study of the social organization of the heroin market in Chicago. A few days before, I had had a conversation with a street dealer who complained about "kiddy-freaks from the suburbs" who were coming to the urban copping areas and trying to score heroin. These young novices did not blend in well with the regulars in "the set," and their presence was causing more enforcement attention to be focused on the local heroin marketplace. This increased pressure was forcing regular dealers and their clients to alter their familiar routines. Since learning of this problematic development in the setting, I had been looking more carefully into the activities and problems of nonregulars who attempted to purchase heroin. With this interest in mind, I asked my student informant, "How do folks who live out here [in the suburbs] go about copping scag?" I should have known better than to pursue the topic this directly with people with whom I had only the most tenuous relationships. My question was understandably interpreted as, "Who is dealing heroin to you high school students?" I was immediately the recipient of a classic cool-out. My question was met with cold stares and, despite my efforts to explain, I was never able to achieve a satisfactory feeling of rapport with the members of this particular network. The excitement of the search for data had precipitated inappropriate behavior which seriously impeded the building of a participatory understanding of the interactants' perspectives and actions.

This is not to say that it is possible or even desirable to entirely avoid *faux pas* during this early period when one is learning the ropes. While the investigator may be embarrased by an obvious normative violation, the mistake and the reaction to it are often (as Garfinkel [1967] has clearly demonstrated) valuable sources of information about the rule system which governs interaction. It is often essential the the researcher become involved in embarrassing situations in order to gain access to important information. This may entail boldly asking for an invitation to a situation which would normally be closed to outsiders, firmly displaying disbelief in certain "facts" provided by informants which the researcher suspects are self-serving misrepresentations, or asking pointed questions about matters which the actors are reluctant to discuss.

Relatively early in my investigation of narcotics enforcement patterns, I became aware that a number of case outcomes were arranged through a "fix" transaction in which the private defense attorney gave the arresting officer money in exchange for altered testimony at the time of the preliminary hearing. While the actual exchange of money generally took place in private settings, the transaction was so traditional and common that I had the opportunity to observe money changing hands in backstage areas near the courtroom. On one occasion, I was fortunate enough to see a lawyer whom I knew to be a notorious "fixer" give money to a young police officer with whom I had a passing acquaintance. Summoning what courage I could muster, I took the officer aside and informed him of my observation. He was, understandably, quite upset that I had witnessed the illegal exchange. I sincerely assured him that I had no interest in blowing the whistle on him and that I was, as a sociologist, ethically committed not to cause harm to the individuals with whom my research brought me in contact. After considerable persuasion, the officer provided me with an extensive description of the specifics of the transaction and what motivated him to participate. While embarrassing and stressful for both of us, this encounter provided me with excellent firsthand data on a key feature of the setting I was researching, and my nonjudgmental possession of secret information greatly aided me in building an ongoing relationship with this knowledgeable informant.

The presentation of oneself as nonthreatening is of central importance for the field worker. Additionally, the researcher is well advised to adopt a relatively naive manner vis-à-vis the interactants. This appearance of naiveté (which Douglas [1976:169] refers to as "playing the boob"; see also Lofland, 1971:100) allows the researcher to legitimately ask questions about taken-for-granted features of the setting and the interaction which takes place therein. Certain established social roles may be effectively employed to legitimate the researcher's apparent naiveté. For example, I have consistently found identifying myself to interactants as a "sociology student" (as opposed to "professor" or "sociologist") to be of considerable value in easing the minds of subjects and in justifying my asking questions about "what everyone knows." It is also the case that women are often defined as "acceptable incompetents." While the subordinate status commonly ascribed to women may be detrimental to the female researcher's access to certain settings (cf. Daniels, 1967; Lyon, 1975:32–35; Wax, 1971), she also has the advantage of being conventionally defined as presenting a minimal threat and is often expected to be rather naive concerning the workings of the "real world."

Presenting oneself as an acceptable incompetent becomes increasingly problematic as the researcher spends more time in the field and becomes identified as someone who knows the ropes. Interactants reasonably assume that the experienced observer has spent sufficient time in the setting to acquire a basic understanding of its routine activities. Similarly, when the investigator is studying a setting or group in which he or she is an accepted and ongoing participant, a naive presentation is difficult to maintain even in the early stages of research.

In the late 1960s, I worked as a folk performer in various clubs in Chicago. Because of my ready access to settings and interactants, I began to collect field notes focusing on the social relationships which were central to the activity of playing in small-scale performance settings (Sanders, 1974). As an accepted and (supposedly) knowledgeable participant, my questions concerning routine activities and interests often elicited expressions of obvious surprise from my fellow performers; why was I asking questions about such mundane and taken-for-granted issues? For the most part, I trotted out my subservient student sociologist role as an understandable rationale for asking such "stupid" questions about things I already knew. I explained to my associates that I was involved in a study which was a part of my responsibilities as a sociology graduate student, and that while I certainly knew the answers to most of the questions, I was required by my professor to ask them of all respondents. Having had at least some experience with the commonly nonsensical requirements of academia, my performing colleagues generally accepted this rationale and provided me with the information I requested. In addition, my acknowledged membership in the group helped to ensure that the respondents were relatively careful not to put me on, as they would have someone who was defined as a naive outsider.

FIELD RELATIONSHIPS AS AIDS OR IMPEDIMENTS TO LEARNING THE ROPES

As noted above, doing field research is essentially a process of being socialized. While observation of situated activity is a good source of data, *understanding* what the activities mean for the actors requires the building of intimate relationships in the field and asking focused questions about the purpose, meaning, and expected outcomes of the behaviors observed. Because of the hierarchical structuring of most settings in which the participant observer operates, and because most organizations have a vested interest in keeping certain aspects of organizational activity secret, building field relationships is commonly a rather complex balancing act. In order to gain access to most formally organized settings, the researcher must acquire the permission of powerful "gatekeepers." Developing these essential relationships upon which initial research access is premised often acts as a hindrance when the researcher later attempts to

build rapport with those who are situated in more subordinate organizational positions. The necessary relationships between the investigator and
the gatekeeper(s) may cause the researcher to be seen by less powerful
interactants as a confederate of those in charge.[4]

After a few weeks of sitting in the section of the courtroom reserved
for the public, I felt that I possessed sufficient basic information to begin
to participate more directly in the ongoing business of the court. At the
close of one daily session, I approached the judge as he was relaxing in his
chambers and introduced myself as a sociologist with research experience
in some aspects of drug abuse. I told him that a major interest which I had
developed in the course of a prior study of a drug-using community
(Schaps and Sanders, 1970) concerned the activities of those who had the
task of enforcing laws against drug use and their relationships with
young people who had had little previous conflictual contact with
enforcement personnel. He was quite cordial and said that he had noticed
my regular attendance and had assumed that I was a law student engaged
in some assigned project.[5] After a bit of small talk, I said that it was
essential for my study that I be able to easily observe and record proceedings before the bench and that this was quite difficult when I was confined
to the audience section. I was gratified, and rather surprised, when the
judge offered to allow me to sit directly behind him on the raised dais in
front of the court. While this was an excellent location from which to
observe and keep fieldnotes, it also symbolically identified me as one who
was in league with the judge and the other regular court officials.
Understandably, this position and my purposefully constructed conservative image significantly hindered my interactions with the young defendants whose perceptions and experiences were also of major interest to
me.[6] This problem of interacting with defendants was partially resolved
by the audience segregation commonly encountered in formal settings. I
found that defendants often awaited the calling of their cases in the
hallway adjacent to the court. I would routinely spend significant
amounts of time in the field engaged in interview/conversations with
defendants away from the official setting of the courtroom itself.[7]

The participant observer must take great care early in the process of
building field relationships to avoid being identified as the agent of any
particular subgroup within the interaction setting. Identification with
authority figures has the potential of hindering the development of
relationships with subordinates, while being identified with those of low
status may adversely affect interaction with persons who are formally in
charge.

During my research on narcotics enforcement, I encountered one
particular marginal member who proved to be of major assistance. While
I was soon well aware that a number of the cases I was observing were

fixed, as described previously, I was having considerable difficulty getting detailed information on this central transaction. Some lawyers were willing to admit that payoffs were made by an occasional lawyer to a few "bad apple" police officers, but all interactants were understandably reluctant to discuss the specifics of this interaction.[8] While talking with lawyers and officers in a waiting room near the courtroom, I observed an individual who seemed to be acting in a legal capacity but whose rather wild countercultural appearance set him off from the other attorneys who handled drug cases. Striking up a conversation, I discovered that he was a lawyer associated with a firm which dealt with a large number of drug-related offenses. As it turned out, we shared a variety of interests and experiences, and after a few weeks we became quite friendly. Tony (a pseudonym) expressed considerable dissatisfaction with various aspects of his occupation. He was uneasy about the responsibility, disliked having to work long hours, and expressed significant alienation from the other regular interactants in the court social system. Because of these negative feelings, Tony was planning soon to resign his position and move to an island in the Mediterranean which he had visited on a previous vacation.[9] As our relationship deepened and a feeling of mutual trust grew, Tony agreed to detail systematically the fix transaction (which he cynically referred to as a "realistic point of law") and to describe transactions in which he had been personally involved. His knowledge was extensive, his assistance was invaluable, and his friendship made this particularly stressful research experience considerably easier for me.

In summary, the careful participant observer should exercise great care in dealing with interactants at various levels of the social structure in the setting. Particular caution in advisable early in the process of building a working understanding of the organization and activity within the setting. During this reconnaissance period, the investigator is commonly uneasy and therefore particularly open to developing close relationships with those actors who are overtly friendly or helpful. In formally organized settings, superordinate members will often agree to assist the researcher out of a desire to acquire information which will be useful in exercising control. At the other end of the social continuum, alienated marginal members tend to latch onto the researcher early in the field involvement because they are seeking the friendship which their marginality often precludes and because they desire social support for their particular perspective. Powerful sponsors and insightful marginal members may be of great assistance to the researcher engaged in learning the ropes. However, the investigator must not allow any interactants to determine the focus of the study, should avoid being identified with any particular interest group, and must interpret the information received in the context of the social position and vested interests of the source.

SUMMARY AND CONCLUSION

The personal involvement which is at the core of participant observation often generates an intense feeling of uneasiness in the sociologist who chooses to employ this investigative technique. Research fear arises from the self-consciousness of the researcher—the perception of violating salient norms of privacy, anxiety about personal rejection, and apprehension that the research may entail physical or legal danger. Should the researcher cater to this fear, the process of discovering the richness of the collective activity which is of interest is seriously impeded or rendered impossible. If the researcher is to gain a minimal sense of comfort in the field, fear must be recognized, confronted directly, and overcome. As with any unfamiliar activity, increased experience with fieldwork techniques tends to decrease the researcher's early feelings of anxiety.

While the nature of participant observation does often generate fear, certain features of the approach also aid investigators in overcoming their apprehension. Since data collection and analysis proceed concurrently, the ongoing thrill of discovery which one experiences soon after entering the field quickly begins to replace the observer's initial feelings of trepidation. Further, the intense personal involvement which fieldwork requires acts as an important personal learning experience. Relationships developed while doing participant observation are often intrinsically rewarding, and the self-knowledge and confidence the disciplined field-worker acquires in the course of the investigation also help to reduce research fear.

From the outset, the observer should carefully monitor his or her subjective experience in the field. Feelings of discomfort, threat, and self-consciousness are important data, as they are recognized, analyzed, and recorded in the researcher's field notes. This data allows the investigator to keep track of researcher bias and changes in the ways he or she ir perceived by various interactants. Field notes on personal feelings also provide a foundation for understanding the discomfort normally experienced by other regular actors in the setting.

During the early process of learning the ropes and reconnoitering the setting, the researcher should be guided by common sense and respect for the autonomy and welfare of the interactants. A certain amount of passivity is advisable during this early stage. As the researcher gains more knowledge and confidence, he or she can begin to take more risks—asking impertinent questions, requesting entry to backstage areas, overtly expressing skepticism, and so on. While this risk taking may (and probably will) precipitate mistakes and conflict, the problems which arise are usually not fatal to the research and do provide a fascinating body of data.

In order to attain a minimal level of comfort in the field, the researcher must take care in constructing the presentation of self to and relationships with the regular actors in the setting. Special caution is appropriate when dealing with those members who are superordinate or marginal. While relationships with both social types are methodologically necessary, becoming identified with actors who are particularly powerful or significantly alienated may severely limit the researcher's access to and understanding of essential data. Statements by actors— particularly those which are volunteered—must be interpreted in the context of the social position and perspective of the respondent.

If the participant observer successfully confronts these problems, he or she is well along in the process of learning the ropes. For the most part, one has learned the ropes when one (1) possesses a basic understanding of the physical and social structure of the setting and the primary activities which take place within it; (2) feels a basic sense of comfort when observing or interacting in the setting; (3) possesses a fundamental ability to use the language of the actors;[10] and (4) can recognize when a respondent is lying, jiving, or otherwise attempting to mislead.

The issues discussed above are problematic throughout the course of the research endeavor. They are, however, particularly troublesome when researchers are engaged in the early process of learning the basic rules and structures which shape the interaction of interest. By directly confronting these issues, making mistakes, making decisions, and sharing themselves and their skills with participants, conscientious field researchers build a grounded understanding of the complex ways in which people make sense of their social surroundings and choose their courses of action. At the same time, involvement in the creative social process of participant observation has the potential of providing researchers with self-understanding and a repertoire of social skills which will prove to be invaluable and personally enriching long after they have left the field.

Notes

1. This discussion owes much to ongoing conversations with Eleanor Lyon, one of the most accomplished and insightful fieldworkers I know.

2. My possession of secret information concerning illegal police behavior was also problematic when I attempted to publish articles based on my research. Prior to the publication of my account in *Law and Society Review* (1975), I participated in a series of interchanges with the journal's editor and lawyers concerning confidentiality, access to raw data, the potential for libel actions, and various other legal issues.

3. While in retrospect I have some ethical doubts about engaging in research designed

to acquire information which can be used by those in power to control the disapproved behavior of subordinates, the ostensible purpose of this research was to provide data useful in constructing an effective and humane drug counseling and education program.

4. Obviously, I am dealing here with the problems of the researcher who openly self-presents as engaged in a sociological investigation. The covert participant observer confronts other problems, which center on the ethics of disguised research and the maintenance of a coherent cover story. The controversy surrounding Laud Humphreys' (1970) research into sexual encounters in public rest rooms strikingly illustrates the various issues raised by covert investigations.

5. In general those interactants who do not know the researcher's specific purpose will place him or her in a role which makes regular appearances in the setting understandable and legitimate.

6. My apparent identification with enforcement officials became particularly problematic when two young men whom I had interviewed in a prior study were arrested for drug dealing on the basis of testimony from an "anonymous informant." Upon seeing me in court, they reasonably assumed that I was responsible for their arrest. With the help of their lawyer, with whom I was acquainted, I eventually convinced them that I had not turned them in. They later provided me with an excellent account of their arrest and processing.

7. In contrast to the court situation described here, my study of the performing world did not entail the same kind of presentational and status problems. As an ongoing member of the more egalitarian and informal performing group, I possessed relatively easy access and was generally accepted as a knowledgeable and bona fide associate.

8. For example, when asked about the fix during an interview, one lawyer whom I had observed passing money became very upset and stated: "*I have nothing to say about that!* Every case is different on its facts. Some people think that everything is fixed. That's not true. Just like in everything there are corrupt cops, corrupt judges and corrupt lawyers. There is corruption wherever there is money. That's what is wrong with this country!" About a year after I completed data collection, this particular respondent was arrested, tried, and convicted of bribery.

9. Tony did eventually carry out his plan and is, to the best of my knowledge, still living in bohemian splendor on his island.

10. The ability to joke with the actors in the setting is a good indicator that the researcher has acquired a working knowledge of the language and meaning system employed by the interactants.

References

BECKER, H. *Sociological Work*. Chicago: Aldine, 1970.

BOGDAN, R. and S.J. TAYLOR. *Introduction to Qualitative Research Methods*. New York: Wiley, 1975.

BRUYN, S. *The Humanistic Perspective in Sociology*. Englewood Cliffs, N.J.: Prentice-Hall, 1966.

DANIELS, A.K. "The Low-Caste Stranger in Social Research." In G. Sjoberg, ed., *Ethics, Politics, and Social Research*. Cambridge, Mass.: Schenkman, 1967, pp. 267–296.

DOUGLAS, J.D. *Investigative Social Research*. Beverly Hills, Calif.: Sage Publications, 1976.

GARFINKEL, H. *Studies in Ethnomethodology*. Englewood Cliffs, N.J.: Prentice-Hall, 1967.

GOFFMAN, E. *The Presentation of Self in Everyday Life*. New York: Doubleday, 1959.

HUGHES, E.C. "Introduction." In B. Junker, *Field Work: An Introduction to the Social Sciences*. Chicago: University of Chicago Press, 1960.

HUMPHREYS, L. *Tearoom Trade: Impersonal Sex in Public Places*. Chicago: Aldine, 1970.

JETTE, P.R., and F. MONTANINO. "Face-to-Face Interaction in the Criminal Justice System." *Criminology*, 16 (1978), 67–86.

JUNKER, B.B. *Field Work*. Chicago: University of Chicago Press, 1960.

LOFLAND, J.A. *Analyzing Social Settings*. Belmont, Calif.: Wadsworth, 1971.

LYON, E. Behind the Scenes: The Organization of Theatrical Production. Ph.D. dissertation, Urbana: Northwestern University, 1975.

MATZA, D. *Becoming Deviant*. Englewood Cliffs, N.J.: Prentice-Hall, 1969.

SANDERS, C.R. "Psyching Out the Crowd: Folk Performers and Their Audiences." *Urban Life and Culture*, 3 (1974), 264–282.

SANDERS, C.R. "Caught in the Con-game: The Young, White Drug User's Contact with the Legal System." *Law and Society Review*, 9 (1975), 197–217.

SCHAPS, E., and C.R. SANDERS. "Purposes, Patterns and Protection in a Campus Drug-Using Community." *Journal of Health and Social Behavior*, 11 (1970), 135–145.

WAX, R. *Doing Field Work*. Chicago: University of Chicago Press, 1971.

Learning the Ropes as Fieldwork Analysis

SHERRYL KLEINMAN   *University of Minnesota*

Learning the ropes of fieldwork is not only coincident with doing the "real work" of field research (jointly collecting, coding, and analyzing the data) (Glaser and Strauss, 1967) but also a part of that process. We become comfortable in the field because we learn what to expect from respondents—how they act in each other's company, with other members of the social system, and with us. As we become acquainted with the life of the group (or organization or community) under study and begin to make sociological sense of it, we learn how to act with participants and

therefore come to feel comfortable in the setting. To begin to learn the
ropes, then, is to begin analysis.

This dictum is a truism for many field researchers but may mean little
to those who have not yet done field research. Common sense suggests that
getting access to the setting, gaining rapport, and acquiring an appropriate researcher role enable us to do the real work but are not part of it.
Some articles on "qualitative methods" unwittingly reinforce this understanding by making few references to the field data in discussions of how
to do fieldwork. Students often get the impression that learning the ropes
is something we do before the real work begins or is a separate process
that goes on at the same time. The suggestion is that time spent in setting
things up is not quite time wasted but is less valuable than time spent
doing interviews or observing. The student, however, should be alerted to
the analytical value of, for example, getting the runaround by respondents or being welcomed with open arms.

In this selection, I will discuss how learning the ropes was an integral
part of my preliminary analysis of the field data. I will do this by looking
at how my own preconceptions changed and at the roles and identities of
the respondents and researcher in the field.

RESEARCH SETTING AND METHOD

I did my research in a graduate professional school of theology of the
United Methodist Church, located on the campus of a large private
university in the Midwestern United States. While the seminary is an
autonomous institution, it has some affiliations with the university.
Approximately 65 percent of the 300 students are enrolled in the ministry
program, 20 percent are doctoral students, and the remainder are special
or nondegree students. Although the seminary offers professional (Master
of Divinity) and advanced (Ph.D.) degrees, the recruits studying to be
ministers are treated (and see themselves) as a separate collectivity. I did
observe and interview some doctoral students but spent most of my time
with students in the three-year Master of Divinity program.

During the six months of research, I participated in and observed as
many activities of ministry students as possible. I lived in one of the two
student dormitories, went to classes in the seminary, ate meals with
students in the school cafeteria, attended chapel services and special
functions, and joined the students during their leisure time. In-depth
interviews were conducted with a sample of students (of all levels), the
faculty, and administrators. In addition, documents such as newsletters,
class handouts, and student projects were examined.

CHANGING PRECONCEPTIONS AND TAKING STOCK OF SURPRISES

Our feelings of discomfort in the first days of fieldwork often derive more from imagined than actual difficulties. Geer (1967) notes that fieldworkers often anticipate problems that do not materialize:

> We do it on each new study. We underestimate people's trust in our neutrality, their lack of interest, perhaps, if we seem to be doing no harm. And we project theoretical problems into the field. Because the process of group formation is difficult to conceptualize, we suppose it will be difficult to observe. We expect ephemeral, unstructured situations . . . to appear incoherent (pp. 382–383).

Further, Geer explains, these anxieties are "a necessary part of our efforts to design the study in advance" (p. 383).

Fieldworkers who study certain categories of persons, particularly deviants or charismatics, have additional fears. They must learn to feel comfortable with people "set apart" from others because of their unusually high or low social position and with whom they are unaccustomed to interacting. Actually, we hold definite ideas about many kinds of people we have had little or no contact with, and even if these preconceptions do not shape much of our everyday life prior to the fieldwork experience, they are likely to surface when we enter the setting. We bring these stereotypes to our work, whether or not the project is planned in advance. These preconceptions, however, can become important to the analysis if we take note of discrepancies (or consistencies) between them and the behavior of respondents.

I did not plan the study prior to entering the setting but nevertheless held strong expectations for what the people would be like. I arranged to take a fieldwork course (for ten weeks) at a university which participates with the University of Minnesota (where I was pursuing the doctoral degree) in a consortium. I corresponded with the instructor, who suggested that I choose a field site after arrival. A student at the host university arranged for me to stay at one of the dormitories of a Methodist seminary affiliated with the university and located on its campus. I worried about sharing living quarters with "religious people" (although I would have a bedroom of my own) but expected to have little to do with them.

I arrived at the dormitory a day before the class began and met some of the ministry students. Since I wasn't yet interested in studying them, I interacted with the students as a new dorm dweller. I asked them where certain facilities were located, such as the cafeteria and the laundry room, and what the surrounding area offered in the way of stores and restaurants. During these encounters I was struck by how "normal" their appearance and talk seemed to be. They looked and talked like students generally, not *ministry* students. Clearly their behavior and appearance did not fit my expectations of "religious" people, and, I thought, surely ministry students must be representative members of that category!

I quickly became intrigued by my ignorance; how could my expectations be so off the mark? After getting settled in the dorm, I asked two female students how they and others would feel about my doing a study of them. I explained that this would entail hanging around with them as much as possible and conducting interviews. These respondents expressed excitement about the prospect and said that others would react similarly. Heartened by their enthusiasm, I decided to try it.

Within a day or so, I was developing questions for myself and respondents as well as becoming comfortable in the setting. Both of these processes were linked to my surprises in the field. By noting the ways in which students violated my expectations, I discovered my implicit "working hypotheses" (Geer, 1967) and could therefore check them out. For example, my reactions indicated that I expected ministry students to act more like ministers than students. And I had definite ideas about what "acting like a minister" meant: engaging in "religious activities" most of the time (such as praying, preaching, reading the Bible, talking about God) and presenting a serious and somber attitude through their tone and appearance. The first students I met did not act in these ways (at least where I observed them), therefore producing a number of questions: Do most students act more like students than ministers, or just the few I have met? Is my reaction of surprise idiosyncratic or reflective my of background characteristics, or would any reasonable person react the same way? If one can reasonably expect such (religious) behavior to be present in a seminary, then how can its absence be accounted for? Does "religious" behavior go on in some places with certain people in the setting, places I have not yet had access to? If so, where, with whom, and why not in plain view?

The public, normal behavior of these students made it easy for me to become comfortable in the field. Because they acted like any student with me, they were letting me know that I could and should act normally, too. They neither expected nor wanted me to treat them as different, which, as we shall see later on, fits with the more general analysis of their problems with outsiders.

It should be noted that unpleasant, as well as pleasant, surprises in the field must be taken into account. Fieldworkers in some settings will have to work hard to gain the trust of respondents and may come up against more resistance than they anticipated. Or respondents may disclose much to fieldworkers but reveal backstage behavior that they find offensive as well as surprising. In order to give the most accurate account of what goes on in the setting, fieldworkers need not become unemotional (which is impossible, anyway) but must make their feelings explicit to themselves. Much has been made of the so-called subjective nature of fieldwork, especially the charge that fieldworkers see what they expect or want to see. While the charge is largely unfounded, the more general notion that fieldworkers' preconceptions affect what they notice in the field is accurate. We are likely to notice events and actions that are *relevant* to our preconceptions. This *includes* observations which contradict or seem inconsistent with our expectations, for it is the surprising nature of these observations that makes us notice them (see Becker, 1970a). In studying groups that people generally stereotype, it becomes quite easy to spot discrepancies between expectations and reality. However, most fieldworkers discover that some of what they observe is not quite what they expected. We must, then, record the observation *and* our reaction to it. And the sooner we recognize these surprises, the sooner we can deal with them sociologically and personally.

RESEARCHER ROLES

What is hinted at in the previous section, and will become explicit here, is the notion that learning one's roles, or how one is expected to act with respondents in particular situations in the setting, is central to learning the ropes. We do not become comfortable until we know how to act with respondents, and we learn this by paying close attention to how respondents act with each other and with us, alone or in groups.

Many sociologists, and fieldworkers in particular, probably see their role as a cynical one. That is, they are not supposed to take the things that people say or do in the field at face value but to " '[see] through' the facades of social structures" (Berger, 1963:31). As Becker (1970) notes:

> Sociologists have had a penchant for the exposé since the days of muckraking. The interviewer is typically out to get "the real story" he conceives to be lying hidden beneath the platitudes of any group and is inclined to discount heavily any expressions of the "official" ideology (p. 103).

Sociologists have the idea that things are not only more than they seem but are also worse than respondents will admit to a researcher.

We feel that we cannot get "the real story," or perhaps any story, without first gaining the trust of our respondents. And because we assume that they will not trust us if we act like cynical sociologists, we try our best to conceal our cynicism from them. After all, how can we expect them to tell us how they "really" feel or what "really" goes on if we challenge what they are telling us (its substance or validity) or let them know that we will check their accounts against others? Consequently, "Interviewers frequently inhibit themselves by adopting a bland, polite style of conversation designed to create rapport with their respondents and to avoid 'leading' them" (Becker, 1970a:59). This fear of expressing cynicism is probably stressful for all fieldworkers, not only those who must set aside their cynical personal style for other audiences.

We may develop an acute case of "cynicism concealment" when we study people whose work is primarily ideological, particularly if we do not share their beliefs. If ideology is conventionally defined as a central aspect of the organization or community, we tend to think that respondents will be overcommitted to their beliefs and will therefore be unable to trust anyone who challenges their doctrine or motives. We assume that these people, unlike others, cannot effect role distance (Goffman, 1961) but are engulfed by their role. Also, because we regard their world view as "false consciousness," we see them as naive people who cannot tolerate cynicism.

I thought this way about ministry students and consequently first used a "bland, polite style of conversation." However, after a few days I learned that I could act cynically (either personally or as a sociologist) without being sanctioned. In fact, I learned the role from the students, who often joked cynically about piety and church community members' unrealistically high expectations of practicing and prospective ministers. I had, of course, expected ministry students to be serious only about religious matters, and the frequency of these jokes (compared with the smaller number of serious talks about theology or faith) meant that something was going on. I wasn't sure what (yet), but I did know that this kidding was important to them and that they seemed to appreciate my joining in.

I became quite comfortable in this role, for it meant that I did not have to deal with the uneasiness of listening seriously to "God talk" or, in my worst fears, being proselytized. However, in adopting this role, there was the danger that students would think it inappropriate to reveal more idealistic attitudes to me, if indeed they had them. Becker and Geer (1958) found that medical students' attitudes of cynicism and idealism appeared in different situations in the setting, and elsewhere Becker (1970b:104) has cautioned that the interviewer may, "by his manner of questioning, fashion a role for himself in the interview that encourages cynicism while discouraging idealism."

Fortunately I conducted a few individual, in-depth interviews during my first week in the field and discovered that, much like the medical students, the ministry students became quite idealistic when they were alone with the interviewer. Some students, I noted, seemed to be transformed in the interview situation. In response to my open-ended questions about how they got to the seminary and their experience in the status of ministry student, they talked seriously about religion, faith, being "called" to the ministry, and the responsibility and problems of ministers.

Students, then, expected me to adopt a serious role in the interview situation. I was at first uncomfortable when students talked this way and even wondered whether some of them were putting me on. I soon became convinced that their performances were sincere but was still left with the problem of learning to take these metaphysical matters seriously. At least, had to act as if I considered, for example, figuring out if one were "called" by God to become a minister a real and serious difficulty. My problem resolved itself quite easily, however, as I (1) learned that the students did not expect me to profess an interest in religion, just in them, (2) developed empathy, and (3) converted what was personally uninteresting into something sociologically interesting.

The first point relates to the general problem of how much subjects will expect the fieldworker to participate in their daily activities, and in what ways they will expect the researcher to be like them. These expectations vary, but the researcher role is always marginal (unless the fieldworker is a covert participant), thereby allowing us to be different from respondents. In my case, it would have been more difficult for the students to discuss their uncertainties about being "called" had I been a churchgoer or even a Christian, for with these people we are supposed to act confident about such matters. Once I realized that I was only a sounding board for them and was not expected to share their beliefs, I became less uneasy during the interview encounters.

To empathize is not only "to imaginatively take the role of another and accurately interpret attitudes and opinions" (Bruyn, 1966:183) but also to develop a personal attachment to the group and a sense that one is "on their side" (Becker, 1970c). Geer (1967) points out that we develop empathy each time we do a study, even if we initially think of the group as boring or unlikable. As we get to know group members better and take their role, we begin to see that their problems are real to them, and insofar as we are interested in their perspective, they are not trivial to us, either. Also, we start to treat their problems as real and important when we ask ourselves the sociological question, Why do these problems exist in the first place? In so doing, we make the apparently trivial or boring personal problems of respondents into something sociologically interesting. As we identify the constraints which operate to produce such problems for respondents and see how they are handled, we learn that *anyone* in their situation would behave as they do, even us! Developing personal empathy, then, and doing the analysis are interrelated processes. We do not empathize with participants merely because they are nice enough to let us study them but because we come to understand why they see things and act in the ways they do.

In this seminary the students' problem was one of identity. Surprisingly, I found that they expressed less concern with the practical difficulties of school life than with what it means to be a minister. Through the research I discovered that their preoccupation became quite understandable when placed in the context of discrepancies in insiders' (faculty, administrators) and outsiders' (parents, friends, church, and the wider community) expectations of ministry students. Not only is "ministry student" a pervasive identity (Travisano, 1970), relevant in many situations and central to interaction, but it is responded to differently by different audiences, thereby creating a situation of "identity confusion" for its encumbents. This analysis also made sense of students' behavior with each other and with me. Outsiders' "traditional" expectations of professionals, and ministers in particular, dictate that they be impersonal and nonequalitarian in their relations with clients and other nonprofessionals. In the case of ministers, outsiders expect them to "[manifest] pious, godly virtues" (Hadden, 1969:214). "Humanistic" professionals (in this school and in some other schools of the personal service professions) wish to demystify the traditional conception of professionals as superior or extraordinary, expecting them to act in a personal and equalitarian fashion.[1] The students' jokes and cynical talk about piety and traditional expectations are a collective response to the "identity problem"; they distance themselves from the unattainable expectations of outsiders. This is their way of telling each other that they *are* normal and that it is acceptable to be that way (despite the expectations of outsiders). By letting me join in, they were able to get confirmation from an outsider—an important validator of self—that they are normal. In sharing their laughter, I was acknowledging that these outsiders are indeed unreasonable. Also, by treating the students as normal, I made it easy for them to admit to me what they could admit to only a few close friends in the seminary (and almost never in public)—that they had not relinquished traditional expectations completely, but in fact had retained a mixture of both traditional and humanistic views. Therefore, they provided me with situational roles that corresponded with their own situational adjustments. I was expected to go along with cynicism about the traditional orientation in group settings and confessions of traditionalism in private.[2]

I also came to understand why the students were so receptive to me, something I had wondered about from the first day of fieldwork. Actually, there are two main reasons. First, the humanistic orientation encourages a ministry of participation; students are expected to be open with, not merely to tolerate, others. Second, and perhaps most important, they were already studying themselves, a self-consciousness brought about by the psychologism prevalent in the school and the situation of identity confusion. They saw me as someone with whom they could possibly discuss their psychological problems and who might provide them with additional knowledge about themselves. This, of course, only makes sense given their rather psychologistic understanding of the work of sociologists, especially those who do fieldwork.

MAKING THE MOST OF YOUR IDENTITIES

We have seen that the researcher role is not of a piece but varies within the setting; we are not expected to act in the same way in different situations.[3] Researcher or sociologist, however, is not the only identity relevant to our interactions with respondents. Mann's (1970) remarks about this in relation to doing fieldwork with people who have little conception of what a researcher does are also relevant to any field study:

> He [the researcher] must recognize that . . . his subjects . . . have some bases on which to predict what he will be like and how he will act. These are generally centered around such characteristics as age, sex, race, perceived class, and other factors which have some cue stimulus value. The expectations that others receive from these cues may limit markedly what a researcher can do in the early phases of a project (p. 120).

In agreement with Mann, our researcher role cannot be separated from other roles and identities that become important to respondents. We present ourselves not only as a researcher or sociologist but also as a woman or man, black or white, young or old. Mann and others discuss these (and other) identities as a hindrance, something that gets in the way of our research and limits what we can do. I want to present the other side of the story, suggesting that we can use our identities to help establish rapport with respondents. Since we cannot eradicate certain identities (they announce themselves through our appearance) and have other, less obvious identities that may "show" soon enough, we should try and use them to our advantage.

During the early stages of research, we try to achieve rapport so that respondents will let us tag along with them as they go about their daily business, ask questions about what we have observed, and perhaps conduct lengthy interviews with them. In my research, I found that identities which were irrelevant to my researcher role became a relevant part of respondents' acceptance of me. These identities were of two types. The first type included identities that I shared with some respondents, such as resident of the Midwest, woman, dorm dweller, and student. Shared identification provided common ground and therefore things to talk about during initial encounters. Further, because respondents, for the most part, positively valued these identities, shared identification also aided the development of trust. The second type included identities I did not share with respondents but which became relevant, such as Canadian and Jew. I discovered that these identities, precisely because they were foreign (but not threatening) to respondents, aroused their curiosity and provided me with something to offer them—interesting stories. This process of using our identities in interaction with respondents is not unique to fieldwork but is characteristic of normal conversation; we make the most of our similarities and differences with others to secure and maintain a level of interest and to achieve rapport.

"Student" was probably one of my most important shared identities. Most of the respondents had been students for most of their lives (about as long as I had) and still were. Also, although ministry students learn different things than sociology students, students generally shared many routines, relationships, and understandings. Respondents could, for example, talk to me about classes, exams, professors, and grades, knowing that I had more than a vague understanding of what they were talking about or doing. (I did, of course, have to learn the ways in which these situations, events, and people took on significance for them, in particular.) Therefore, being a student was important because it offered shared identification as well as shared knowledge.

Given the general stereotype of ministers (and ministry students) as people who are primarily "religious," I presupposed that "Jew" would become my most important identity in the setting. I also anticipated that this would be a negative identity; mightn't they think that only a Christian could really understand what goes on in their seminary? It turned out that this identity did not even become relevant for a while, since they could not tell I was Jewish. When they did ask questions about my religious background, being Jewish became an asset. Most of the students had had little contact with Jews and equated being Jewish with being a religious Jew. They were quite interested to learn how Jewish people differ in degree of religiosity and life style. Further, I have no evidence to indicate that they thought my religious identity would interfere with my ability to do the study. Other identities also took on "difference" value, such as being a Canadian from newsworthy Quebec.

By bringing a number of identities to the interaction, both respondents and researchers get to know each other better and learn to feel comfortable in each other's presence.[4] Also, by broadening the range of relevant identities, researchers can acquire data they might not get otherwise. For example, after learning that my interest in them as ministry students did not preclude an interest in their other identities, students thought it reasonable to include me in leisure activities and tell me about their interpersonal relationships. Further, in this setting, treating the respondents as people who hold many identities helped me achieve rapport because I was granting them a right which many outsiders deny them—the right to act like "regular" people.

I do not mean to suggest that none of a fieldworker's identities will interfere with the research process or alienate respondents. Some familiar identities may bring out an old contempt, just as a foreign identity might produce an immediate response of distrust. Fortunately, in one sense, the researcher is likely to find out about these identities soon enough and can therefore try to deal with the conflict. Respondents, like fieldworkers, can change their preconceptions, but because the latter have a greater interest in developing empathy, it is up to them to actively convince the former that they are not really that bad. For example, a few of my respondents had taken some sociology courses as undergraduates and in the process had acquired a rather negative view of the field and its practitioners. They would, off and on, make snide remarks to me about "being a sociologist." I decided to confront them about this and probe their attitudes. These students shared a positivistic conception of the field and felt that I would purposefully avoid taking their perspective into account. Their distrust (and remarks) subsided after I explained to them that I was using a sociological framework that made their meanings central.

Nor am I suggesting that the researcher bring every identity to initial (or later) encounters. If there is good reason to believe that particular information might alienate respondents and can easily be kept out of the interaction, then it is probably best not to reveal it. Fieldworkers should exercise some caution in deciding what to reveal at the outset, because certain identities will tend to stick with them throughout the research; others will become relevant only on a few occasions.

CONCLUSION

Learning the ropes, in the sense of becoming comfortable in a particular setting, does seem to happen somewhat magically. We begin our study with apprehension and suddenly, within a few days or weeks, we quite comfortably go about our work, as if we had always felt this way.

However, this sudden change seems less magical when we go back to our notes and find that it was in fact a *process*, and one that entailed work. We become increasingly comfortable in the field because we learn more about the people we study, what to expect from them and how we should act. In looking at how we learned the ropes, we see our surprising observations, the questions we asked ourselves and respondents, and the hypotheses we developed and modified—in short, the beginning of our analysis.

Notes

1. My use of the terms "traditional" and "humanistic" is similar to that of Sanders and Lyon (1976).

2. Students also expressed cynicism about the humanistic orientation on particular occasions, but I will not go into that here. For further discussion of the analysis, see Kleinman (1970) and Kleinman and Fine (forthcoming).

3. Or with different groups, such as faculty or students.

4. Getting to know each other "too well" can also pose problems. See Miller (1969).

References

BECKER, H.S. "Field Work Evidence." In H.S. Becker (collected papers), *Sociological Work: Method and Substance*. Chicago: Aldine, 1970a, pp. 39–62.

BECKER, H.S. "Interviewing Medical Students." In W.J. Filstead, ed., *Qualitative Methodology*. Chicago: Markham, 1970b, pp. 103–106.

BECKER, H.S. "Whose Side Are We On?" In W.J. Filstead, ed., *Qualitative Methodology*. Chicago: Markham, 1970c, pp. 15–26.

BECKER, H.S., and B. GEER. "The Fate of Idealism in Medical School." *American Sociological Review*, 23 (1958), 50–56.

BERGER, P.L. *Invitation to Sociology: A Humanistic Perspective*. Garden City, N.Y.: Doubleday, 1963.

BRUYN, S. *The Human Perspective in Sociology: The Methodology of Participant Observation*. Englewood Cliffs, N.J.: Prentice-Hall, 1966.

GEER, B. "First Days in the Field." In P.E. Hamond, ed., *Sociologists at Work*. Garden City, N.Y.: Doubleday, 1967, pp. 372–398.

GLASER, B., and A.L. STRAUSS. *The Discovery of Grounded Theory*. Chicago: Aldine, 1967.

GOFFMAN, E. *Encounters*. Indianapolis: Bobbs-Merrill, 1961.

HADDEN, J.K. *The Gathering Storm in the Churches*. Garden City, N.Y.: Doubleday, 1969.

KLEINMAN, S. "Making Professionals into Persons: Conflicts Between Traditional and Humanistic Views of Professional Identity." Unpublished manuscript, 1979.

KLEINMAN, S., and G.A. FINE. "Rhetorics and Action in Moral Organizations: Social Control of Little Leaguers and Ministry Students." *Urban Life*, forthcoming.

MANN, F.C. "Human Relations Skills in Social Research." In W.J. Filstead, ed., *Qualitative Methodology*. Chicago: Markham, 1970, pp. 119-132.

MILLER, S.M. "The Participant Observer and 'Over-rapport.'" In G.J. McCall and J.L. Simmons, eds., *Issues in Participant Observation*. Reading, Mass.: Addision-Wesley, 1969, 87-89.

SANDERS, C.R., and E. LYON. "The Humanistic Professional: The Reorientation of Artistic Production." In J.E. Gerstl and G. Jacobs, eds., *Professions for the People: The Politics of Skill*. Cambridge, Mass.: Schenkman, 1976, pp. 43-59.

TRAVISANO, R.V. "Alternation and Conversion as Qualitatively Different Transformations." In G.P. Stone and H.A. Farberman, eds., *Social Psychology Through Symbolic Interaction*. Waltham, Mass.: Ginn, 1970, pp. 594-606.

3

Maintaining Relations

At first, the problems of getting along with the people in the field may appear to be of little scientific interest. Such an outlook, however, is hardly correct. The validity of the data hinges, in part, on achieving that delicate balance of distance and closeness that characterizes effective researcher-subject interaction. Further, workable field relations must also be sustained among members of the research team, if one exists. Since most of the selections in this section center on relations with subjects, we will turn to this topic first.

The key to success in interacting with subjects is the establishment and maintenance of rapport. Basically, rapport is a blend of the external and internal ingredients of day-to-day involvement. When rapport is established, the subject shows a willingness to cooperate in achieving the goals of the study and trusts the researcher to handle personal and often sensitive information with tact and objectivity. When rapport is achieved, the aims of the study are balanced by the human qualities of warmth, harmony of interest, bonhomie, and the like.

Relations with subjects may be strengthened or weakened during the research project at four points. One of these is the discussion or observation of sensitive topics, behaviors, or events. Trust must be firmly established if fieldworkers are to succeed in collecting valid data. For example, Junker (1960:34) points out how researchers develop sensitivity to the many kinds of distinctions subjects make about public versus private events. An inability to take the role of the subjects may cause researchers to treat this information inappropriately. For the fieldworker, the outcome is soured relations with people on whom he or she depends.

The maintenance of trust is most critical in situations such as that faced by Bromley and Shupe, who demonstrate how to maintain relations in spite of shifting goals. Fluidity is inevitable in fieldwork. Although they did not anticipate the problem, Bromley and Shupe gradually became aware of the necessity of gaining the confidence of two antagonistic groups. Both the Unification Church and the National Ad Hoc Committee Engaged in Freeing Minds knew that the researchers were studying their opposition. As the researchers learned more about the groups' ideologies and began to show signs of less than complete acceptance of them, the trust, so painstakingly cultivated, began to wane: each side suspected the investigators of providing inside information to the other.

A second area is maintaining ties with informants, those subjects who routinely provide inside information about individuals and events of interest to the project. Since informants usually discuss their associates instead of themselves, their trust in the researcher's confidentiality is somewhat different from that of the usual subject. The researcher must not reveal the informant's identity or interpretation of an event or person.

Additionally, informants get something in return for their special contribution. Usually they have closer ties with the researcher than do other subjects and also a unique opportunity to discuss the people and events focused on in the study. This means that a fieldworker must be prepared to spend more time with an informant than with other subjects, often becoming more of a friend with that person (more internal involvement) than with the others.

Bogdan's paper centers on two mental retardates named Ed and Pattie. Throughout his many interviews with them, it was necessary to pay constant attention to their sensitivity about being treated as inferiors. Rapport here meant being defined by the subjects as being on their side in their continual struggle against stigmatization and discrimination.

Another strategic point in the maintenance of field relations is the offering of assistance to some or all of the subjects. This does not mean giving advice, professional or otherwise, for that can be most risky (e.g., Johnson, 1975:130–131). Rather, the researcher does something useful, such as serve as "watch queen" in a homosexual tearoom (Humphreys, 1970:26–28), convey messages or materials among members of a Gamblers Anonymous chapter (Livingston, 1974:11), or provide transportation and money for a group of urban blacks (Liebow, 1967:253). This way of maintaining relations involves reciprocity with one's subjects. In partial repayment for their cooperation, the researcher lends a hand with an appreciated form of help.

Pepinsky's study of the Minneapolis police illustrates a moral dilemma that field researchers often face. They commonly feel obliged to help their subjects in return for the privilege of observing and interviewing them. Fieldworkers may also be asked to help in ways they find personally objectionable. Where does one draw the line? What are the consequences of the stand finally taken?

A fourth strategic point involves living up to the bargains fieldworkers often have to strike with their subjects in order to gain access to them and the field setting. One such bargain is the promise to cause little or no disruption to organizational or group affairs (Bogdan and Taylor, 1975:36). Furthermore, confidentiality of detailed interview and observational data may be an implicit bargain that is as crucial during the fieldwork as during the writing of the report. In short, when a researcher defaults on a bargain, smooth relations with subjects, as well as rapport, are threatened.

Haas and Shaffir write about the sometimes delicate process of living up to the bargains struck with the gatekeepers of the setting. What those bargains are and how they are met as the study progresses are matters that are subject to wide interpretation and subsequent negotiation by all concerned. They are an area of potential conflict.

Clearly, maintaining field relations is hardly an easy task. For one thing, rapport sometimes becomes the basis for deeper friendships, stronger identification with the group under study, or both. This "over-rapport" (Miller, 1952) or "going native" (Paul, 1953:435) tends to destroy the delicate balance of external and internal considerations so painstakingly achieved in ideal field relations by allowing the latter to predominate. In the process the investigator's objectivity is weakened, if not destroyed. Indeed, the very goal of presenting a scientific account of the group may be effectively scuttled. Cooperation and trust, however, are likely to remain strong in overrapport, though these now make little difference since the erstwhile researcher has disappeared into the subject group. It should also be mentioned here that overrapport is especially problematic for covert observers. They are trying to balance the internal and external aspects of field research, while their subjects see only the internal (and possibly the nonscientific external) reasons for their actions.

Yet, the fieldworker can also err in the opposite direction by trying to function in an atmosphere of underrapport. Here a number of factors may combine to chill social relations. One of these is a desire to rush the interviews or cut short the observation sessions in an attempt to complete the project quickly; another is a reluctance to consider suggestions from subjects on how to conduct the study (scientist as singular expert); and finally, there is a penchant for conspicuous note taking, which, under certain conditions, creates suspicion or self-consciousness among subjects.

Another set of factors may be inferred from Bogdan and Taylor's (1975:46–48) prescriptions for generating rapport, which suggest how some researchers fail and thereby seriously lessen the quality of their work. One way to gain rapport is to talk for a while about those aspects of daily life that researcher and subject have in common. But investigators who refuse to open up in this manner, even though they expect their subjects to do so, miss this opportunity to promote good field relations. Similarly, those who avoid participating in the subjects' activities, when it is possible to do so and makes good sense from the research standpoint, lose another opportunity.

Otherwise, insensitivity to subjects' routines, observing and scheduling interviews in ways that violate the local code of etiquette, airs of superiority, obnoxious personal mannerisms, and other characteristics contribute to underrapport and hence ineffective field research. In Lofland's (1976:13) words: "many of those who populate the social science disciplines are temperamentally unsuited for the less than traumatic mucking around in the real world outside the academy." Nevertheless, some of them try their hand at fieldwork while failing to develop the necessary rapport with their subjects.

Posner faced the lack of rapport inherent in covert observation: How does the researcher maintain a level and quality of interaction with subjects that facilitates research but looks normal in the setting under study? She recounts how she managed, sometimes tenuously, to maintain relations (and her research aims) as her official position changed within the nursing home she was studying. As she moved through these positions, adjustments had to be made to both the residents and the staff without revealing that she was a fieldworker.

In sum, maintaining relations through sustained rapport involves keeping the goals of the study in mind but pursuing them in ways that gain subject cooperation and trust. In working toward this end, one must often tactfully remind well-intentioned subjects that these very goals prevent such forms of participation as giving advice, taking sides in a dispute, and engaging in certain tasks or activities. And to complicate matters further, the goals may change during the course of the study, requiring further explanations to the subjects most directly affected. If this is handled ineptly, relations can be weakened at this point as well.

OTHER FIELD RELATIONS

When fieldworkers join together to do a project, the possibility of interpersonal problems will also emerge. Remarkably little has been written on this subject (but see the selection by Haas and Shaffir), though there may be severe differences of opinion on how best to surmount an entry problem, what to do when a moral issue arises, or how much time to spend collecting data. The level of commitment among team members may vary. Some members are probably better suited as personalities to do fieldwork than others, resulting in an uneven quality (validity, completeness, accuracy) in the data collected. In short, besides trying to maintain relations with subjects, team members must try to maintain them with each other.

Turning to another area of field relations, it may be noted that the need, even the desire, to maintain relations with subjects may continue well beyond the data collection phase of the project. One of the common bargains reached with gatekeepers, and frequently with all subjects who participate closely in the study, is to give them a report of the findings. The writing of this report may require occasional consultation with some of them as to accuracy and readability. Moreover, fieldwork projects tend to raise more questions than they answer, driving some investigators back to the original setting to do more work. Or they may simply wish to see what changes have taken place over the intervening years. These enduring research interests are accompanied at times by friendships that have sprung from the initial contact between researcher and subject. By means of telephone calls, personal visits, or letters, the fieldworker maintains contact with members of the focal group and thus remains informed about at least some of the developments that bear on his or her professional interests.

The article by Miller and Humphreys demonstrates how ties with former subjects can be maintained over the years. These relationships enabled the authors to conduct further research on new questions that emerged in subsequent interpretations and reinterpretations of their data. Maintaining extended relations of this sort is a mixed blessing in terms of time and effort.

The maintenance of effective relations with subjects and collaborators is central to the social experience of fieldwork. The selections in this section offer us several insiders' accounts of what it is like to nurture and manage these ties under a variety of research conditions.

Evolving Foci in Participant Observation: Research as an Emergent Process

DAVID G. BROMLEY
ANSON D. SHUPE, JR.   *The University of Texas at Arlington*

Although social scientists have observed that a researcher's understanding and perception of informants often changes over the course of a project as one gains knowledge about them (e.g., Becker, 1958; Vidich, 1970), there is also a tendency to present the research process as a largely predetermined series of steps. Indeed, unless a researcher's goal is pure ethnographic description or theory construction, it is expected that he or she has usually decided in advance which types of observations are of interest. The theoretical perspective from which the research is conducted or the simple need for parsimony does, in fact, channel the researcher's observational activity. However, in many participant observation situations the initial formulation of the research problem constitutes merely the beginning of an interactive process between researcher and data. The subsequent questions flow out of this interactive process and provide much of the direction and substance of the project. Since data are obtained from informants in the ongoing social milieu under observation, it follows that as new questions are raised and new perspectives formed with regard to the group(s) under study, the researcher's relationship with informants also changes. In this selection, we shall describe how the focus of research shifted over time in a participant observation project as we interacted with the data and how our changing conceptions of the informants influenced our relations with them.[1]

The situation we will describe was somewhat unique in that it involved studying two groups that were in open conflict. The substantive findings which emerged from studying both groups simultaneously revealed (1) how each group sought to legitimate its own activities and

191

discredit those of its opponent and (2) how the strategy and tactics of each group tended to be influenced by those of its opponent. However, we are more concerned here with the emergent process by which those findings evolved; what follows is an attempt to reconstruct that process and its implications for ongoing relationships with our informants.

Over a two-year period (1976–1978), we were involved in an investigation of two groups mutually opposed to each other: the Unification Church (founded by Korean evangelist Sun Myung Moon) and a national coalition of anticult organizations dedicated to the exposure and restraint of Moon's church (among others) that eventually became known as the International Foundation for Individual Freedom. Our data were collected from published literature of the two groups, from interviews with national leaders and rank-and-file members of both, and from participant observations in their respective activities. Moon's church, which had as its goal the unification of all religions worldwide according to a particular neo-Confucian version of Christianity and the establishment of a worldwide theocracy, drew its members disproportionately from the ranks of white, middle-class American college-age youth. The anticult organizations, whose members consisted primarily of ex-members and the families of members of such religious groups as the Unification Church, accused Moon of "brainwashing" or using deception in recruitment, and of exploiting idealistic young persons by using them as fund raisers to enhance Moon's personal wealth. The latter group achieved notoriety in the mid-1970s as a result of its condemnation of such new religions for its practice of coercive "deprograming"—that is, the involuntary detention and pressuring to recant their new faith, through extended argument, of marginal religious group members.

PRECONTACT IMPRESSIONS OF THE GROUPS

The project began even before we commenced participant observation with either group. Like much of the American public, we had become aware of the existence of new religious groups and had been exposed to the allegations of exploitation and deception leveled at them through the news media. We became intrigued by the enormous amount of adverse publicity these groups received and the degree to which they were perceived as threats, particularly given their relatively small membership size. Further, we wondered why the Unification Church, among all the various new religious groups, had been singled out for condemnation.

In an effort to answer this question for ourselves, we wrote an initial speculative paper (Shupe et al., 1977) which argued that the Unification Church in particular had been vilified for several reasons. First, Moon's group had violated several cultural norms, such as overt involvement of a religion in political activities and failure of its members to identify their church affiliation when soliciting funds. Second, Moon offended both liberals with his staunch cold-war, anti-Communist rhetoric and conservatives with his radical reformulation of orthodox Christianity. And third, the church's demand that members postpone or sacrifice conventional careers and close family ties for a communal life style of celibacy and self-denial had outraged families with more conventional aspirations for their maturing children. Although we thought we could identify some real violations which had precipitated a hostile public response to the Unification Church, still it seemed to us that the church had become something of a symbolic political whipping boy for a number of main-line religious and political interests.

In the process of preparing the paper, we requested information on the Unification Church from anticult groups, the national headquarters of which fortuitously was located nearby in the Dallas-Fort Worth metropolitan area. They supplied us with case histories, anecdotes, newspaper accounts, and other public testimonies related to various alleged social and cultural violations by the new religious groups. At the time we were impressed that, even allowing for the exaggeration of their sense of threat, there must have been some substance to their concerns. Why else, we asked, would a group of seemingly moderate middle-class citizens go to such great lengths and personal inconvenience to attack these small, seemingly insignificant religious groups?

Prior to any participant observation of either group, then, we had already formed some impressions of them. We saw the Unification Church as an organization which had committed some social and cultural violations, but the reactions to the church appeared to be out of proportion to the violations themselves. We pictured the anticultists as somewhat overzealous but also as legitimately concerned about exploitive activities by new religious groups. In short, we felt a certain sympathy both for members of the Unification Church as an underdog minority and for anticultists as a well-meaning civic group. These two conceptions were to some extent inconsistent with one another, and these incongruities in part motivated our subsequent participant observational activities.

GETTING OUR BEARINGS

Our original conception of the research project was simply to produce a paper on the Unification Church which explained to our own satisfaction the hostile public reaction. We had anticipated no participant observation activity nor an investigation of the anticult movement. However, once we discovered that the national coordinating center for the anticult movement was located in the Dallas-Fort Worth metropolitan area, and when a witnessing/fund-raising team from the Unification Church appeared in the area, we began to realize that a unique opportunity to explore our speculations further had presented itself. Having decided to become involved with both groups, we shifted the focus of the research from reliance on secondary sources to direct observation and from the study of a single group to the study of intergroup conflict. For the first time, we had to gain entry and develop rapport with informants in both groups, and our initial task was simply to understand each group in its own terms.

Our observation activity formally began after a phone call to an anticult organization called the National Ad Hoc Committee Engaged in Freeing Minds (CEFM). Upon being invited to visit its headquarters for an interview with the interim director, we found that "headquarters" was the living room of the director's home. His "staff," busily engaged in filing and responding to letters, answering phones on three separate lines, and mimeographing and copying equipment, consisted of his wife, a volunteer friend of the family, and (for a short time) a paid secretary. Our first impression was one of frenetic activity. Leaflets, letters from parents seeking information on religious groups and children's whereabouts, and files on various cults covered all available surfaces, including the dining-room and coffee tables. The telephones rang constantly.

After several visits to CEFM headquarters, we began to recognize that the organization and its affiliates fulfilled several unique functions. Thousands of young persons nationally had joined "fringe" religious groups and had, for all practical purposes, broken contact with their families. Frequently their families did not know their whereabouts or the nature of the group they had joined. One important function of CEFM, therefore, was to help families locate either their children or the group they had joined. Another was to "educate" concerned families, albeit with generally negative information, about the various religious groups. Still another was to provide social support for parents who were distraught with fear, confusion, and guilt over their offsprings' conversions. Finally, CEFM also fulfilled a political function, helping to coordinate a lobbying effort by providing the vehicle for expressing the common grievances of these families. The impression we got of the people we first met was of a harried, overworked group of volunteers responding to what they perceived to be a crisis situation.

Our grasp of their movement's ideology also increased. Rather than simply chasing runaways or young adults gone astray, they were concerned about a conspiracy by cults to capture, "brainwash," and exploit their children and subvert such institutions as democratic government and the family. They regarded themselves as ordinary patriotic citizens attempting to cope with a problem to which the public at large and various levels of government were paying scant attention (see Shupe, Spielmann, and Stigall, 1977a, 1977b).

A few months later, a Unification Church witnessing/fund-raising team appeared in the area and attempted to establish a campus student organization as part of a two-month recruitment campaign. Fortunately, the group maintained its base of operations in a motel adjacent to the campus, affording us the opportunity to engage in participant observation of its activities. Since we had just completed the previously mentioned paper and research on the anticult movement, we were eager to compare our speculations about the "Moonies" and the allegations of others with our own firsthand observations.

Our first contact with the Unification Church involved the standard dinner/lecture introduction offered to all interested outsiders. We had little idea of what to expect and were even slightly apprehensive. In actuality, the occasion turned out to be rather bland and conventional. An hour-long lecture describing the Unification Church and its theology was followed by an oriental-style buffet dinner, interspersed with revival-style group singing and prayer. If the situation seemed slightly artificial and orchestrated to us, it nevertheless did not appear to be coercive or manipulative. These initial experiences increased our sense of dissonance between prior expectations and what we actually found, motivating us to investigate further.

After our first few evenings with the Unification Church members, our conception of the group began to change. Our first struggles had involved simply trying to understand the concrete events occuring around us. Soon, however, our focus on the cultural "landscape,"—understanding the group in its own terms—became sharper in several ways.

First, the group's organization and nightly routine became more apparent. What initially appeared to be spontaneous or even random behavior later could be identified as the acting out of specific group roles, whether as song leader, lecturer on *The Divine Principle*, or even dinner companion for a prospective recruit.

Second, we lost our sense of awkwardness and felt almost part of the routine itself, conducting our interviews and observations inconspicuously so as not to upstage the Moonies' proselytizing efforts with their guests.

Third, as we came to know individual members on a more personal basis, our views of the group became more complex. Some of our stereotyped expectations—for instance, that most members would be either extremely naive or alienated from the larger society—were difficult to substantiate as we encountered a number of members who were extremely perceptive, articulate, and optimistic.

Fourth, over time we became familiar with the theology of the church

196   DAVID G. BROMLEY AND ANSON D. SHUPE, JR.

and came to realize that activities which otherwise seemed to be nonreligious, such as fund raising, were in fact directly linked to and justified by the doctrines. For example, members did not view money received from strangers on the street for such items as cookies and flowers as mere economic transactions. Rather, the Moonies saw themselves as giving a gift; if they were successful in expressing love, the recipient, in return, would be motivated to donate money. Further, the gift-donation sequence became a concrete test of the members' ability to love others (even those who rebuked them) and to reach the latter on what members referred to as a "heartistic" level. Thus, in this situation, a theological context analogous to Max Weber's Protestant ethic justified an otherwise mundane secular activity. As we began to appreciate the symbolic significance of numerous other daily events, we began to understand why members' involvement was so intense and complete.

We emerged from these observations with a much more complex and relativistic view of both groups. From our perspective as sociologists, each group initially reacted to a structural problem which, in turn, generated a social reaction against it. In the case of the Unification Church, which was basically an idealistic youth movement seeking socioreligious reform, the members took as problematic the widespread discrepancies between ideals and reality. Their means of reducing that gap, however, involved a reformulation of orthodox Christianity and a merging of philosophy, science, politics, and religion, all of which was viewed as heretical both religiously and politically. In the case of the anticultists, the problem was the widely discussed lack of continuity between adolescence and adulthood. As numerous social critics have pointed out (e.g., Goodman, 1960; Rozak, 1969), there was no clearly defined process through which young people could mature and assume full adult responsibility. As a result, in the interim years (i.e., between the late teens and mid-twenties), individuals became increasingly independent of their parents but had not yet fully assumed role obligations in the workplace or in families of their own. It was during this transitional period that most individuals joined groups such as the Unification Church. Since such commitments had at least the appearance of being permanent and lifelong, parents understandably became concerned for the future of their offspring. From the parents' perspective, all of their efforts and sacrifices to ensure that their adult children would have the maximum chance to lead happy and successful lives suddenly seemed in danger of having been for nothing. Their solution to the problem was to reassert parental authority and to redirect their maturing children into more acceptable life styles via the deprograming.

On a personal level, as we began to understand each group's ideology in greater detail, our ability to comprehend and empathize with both increased. We perceived both groups as basically well-meaning, and both were forthright in their dealings with us. Members of both groups also began to manifest greater trust in us, readily sharing confidential and even intimate thoughts and feelings. If they did not reveal all the details of their beliefs and activities to us immediately, this apparently was out of concern for not being understood. Both groups actively sought our understanding and approval. We sought to reciprocate with a patient hearing of their case and by getting to know them as individuals. As we got to know members of both groups better, we felt greater sympathy for their respective causes and greater acceptance of them personally. Our sense of detachment decreased, and we developed relations as friends and confidants.

TAKING ON THE MYTHS

After completing the participant observation activity with each group (Bromley and Shupe, 1979), we shifted the focus of the research once again. If both groups turned out to be considerably less sinister than we had been led to expect, what was the significance of the media images which had led us to undertake the research in the first place? Our attention thus moved to the conflict between the two groups, and specifically to the process by which each sought to legitimate its own values and activities and to discredit those of its opponents. Since the information we now sought related to the conflict process, and since we were dealing with both groups simultaneously, our relations with our informants obviously became more delicate. Each interaction with either camp took on increasing significance because we were now in possession of information which, if misused, would be potentially damaging to our informants.

Our efforts to understand the conflict process began when through serendipity we gained access to a large national sample of negative newspaper accounts of the Unification Church's recruitment techniques, activities, and life style. They were so clearly at variance with our own observations that we began to regard them as social "constructions" (i.e., as events which might or might not have occurred as related but which, even if they did occur, were reported in an inflammatory and exaggerated style). For example, after reading allegations of food deprivation brought about through nutritionally poor meals and irregular eating schedules, we were surprised to observe just the opposite. Instead of humorless, grim automatons with glassy-eyed and expressionless faces, we encountered the same range of youthful enthusiasm, humor, and energy one might expect among any teenagers and young adults. Nor did we see any evidence of "sinister" mind-control techniques; in fact, the Moonies' success rate for retaining the interest of persons after the initial lecture was astonishingly low. A detailed analysis of what we came to refer to as "atrocity stories" showed that they typically portrayed a series of social and cultural violations that were designed: (1) to outrage the uninvolved reader with accounts of violations of important norms and values; (2) to strip the target group so negatively depicted of the rights and legitimacy otherwise accorded to conventional groups; and (3) to mobilize sentiments of outraged anger and transform them into punitive sanctions (Bromley, Shupe, and Ventimiglia, forthcoming).

The realization that the atrocity stories represented social constructions tended to swing our sympathies toward the Unification Church. We began to see the Moonies as composing a relatively innocuous marginal religious group which for complex reasons had elicited repressive social action. We also began to wonder if indeed the anticultists were not simply intolerant of religious diversity (at least when it occurred too close to home), rationalizing the imposition of their own particular values through the construction and repetition of atrocity stories. Our concept of the anticultists was reinforced by the growing rejection of deprograming by the courts, religious leaders and civil libertarian groups, and other social movements.

Having begun to perceive the Unification Church as the underdog in the conflict, we became aware of an emerging stereotype of the anticultists as reactionary fanatics, sometimes brutal in their callousness toward the civil liberties of others and generally hostile to all but mainline religions. After a series of negative television documentaries on the news and several years of hostile newspaper coverage, a sort of "underdog" effect had generated sympathy for such minorities as the Unification Church. For example, in 1978 the popular *Lou Grant* television series about a newspaper editor contained an episode in which a young man's parents were distraught when he joined the Hare Krishna sect. Their overall portrayal in the program, as well as that of the deprogramer whom they hired, was of parochial middle-class "red-necks." A source that conveyed the same image and that was perhaps more influential among professionals, *Deprogramming: Documenting the Issue* (1977) was published by the American Civil Liberties Union. This report contained a set of atrocity stories about the anticultists and deprogramers parallel to those dealing with the Unification Church.

We also began to realize that the term "deprograming" actually referred to a range of activities: from a parent's phone call to a son or daughter pleading for the latter to reconsider the new religious commitment, to a clergyman counseling a novitiate who has just joined, to the much more widely publicized and sensationalized coercive type involving literal "body-snatching" and browbeating. While the stereotype of deprograming connoted only the last extreme activity, in fact we found that such coercive deprogramings constituted only a tiny fraction of the anticultists' activities. Most of the time, deprograming involved concerned parents attempting to "restore" earlier family relationships as they perceived them and to redirect their offspring into more conventional life styles. For this reason, although we could not accept all of their claims about how young persons came to join movements such as the Moonies or condone all their activities, we did sympathize with the anguish they felt in the difficult situation they confronted.

We emerged from these new experiences with a much more complex and relativistic view of both groups. The arbitrariness of the definition of the Unification Church as evil and the anticultists as intolerant fanatics was fully apparent to us. Each group misunderstood the other, and, as a result of their mutual attempts to discredit each other, the public misperceived both. Our relations with our informants became more complex for us as we began to understand the process whereby each group had been labeled. We could not in good conscience accept each group's stereotype of the other as long as the conflict persisted. As a result, we were forced to limit the bargains and the involvement we maintained with each group both because they increased suspicion of us by both sides and because they implied a level of acceptance and approval which did not reflect our own attitudes and feelings.

MAINTAINING RELATIONS

As the focus of the research project shifted and expanded, so did the delicacy and complexity of maintaining relationships with each group. At the outset of our research, maintaining relations was not particularly problematic. Our sympathy for both groups and our interest in resolving the discrepancies in each group's portrayal of the other allowed us to express a genuine interest in learning more about both groups. Since we did not anticipate an extended relationship with either group nor did they foresee our having extensive access to them, relationships were maintained at a cordial if superficial level.

At the second stage of the research, getting our bearings, relationships were facilitated by our outside status in the community. Each group saw itself as an underdog and welcomed allies as well as adherents. There is little doubt that in our professional roles as social scientists we had positive public relations value for both groups, lending legitimacy merely by association with them. Matters of legitimacy aside, each group saw us as potentially useful as disseminators of "the truth." Both sides fervently believed in their version of reality and therefore tacitly assumed that to understand was to believe. From their perspectives, then, our association with them would eventually bring us around to their point of view. Finally, as our fluency and sophistication in communicating with them in their terminology increased, they credited us with greater interest and sympathy and then were willing to share with us some of the more esoteric and controversial aspects of their ideologies. And, importantly, we developed personal relationships with a number of key informants that tended to be self-sustaining. To the extent that informants felt that they were supplying information to us as individuals rather than as sociologists, they were more open and responsive.

Certain problems did arise at this stage, however, that required diplomatic resolution. There were occasions when we as outsiders over-stepped our boundaries as they perceived them, seeking information or access to events that were restricted to the faithful. In these circumstances we generally pursued one of two alternatives. If the information we sought could not be obtained from one group, we discreetly sought it from the other side. We discovered that if we obtained information about either group in this fashion, they were willing to discuss it with us although they never would have initially provided it to us. The other tactic was to request the same information from several informants within the appropriate group. Each group was so decentralized that there was no common definition of public and private; thus what one informant refused to divulge was often freely available from another.

The other major problem we encountered at this stage was one that often plagues members of our discipline—namely, that our informants lacked any meaningful definition of sociology. Since they had no sense of our disciplinary perspective, it was difficult for them to comprehend why we sought certain information or the uses to which it might be put. They were frequently perplexed by our intense interest in innocuous organizational detail and by our relative disinterest in the more spectacular charges and countercharges surrounding their activities. To some extent, we were able to allay their anxieties by supplying informants with copies of papers which had already been completed, although that tactic was not always successful. Not infrequently we miscalculated their reaction to our ideas and were forced to engage in interminable discussions to regain credibility. In the end, it seemed that our willingness to submit to their criticism and convincingly show our efforts to understand their perspectives was the key determinant of our continued access to confidential information and activity.

At the third stage of our research, "taking on the myths," we began testing the myths that each movement constructed of itself and its opponents' motives and behaviors. In large measure, we became aware of these mythologies as our relationships with each group broadened and deepened. It was the combination of having accumulated extensive "insider" knowledge about each group and investigating these much more sensitive issues that produced a new set of relational problems.

As we became more knowledgeable about each group, investigating their perceptions of reality, they began to wonder how we could have been exposed to so much of their respective groups and still raise such fundamental questions. At this point, pressures to "go native"—to align ourselves with goals and espouse beliefs of the respective movements—intensified. They now perceived that we were no longer dealing with ethnographic description but rather with analysis and evaluation of their ideological constructions. Their reliance on our integrity, trust, and good will was tempered by their awareness of our reservations about aspects of each movement, a further source of tensions. They developed a sense of uneasiness that we had seen so much and yet remained unconvinced, and our failure to embrace their respective points of view tended to threaten their faiths (and our positions, dependent as they were on our informants' cooperation and goodwill) in the self-evident rightness of their causes. We were unable to satisfy fully these pressures for reasons of both professional neutrality and personal feelings. As our informants began to perceive this, they also began to demand more and more explicit assurances of the uses of our data. (Yet they also knew that, having given us a good deal of information, their refusal to give more would appear as if they were harboring secrets.)

Despite our assurances, however, we frankly acknowledge that the tensions inherent in such situations were never completely resolved. If anything, they began to mount as both sides became aware of our intentions to publish our findings.

SUGGESTIONS FOR MANAGING RELATIONS

Suggestions which we might offer other researchers based on our own experiences relate specifically to the two-group situation but do have more general implications for any participant observation fieldwork. The following, in our opinion, are salient considerations:

First, it is axiomatic to remind researchers that participant observation is an ongoing, emergent process in which the observer constantly absorbs new information and integrates it with previous observations. This often leads to ongoing reinterpretations of data. Likewise, just as the researcher's perspective of site and informants evolves, so also do the latters' perspectives of the researcher. Their interpretation will often move from regarding the researcher as a naive outsider to crediting the researcher with considerably more knowledge. Anticipating this evolution of perspectives will help the field researcher guard against locking into any single set of realtionships (e.g., with factions, informants who have ulterior motives for passing on information, and so forth) early in the research.

Second, it is pragmatically wise as well as ethically proper to inform each side that you are studying the other. This will probably create fewer problems than it might initially appear. Since one objective of the research is to understand the relations between the two groups, respective "gatekeepers" will usually appreciate, out of a sense of "fair play" if for no other reason, the researcher's desire to independently investigate both sides. Such a position will be much more readily accepted than covert research that is later discovered by one or both sides. Of course, each side, because of its confidence in the self-evident justice of its perspective, often believes that the research will ultimately vindicate that perspective.

Third, as a researcher becomes more deeply involved with groups engaged in conflict, each will subtly or directly exert pressures on the researcher to "go native." Since each group will be highly sensitive to any hints of such an alliance with its opponents, it is imperative for the researcher to decide consciously how much compromise to make without jeopardizing neutrality and integrity. Even if compromises can be made without acting dishonestly, it is worth considering whether or not such compromises will yield worthwhile findings. In this sense, as a rule of thumb, the researcher should structure relations with informants on the basis of the former's relation to (i.e., how close to achieving) the research goals.

Finally, researchers may conclude as individuals, outside of their professional roles, that they feel compelled to support one side over the other. From an ethical standpoint, some honest introspection of personal values is necessary lest the researcher obtain information under false pretenses. Informants have a right at all times to be kept informed of any changes in the researcher's stance so that they have an equal ability to renegotiate the research arrangement.

Notes

1. This paper is the product of a joint effort. The order of authorship is random and does not imply any difference in the importance of contributions.

References

BECKER, H.S. "Problems of Inference and Proof in Participant Observation." *American Sociological Review*, 23 (1958), 652-660.

BROMLEY, D.G., and A.D. SHUPE, JR. "'Just a Few Years Seem Like a Lifetime:' A Role Theory Approach to Participation in Religious Movements." In L. Kriesberg, ed. *Research in Social Movements, Conflict, and Change.* Greenwich, Conn.: JAI Press, forthcoming

BROMLEY, DAVID G., ANSON D. SHUPE, JR., and JOSEPH C. VENTIMIGLIA. "The role of anecdotal atrocities in the social construction of evil." In James T. Richardson (ed.), *The Deprogramming Controversy: Sociological, Psychological, Legal, and Historical Perspectives.* New Brunswick, N.J. Transaction Books, forthcoming.

GOODMAN, P. *Growing Up Absurd.* New York: Random House, 1960

ROSZAK, T. *The Making of a Counter Culture.* New York: Doubleday, 1969.

SHUPE, JR., A.D., J.C. VENTIMIGLIA, D.G. BROMLEY, and S. STIGALL. "Political Control of Radically Innovative Religions." Paper presented at the annual meeting of the Association for the Scientific Study of Religion: Southwest, 1977.

SHUPE, JR., A.D., R. SPIELMANN, and S. STIGALL. "Deprogramming: The New Exorcism." *American Behavioral Scientist,* 20 (1977), 941–956.

SHUPE, JR., A.D., R. SPIELMANN, and S. STIGALL. "Deprogramming and the Emerging American Anti-Cult Movement." Paper presented at the annual meeting of the Society for the Scientific Study of Religion, 1977b.

VIDICH, A. "Participant Observation and the Collection and Interpretation of Data." In William J. Filstead, ed., *Qualitative Sociology.* Chicago: Markham, 1970, 164–173.

Urban Anthropology: Fieldwork in Semifamiliar Settings

JUDITH POSNER *York University*

Numerous textbooks and firsthand confessionals such as Hortense Powdermaker's *Stranger and Friend* (1966) and Elenore Bowen's *Return to Laughter* (1964) describe in detail the trials and tribulations of doing fieldwork in a foreign culture. But anthropologists and sociologists alike have tended not to dissect the urban fieldwork process to the same degree. Obviously, to become a complete observer (if there is such a thing) in your own society is quite different from attempting to be an observer elsewhere. And the same is true for the participant role.

A further gap in the ethnographic literature involves the analysis of research done in one place from a variety of fieldwork roles, thus experiencing the same society from various perspectives. By this, I do not refer to the ordinary process of becoming increasingly involved with the setting under study—rapport. Rather, I am referring to the fieldworker's capacity to take on a number of different official structural positions in a milieu and the effects such positions have on social perception, self-perception, and the nature of one's reporting. While the concept of role maintenance is discussed in the fieldwork literature, it is usually approached from a static perspective which implies that once a fieldworker establishes a certain role or position in a setting (covert/overt, observer participant/participant observer, etc.) it remains relatively permanent. But the truth is that one may enter a social scene in one role and leave in another. And in between, a variety of social roles may occur. In short, the researcher's roles, like real roles in society, are quite flexible, thus altering one's slant on the social world under scrutiny. The following selection, which discusses these issues, is based on two years of intensive fieldwork and intermittent follow-up contact in a home for the aged in Canada.

ON HOUSEWIFE ANTHROPOLOGY:[1]
THE STIGMA OF STAYING HOME

As an anthropologist who was officially equipped to enter another culture in the early 1970s, I suddenly came to the realization that I was hopelessly fascinated with my own, a stigma I have never quite lived down. And because of this attitude among their colleagues, there is sometimes a tendency for urban anthropologists to overcompensate. While my colleagues can produce yet another boring genealogical study of a preliterate culture, an urban fieldworker is more likely to turn to a more bizarre substantive topic—as evidenced, for example, in anthropologist Ester Newton's sensational study of female impersonators in America, *Mothercamp* (1972). Of course, the basis of the stigma is the notion that it is more adventurous, and indeed more difficult, to do fieldwork in a foreign culture. If we were to take this notion to its absurd conclusion, it would mean that anthropology is more difficult than sociology. Obviously, the issue is not that simple. There are both advantages and disadvantages involved in working in one's own milieu. While the positive (easy) aspects of doing fieldwork at home are obvious, little attention has been directed to the negative, or difficult, side of doing fieldwork in semifamiliar settings. The importance of this fact for role maintenance is obvious. Not only do we tend to take it for granted that fieldwork is relatively static, but we also tend to assume that role maintenance is less dynamic in familiar settings. But as this selection will attempt to demonstrate, role maintenance may be even more precarious for the fieldworker at home. For one thing, it is more difficult for home fieldworkers to keep the lines drawn between their research and their personal lives. Their participant observer roles are constantly intermingling in an exaggerated form vis-à-vis the situation in foreign milieus.

FIELDWORK SCHIZOPHRENIA

Aside from the obvious lack of status and the exotic aura associated with those who returned from more glamorous sections of the globe, accompanied by bizarre artifacts ranging from woven ponchos to hash pipes (all I had to show for my efforts was one potholder and two mosaic tile ashtrays from the senior citizen gift ship), the urban fieldworker faces special problems. The first of these is the methodological paradox of studying subcultures in our own society that are familiar and foreign at the same time. Whereas we go to a foreign culture with a more or less complete assumption of relativist rhetoric, and so are quite prepared to find things different, even strange, in our own society things may be just as strange but we are ill prepared. For example, many of the people in the senior citizens home spoke languages that I did not understand, and others were unintelligible due to strokes or senility.

Another feature of doing fieldwork at home is a perpetual state of schizophrenia. Whereas my colleague in Tanzania definitely undergoes a more dramatic form of culture shock (although, as I have tried to suggest, it is sometimes more shocking to find out that our neighbours are not as they seem to be), once this transition is made, the traditional fieldworker can settle somewhat comfortably into the new culture. Still, it must be emphasized that one should never become too comfortable—that is, "go native"—this is the most heinous of fieldwork sins. In the case of fieldwork at home, however, the researcher is constantly darting back and forth between one world and another. In my case, fieldwork schizophrenia involved the unusual world of a senior citizens home and my more usual downtown social milieu in which I barely see old people from day to day. While this shuttling process has certain methodological advantages over those of my colleagues in other cultures, it is extremely emotionally stressful. The energy involved in switching cultures daily is exhausting. From time to time I actually forgot where I was, who I was, and what I was doing. The transition period—a sort of daily rite of passage—involved getting into my car each morning to drive up the street where the home was located. This drive enabled me to prepare myself psychologically for entering the world of the total institution. More importantly, it prepared me to enter the world of the decrepit, partially mobile, and hard of hearing. Although I consciously refused to engage in the baby talk or other strange speech intonations that frequently accompany working with the aged, I am sure that I persisted in talking too loud at the end of the fieldwork day. My husband reminded me of this fact from time to time with a polite: "Why are you screaming at me?" Who would argue that the culture I studied was not exotic?

ROLES WITHIN ROLES: FIELDWORK IN ALTERED STATES

As any ethnographer knows, upon entering the field one may find a variety of roles, informal or formal, which allow for comfortable absorption into a social setting. And it is a matter of no small significance which one you choose. Junker (1960) presents a neat typology of fieldwork roles which reflect varying degrees of involvement in the milieu under study. He refers to the complete observer, the participant observer, the complete participant, and the observer participant. Most writers, like Junker himself, consider these roles from the perspective of rapport with informants and information retrieval. It is equally important, however, to consider the consciousness—the intellectual-emotional frame—of the fieldworker. Fieldwork in different structural positions in a single milieu changes the perceptual and emotional frame of the researcher in a dramatic way. The following is an attempt to document such variations and their implications for the field experience.

PHASE I: PARTICIPANT OBSERVER— THE GIRL IN THE PINK SMOCK

I became familiar with the home for the aged through a public relations tour. My grandmother had come into town for a visit, and because she is active in a local nursing home she was interested in taking a tour. I was immediately struck with its research possibilities and made an appointment with the public relations office to discuss it further. The fact that such an office even existed reflects the ease with which I was able to enter the fieldwork setting. The home was ripe for study. The cooperation I received throughout my stay there was overwhelming. While this is not uncommon for many facilities, this particular one has such an excellent reputation in the geriatric field that it had nothing to hide. Many people seemed to forget that I was actually an outsider, an anthropological observer. In short, I was not covert, but neither was I really overt in my research role.

At the suggestion of the public relations officer, I became a volunteer worker. This tactic allowed me an official role at the home and one that was explicitly visible in the form of a pink volunteer smock, complete with name embroidered on the left-hand breast pocket. However, it should be noted that I took this role not to disguise the fact that I was doing research but merely to downplay my voyeur status. This would be less plausible in a foreign setting. Since no one likes being observed in a blatant way, I preferred not to call attention to my ambiguous role. I also avoided taking notes at programs and entered into activities instead. Every hour or so, I sat in a lobby or washroom to jot down notes. However, to some extent this volunteer role backfired. Because most people viewed me as a volunteer worker, I frequently acted like one and gradually absorbed many features of the "do-gooder" volunteer role. Some of these, such as the paternalistic aspects of volunteering, were personally alienating, yet it was difficult to resist the pink smock world view by which I was surrounded. As proponents of the Chicago school suggest, "You are as others see you." Secondly, while the pink smock allowed me inconspicuous loitering and access to a wide range of institutional life, it also made me public property. Residents feel, and rightly so, that they can make almost any demand of a volunteer worker—and they did. Although such tasks frequently kept me away from other activities that I wanted to observe, it also helped assuage my guilt.

Ethnographic exploitation—no small issue in the anthropological literature—was compensated for by the many service hours I donated to the home. I got constant feedback on this matter—how wonderful it was that a young, educated person like myself was willing to give up so much time to help the elderly. But various members of the home with whom I had less direct contact (maintenance, dietary, etc.) may well have wondered what on earth I was doing there. For one thing, most volunteers do not work five days a week, as I sometimes did. More importantly, why wasn't I in school or working? As a young person (age twenty-six), I was quite distinct from most of the volunteer population, which consists of women over forty. In fact, I was in an age range more compatible with social workers, and I was frequently identified as one of them. This perception was perpetuated by the fact that my pink smock arrived late (nearly six weeks after I began fieldwork), and by that time many first impressions were already established. Throughout my stay, some people saw me as a volunteer worker and others as a social worker, but only a few seemed to maintain consistent cognizance of my true identity (graduate student) and observer role. I should add here that the fact that I belonged to the ethnic group served by the home was also a factor in my speedy assimilation. I couldn't help but pass in spite of myself. And my charitable (nonexploitive) role was well institutionalized.

In spite of all of this, however, I continued to feel marginal, and this probably affected my fieldwork. I was not especially assertive in asking questions and investigating. Moreover, I frequently used my passivity as a strategic device to avoid being too closely affiliated with any one group at the home and thus biasing my research. My feeling of marginality stemmed from the fact that I did not quite identify with the do-gooder role, though it was convenient (and I was "doing good"). While this discrepancy was mainly in my own mind, it weakened my position by accentuating the contrast between my self-perception and my social perception. My attempts to use my passivity and marginality to neutralize my bias at the home were not especially successful, however. As in many social service settings, various professional groups tend to stake out claims in the treatment process and segregate themselves from one another. Partly because of my age, initial lack of uniform, and other visible characteristics, I was generally regarded by most medical staff who knew nothing about me as a social worker. Since nurses and social workers do not have particularly close relationships at the home, this produced a definite bias in my research. To them, I was too easily identified as an insider, but not one of their particular subgroup. Looking back, I might have done better to play up my observer status with this particular segment of the home population. To them an observer might have been preferable to another social worker.

One of the most fascinating aspects of this stage of my research was that although most social workers knew why I was there, they seemed to prefer to forget. They immediately incorporated me into the setting. One poignant incident occurred when I was chatting with a social worker and a colleague joined us and began to talk about very confidential matters pertaining to a resident. Halfway through her story, she suddenly remembered that I was really an outsider and said, "Oh, I forget—I shouldn't be saying this in front of you." In other words, people are eager to find ways to take you in—if you agree. I remember wondering whether to remind her that I should not be privy to such information. I felt guilty listening, but it would have been hard to walk away.

Ironically, some professional social workers had more difficulty being accepted by their clients than I did. This is largely the result of perception of ethnic identity. Social workers who were clearly not of the "appropriate" background were initially regarded with some suspicion. (If residents were unsure, they had little hesitation asking, "Are you _____?") On the other hand, once residents decided that they liked a particular social worker, this person was quickly adopted by the ethnic group as one of their own. They might even refer to one of these ethnic outsiders as an insider—even though this was fiction. This process is pervasive in anthropological literature, which suggests that in most societies new persons are regarded as fitting in to one of two categories—kin or enemies. From the residents' point of view, my ethnic affiliation was more significant than my professional role or lack of view; thus, I was an insider by definition. I was virtually always treated as a participant by the elderly population. In fact, one of my greatest difficulties in doing research was extricating myself from the participant role vis-à-vis residents. It was difficult for me to ask them certain kinds of questions because I was usually treated as an official representative of the home who wanted to hear the party line.

TRANSITION PERIOD: FLOATING

As I got to know the home, physically and administratively and became increasingly comfortable socially, I became less involved in formal programs and activities and instead investigated on my own. The staff also used me for special tasks, such as supervising large fieldtrips and working with problem individuals such as stroke victims. I also ran my own program—the Women's Discussion Group. This stage was also problematic. I was free to do as I wished, but I always felt somewhat confined by the social work perspective. While I was able to take advantage of a wider variety of activities in this role, including important staff conferences, I was also starting to feel more and more responsible. I began to feel increasingly uncomfortable observing and increasingly obliged to "work." It was during this time that I found myself sliding more and more into the role of social worker, whether I liked it or not. This prepared the way for the second stage of my research.

PHASE II: OBSERVER PARTICIPANT: GOING PROFESSIONAL

After I'd been at the home for over a year and had even withdrawn for a brief time to write and maintain some psychic breathing space, an unusual opportunity arose. I had become friendly with the supervisor of one of the programs, and when a temporary position became available, he offered me a summer job. The agreement was that my schedule would be somewhat flexible, to allow me time to write up my notes. As it turned out, however, the real problem involved my role. As I got more and more involved in the social work job, I found it difficult to continue with my dissertation. *I was clearly approaching the role of complete participant.*

Even though my observation activities continued, and even though I still perceived myself as an outsider, I also found it difficult to transcend my role as social worker because this was my official social position. I suppose that this period was somewhat analogous to the anthropological notion of "going native," but not entirely. The fieldworker who goes native in a foreign culture does not have to confront the magnitude of the change until a return from the field, when reverse culture shock sets in. In contrast, the fieldworker in semifamiliar settings is continuously cognizant of two cultures. This dichotomy presents two related problems.

From the perspective of being a good participant—in this case, being a good social worker—it was difficult for me to give my full attention to residents when my thoughts were sometimes elsewhere. The home was a large, complex institution full of fascinating data. It was even difficult to focus on specific issues or themes, and it was at least a year before I was able to narrow down my thesis topic. As involved as I became in home life, I never lost sight of the fact that I was ultimately an observer, an outsider, a temporary member. This was especially reflected in my lack of ego investment at the home. I did not have to worry about salary level, advancement, or even being fired. On the other hand, in many ways this detachment allowed me to be a more effective social worker. Certainly some supervisors and administrators viewed me in this light and treated me as a sort of objective observer—detached but sensitive to home issues— a confidant or mother confessor. It was not unusual for staff to express to me their frustrations with aspects of the home. Similarly, I was expected to play the role of disinterested listener, which was wholly compatible with my real role as observer. I found myself nodding politely, head cocked to one side, taking copious mental notes. (It would have been insulting to take notes openly at such times.) On one occasion I had a spontaneous phone call with a top home administrator which turned out to be the best encounter of my field experience. Afraid I would never hold on to it, I grabbed my tape recorder as soon as we hung up and spewed forth for half an hour. In short, I was always doing two things at once— social work and social analysis—and the two were sometimes complementary and sometimes antithetical.

At times, I felt more than a little guilty about the fact that I was listening to people's problems with an ulterior motive. While my detached role was necessary, and may have even been helpful at times in terms of my contribution, it certainly meant that my perspective was quite different from that of an ordinary participant. Perhaps all this means is that participant observation, even in one's own culture and even when it favors participation, is never fully synonymous with being an ordinary member of a social group.

Second, as a social scientist, but one not trained in the helping professions per se, I developed my own ideas about programming and policy with the aged. But being an outsider, I did not often feel inclined to express myself among professionals, although I frequently felt critical of home practices. For example, some social workers tended to cajole or push residents into activities, which I believed was wrong. However, I was aware of the fact that my opinion, unlike those of my colleagues, was based on limited practical experience. Similar to the role of volunteer worker, which put me into the unwanted position of a do-gooder, the role of social worker was helpful in understanding the complex bureaucracy that is part of any institutional setting. Many of the practices I found ridiculous were now part of my job. I suppose I developed a certain empathy with social workers, while at the same time becoming frustrated with their acceptance of the status quo. But I certainly began to appreciate the difficulties involved in instituting change in a large organization. Since I had been a professional student until this time, my field experience instructed me in the wider ways of postindustrial bureaucracy.

I should add here that since I have left the home, it has become easier for me to see its strengths and weaknesses, and I am generally able to defend the institution, at least in principle. While I might be critical with other insiders, I identify with the home vis-à-vis the outside world. This too is an aspect of the participant role. I tend to feel protective about the home staff and sympathetic to their frustration with the wider society with which they must deal and which understands very little about the intricacies of total institutions. In anthropology this is referred to as "fission and fusion"; I disidentify with the home when I am there and identify with it vis-à-vis the rest of the world. This fact seems to express the participant/observer dichotomy.

While much has been written about this dichotomy, it must be emphasized that the conflict can never be resolved. In fact, it is the discrepancy itself which stimulates ethnographic reporting. And as this brief discussion has attempted to show, the discrepancy is heightened in semifamiliar settings. Because others in the social milieu may be convinced that we are one of them when detachment is necessary, field research may be hindered. And at the same time, the ease with which we can pass in our own society tends to exacerbate guilt about ethical and moral issues surrounding voyeurism and exploitation. And lastly, the schizophrenic life style of the fieldworker who does research at home may be methodologically useful but emotionally draining. While introspection is useful, too much of it is crippling. And fieldwork in semifamiliar settings demands repeated cycles of cultural emersion and withdrawal. Perhaps I did no more work than my colleagues in Tanzania, but I certainly felt that I did. As the Queen said to Alice, this is a fast country, and you have to run as fast as you can just to stay in one place.

Notes

1. I am definitely not responsible for coining this term. In fact, it originated with one of my professors, who thought rather disparagingly of those of us who wanted to undertake a P.O. project at home.

References

BOWEN, ELENORE. *Return to Laughter*. Garden City, New York: Doubleday, 1964.
JUNKER, BUFORD, H. *Field-Work: An Introduction to the Social Sciences*. Chicago: University of Chicago Press, 1960.
NEWTON, ESTER. *Mothercamp: Female Impersonators in America*. Englewood Cliffs, New Jersey: Prentice-Hall, 1972.
POWDERMAKER, HORTENSE. *Strangers and Friends: The Way of an Anthropologist*. New York: Norton, 1966.

Keeping in Touch: Maintaining Contact with Stigmatized Subjects

BRIAN MILLER   *University of Alberta*
LAUD HUMPHREYS   *Pitzer College*

INTRODUCTION

In the course of dissertation research, both of the authors conducted lengthy interviews with separate samples of fifty men, all of whom had been identified as engaging in homosexual behavior and a majority of whom had experienced both heterosexual marriage and parenthood.[1] Miller studied gay fathers and Humphreys investigated homosexual acts in public restrooms. There were, however, many dissimilarities between the two groups of subjects. The first, for example, shared a homosexual identification, whereas many of the other set steadfastly avoided such an identity and were even unaware that the researcher had observed their involvement in homosexual acts. The authors nevertheless found similar advantages in maintaining contact with many of their respondents and encountered comparable difficulties in keeping in touch.

Several writers of monographs and methods texts discuss the problems and strategies of terminating relationships with respondents. As yet, however, none has dealt with the contingencies of maintaining contact with subjects. Both Bogdan and Taylor (1975) and Weinberg and Williams (1972) note that investigators never wholly complete the cessation stage of research. Weinberg and Williams, however, say that it is because researchers never escape their research reputation; and Bogdan and Taylor credit the lack of cessation to the likelihood that one study may lead to further research. We have been unable to find any methodology in the sociological literature for purposeful continuation of interaction with respondents after termination of the formal interview stage. This selection addresses the issue of contact maintenance with research subjects.

After discussing each of our projects, we shall detail some of the advantages of keeping in touch with respondents. For example, the methodology of triangulation is greatly enhanced by the maintenance of contact. Indeed, later events in the respondents' lives may reveal consequences of their behavioral patterns and the impact of the study on their life styles, and suggest unanticipated implications for further research. We then explore strategies for maintaining contact and possible negative implications of such extenuated study for subjects, as well as several disadvantages for investigators. Finally, we discuss the impact of the research process on the lives of both respondents and researchers.

SUMMARY OF THE GAY FATHER RESEARCH

From 1976 to 1978, Miller studied the life styles of gay fathers (1978a). The purpose was to determine how these men construct a reality to solve the seemingly contradictory statuses of homosexual and father. Audio-recorded, semistructured, depth interviews lasting up to four hours were conducted with fifty of these men. Respondents were located through multiple-source, snowball samples in large and small cities in Canada and the United States. Since the study was exploratory, the broadest range of gay fathers was sampled. They manifested many degrees of overtness, a variety of ages, different living and child-custody arrangements, and a broad range of occupations representing a spectrum of socioeconomic backgrounds. The interviews probed for information concerning the men's family of orientation, family of procreation, and domestic, career, and social relationships. The men completed scales and answered questions that determined the mix of their homosexual to heterosexual behavior and fantasy responses, as well as the level of their social and occupational resources.

Additional details and inferences about life style were recorded, where possible, by interviews in the father's residence and by interviewing wives, children, and gay lovers. Interaction with significant others and peers was also noted at parties, cruising spots, gay baths, and bars. All respondents were informed prior to the interview about the nature and purposes of the research, and all were sent copies of the articles published from the study.

SUMMARY OF THE RESEARCH ON TEAROOM SEX

Humphreys' research investigated impersonal sexual encounters in public restrooms ("tearooms," as they are known to participants). It involved both observations of the interaction in those settings and later interviews with a sample of fifty men observed in the restrooms. Conducted in the St. Louis metropolitan area from 1965 to 1968, the study involved a combination of several research strategies: participant observation, archival data, the observation of physical traces (Webb et al., 1966), systematic observations, structured interviews, and depth interviews (Humphreys, 1975:26–44).

Observing the sexual encounters in their natural setting required Humphreys to assume the role of a lookout in these public facilities, a strategy which some have criticized as "disguised observation," in that he was unable to make his identity as a sociologist known to the participants. His sampling technique involved tracing automobile license numbers in order to locate the names and residences of the men who engaged in these furtive encounters. When administering interview schedules to respondents in their homes, he explained only that they had been chosen as part of a sample of men for a "social health survey" of the community. Those interviewed were not informed of the true purpose of the study, and the researcher took precautions to alter his appearance in order to avoid recognition as the lookout who had observed them in acts of fellatio a year earlier. The ethics of such subterfuge have been criticized and defended in subsequent publications (Glazer, 1972:160–164; Humphreys, 1975:167–232). At issue in this selection, however, are only the depth interviews and subsequent contacts with a dozen "cooperating respondents," all of whom were fully informed of the researcher's identity and purposes of the study.

Although participant observation and structured interviews provided vital information on the structured interaction of impersonal sex in public settings, along with a general profile of those who engage in such behavior, the study's richest data were provided by depth interviews with the fully informed subjects. It is the continuation of observations, correspondence, and conversation with these men subsequent to completion of the project's final interview stage that will be discussed throughout this selection.

WHY KEEP IN TOUCH?

At least three advantages accrue from keeping in touch: triangulation is enhanced, a longitudinal dimension is added to the data, and new areas of research are fostered. Triangulation is a method that seeks ancillary data to corroborate statements made by the focus population. Primarily, it is a means of testing the internal validity of data. Triangulating methods enable the researcher to check the candidness of respondents' replies, illuminate various perceptions of events, and offer competing interpretations of respondents' worlds.

Such safeguarding of data validity is particularly important in qualitiative research, where subjects, lacking anonymity, may engage in deception. Wiseman (1970), for example, studying skid row alcoholics, found marked variations between self-reports of the men's behavior and their court records.

By stressing the importance of triangulation, we do not mean to imply that respondents intentionally set out to deceive. Although most people have fronts, we are less certain than Douglas (1976) that subjects deliberately intend to hoodwink the researcher. Most discrepancies we uncovered through triangulation stemmed not from deliberate falsehoods but rather from omissions and differing perceptions of events. Often, these differing perceptions are exacerbated by the passage of time, as Bogdan and Taylor note: "Contradictions in a subject's perspectives should not be a source of concern. People can honestly see and feel different things at different times" (1975:122).

Few people possess such great powers of recollection as to preclude the need for further substantiation. It is common knowledge, expressed in a familiar parlor game, that different witnesses provide varying accounts of what they have seen or experienced. An example of differing perceptions appears in Klockars (1974). Vincent, a professional fence, claims that the jail term he served was like a vacation. Vincent's wife, however, said that he was severely depressed in the months he spent there. Klockars notes the likelihood that both assessments are accurate in part.

Many accounts that appear as deliberate attempts to fool the researcher may actually stem from the respondent's self-deception. Keeping in touch via triangulation reveals this. One respondent in Miller's study, for example, expressed deep concern that his wife never learn of his homosexual orientation. On the basis of an interview, this man would appear to be circumspect in his nonmarital sexuality. Personal observation, on the other hand, indicates that this subject is quite daring in his pursuit of homosexual outlets. For instance, after dining with the researcher, the respondent returned to the restaurant to proposition a waiter, not realizing that the waiter was an acquaintance who subsequently reported this indiscretion to the researcher. Another respondent claimed that his children were unaware of his homosexual relationships. Later, his son, taking a course from the researcher, recounted in his journal discussions between himself and a sibling of their father's homosexuality.

"Between-method triangulation" (Denzin, 1978:302) is a relatively common practice among field researchers, even if, like Klockars, they do not call it such. Seldom can ethnographic triangulation be confined to a predetermined research schedule. Often the corroborating data are not immediately available or appear later through serendipitous circumstances.

Our second reason for maintaining contact is in the interest of research economy. Providing a longitudinal dimension is especially important when subjects are relatively covert and inaccessible. Efficient deployment of research energies demands that the extraordinary time and resources required to obtain samples and gain the trust of stigmatized persons be balanced by expansion of research production and significance. Such samples, in our opinion, should be studied over extended time periods in order to maximize knowledge gained from the great investment of effort in developing initial relationships with respondents.

There are a number of examples in the literature of such increased returns through longitudinal investigation. Certainly, Liebow (1967), Polsky (1967), and Whyte (1943) set standards for research over extended time periods. Carrier (1976 and in private communication) reported that be maintained contact with 20 percent of his Mexican homosexual males for a decade. The resulting research has set a standard for cross-cultural analysis in the field. Feinbloom et al. (1976) followed up a sample of male-to-female transsexuals and found that, over time, they developed a feminist ideology. Garfinkel's follow-up (1967) of another transsexual, Agnes, led him to reconsider his original conclusions. Similarly rich data might have resulted had Cork (1969) maintained contact with her sample of alcoholics' children.

Finally, maintaining contact facilitates expansion of research into previously neglected areas. Subsequent to interviews with gay fathers, Miller interviewed a number of their wives and children. Research among these tangential respondents not only added a great deal to understanding of the target population but also led to research papers on the new samples (Miller, 1979a, b, 1980) and the opening of fresh opportunities for investigation. Both authors have been introduced to the study of crime victimization (Miller and Humphreys, 1980) and cultural impact on identity formation (Humphreys and Miller, 1980) through data gained from extended contact with their original respondents. Had we said goodbye after the initial interviews with the subjects, it is unlikely that we could have done direct research in these related areas.

PROFITABLE DATA GAINED

In the research projects under discussion, postinterview correspondence, telephone contacts, newspaper accounts, and personal encounters were found to yield rich data on the development of moral careers, criminal victimization, political involvement, and details overlooked by the subjects during interviews. Humphreys, for example, committed the names of his fifty respondents to memory. By careful reading of local newspapers during the year following the interviews, he discovered a number of interesting facts about the tearoom participants. One, for instance, became a candidate for political office for a rightist party and another assumed a position of leadership in a League for Decent Literature, adding support to the researcher's conclusions about the political conservatism of men involved in public restroom sex. The propensity of the more covert tearoom respondents for criminal victimization became evident when, through newspaper accounts, it was learned that two members of Humphreys' original sample were murdered by the same offender under similar circumstances.

Contacts subsequent to the depth interviews disclose that 12 percent of Miller's respondents have become active in gay organizations. Of the twelve cooperating respondents in Humphreys' study, a third joined such organizations within four years of the initial interviews and simultaneously terminated their impersonal tearoom activity. Miller was able to follow respondents through attempted suicides, therapy, divorces, the improvement of body image, and the strain of informing children of their homosexuality. Data on their moral careers would have been largely impossible without this longitudinal contact.

One-shot measurement techniques allow, at best, for analyses of correlation. With longitudinal data, on the other hand, it is possible to observe causal relationships in process. Consequences of behavioral patterns are revealed. Gay fathers who ceased impersonal homosexual activity in favor of a gay love relationship were shortly thereafter observed to terminate heterosexual marriage. Comparably, Humphreys observed a tendency of respondents to change political and social views after they turned from tearoom sex to more affectional homosexual relationships.

STRATEGIES FOR MAINTAINING CONTACT

The quality of data gathered through contact maintenance differed in accordance with the relative geographic diffusion of the two samples and with strategies we employed for keeping in touch. Contact with gay fathers, for instance, was maintained by mailing notes of appreciation to respondents and by supplying each with copies of research publications. Since subjects were scattered across the North American continent, regular correspondence and phone calls, more than personal visits, supplemented these procedures. Such formal and informal contact strategies helped us keep in touch with virtually all respondents.

The tearoom patricipants, all of whom initially resided in one metropolitan area, received no formal communication. Instead, contact was sustained with the cooperating respondents by means of telephone and personal meetings, and all were involved in reactive research through solicitation of their comments on the resulting dissertation. Although names of other participants in impersonal sex were committed to memory, the list of respondents was destroyed upon completion of the study. For this latter group, therefore, newspapers were the principal source of postinterview data.

Subsequent data on tearoom respondents tended to be of a newsworthy or "running record" variety, while those gathered from the homosexual fathers were of the "private record" type (Webb et al., 1966:53–111). Only the cooperating respondents in the tearoom study provided personal material on career processes and reaction to the research intrusion comparable to self-reported, postinterview data gathered in the research on gay fathers.

Many respondents became friends of the researchers. Visiting and vacationing with them over twelve years after initial contact, Humphreys still has correspondence and meetings with 25 percent of his cooperating respondents. These contacts provide observational data to accompany the archival material discussed above.

CAUTIONS ABOUT KEEPING IN TOUCH

Continued contact with the covert respondents is more problematic than with the relatively overt research subjects. The possibility exists that families and friends of covert respondents might discover their secret as a result of longitudinal interaction with researchers. To date, this has not happened in our research, perhaps because of the precautions we have observed. For example, respondents who are unable to receive mail from Miller at their home or office addresses for fear of discovery are contacted through intermediaries willing to forward correspondence. We have minimized the chance of accidental disclosure by urging respondents to terminate contact with the researcher if they fear any danger of exposure.

One risk of keeping in touch with highly discreditable subjects is indicated by Humphreys' experience following the conclusion of his tearoom research. Political and personal tensions in the sociology department at his university erupted in a flurry of fists, charges, countercharges, administrative investigations, and resignations. The research for which Humphreys had just been awarded his doctorate was involved in that controversy, the Chancellor of Washington University charging that, in observing and failing to report more than 200 acts of fellatio, the researcher had served as an accomplice to the acts. Ultimately, banner headlines across the front page of a St. Louis newspaper proclaimed: "W.U. Furor! Homosexual Study Involved."

Not surprisingly, several of the cooperating respondents phoned to ask if they were in danger of exposure. Having already destroyed all tapes, notes, lists of names, and identifying tags on interview schedules, Humphreys assured the men that their reputations were in no danger and urged them to pass the word around the city's public restrooms. A lawyer contacted the state attorney general, who assured him that no charges would be pressed, subpoenas filed, or testimony demanded of the researcher.

Other respondents, who were not aware of the true purpose of the tearoom research or of how they had been added to the sample, may have experienced alarm. Having been told only that they were part of a "social health survey" (which Humphreys was also supervising at the time and from which he gathered a control sample), they could always claim to wives or others who knew of their being interviewed that they were members of the control group. On the other hand, the researcher had formed friendships with several cooperating respondents and had even met a few of the wives. These relationships enabled him to triangulate data and add a great deal to his understanding of the participants in impersonal sex. Continued association with these persons, once the research had become an issue for press coverage and community gossip, threatened to expose these subjects to embarrassing questions from friends and family members. Because the researcher had lost his job as a result of the controversy, however, it became necessary for him to move to another city. Contact with most of the cooperating respondents was terminated by phone calls, but several participants still continued to keep in touch. All continuing contacts were initiated by them through visits, letters, and long-distance calls.

What we have been discussing in regard to Humphreys' study is that the stigma attached to a research project and an investigator may rub off on respondents. In contrast to research that terminates prior to any dissemination of findings, longitudinal research in which contacts are maintained poses the possibility of stigma contamination. Colleagues, aware that the investigator is studying a disvalued population, occasionally assume that unknown persons seen with the researcher are interviewees. For example, one associate, observing Miller with two men, a respondent and his lover, approached and said, "Don't tell me these are gay fathers!" Other than this single incident, however, there is no indication that respondents suffered exposure or stigmatization as a result of association with the research.

RESEARCH IMPACT ON RESPONDENTS

We have already mentioned that postinterview contacts with respondents show that in-depth interviews affect the lives of subjects. Many have poured out their concerns by long-distance telephone calls and correspondence, along with the ever-present comments about intensive self-examination and reassessment of life histories following the interviews. One of Miller's subjects commented: "The chance of telling my story to you helped me put it all together. That afternoon, I faced the contradictions in my life for the first time." For many, the interview ended a lonely period of isolation and the feeling of being the only gay father in the world. Information given by Miller after the interview put some in touch with gay father organizations. Several wives were assisted by the researcher to form a self-help rap group for spouses of gay men.

Reading products of the study also affects respondents. One man Miller kept in touch with made the following statement in a letter:

> I just read the article you sent of your study. Wow, did I see myself! It's like you peeked at my diary or read my mind. Scary. I'm surprised I was so open in the interview. I'm not usually the type that bares my heart or talks about my sex life. I don't know how you got it out of me. . . . I loved reading about the other gay fathers' situations too. It's a relief to know there are more in my shoes. I'm going to give some of their suggestions a whirl and see how they work for me.

Humphreys was approached by a familiar person during refreshments following a speech he had presented in Los Angeles. "Do you remember me?", the man asked. "I'm [Doug], one of the tearoom gays in your St. Louis study." During the lengthy conversation that followed, the former respondent said:

> You know, that research really changed my life. I had a terrible opinion of myself in those days—almost got married to escape myself and the gay world. Then I read the book you wrote, recognized myself, and never went back to a tearoom again! I realized it was really dumb and self-defeating—a dead end. So I got involved in gay liberation, went back to school, became an accountant, found a lover, and moved out here. God knows where I'd be if you hadn't seen me sucking cock in that tearoom!

Another respondent in that study, the model for the self-hating, conservative "Karl" in *Tearoom Trade* (1975), phoned the researcher years later from a Midwestern city. He, too, had become moderately active in the movement, had grown a beard, and had become an antiwar liberal. "I couldn't stand the portrait of me in that book," he reported. Another cooperating respondent went back to college and graduated, worked on a master's degree, and has become a clergyman. Only by keeping in touch can the investigator assess the impact of research on respondents.

IMPACT ON RESEARCHERS

The study of stigmatized, socially oppressed individuals brings researchers into significant contact with persons who, in many cases, suffer from acute or chronic depression, feel trapped, and need desperately to find a neutral listener. It was not uncommon for Miller's respondents to break into tears during the interviews. Both authors found it impossible to do more than two interviews per day and, in nearly every instance, reacted to interviews with emotional and physical exhaustion. A major part of this postinterview reaction was an awareness of the ethical and intellectual responsibilities of dealing fairly and objectively with respondents who were often emotionally fragile.

Such a drain on the energies of researchers is compounded by keeping in touch with respondents. When there is no follow-up, no contacts or letters subsequent to interviews, students of human behavior probably remain blissfully ignorant of the results of their obtrusive research methods. It is serious enough to be instrumental in the opening up of old wounds and the disclosure of buried motivations, but the blood from those wounds continues to drain into letters and midnight phone calls. The valuable knowledge to be gained from maintaining contact includes information that can be painful to a concerned researcher.

On balance, the authors believe that the rewards of maintaining contact, except in those cases where it poses a threat to respondents, far out-weigh the costs. Many of our findings, not to mention ideas for future research, would have been lost had we not kept in touch. In addition, as evidence accumulates that the research impact on the respondents' lives is positive and constructive, it produces satisfactions for the investigator that exceed the rewards of publication and professional recognition.

Notes

1. This is a revised version of a paper presented at the meeting of The Pacific Sociological Association, Anaheim, Calif., April 1979.

References

BOGDAN, R., and S. TAYLOR. *Introduction to Qualitative Research Methods.* New York: Wiley, 1975.

CARRIER, J. "Cultural Factors Affecting Urban Mexican Male Homosexual Behavior." *Archives of Sexual Behavior,* 5 (1976), 103–124.

CORK, M. *The Forgotten Children.* Don Mills, Ontario: General Publishing, 1969.

DOUGLAS, J. *Investigative Social Research: Individual and Team Field Research.* Beverly Hills: Sage Publications, 1976.

FEINBLOOM, D., M. FLEMING, V. KIJEWSKI, and M. SCHULTER. "Lesbian/Feminist Orientation among Male-to-female Transsexuals." *Journal of Homosexuality* 2 (1976), 59–71.

GARFINKEL, H. *Studies in Ethnomethodology.* Englewood Cliffs, N.J.: Prentice-Hall, 1967.

GLAZER, M. *The Research Adventure: Promise and Problems of Fieldwork.* New York: Random House, 1972.

HUMPHREYS, L. *Tearoom Trade: Impersonal Sex in Public Places.* Enlarged ed. Chicago: Aldine, 1975.

HUMPHREYS, L., and B. MILLER. "Identities in the Emerging Gay Culture." In J. Marmoor, ed., *Homosexual Behavior: A Modern Reappraisal.* New York: Basic Books, 1980.

KLOCKARS, C.B. *The Professional Fence.* New York: Macmillan, 1974.

LIEBOW, E. *Tally's Corner.* Boston: Little, Brown, 1967.

MILLER, B. "Adult Sexual Resocialization: Adjustments toward a Stigmatized Identity." *Alternative Lifestyles,* 1 (1978a), 207–234.

MILLER, B. "Stigma Contamination: Attitudes and Adjustments of Women Married to Gay Men." Paper presented at the meetings of the Canadian Psychological Association. Ottawa, Canada: June 1978b.

MILLER, B. "Unpromised Paternity: Lifestyles of Gay Fathers." In M. Levine, ed., *Gay Men: The Sociology of Male Homosexuality.* New York: Harper & Row, 1979a.

MILLER, B. "Gay Fathers and Their Children." *Family Coordinator* 28 (1979b).

MILLER, B. "Gay Men's Relationships with Women." In D. David and R. Brannon, eds., *The 49% Majority: The Male Gender Role*. 2nd ed. Reading, Mass.: Addison-Wesley, 1980.

MILLER, B., and L. HUMPHREYS. "Lifestyle as a Neglected Variable in Criminal Victimization." Paper presented at the meetings of the Sociology of Lifestyles Conference. Los Angeles: September 1978.

MILLER, B., and L. HUMPHREYS. "Marginality and violence: Lifestyle as a variable in victimization." *Qualitative Sociology* 3 (May, 1980).

POLSKY, N. *Hustlers, Beats, and Others*. Chicago: Aldine, 1969.

WEBB, E.J., D.T. CAMPBELL, R.D. SCHWARTZ, and L. SECHREST. Unobtrusive Measures: Nonreactive Research in the Social Sciences. Chicago: Rand McNally, 1966.

WEINBERG, M.S., and C.J. WILLIAMS. "Fieldwork among Deviants: Social Relations with Subjects and Others." In J. Douglas, ed., *Research on Deviance*. New York: Random House, 1972.

WHYTE, W.F. *Street Corner Society*. Chicago: University of Chicago Press, 1943.

WISEMAN, J. *Stations of the Lost: The Treatment of Skid Row Alcoholics*. Englewood Cliffs, N.J.: Prentice-Hall, 1970.

A Sociologist on Police Patrol

HAROLD E. PEPINSKY   *Indiana University*

In recent years in North America, there has been growing concern about social science researchers' "use of human subjects." The American Psychological Association long ago promulgated a professional code of ethics, including guidelines for the kind of relationship researchers were supposed to maintain with those they studied. Today, practically every social scientist who collects data from people—in the field as well as, for instance, in the laboratory—must file a statement of how the interests of those they plan to study will be safeguarded, and the statements must be approved by one or more review panels.

For all the concern over the quality of relations researchers establish and maintain with those they study, we researchers are just beginning to think through what our ethical responsibilities might be. The most pressing issue of the last several years—a concern that came to prominence after the police study described in this chapter was completed—is of whether "subjects" give "informed consent" to be studied. This in turn raises a larger, seldom addressed question: Whose interests is the researcher to serve while trying to maintain relations in the field—the interests of those providing the data or of others?

Like it or not, researchers like everyone have their personal biases. One very common bias among those who study issues of crime, deviance and social control is that they dislike the people they study. It is the problem that Alexander Liazos, in a widely read and reprinted 1972 *Social Problems* article on "The Poverty of the Sociology of Deviance: Nuts, Sluts, and Perverts," decried as a propensity for students of deviance to concentrate on collecting data on weird people whom the researchers implicitly look down upon.

One of the most difficult ethical problems confronting social scientists in the field is the potential for conflict between their obligations to help the people they study and their larger mission as scientists. Researchers in the field ask the people they observe to trust them, to open their lives to scrutiny and evaluation. Researchers owe the knowledge they gain to the people observed, and it would be ungrateful indeed for researchers to use that knowledge to attack or expose weaknesses or foibles of those who have provided the data.

On the other hand, a researcher may discover that the people being studied are engaged in what appears to be objectionable behavior. Moreover, in return for their trust, the people being studied may even ask the researcher to participate in or help cover up the wrongful activity. The moral dilemma this presents is especially strong if the people being studied, such as police officers, hold a public trust.

In the field of police research, many departments have learned to their chagrin that researchers who study their work will turn around and publish exposés of how poorly police are doing their jobs. Not surprisingly, many of these departments have become loath to let more researchers see what police do in the field. This makes issues of how or whether to establish and maintain relations with police in the field especially delicate.

This is the conflict I faced when I went into the field to study police behavior for my sociology dissertation. Here is an account of how I dealt with the conflict while trying to maintain helping relations with the police.

THE BEGINNING—GETTING ACQUAINTED

It was a bright, sunny day in March 1971, but I was nervous as I drove to the Model City Police Precinct Station in Minneapolis for my first ride-along. I felt the way I had the first time I got to the edge of a high diving tower. I was about to take a long plunge, and I was not so sure that I would be able to cope when I got to my destination. I had planned my research on how patrol officers decide whether to report offenses scrupulously. I wanted to find a connection between what happened on the street and what got into police crime statistics. I had an observation schedule to fill out each time the officers got a call to respond to just about anything except a traffic problem. The schedule contained eighty items describing everything from the time and place of the call, to how complainants, suspects, and witnesses looked and what they said, to characteristics of the officers and how they responded to the call. My hardest job so far had been to get permission to conduct the observation of the police. I had had to negotiate six months and had suffered a number of refusals before getting permission to ride along in this one precinct, which, happily for me, was the high-crime area of the city. I still had to get permission from each pair of officers I was to accompany for an eight-hour shift and was obliged to sign a waiver of liability for each shift I rode. I planned to pretest the observation schedule for ten patrols, revise it, and then gather data on seventy more patrols. Would any officers let me ride with them? Would I be able to fill out such a long schedule for each call? Would I get any meaningful data? I wondered and worried.

The first trick was getting in the door to the station house. It was locked, and the officer on desk duty sat behind a glass panel. Not that attacks were imminent, but the locked door symbolized the suspicion with which the police regarded outsiders. I would be told later by an officer that young police soon learned not to socialize with outsiders because of harassment they received. Officers are fun to be around for they are outspoken on political and social issues, but they do not trust lay citizens enough to get too close to them.

Some of the officers were in my criminology classes. (The officers in this precinct were an elite group, most of them young and many of them in college. They had volunteered to work in this new precinct, which had been set up with federal funding.) I had gotten especially friendly with one young sergeant. He welcomed me to the precinct and allayed my anxiety somewhat. He took me to roll call, in which the officers who were about to start a shift (in this case, the "middle watch," which lasted from 3 to 11 P.M.) sat in rows looking much like a high school class, listening to their sergeant read their assignments and give them any special instructions, such as concentrating on writing tickets for running red lights at particular intersections. I sat on the side. The sergeant introduced me. I could sense wariness in the looks I got from some of the officers. The sergeant asked for volunteers to take me along, and one pair of officers obliged. As it turned out, they had taken a number of previous ride-alongs and enjoyed introducing lay persons to the reality of the street as they saw it.

Before this and every other patrol, I had to sign a waiver of liability.

In one of my rare academic opportunities to use my legal training, I had composed my own waiver. It stated that I assumed the risk of any injury I might suffer from the officers' negligence. I signed the waiver and we walked out to begin the patrol, two neatly uniformed officers and a young, long-haired sociologist in a jacket and tie. I carried a valise containing my observation schedules, a clipboard, and a number of freshly sharpened pencils. I got in the back seat of the squad car behind the grill. The handles had been taken off the doors so that prisoners could not escape. One of the officers took a window crank out of the glove compartment and handed it to me. I eventually carried a crank in my valise (which I forgot to return to the police and have to this day). By inserting the crank into its aperture, I could roll down the window, reach out, and open the door from outside. I got to be pretty adept at this maneuver.

We had a call waiting for us. No sooner had the officer "riding shotgun" called the dispatcher to say "661 in service" than the dispatcher sent us to an address to "check neighbor trouble." I busily set about marking a schedule. Much to my relief, it proved simple to fill out during the response to the call. I did find some room for changes. The most important addition was suggested by a psychologist who was consulting with the department on training officers to handle domestic disturbances (family fights and quarrels). He suggested that I add an item describing the call as the dispatcher gave it. Here is an example of serendipity in research, for it turned out that the officers' offense reporting decisions were almost fully accounted for by what the dispatcher said in his call. If he named an offense in the call (e.g., "check a burglary"), the officers required only corroboration from a complainant in order to file a report. If the dispatcher did not name an offense in the call, even if a complainant subsequently indicated that an offense had occurred, the officers almost never filed a report. But I discovered this pattern only about halfway through the data collection, and I am getting ahead of my story.

After we had responded to the call, we had some leisure time. In fact, this was generally true of the officers I rode with. On the average, there would be only five or six calls during an eight-hour patrol, and the activity was just as likely to be light on a weekend night as at any other time. I was to discover that the biggest feature of a patrol was tedium. Most of the time, the officers had nothing to do. They would ride around aimlessly. Often they would stop for a cup of coffee. (They had portable radios if they got out of their cars and could answer calls from inside cafes.) If they got too bored, some hapless motorist—generally a youth or minority group person in an old, beat-up auto—would get stopped to see whether his (rarely her) license and registration were in good order and whether he had an arrest warrant outstanding. Indeed, the most common arrest was for failure to have paid a $3 parking ticket, for which the culprit would be taken to jail to be released after posting a $25 bond. Sometimes the officers would stop a suspicious-looking person who was walking down the street or through a yard, although I never saw any useful information come from this street questioning. Most of the time, though, the officers just rode around and chatted together on miscellaneous topics. It is small wonder that officers who ride in pairs are so outspoken; they have a lot of time to practice their skills.

During this first interlude, the officers wanted to know about me. Why was I doing the study? (My dissertation for my doctorate in sociology.) What was I studying? (How the police decided when to report offenses. Here I was assured, as I was repeatedly to be told, that officers exercised individual discretion and that I would find no system in their decisions.) But what did I expect to find?

This last question confronted me with my first ethical dilemma. On the one hand, I wanted to be as open as I could in order to earn the officers' trust. On the other hand, I did not want to be so specific about my expectations that I encouraged the officers simply to do what they thought I wanted and expected for my benefit. The first thing I emphasized was that I was doing the study precisely because I had no preconceived notion of the wrong and right ways to make the decisions. This was in fact the case. Then I showed them a copy of the observation schedule and pointed out the many items, emphasizing that I was collecting a lot of data because I had no idea of what to expect.

The officers pressed a little further. Surely I must have some idea of what I would find. I told them that there had been one prior study of offense reporting decisions, indicating that such things as wishes of the complainant and demeanor of suspects might enter into the decisions. I thought this was all the officers wanted to know, but I was mistaken. Later in the patrol, one of the officers, older than most in the precinct, after a traffic stop, asked me whether they had handled the matter correctly. Here I must admit to a little less than complete candor. I noticed that the car they had stopped was old and had been driven by an American Indian; this appeared to be the only reason that this driver rather than another had been stopped. But I told them that the response had looked all right to me. The officer stressed that whenever I had a criticism to offer, I should do so freely. I had doubts that open criticism would be well received, and a later experience on patrol confirmed this view.

On that subsequent patrol, I got into a discussion of school busing to achieve racial balance. My liberal thinking on the matter, which I expressed openly, was not taken well. The officers had worked hard to be able to buy homes in neighborhoods with good schools, one officer was angry over the possibility that a black student might touch his white daughter, and both officers thought it unfair for the poor to get a free ride while they had to work. I thought that we had had a restrained and interesting debate, but these officers refused to ride with me again. Some officers never took me with them. But before long, I had gotten friendly and relaxed with many officers, and by the time I finished my observations I had collected data with fifty-six of the seventy officers in the precinct.

I must nonetheless confess that I became friendly and relaxed only up to a point. For one thing, police officers tend to be wary, even with one another. Some officers made it a point not to ride with certain others. To illustrate, there was one young threesome who habitually rode together, and who habitually got into fights as well. They had just returned from Vietnam and seemed to regard the street as another battleground. One other officer in particular, who prided himself on never having had to use force to make an arrest, thought it a poor reflection on the precinct that these three kept getting assaulted because they were so aggressive. Another officer told me, "You couldn't pay me to ride with those three. I might get killed."

It is not that police work is so dangerous, but that police officers are especially concerned about getting into trouble by associating with the wrong people. If, therefore, I had let my liberal ideas be too well known, or if I had been openly critical of anything an officer had done, I feared that my riding days would be over. To be perfectly frank, I was too anxious to get my Ph.D to take that risk.

This raises the point of how my attempts to get along with the police differ from my attempts to get along in other situations. For one thing, other social relations are not normally so formally circumscribed as those I had with the police. I knew that my data collection would be over in six months, and so I was able to put up with a kind of duplicity I could not so easily have maintained in relationships with no prescribed end point. On the other hand, unlike some of my other relationships that were limited, expedient, and short-lived (as in some professional dealings in academia), I could not afford to speak my mind and simply walk away if the police officers rejected what I had to say.

Off-duty socializing with the officers was out of the question for me. I faced the attitude at home that I was spending too much time with the police as it was. Furthermore, after-hours socializing among the police usually meant going out drinking and picking up women, a personal life style I was unwilling to share. There were groupies (one of them known among the officers in the precinct as "Easy Mary") who frequented bars and thrived on sleeping with policemen. One married officer, who enjoyed the unusual distinction of no longer partaking of the after-hours carousing, said, "There is only one difference between married coppers who sleep around and those who don't; some stop after they get caught by their wives." And so, here I was, with a group of men who in self-defense felt unable to separate their professional and social lives, and whose social life I was unwilling to share. To some extent, my status with the officers was bound to remain tenuous.

THE MIDDLE—WANTING TO HELP

As I got to know the police officers, I grew tempted to become a policeman myself. The temptation came especially on day shifts. Many of the officers had to appear in court, and the chances were good that I would be able to ride up front with one of them. I would work the radio and keep the log, which was innocent enough in itself but began to give me a feeling of power. Perhaps I began to feel like many young police officers, excited by the authority that goes with their job. The things I began to do were small and probably not too harmful; in fact, some of them were even silly. In any event, in retrospect I am not too proud of my behavior. If we had a call to look for children sniffing paint or glue, I would look hard and feel something of a thrill when I could shout, "There goes one, behind the garage," to the officer driving. I once saw a driver run a red light, pointed it out to the driver, and then called out over the public address system, "Green Buick, pull over," as we came up behind with our red lights flashing. I took it upon myself to manage the lives of people even though no one had trained me, hired me, authorized me, or even invited me to do so.

My behavior carried over to night patrol. We might get a call to look for a prowler, and I would set off through a backyard with my flashlight, scared mightily that I might find someone, and then come back and report proudly, "It's all clear out back." Some of the officers asked me whether I would back them up in a fight, and I assured them that I would (although I never did, or rather rationalized that I never had to).

At one point, one of the officers at the station said, "You might as well strap on a gun. You're just like one of us." That felt good at the time. It was several years before I became convinced that I would never want to become a police officer, just as I had earlier decided that as a lawyer I was quite willing to defend clients in criminal court but never to be a prosecutor.

The officers and I shared some embarrassment about my role. One morning, at about 7:30, I parked my car around the corner from the station and went in to ride along on the day shift (8 A.M. to 3 P.M.). When the patrol was over, I went back around the corner, and my car was gone. Temporary "No Parking" signs were up, and a city crew was laying a new sidewalk. I walked back into the station and announced, "My car has been towed. I parked it before the signs went up. What should I do?" The officer who had said that I ought to strap on a gun (only a few days earlier, in fact) blushed furiously. "I'll take care of it," he said. He took me down to the lot to which the car had been towed and got the car out with no charge. Then he wrote in to have the ticket taken care of, which was no mean feat. Tickets did not get fixed in Minneapolis, and the officer's procedure was extremely unusual. The experience made me take note of my privileged position. If I had not been riding with the officer—if I had parked my car at 7:30 and come in to complain as an ordinary citizen—I probably would have been told to take up the matter with the City Attorney and would certainly have had to pay the towing charge.

I kept getting embarrassed by seeing police conduct I did not approve of and keeping it to myself. I continued to rationalize that I could not do much to help by objecting, and that I would jeopardize my data collection in the process. There was one occasion when I now judge that my failure to act was inexcusable. The officers I was with followed a car full of black youths driving through a white part of town. The police are trained to react to the unusual, and unfortunately, most of the unusual events they take note of seem to involve minority group persons or children. Police investigation of the unusual seldom bears fruit, but it does so just often enough to keep many officers' hopes high and reinforce their prejudices.

The car we were following tried to evade us, turning this way and that and finally making an illegal U-turn. Then the officers stopped the car. One of the passengers came up to shout objections to the officers' actions. One of the officers, six months on the job, demanded to see the youth's identification. The youth refused. The officer told the youth that if he did not produce identification, he would be arrested. The youth still defied him and was taken into custody. Down at police headquarters where the jail was, after the youth had been booked, the officers sat down to fill out an arrest report. They discovered, to their chagrin, that there was no legal requirement for anyone other than a driver or a bar customer to produce identification. The arresting officer decided to cover himself by charging the youth with disturbing the peace.

There is no such thing in Minneapolis as disturbing a police officer's peace. The street where the arrest had taken place had been deserted. The youth was clearly not guilty.

I was subpoenaed to testify. This was the only subpoena I ever received, which reflected the officer's sense of the tenuousness of his own situation. I obsessed over what I would say on the witness stand and decided that I had no alternative but to tell the truth. I wondered whether I would then be welcome in the precinct. When I got to court, the arresting officer went into the hall to talk to the City Attorney while I stood by. The City Attorney told the officer that the defendant had agreed to plead guilty in exchange for a fine of $25. The officer was overjoyed, and

I breathed a sigh of relief. But I could have told the City Attorney the circumstances of the case and probably gotten the charges dismissed. What I gained in trust from the police I lost in self-respect.

To cover my embarrassment and loss of self-respect, I overcompensated by exaggerating my feelings of admiration for the good things I saw the officers do. One incident in which an officer produced a reconciliation between a couple of neighborhood women who had been squabbling actually brought tears to my eyes, and for months afterward I kept telling people what a wonderful thing this officer had done. I kept talking with ʼ the officers about how great the appreciation seemed to be from citizens they helped in medical emergencies. (In fact, I think the officers themselves thrived on these situations. They were marvelously responsive, driving more recklessly to answer medical emergency calls than they did even in cases of possible robberies in progress. In retrospect, I have come to appreciate just what a thankless job police patrol usually is. The police seldom receive any indication from citizens of gratitude for or satisfaction with the services they perform. For the most part, the citizens I saw simply complained. One of the officers I rode with, who was enrolled in a criminology class in which I conducted a victim survey of students, came up after class to express his amazement that the students so seldom encountered crime: "From what I see on the street, I assumed that everyone constantly had problems.")

My change of heart is described below. But while I rode with the police and for some time thereafter, I unconsciously went out of my way to glamorize and romanticize their work. Otherwise, I doubt that I could have coped with having to restrain my criticism for six months of life in squad cars.

As noted earlier, about halfway through the data collection I became aware of the pattern of the officers' decision making, of how thoroughly they seemed to depend on what the dispatcher told them. From an ethical perspective, I felt an obligation to tell the officers what I knew about their decisions, but I did not for fear of its effect on their behavior. Instead, I tested them about their rationales for their decisions. For instance, there was one interesting anomaly. If the dispatcher told the police to check a burglary or damage to property (vandalism) and they found evidence of damage from an attempted break-in, they would report an offense. If the dispatcher told the officers to check a break-in (not in itself an offense in Minnesota) or an attempted burglary (attempted offenses were never reported) and the police found the same evidence, they would *not* report an offense. I repeatedly asked officers how they decided whether to report property damage, telling them that I had seen that they sometimes did and sometimes did not file reports. Their stock response was that the most important determinant was whether the complainant had insurance and needed a report to file a claim. My data told me that the officers did not conform to this rule, but I never let on during my observations. In sum, much as I would like to think of myself as someone with high moral standards, I acted expediently—doing what I needed to get the data I wanted and otherwise acting in sympathy with the officers out of the thrill of acting with police authority.

I did come to like, trust, and genuinely respect many of the officers I rode with. Eventually I was even able to confess that I had smoked marijuana while one officer was declaring his belief in strict drug enforcement. I came away from my observations with the conviction that most of the officers were genuinely concerned with serving the public and were capable of showing warmth and compassion in doing so. I left the field still dreaming of becoming a cop.

THE END—BECOMING DETACHED

Several years passed. One day, I went to visit a police academy, and there I discovered how detached I had become from my former identification with the police. While I could see a lot of nice personal characteristics in individual officers, I found the behavior and attitudes of the officers in their professional roles unattractive, particularly as men to women and to the officers' claim to a kind of legal impunity they would deny to ordinary criminals. I no longer wanted to help the police. And in retrospect, I suddenly became aware of the demands on researchers who try hard to understand persons they study in the field—of how the sympathy the researcher needs to do good field research impedes the exercise of independent ethical judgment. I have become wary of going into the field again, and I am inclined to believe that the ethical dilemma I confronted in Minneapolis—of serving those one studies versus serving one's own research—can be resolved only by studying those whose objectives the researcher has a prior commitment to furthering. I have become detached from the police, but I now realize that I could not be detached from any persons I might later study in the field.

CONCLUSION

Kings and queens have subjects, researchers should not!
(Leslie T. Wilkins, 1976)

It is, I think, an occupational hazard for social scientists who study deviance and crime, and who study systems for controlling them, that they hold themselves superior to the people they study. By describing the behavior of their subjects, researchers manage to displace attention from their own foibles, as though to say, "It is they, not I, who have the real problems." We researchers function in the tradition of journalists who muckrake in the guise of value neutrality, limiting their criticism to others rather than exposing themselves to the same kind of criticism. In our field of research, this form of arrogance is especially unfortunate. The fundamental moral and political problem posed by notions of deviance, crime, and their control is social intolerance, and by treating our research informants as subjects whose ways of life are beneath us, we add our credentials—our purported expertise—to intolerance.

The conscientious researcher who goes into the field to study the activities of social control agents faces a difficult ethical dilemma. Although research informants should be treated as peers rather than as subjects, it is the job of social control agents themselves to treat people as subjects. How can one who is committed to the principle of treating others as peers fully share the experience of those who are paid to treat others as subjects? It is not easy.

It would be too glib to conclude that no one should go into the field to study the activities of social control agents like the police. After all, I myself went there, and I do not hesitate to draw on that experience in my research, writing, and teaching even today. Speaking of arrogance, who am I to say that my own experience in the field should prevent others from gaining such experience of their own?

The best advice I can give to the prospective field researcher is to study social control activities with the conviction that the subjects are doing no worse than you would in their situation. While it may be your job to pass judgment on the roles social control agents are asked to play, it is also your job to understand—to sympathize with—the individuals you study. If you do your job correctly, you will to some extent share their moral burden. You will participate in the role of social control agent, sharing the blame for whatever actions you see that should not be done. And if you work self-consciously, as you should, you will find yourself in a constant state of moral turmoil.

If you are like me, the time will come when you must either put on a badge yourself or get out of the field. I think that in the final analysis, the only justification for spending time in the field is to find out as much as you need to know in order to decide whether you yourself want to assume the role of your informants. If you decide to do so, that is all well and good. All of us have to engage in some form of moral hypocrisy in order to play the roles we assume. I, for instance, who choose to teach but who cannot justify treating others as subjects, have to engage in the moral hypocrisy of grading. But as long as I continue to play the teaching role, I cannot treat the other teachers, whose problems I share, with disdain for doing their jobs.

234   HAROLD E. PEPINSKY

On the other hand, if and when you know enough to decide that you cannot accept the role of social control agent for yourself, you know enough to get out. To continue to ask your informants to share the privacy of their social world with you would be an act of betrayal. And as far as your quest for research knowledge is concerned, you have learned as much about the world of the social control agent as you can.

The researcher of social control who has left the field can still do further research. The understanding, the field experience, remains as a foundation upon which to build. If, then, the researcher chooses to specify conditions in which the role of social control agent could be made more palatable, two options remain. On the one hand, the researcher can go back into the field in other settings where potential informants may have achieved a more palatable way of life in order to describe and try to account for it. On the other hand, the researcher can use the prior field experience as a foundation for interpreting data that social control agents publish. Once the data are in the public domain, the researcher has no special position of trust to uphold in using them. Also, it is clear that the data published by social control agents, such as the Federal Bureau of Investigation's offenses-known figures, pertain to roles rather than individuals. For the time being, this is the path I myself have chosen. I can engage in social criticism of police-produced data with impunity without treating police officers who have entrusted me with their private worlds as subjects.

In any event, I found that observing police activity in the field was anything but dull. I commend such a field experience to you for as long as you can reconcile sharing the role of the police officer with your own conscience.

These are some personal reflections based on my own experience of maintaining relations with police officers whose behavior I studied in the field. There are many field researchers who would disagree with me. Some I have talked with would place the quest for knowledge about police behavior ahead of any concern for officers' personal interests. From this point of view, the question of how to maintain relations boils down to practical considerations: Within the limits of the terms upon which the police give consent to be studied, what does it take to collect the data one needs? By contrast, from my point of view, as you have seen, I find it impossible to separate issues of what I ought to find out in the field from issues of what I owe both to the people who trust me to observe their behavior and to those with whom they interact.

Notes

*The findings of the study described here can be found in "Police offense-reporting behavior," Journal of Research in Crime and Delinquency, 13 (January 1976): 33–47.

Interviewing People Labeled Retarded

ROBERT BOGDAN   *Syracuse University*

In fieldwork studies, interviewing is integrated into the total research process. It is one of the things that a participant observer does in the course of work. But in-depth interviewing with one or two subjects over an extended period of time as the major method of collecting data has been closely associated with the fieldwork tradition. In this selection, I will discuss research I am presently conducting with people labeled mentally retarded. With all long-term interviewing arrangements, maintaining positive relations with the subjects is crucial. Thus, maintaining relations is a central theme in the discussion that follows.

The memory is vivid of the first time I approached the locked dayroom of a back ward of an institution for the mentally retarded. The fear of coming face to face with what was described by my staff guide as "ambulatory, aggressive young males who were severely and profoundly retarded." The smell of urine and feces as I climbed the stairs. The walk across the dormitory with eighty beds in three lines. The door to the dayroom. The key in the lock. He in first, and then I. And there they were: some nude, some in straitjackets, all with close-cropped hair, and those that were dressed in baggy institutional clothing, many with scars, some hunched over, some drooling, most shaved with patches of hair on their faces. As we entered, some ran toward us. The fear of being attacked by these creatures. I wanted to run before I was scratched and bitten.

Three of these men came up to me and stopped. One reached out and touched my hand lightly. Another began to hug me and then was reminded with a gesture from an attendant that he was stepping out of bounds. One of the three began talking. He told me his name and asked me mine, and held out his hand to shake. Out of fear of facing the mass of others, I moved off to the side with him and began a conversation. He told me that he had been taken from his family and hadn't seen his brother in ten years, although he was one of the 3,000 other residents in the same institution. He told me that he missed him and wanted to see him. When I left, before the door was locked on him, he gave me a piece of paper. He said it was a letter for his brother, and asked me to find him and see that he got it. As I walked across the dorm in which he would sleep that night, I opened the note. There on the piece of lined looseleaf paper, on every line, was a row of joined-together cursive lowercase e's.

When I first visited these institutions in 1972, I was new to the field of mental retardation. I learned a great deal from those trips, and more as I pondered the questions raised by that first and later visits. Why had those men run to me? Why had I feared them? Why did I assume that they would hurt me? Why were they there? In those conditions? Why wasn't that man allowed to find his brother? How did these men get where they were? How did they think about themselves? Did they think about themselves? What was it like to live in a place like that? What was the meaning of "mental retardation" in their own minds and lives? What had being labeled "mentally retarded" done for them? What did "mental retardation" mean in our society? Being trained as a social scientist, I framed these questions in a way that required answers not only for the people I had met in these facilities but for all people similarly situated and, for the last two questions, for all people who have come to be called "mentally retarded." My relationship with the people I interviewed is born in a sense out of both my previous experience in institutions and a commitment to these qeustions. The research is my way of maintaining relations with certain issues and with those people I met when I visited the man who lost his brother.

These are difficult questions to think about, no less try to answer. Over the last few years, I have spent hundreds of hours talking to residents and former residents of state schools, some of whom lived in the wards I visited. My research strategy was to get to know these people, to get them to feel free with me so that they could share as openly as possible what their former lives were like, what it meant to be a resident in such facilities, and what it is like now. I have recorded many of our conversations, and transcribed and studied them.[1]

In a book currently in progress, my colleague and I present the life stories of two "retarded" people from their own point of view. We offer the autobiographies of a twenty-seven-year-old man called Ed Murphy (see Bogdan and Taylor, 1976) and a twenty-year-old woman called Pattie Burt.[2] Both have been labeled "mentally retarded" by their families, schoolteachers, and others in their lives. At the age of fifteen, Ed Murphy was placed in a state institution for the "retarded" (Empire State School), where he lived for four years. After a series of "family care" placements subsequent to his release from the institution, he moved to his current residence, a boarding home which houses four other former residents of state institutions. For the past several years, Ed has worked as a janitor in a large urban nursing home.

Pattie Burt lived in more than twenty homes and institutions before being committed to the same institution as Ed Murphy. She was ten at the time and spent approximately six years there. She was later transferred to another state school closer to her original home. After living there on and off and with a number of families and in other arrangements, she moved to a small town, where she now lives in her own apartment. She has been employed for six months packaging fish hooks at a local factory.

The purpose of the book is to convey what life has been and is for these people, how they see the world and themselves. But it is more than that. These are life histories collected and presented to accomplish what social scientists hope to achieve: a better understanding of society, its institutions, and those who pass through them.

Our interviewing procedures have been discussed in detail elsewhere (Bogdan and Taylor, 1975). However, I want to describe briefly how we went about our work in order to convey how the subjects stories are constructed and how we maintained relations with our subjects.

Ed Murphy and Pattie Burt were not chosen for our research by some random selection process. Rather, they emerged as subjects in the course of our everyday activities. They were not chosen because they were typical of those labeled "retarded" but because they revealed themselves as having special insights and understandings and proved to be articulate representatives of that category of people.

When we first met Ed Murphy, he worked at a local branch of the Assocation for Retarded Children. He was recommended to me as the guest speaker for a course in architecture and social science I was teaching. Ed was engaging and instructive in his presentation. Students in the course were being asked to design a living center for the retarded, and his purpose was to tell them what he thought was appropriate. His words revealed what became obvious—that they, the retarded, want the same things that other people want in living situations. To think that they needed a specially designed facility was the concretization of my own preconceived notions of what the retarded are like. In fact, the word "retarded" lost some of its meaning as he spoke.

We kept in touch with Ed after that experience. Since we were familiar with the institution in which he lived and the organization where he worked, we had a number of things in common and had frequent opportunities to talk with him. In contrast to other social science respondents, Ed was someone we knew quite well before the project began.

Approximately two years after we had first met him, the idea of working on his life story began to be seriously considered. I called and arranged to meet him in order to talk about it. Matters of our motives and intentions, anonymity, royalties, the overall plan, and the logistics of getting started were discussed and agreed upon. Our relationship with Ed was more like a partnership than a traditional research relationship. We knew that Ed had experienced certain institutions and treatments we were interested in exploring. I knew he had been declared "retarded" and was interested in that concept.

Ed was not a reluctant participant in the project; when we first started, he was most enthusiastic. He had friends at work and at home, but the idea of talking to us on a regular basis was special to him. Whether our affiliation with the university gave us special status or just the fact that we were not part of his regular world, he looked forward to our sessions. The early interviews did involve some misunderstandings. Problems in regard to the time of appointments were minor compared to the difficulty that arose over not having a shared understanding of what was supposed to happen at the interviews and Ed's self-consciousness in front of the microphone. While we thought we were clear in describing the project to him, he apparently did not understand or just could not enter the relationship we expected. He did not seem to understand that we were interested in the details of his life. He seemed to think that these were unimportant and skipped over his opinions about current events. We gradually taught him to be a respondent, one closer to what we had in mind, but the relationship was also flavored by Ed's original concepts.

When he spoke, we paid careful attention to what he said. Although the tap recorder was listening, we knew it was important to him that we listen too. He needed reassurance with a word or gesture that he had something interesting and important to say. We taught him that he did.

We also had to teach Ed that we were not evaluating him—not making judgments as to his intelligence or his worth. We tried to convey to him in as many ways as possible that it was not our intention to criticize or to judge, but rather to understand. Throughout the months of our interviews, Ed wanted to be reassured that he was "all right" in our eyes. We went out of our way to provide such feedback.

We met with Ed over a two-year period. During that time, we got together once and sometimes twice a week. We usually met at night or on Saturday in an empty office building located in Ed's neighborhood. Most interview sessions lasted about three hours. The interviews, which were taped, followed an open format. We tried to create a free and open atmosphere in which Ed expressed his understanding, hopes, joys, and fears. We attempted to pay careful attention to what he said so as to comprehend how he ordered and understood his world. If he said things that we did not understand, we assumed that it was a deficiency of our ability to understand. We tried to suspend the clinical view of Ed: that he had been classified as "retarded." We did not want to understand him in terms of preconceived diagnostic categories; rather, we wanted under- standing to emerge as we got to know him better. We tried not to concentrate on the differences between us but rather on what we had in common. We tried to be reflective, letting our own feelings and reactions to what he told us be the barometers of the prejudices and preconceived notions we carried around as transmitters of our culture. This necessitated our being nonevaluative in our thinking about Ed's experiences and values. Thus, we wanted to learn as much about ourselves as about him— or, perhaps, more accurately, our research strategy assumed that the two were inseparable.

We were not completely passive in our interviewing. There were times when we probed in areas that were of interest to us. We asked Ed to repeat things that we didn't understand, and we pushed for descriptions and details when he would have been satisfied with a more superficial rendering of events. We brought up things that perhaps he wouldn't have talked about if we hadn't asked.

Everything did not go smoothly. As with any relationship, tensions arose between us during the course of the project. After we had been conducting the interviews for a while, Ed seemed to lose interest in the project. He became less willing to talk openly as the topic of conversation moved from his institutional experiences to his early childhood and family life. He would dismiss questions with an abrupt "That's not important" or "I don't want to talk about that now." Even more distressing, however, was Ed's tendency to talk around certain painful topics. He would conveniently misinterpret uncomfortable questions and give inappropriate answers. While after our initial interviews our talks had become a time of fellowship and enjoyment, they became more of a heavy experience for him and something to which he did not look forward. For a while he broke appointments, and the project seemed to be in danger. In interviewing of the type we are discussing, the relationship has to be one of give and take. Ed, while continually uncomfortable with some issues and with some period of his life, did eventually get over the period of resistance. We learned that we had to be sensitive to his low spots and feelings. Relations improved, and we did get back to interview- ing on a more regular basis. We learned the importance of being sensitive to Ed's moods and the ups and downs of his life. We began to see that his interest in the project was not unrelated to how tired he was and how things were going at work. We tried to be sensitive to his moods and ours, and when we felt that he could not take being too task oriented, we spent more time getting coffee and taking breaks. Occasionally we had lunch together, and sometimes more time was spent with the recorder off than on.

It is difficult to remember how our interviewing came to an end. We had recorded over a hundred hours of conversation and felt that what we were hearing was redundant. Other responsibilities seemed more pressing.

About two weeks ago, I was driving up one of the main boulevards in the city in which I live. I saw a short man who was hunched over waiting to cross the street. He looked disheveled, and his out-of-style mod dress did not quite fit his thin frame. He hopped off the curb and then back again. His gestures and appearance made me think that he was an ex-resident of the state school. I categorized him as a retarded person. I looked more carefully, and it was Ed. I waved to him but he did not look. The traffic was heavy, and I moved on. Although I went over to his place a few times since the interviewing ended, I have not maintained my relationship with Ed. Seeing him on the corner reminded me of how I used to think about people labeled "retarded." When I realized it was he, I noted how easy it is to forget what you have learned. I resolved that I would have to see him soon.

Our relationship with Pattie differs from Ed's only in detail. We had struck up a friendship with her when she was a resident at Central State School. On visits to the institution, we had been impressed with the perceptive, outspoken teenager. When we were told that Pattie wanted to leave the state school but had no place to go, we began looking around for a family that might be willing to provide a place for her to stay. We found a home; it was mine.

The first night she stayed with us we, my wife and I had close friends over for dinner. We asked Pattie if she wanted to join us or eat earlier with our children. Her presence was a pleasant addition to our dinner. My reservations about her feeling uncomfortable or the fear that she might act inappropriately revealed my assumptions, not her capabilities. It was a cold winter night, and we sat around the fire in the living room after dinner talking. At first, Pattie was quiet but obviously not uncomfortable. At one point she said, "I have never been in a place that had a fireplace and where people listened to each other." She began talking about her childhood and the coldness of the institutions. What she said was moving. She related emotional events with control and dignity. That night, I began listening to Pattie's life history.

As she relates briefly in her own story, Pattie enjoyed a pleasant stay with my family until officials from the Department of Mental Hygiene inspected our house to see that it was in compliance with regulations for foster-home placements. Since it was not in compliance, she was forced to move to another home. It was during that six weeks, through long conversations, that some of the details of her life began to emerge. While there was no thought of collaborating with her in telling her when we arranged for her to move in, the thought did cross my mind that first night in front of the fire. Because she had a personal relationship with us, interviewing was not pursued; it was felt that it would complicate that relationship as well as bias the content of our conversations.

After Pattie left, I kept in touch with her. She moved into another foster-care placement with which she soon became dissatisfied. She walked out of that home and struck out on her own, living in an apartment near the state school in which she most recently had lived. I drove past her house regularly and would stop to see how things were going. I remember that once she came up to the car and told me she had just "stole" her records. I asked, "What do you mean?" She told me that she went for a placement conference with her social worker and that he had put the folder containing her institutional records on the table and left the room. She had quickly taken some of the papers, put them in her bag, and taken them to her apartment. She told me that she thought the professionals had no right to write all these things about her without her seeing them. She told me that no one had the right to say she was retarded, much less to write it. I had come to understand that Pattie hated the word "retarded," and using it in relation to her filled her with anger. It was through these contacts that I began to understand enough about her and the way she saw the world so as not to be offensive. She came to define me as someone who was on her side.

It wasn't until fifteen months after she moved out of my home that I spoke with her about the project. I had a difficult time reaching her, since she had moved to a town approximately one hour's drive from my home and did not have a phone. After many calls, the idea of the project was discussed over the telephone. The week after that conversation, I drove down to her apartment, discussed the idea more fully, and began recording her story.

The apartment was a good place to talk. It was filled with the objects that were central to her life—her hi-fi set, records, and pictures. When she offered me coffee and went to the refrigerator to get milk, it reminded her of the difficulties she was experiencing living on a fixed income with increasing food costs. It reminded her of how stupid she felt leaving the institution and living on her own because she had never learned some of the basic skills, like shopping, that everyone took for granted. The apartment almost served as our research interview guide, since the various things in it had a story behind them. While sitting on her couch, for example, Pattie told me:

> I remember one day I came home from work and sat down on the couch, right here, and I just burst out crying. I didn't have anything

to cry about. But the tears just came. Nobody was here. I just felt that I wanted to be in the dark all closed in. I can't give an explanation why I felt like that—and that wasn't the first time. Just everything goes through my mind. I remember the state school. Why did Mom ever say Pat needs professional help, she is retarded, she does things a normal girl wouldn't do? This is what goes through my mind. Mom didn't have that much love she had to call me retarded.

Interviewing people in their own settings is similar to participant observation in that you are interacting with them in the place that they normally spend their time and they can be observed interacting with the objects of their world.

There were seven three- to four-hour tape-recorded discussions. We conducted the interviews with the same perspective as we did with Ed. Five of the sessions were conducted in Pattie's apartment. One was held at my office at the university where I was working. The last took place at the home of a family that she moved in with. The shorter amount of time spent interviewing Pattie as compared to Ed is related to a number of factors. First was the amount of material we were able to cover in one session. Pattie proved to be much more verbal and quick. In addition, we had already conducted interviews with Ed and were better listeners. Also, after Pattie left her apartment, it was more difficult to arrange for a time and place to talk in private without fear of being interrupted or overheard. Knowing that this might be the case, an attempt was made to cover as much ground as possible while she was still living alone. Thus the discussions contained much less small talk.

In putting the transcripts into their present narrative form, we rearranged and edited the materials. The clarity of Ed's and Pattie's message was certainly intensified by this process, but our goal was not to distort the content of the message. In editing, we combined material in order to provide the fullest possible description. I clarified what might be difficult to understand. We cut material that was repetitious. We edited for wordiness and tense, but by and large, our book consists of Ed's and Pattie's stories as they were told to us.

Social science research must be understood in terms of the balance between what is lost using a particular procedure and what is gained. Using a large random sample provides some assurance of representativeness of the population being sampled while losing the depth and uniqueness of understanding of the lives of a few in detail. Not knowing the subjects intimately puts some controls on the possible effects of the distortion by affect but loses the potential insight that in-depth sharing, with its resulting empathy, promotes. Including in a research report the unedited transcripts and background details provides more information by which the readers can draw their own conclusions, but it clouds the analysis and insights of the researchers. We chose our method and procedures with these losses and gains in mind, hoping to be judged by the criterion of possible gain, not definite loss. Some will argue that the procedures we have used and the gains we have emphasized have more in common with literature or journalism than with social science. We have been systematic; we have attempted to control for bias as much as our method would allow; we have checked the "facts" of the stories with other sources; we have been concerned with social science questions and the contribution to social science knowledge and theory. We are not as concerned with others' evaluations as with our success in accomplishing our objectives. In short, we have not been slaves of procedure and role, but rather the goals of our discipline.

In approaching people labeled "retarded," is it often assumed that they are not articulate, do not have the ability to think abstractly, and have little to say that is worth hearing. Clearly the stories we present deny these stereotypes. They are anomalies to commonsense notions. One way to deal with the dissonance created by anomalies is to treat them as exceptions to the rule—that is to believe that they were misdiagnosed and are not really retarded. While we don't present Ed Murphy and Pattie Burt as representative of that category of people, we can assure you that they are legitimate members of that classification. As their stories reveal, they have been officially diagnosed and are treated and related to by professionals and others as being retarded. We have met, talked to, and interviewed other ex-state school residents as well as people who are presently in state schools who are as articulate and intelligent as Ed and Pattie. In our own work in the field of retardation, we resolved the dissonance created by these anomalies not by treating them as nonauthentic cases but by questioning the value of the system that classifies people as being either "retarded" or "normal."

Notes

1. Steve Taylor has been a co-worker on this project.
2. Ed Murphy and Pattie Burt are pseudonyms as are the other names of people and places in this book. Steve Taylor is co-author on this project.

References

Bogdan, R., and Taylor, S.J. *Introduction to Qualitative Research Methods.* New York: Wiley, 1975.
Bogdan, R., and Taylor, S.J. "The Judged Not the Judges: Insiders' Views of Mental Retardation." *The American Psychologist*, 31 (1976), 47–52.

Fieldworkers' Mistakes at Work: Problems in Maintaining Research and Researcher Bargains

JACK HAAS
WILLIAM SHAFFIR   *McMaster University*

INTRODUCTION

Fieldwork has moved from an oral tradition, passed on in the mentor-student relationship, to a methodology increasingly examined, codified, and communicated in published form.[1,2] This development helps meet the "need for working students in sociology to communicate the procedures and strategies of field research they have found consequential in their own studies to the less instructed or less experienced" (Habenstein, 1970:1). At the same time, fieldworkers, researchers, and teachers know that there is no single best way of conducting field research or disentangling their method from social influence (Vidich et al., 1964:vii). We are correctly cautioned that field researcher experiences are highly variable and that approaches and guidelines must be adapted to the particular research problem and setting (Bogdan and Taylor, 1975).

The interactional, situational, and ever-changing character of field-work roles and relationships militates against the development of exact procedures. Hence the difficulty of delineating the "do's and don'ts" and "ropes" (Geer, et al., 1968) of social research.

Ironically, fieldworkers often focus on problematic relationships in the groups they study, while at the same time ignoring their own mistakes and research problems. Understanding the research process, it seems, is viewed as peripheral to the research analysis. Such studied inattention to our mistakes at work (Hughes, 1951) assures us of a serious gap in understanding the process whereby researchers affect and are affected by research and researcher problems.[3]

This selection, based on our experiences in studying medical student

244

professionalization,[4] focuses on our problems of maintaining bargains with gatekeepers and among ourselves and the necessity of viewing such relationships as temporal, fragile, inherently contraditory, and subject to change. Field researchers use such phrases as "making the bargain," "developing rapport," and "working as a team." These phrases abstract aspects of the research process. The implicit assumption, it seems, is that once the bargain is made, rapport developed, and the team organized, no further negotiation is necessary. Our experience tells us that these are not fixed "stages" but continuous *processes*. This conceptualization of the research process shifts our attention to the important problems of maintaining (negotiating and renegotiating), not only establishing, research and researcher relationships.

PROFESSIONAL BARGAINS

The nature of any bargain relationship is likely to shift and alter (Johnson, 1975). What is referred to as the "bargain stage" of the research is more accurately conceptualized as a series of negotiations throughout the research endeavor wherein the researcher continually attempts to secure others' cooperation. Bargain negotiations typically require the development of relationships of equality, involving an idea of exchange or give and take. This is particularly true in relationships between professionals. These relationships are symbolically communicated in interactions and negotiations that indicate the development and mainte-nance of a collegial relationship (Haas, 1972; Strauss et al., 1964) and at the same time demonstrate professional control over the situation (Blank-enship, 1977; Freidson, 1975; Larson, 1977).

Our analysis focuses on our negotiations with gatekeepers and among ourselves, respectively. We observe that in both sets of relation-ships, participants' concerns with developing and maintaining profes-sional reputations—the basis of professional legitimacy—conflicted with the development and maintenance of professional collegiality and equality—the basis of cooperation. Gatekeepers of a new, innovative, and internationally recognized school and young Ph.D.'s in sociology shared similar concerns about professional reputation, thus creating strains and conflicts which led to the breakdown of collegiality and cooperation. Professionalism is rooted in contention for professional dominance of the situation.

The negotiations and renegotiations with gatekeepers and among ourselves reveal a cyclical pattern or "career"—a struggle for equality if not superiority. Bargains were made on the participants' symbolically negotiating a context of collegiality. Conflicting interests and commitments in establishing and maintaining professional reputations created strains. These difficulties were exacerbated by the development of a context of pretense awareness (Glaser and Strauss, 1964) in which parties refrained from confronting each other because of the assumption of collegiality. This context was disrupted when one party formally expressed its interests and grievances, thus challenging the veneer of collegiality and forcing a renegotiation and reconstitution of the relationship. Conflicting professional interests and commitments created difficulties in maintaining professional collegiality and agreement. Professional competition for control of the situation was a structural impediment to the cooperation that all parties desired. We became observers of an important social scientific problem.

GATEKEEPER BARGAINS

An irreducible conflict exists between the interests of the researcher and representatives of the organization (Becker, 1964: 272–276). It is not surprising, then, that organizations attempt to define, limit, and control others' investigations of their activities. They want to ensure that the research is compatible with their interests and casts their activities in a favorable light. This underlying concern is likely to be increased when researchers examine the underside of an institution or when that institution is highly organized and powerful (Habenstein, 1970: 99–121).

We met our first problem in trying to secure a bargain with representatives of an image-conscious profession in a new and reputation-conscious school. Though sociologists routinely make bargains to study people with less power, status, and prestige, the study of the most powerful profession makes bargains based upon shared interests and collegiality inherently problematic and difficult. The professions are, by definition, groups that attempt to control the definitions of the situation. This control is threatened by outsiders, such as ourselves, who observe the professionalization process firsthand. The basis of professional power and control centers upon the process by which professionals mystify their competence, thus obscuring the basis of authority and providing a justification for inequality of status, closure of access, monopolization of knowledge, and control over constructions of reality and definitions of the situation (Haas and Shaffir, 1978; Larson, 1977). Our interest in observing the professionalization process firsthand was met by a wary, uncertain, and powerful set of gatekeepers.

In order to receive official permission to study the socialization of medical students, we attended a series of meetings with medical school faculty, administrators, and students. We prepared and submitted a proposal to examine the socialization process from the students' point of view. We described the theoretical underpinnings of our research and methodology. Our discussions of the proposal in committee and public meetings were characterized by two central gatekeeper concerns and reservations: (1) How can a methodology lacking in rigorous design result in a scientifically accurate analysis? (2) To what extent would our analysis make statements about program success and failure? Although we expected that our proposal would be carefully and critically examined, we did not fully anticipate the strength of the institution's reluctance.[5]

From the beginning, we felt that we were parties to a reluctantly granted bargain. Our first days in the field (Geer, 1964) indicated that we would continue to have problems with the gatekeepers. An agreement that we would have an opportunity to introduce ourselves and our research to incoming students at their first meeting was violated, hampering our early efforts and indicating that the relationship might not proceed smoothly.

While initial discussions with the school's administration indicated that frequent meetings would be mutually desirable, we did not meet to discuss our work or problems related to it. The relationship became characterized by "pretense awareness"; both parties were aware of strains in the relationship but pretended otherwise (Glaser and Strauss, 1964). At the beginning of the third and final year of the research, we met with the school liaison to request institutional data about the cohort we studied. In spite of our avoidance relationship and a research bargain which did not clearly identify expectant rights and obligations, we presumed that such materials (admission letters and background information), properly treated through norms of confidentiality and anonymity, would be forthcoming.

After six months without an answer, we knew there was trouble; the procrastination was a warning. Yet even our trepidations did not match the fierceness of the belated reaction. We learned that our request had "prompted a thorough review of the entire project by members of the medical faculty," that the "history" of the project was explored and summarized. We were informed that an executive committee discussed and approved that: (1) the medical school would "continue [their] agreement to provide access to the research team, with the understanding that the study is to be completed this spring"; (2) our request would be considered as an additional study, approval of which would be contingent upon a further review of "a detailed progress report of the main study" and "an expanded statement of the rationale, objectives, methodology and intended analysis of the additional study"; (3) ". . . as some serious concerns [had] arisen over the course of the main study," the Program Executive Group . . . [was] anxious to have these concerns discussed in a constructive and critical manner." These concerns centered on research design and methodology, implementation of the project, and communications.

Prior to our first meeting with this executive committee, we formulated a reaction to the memorandum, including our own interpretation of situations and events. We contended that our bargain, permitting us access to the students and institutional settings, was being modified to the point of violation. We claimed that not only was the bargain being altered but also that an attempt was being made to redefine the relationship as one of inequality.

We prepared ourselves for a protracted period of negotiation. We were informed that decisions about such requests were not left to any individual's discretion but would require a recommendation from a hierarchy of special committees. We were to provide the committee members with a detailed written description of why we needed these data and how we would use them.

We could not immediately agree (among ourselves) about the appropriate nature and extent of our cooperation with the committee's requests. We carefully weighed various alternatives, developing and following compromise approaches.

As negotiations progressed, it became apparent that the committee's fundamental concern related to our preliminary findings about the students' socialization. The committee members' comments and questions about our methodological design and the representativeness of our data were indicative, we believed, of their main concerns about how the developing findings, analysis, and model would affect the school's reputation. Faced with researchers employing, by their definition, a highly subjective methodology and developing an analysis attaching credibility to the students' views, the committee was anxious to organize a regular exchange of views concerning both the direction of the project and the analysis.

The executive committee claimed that our methodological approach lacked sufficient rigor and clarity and invited a methodologist affiliated with the medical school to appraise and evaluate our research design. In a meeting during which we justified our methodological orientation, and much to our surprise, an executive committee member announced that steps would be taken immediately to give us access to the requested data. The verbal agreement stipulated that we would provide the committee with a draft of analyses containing those data.

Our relationship with the medical school gatekeepers was influenced by conflicting and changing definitions of the situation, which affected the collection of specific data.[6] The deteriorating nature of this relationship was paralleled by the changing relationship among members of the research team. Again, in the face of conflicting personal and professional interests and commitments, the problems of maintaining a relationship based upon collegiality led to a process of renegotiation. This eventually caused the breakup of the research team.

COMPETING COMMITMENTS AND RESEARCHER BARGAINS

Joint endeavors, such as team research, involve negotiations among team members that are fragile and tenuous. Problems can arise over differences in theoretical and methodological perspectives and in attempting to leave personal differences out of the work relationships (Valentine, 1968:181).

In our case, conflict in our three-member team resulted primarily from the additional side bets (Becker, 1960) we were making to establish and protect our professional careers and reputations. One of us accepted a role on another research project in the same medical school, the full scope of which was neither discussed by the others nor recognized by him. At the same time, the two remaining team members agreed to edit a book. All of us were writing up other research for publication. In short, professional, career, and family pressures led each of us to pursue alternative commitments that detracted from our joint project. Due to the longitudinal nature of our medical socialization project, we anticipated that a period of time would elapse before publication. Conflicting interests—particularly pressure to publish and establish individual professional reputations—strained our commitment to the project.[7]

As a result of these conflicting priorities, barriers of communication developed that affected both the research and the researchers. We were less able than we wished to read and comment on fieldnotes, generate memoranda, and meet together about problems and directions of the research. We had difficulty finding time to read bibliographic materials which would provide strength and support for the notions we were developing in the field. Meetings for maintaining collegiality, sharing and analyzing our observations, and generating new theoretical directions occurred sporadically.

As disagreements developed, our initial response, as with the gate-keepers, was to downplay or ignore them. We again developed and practiced a pretense awareness of collegiality. Each of us was aware that the problems in the project required discussion and each was sensitive to the others' awareness, yet seldom did any of us acknowledge our problem. We wished to preserve collegiality and hoped that problems would vanish by themselves.

The focus of our individual and intermittently expressed collective anxieties about our ambivalence toward the project was the quantity of our observations. We justified periods of absence from the field to each other in the hope of gaining sympathetic understanding. Such understanding was almost always offered and, when confronted with a similar situation, reciprocated. When unable to enter the field for a period of time, we would reassure one another that the lost time would be recovered, even specifying precisely how this would be accomplished. Usually, however, such absences were not discussed. Each of us feared that raising the topic might lead to recriminations and bad feelings. This reciprocity of avoidance sustained the bargain but built up an emotional strain for the inevitable facing-up encounters.

Again, as with the gatekeepers, differences of opinion and lack of agreement arose from competing professional interests and commitments and our failure to establish effective and regular opportunities for communication. Because of the time we needed for other inportant personal or career-related priorities and the fear of recriminations, we did not meet regularly to give realistic accounts of our individual roles, participation, contribution, and commitment. Differences of opinion about research roles, methods of collecting and analyzing data, and the publication and authorship of findings created strains among the researchers and threatened the veneer of collegiality. One member, breaching our gentlemen's agreement, resorted to a written memorandum, in which he tabulated the number of transcribed pages of fieldnotes dictated by each of the researchers and seriously questioned his further participation. In frustration over his colleagues' absence from the field, he wrote:

> This memo is of critical importance to my own continuing involvement in this project. . . . This situation [his co-investigators' absence from the field] is unacceptable to me. First, I feel the situation is not just. I do not wish to carry what is ostensibly a joint project largely on my own shoulders. Secondly, I'm rapidly losing any confidence which I initially had, that the project would be successful. I am putting as much time into the project as I can and this time is not being matched by my co-participants. . . . This may sound nasty, but under these circumstances, I feel I must ask for an agreement in writing between us concerning ownership, including order of authorship of any material which is written from this project.

Use of a memo and the disruption of our "gentlemen's agreement" was resented by the others. The ensuing discussion, however, provided an explicit recognition of the "competing commitments" and bargaining problem, and the conditions of a renegotiation. We temporarily repaired relations and collegiality by developing supplementary methodological approaches to help us meet students and obtain an increased and regularly scheduled amount of data. In this way we renewed and reexpressed full commitment to the project and forestalled a more fateful renegotiation.

For a time, the pressure that led to conflict drew us together, reemphasizing our sense of interdependence. As time passed, the side bets we made on successful continuance of the study had accumulated. These bear enumeration. The research bargain with the medical students morally committed to us to carrying out the project. Our professional reputations with colleagues, the funding agency, and the discipline's reputation within the university community were at stake. Public presentations extended our side bets and renewed our commitment.

At the same time, however, we began to hedge our bets. Rather than fully commit ourselves to a troubled project, each of us further developed alternative interests in research and teaching, thus exacerbating our competing commitments, the chief source of our difficulties.

As Simmel (1950) has described them, triadic relationships are inherently stressful because of the emergence of coalitions. As the project developed, one of the researchers became isolated, having little opportunity for interaction with the others, who met regularly about their joint work. At the start of the second year, the isolated researcher formulated a proposal to reduce his fieldwork role in order to balance his contribution with those of his co-researchers. This proposed reduction led eventually to his total withdrawal from the field to observe the seriousness of his colleagues' fieldwork contribution. His withdrawal was another signal that irresolvable difficulties were affecting the team. The situation worsened until, in an explosive confrontation, the team was reduced from three to two members.

CONCLUSION

Field researchers use phrases to describe their relationships with gatekeepers, subjects, and each other that capsulize processes which culminate in desired conditions of collegiality and shared interests. "Making a bargain," "developing rapport," and "working as a team" all imply phases of the research process with limited and determinate careers based upon communication, cooperation, and equality.

The concept of the research process as having a determinate career with specific "stages" contributes to our neglect of the changing relationships that characterize *all* social interaction. Our research experiences lead us to call attention to the methodological neglect of the problems of maintaining field relationships and suggest that in ignoring the inherent structural contradictions of the professional research relationship we limit our understanding of the research process. Researchers are obliged to describe their theories and methods but typically do not discuss their problems and mistakes. An unspoken part of our work is the implicit agreement to avoid focusing on the more personal aspects of our research activity. We uncritically and reflexively limit ourselves to concerns about how we affect research subjects (Rosenthal and Rosnow, 1970), failing to describe how we and the research itself are affected by other interests, commitments, and relationships.

This selection has described two sets of major conflicts that developed in the course of our research over the nature of our peer relationships with outsiders and among ourselves in negotiating a successful research bargain. In both examples we observed a similar process of maintaining cooperative relationships in the face of conflicting interests and concerns about professional reputation and control. Concerns about professional reputation and the absence of opportunities for maintaining "collegial," professional relationships and shared definitions of the situation resulted in unavoidable, structurally rooted conflict. Because these relationships were based on the concept of collegiality in a competitive context, we noted the development of a context of pretense awareness, wherein participants perceived a changing and deteriorating relationship, but acted as if past understandings would serve as a basis for continued cooperation. This context was disrupted in both sets of relationships by the raising of background issues by one party of the relationship. The formalization of issues produced a new situation requiring remedial attention and, ultimately, renegotiation. Competing interests and definitions of the situation created strains and conflicts that disrupted the concept of collegiality altering the basis of the relationship, threatening the basis of cooperation, and leading to a renegotiation and reconstruction of the relationship.[8]

A look at our problems and mistakes helps us learn and communicate about general features and dilemmas of our work. Our experience reveals that there exist basic contradictions wherein professional careers are individualized and professional groups solidified by threats to their control of the situation. Conflicting interests and commitments affect professional groups in their internal and external relations. These structural problems pose a continuing dilemma in professional careers.

Relationships between researchers and gatekeepers remain fragile. The struggle for equality in a framework of competition for reputability and defined control continue to plague personal and scientific trust. The alienating character of these relationships deserves our careful and continuous attention.

Notes

1. We wish to thank Richard Brymer, Sherryl Kleinman and Robert Stebbins for their helpful comments. We are grateful to the Social Sciences and Humanities Research Council of Canada and McMaster University for their generous support of the research.

2. For examples, see: Becker, 1970; Bogdan and Taylor, 1975; Douglas, 1976; Filstead, 1970; Golde, 1970; Habenstein, 1970; Hammond, 1964; Johnson, 1975; Junker, 1960; Lofland, 1971 and 1976; Powdermaker, 1966; Schatzman and Strauss, 1973; Shipman, 1976; and Vidich et al., 1964.

3. There are few published personal accounts of fieldwork problems. Although sociology contains an enormous literature on the subject, Robert K. Merton noted some time ago that it is primarily concerned with what social scientists ought to think, feel, and do and fails to draw necessary attention to what they actually think, feel, and do (1962:19). There are exceptions, however, and a number of researchers have provided personal chronicles of their research in which attention is focused on the process of interaction between the researcher and community members and on the personal considerations affecting both the organization and outcome of their research activity. It is impossible to mention all of the scholarly articles that have addressed these issues. Some of the better ones include: Bell and Newby, 1977; Gans, 1968; Golde, 1970; Hammond, 1964; Liebow, 1967; Powdermaker, 1966; Roth, 1966; Shipman, 1976; Vidich et al., 1964; and Whyte, 1955.

4. The medical program spans three academic years, each of eleven months' duration. The training period is divided into five sequential phases but is otherwise completely integrated. Except for elective periods, the students are assigned randomly to tutorial groups of five students and one tutor. There is little emphasis on large-group teaching methods, although a number of lectures and seminars are available. It is in the framework of the tutorial group that objectives are developed, problems presented, solutions discussed, and where students and tutor interact with and evaluate each other. There are no traditional examinations in the program. See Haas and Shaffir (1977, 1978) for a fuller description.

5. The conflict continues in the struggle for professional control over the legitimation of our analysis. The medical school continues privately to dispute the science of our methodology: we have seen a letter critical of both our "cloak of competence" paper (1977) and our presentations at committee meetings.

6. Our rapport with students was, by dramatic contrast, very favorable. Students actively cooperated from the beginning, their honesty and trust based upon an equality shared with the researchers.

7. For a more complete description and analysis of our problems in working as a team, on which this section relies heavily, see Shaffir et al., forthcoming.

8. The stages involved in negotiation and renegotiation of our research and researcher relationships generally parallel the insightful conceptualization of negotiations of teacher-pupil and teacher-teacher interactions by Martin (1976).

References

BECKER, H.S. "Notes on the Concept of Commitment." *American Journal of Sociology*, 66 (1960), 32–40.

———. "Problems in the Publication of Field Studies." In A.J. Vidich, J. Bensman, and M.R. Stein, eds., *Reflections on Community Studies*. New York: Wiley, 1964, pp. 267–284.

———. *Sociological Work: Method and Substance*. Chicago: Aldine, 1970.

BELL, C., and H. NEWBY (eds.). *Doing Sociological Research.* London: Allen & Unwin, 1977.

BLANKENSHIP, R.L. *Colleagues in Organizations: The Social Construction of Professional Work.* New York: Wiley, 1977.

BOGDAN, R., and S.J. Taylor. *Introduction to Qualitative Research Methods: A Phenomenological Approach to the Social Sciences.* New York: Wiley, 1975.

DOUGLAS, J.D. *Investigative Social Research: Individual and Team Field Research.* Beverly Hills, Calif.: Sage Publications, 1976.

FILSTEAD, W. (ed.). *Qualitative Methodology: Firsthand Involvement with the Social World.* Chicago: Markham, 1970.

FREIDSON, E. *Doctoring Together: A Study of Professional Social Control.* New York: Elsevier, 1975.

GANS, H. "The Participant-Observer as a Human Being: Observations on the Personal Aspects of Field Work." In H.S. Becker, B. Geer, D. Riesman, and R. Weiss, eds., *Institutions and the Person.* Chicago: Aldine, 1968.

GEER, B. "First Days in the Field." in P. Hammond, ed., *Sociologists at Work: Essays on the Craft of Social Research.* New York: Basic Books, 1964.

———, J. HAAS, C. ViVONA, S.J. MILLER, C. WOODS, and H.S. BECKER. "Learning the Ropes: Situational Learning in Four Occupational Training Programs." In I. Deutscher and E.J. Thompson, eds., *Among the People: Encounters with the Poor.* New York: Basic Books, 1968.

GLASER, B., and A. Strauss. "Awareness Contexts and Social Interaction." *American Sociological Review,* 29 (1964), 669–679.

GLAZER, M. *The Research Adventure: Problems and Promise of Field Work.* New York: Random House, 1972.

GOLDE, P. (ed.). *Women in the Field: Anthropological Experiences.* Chicago: Aldine, 1970.

HAAS, J. "Binging: Educational Control Among High-steel Iron Workers." *American Behavioral Scientist,* 16 (1972), 27–34.

———, and W. SHAFFIR. "The Professionalization of Medical Students: Developing Competence and a Cloak of Competence." *Symbolic Interaction,* 1 (1977), 71–88.

———, and W. SHAFFIR. "Do New Ways of Professional Socialization Make a Difference?: A Study of Professional Socialization." Paper presented at the Ninth World Congress of Sociology. Uppsala, Sweden: August 1978.

HABENSTEIN, R. (ed.). *Pathways to Data: Field Methods for Studying Ongoing Social Organizations.* Chicago: Aldine, 1970.

HAMMOND, P. (ed.) *Sociologists at Work: Essays on the Craft of Social Research.* N.Y.: Basic Books, 1964.

HUGHES, E.C. "Mistakes at Work." *Canadian Journal of Economics and Political Science,* 17 (1951), 320–327.

JOHNSON, J.M. *Doing Field Research.* New York: Free Press, 1975.

JUNKER, B.H. *Field Work: An Introduction to the Social Sciences.* Chicago: University of Chicago Press, 1960.

LARSON, M.S. *The Rise of Professionalism: A Sociological Analysis.* Berkeley: University of California Press, 1977.

LIEBOW, E. *Tally's Corner.* Boston: Little, Brown, 1967.

LOFLAND, J.A. *Analyzing Social Settings: A Guide to Qualitative Observation and Analysis.* Belmont, Calif.: Wadsworth, 1971.

———. *Doing Social Life: The Qualitative Study of Human Interaction in Natural Settings.* New York: Wiley, 1976.

MARTIN, W.B. *The Negotiated Order of the School.* Toronto: Macmillan of Canada Ltd., 1976.

MERTON, R.K., G.G. READER, and P.L. KENDALL (eds.). *The Student Physician.* Cambridge, Mass.: Harvard University Press, 1957.

———. "Forward." In B. Barber, *Science and the Social Order.* Rev. ed. New York: Collier, 1962.

POWDERMAKER, H. *Stranger and Friends: The Way of an Anthropologist.* New York: Norton, 1966.

ROSENTHAL, R., and R. ROSNOW (eds.). *Sources of Artifact in Social Research.* New York: Academic Press, 1970.

ROTH, J. "Hired Hand Research." *American Sociologist,* 1 (1966), 190–196.

SHAFFIR, W., V. MARSHALL, and J. HAAS. "Competing Commitments: Unanticipated Problems of Field Research." *Qualitative Sociology,* forthcoming.

SCHATZMAN, L., and A. STRAUSS. *Field Research: Strategies for a Natural Sociology.* Englewood Cliffs, N.J.: Prentice-Hall, 1973.

SHIPMAN, M. (ed.). *The Organization and Impact of Social Research.* London: Routledge & Kegan Paul, 1976.

SIMMEL, G. "The Triad." In *The Sociology of George Simmel,* ed. K.H. Wolff. New York: Free Press, 1950.

STRAUSS, A., L. SCHATZMAN, R. BUCHER, D. EHRLICH, and M. SABSHIN. *Psychiatric Ideologies and Institutions.* New York: Free Press, 1964.

VALENTINE, C. *Culture and Poverty.* Chicago: University of Chicago Press, 1968.

VIDICH, A.J., J. BENSMAN, and M.R. STEIN (eds.). *Reflections on Community Studies.* New York: Harper & Row, 1964.

WHYTE, W.F. *Street Corner Society.* Chicago: University of Chicago Press, 1955.

4

Leaving the Field

The previous sections of this text suggest that issues in field research have recently been considered in detail. Problems such as gaining access, collecting data, establishing a network of key informants, and handling moral obligations are routinely covered in the literature (Denzin, 1970; Filstead, 1970; Glazer, 1972; Lofland, 1976; McCall and Simmons, 1969). One area equally deserving of investigation which has been ignored, however, is that of leaving the field. This section examines the process whereby researchers disengage themselves from the field setting and the social relationships formed during the research.

While much attention has been given to the relationship between the researcher's entrance and presence in a particular research setting and the resulting constraints for data collection, the researcher's departure from the setting deserves the same systematic treatment. Erikson (1965:368) has argued that if sociologists do not conduct their work in a responsible manner, they are ". . . liable to damage the reputation of sociology in the larger society and close off promising areas of research to future investigators." In fact, the researcher's departure from the field, if misunderstood or viewed unfavorably by the subjects, may strongly affect the efforts of future investigators in the same or similar research milieus.*

Basic to an understanding of the process of disengagement is the review of the fieldworker's experience. Often we are left with the clear impression that the researcher's time in the field was patterned after a model of how fieldwork ought to be done. In describing how access was obtained and data were collected, the authors typically describe the

*In contrast, Herbert Gans, in correspondence with two of the authors, suggests that one cannot entirely control the future, and that simply by having been there, a fieldworker could make it difficult for a successor; even if he or she behaved properly, people may feel that they don't want to be studied again. Or later, they may dislike the final report and then take it out on the next researcher.

257

unique difficulties posed by the research setting and the strategies used to overcome them. In spite of these challenges, the researchers' account almost always fits within the boundaries of how such research should proceed. Drawing from Deutscher's (1965) analysis of a disjuncture between words and deeds, there is probably a discrepancy between sociologists' discussions and suggestions of how the fieldwork should be done and how, as a result of both foreseen and unforeseen contingencies, it is actually executed. Such contingencies might include mistakes in participant observation, fractious relations with respondents, or the betrayal of confidences. It is precisely these contingencies and their handling by the researcher that help to shape and define the problem of leaving the field.

Another related point is the research bargain between researcher and subjects. During the initial stage of the research, the bargain consists of a written or unwritten agreement between the researcher and those who provide access to the research setting. While the bargain is usually important at the beginning of the project, it is rarely remembered and discussed later on. The nature of the bargain may shift, often subtly or even dramatically, as the research unfolds. Regardless of this shift, the nature of the bargain helps to shape and influence role disengagement.

The Maines, Shaffir, and Turowetz selection—case studies of post-doctoral students, professional wrestlers, and Chassidic Jews—traces the histories of three bargains. Generally, the authors discuss numerous avenues for leaving research settings. More specifically, they explore the notion that the social relationships formed and maintained during the research help to shape the ways in which the researcher can leave. The authors conclude that all phases of the field research influence exit strategies.

Similarly, Altheide argues that the leaving process is a stage in the ongoing interplay between the researcher and the community being investigated. The nature of Altheide's role as researcher, his periodic leave taking, and his informant's accounts of insiders' perceptions of both his character and his work during those leaves of absence helped to determine his exit strategies. Through a set of systematic announcements to all of the newsroom staff of his intentions to leave, Altheide was able to disengage himself from the setting gradually.

Yet another factor in leaving the field is that potential subjects are less than enthusiastic about being studied. For a variety of reasons well known to us, they do not share our excitement about our work. As they see it, they stand to gain little, if anything, from our research findings and may even lose. A related reason for their reluctance is their impression that our work will add little to their own lives. While we may not be perceived as a direct threat, we are seen as a nuisance since we occupy their time by asking thorny questions. As such, the ultimate purpose and net gain of our activities seem unclear. While we are occasionally informed that our research will have to be postponed or terminated, usually our efforts to continue working are met unenthusiastically.

Such a situation is both discouraging and despairing to the researcher. Convinced that the research will shed light on a particular problem or may make a special contribution to the discipline, he or she seeks ways to pursue the study. Familiar with the potentially disruptive consequences of becoming personally involved with and obligated to the subjects, or possibly even going native, the researcher is prepared to temporarily abandon such warnings in order to solicit their help. In short, the researcher's involvement in the work extends beyond the expected academic requirements. We suspect that it is precisely in such situations that leaving the field becomes problematic.

Although moving to another province necessitated Letkemann's exit from the research setting, the nature of his research and his association with the respondents prevented him from leaving the project permanently. As a consequence of having worked with vulnerable and subordinate subjects to whom he was committed, Letkemann found extricating himself from the research problematic. Furthermore, with the publication of his dissertation in book form, he assumed a quasi-political responsibility to his respondents.

Another area of concern, which underscores the complex nature of the leaving process, deals with the misrepresentation of the researcher's identity. Many studies using qualitative research illustrate the intimate relationship between the researcher's academic and personal involvement with the subjects (Gans, 1962; Liebow, 1967; Whyte, 1943). While researchers tread a fine line between such personal rapport and the ensuing consequences of data contamination, we are typically led to believe that they are aboveboard in their dealings with subjects. Although the majority of researchers are overt in their conduct most of the time, we suspect that a significant number of cases go unreported in which researchers intentionally and deliberately misrepresent their interest in and commitment to the research activity.

Personal commitments to those we study often accompany our research activity. Subjects often expect us to continue to live up to such commitments permanently. On completing the research, however, our commitment subsides and is often quickly overshadowed by other considerations shaping our day-to-day lives. When our subjects become aware of our diminished interest in their lives and situations, they may come to feel cheated—manipulated and duped.

We inevitably take some responsibility for the feelings of our respondents. Roadburg's selection emphasizes that leaving the research setting is as much a psychological problem as a tactical one. Like other researchers, Roadburg was overcome with feelings of guilt and alienation when his project with the British professional soccer players came to an end. His decision to terminate the project involved breaking a routine that was not only intellectual but physical: he had trained with his subjects. In an effort to alleviate some of these problems, the author advises that the researcher withdraw gradually, clearly define the time-frame involved in the project, and maintain a degree of social distance from the project's subjects.

Just as there are no sure ways to handle the problems associated with gaining access, learning the ropes, and maintaining fieldwork relations, there are no right or wrong strategies appropriate to leaving the field. The potential variations in leaving strategies were brought to the attention of one of the authors (Turowetz, 1974) when he was contemplating his exit from the world of professional wrestling. Searching for the appropriate strategy, he asked several colleagues, all of whom, not surprisingly, suggested different methods. Some said that to distance oneself totally was mandatory. Others warned that a total disengagement might prohibit the collection of critical data during the analysis and "write-up" phases of the research project. Still others stated that one never has to leave entirely; social relationships can be maintained after the project has been completed.

It may well be that leaving the field is rarely discussed in the literature because it is taken for granted as the natural and routine way of ending researcher-subject interaction. The selections in this section, however, suggest that sociologists should seriously attend to the process of disengagement, for each situation has its own set of properties which must be addressed.

Leaving the Field in Ethnographic Research: Reflections on the Entrance-Exit Hypothesis

DAVID R. MAINES   *Northwestern University*
WILLIAM SHAFFIR   *McMaster University*
ALLAN TUROWETZ   *Dawson College*

In this selection, we examine the process of disengagement from the ethnographic research project, which we refer to simply as "leaving the field."[1] This topic pertains to a process which is generic to social orders. Of all the many ongoing processes of societies, leaving and arriving are perhaps two of the most universal.[2] We are continually being caught up in the formation of new alliances and relationships, taking on new obligations, and modifying our circle of friends and contacts as we encounter new social networks. Yet, this is no simple linear process, for we are also simultaneously involved in dissolving relationships and group affiliations, with or without intent, and losing interest in others. We can think of these processes in terms of each group or individual being in a particular career line involving multiple group affiliations, with each affiliation containing an entrance phase and a potential exit phase. Some entrances, such as sales transactions, imply a rather quick exit, while others, such as professional careers, imply lifetime commitments.

Our point of view in this analysis is that ethnographic field exiting is at least partially structured by the field entrance phase. The nature of the "research bargain," to use Geer's (1970) term, with its manifold subprocesses involving research identities and relationships, allocation of tasks, moral obligations, and the like, sets conditions on the nature of research role disengagement and also charts courses through which exiting will take place. The issues and problems raised by some projects will sometimes not let the researchers leave in the phychological sense. The sense of harm felt by the residents of Springdale, for example, caught the attention of Vidich and Bensman (1968), while the view held by the Belgian medical practitioners that Renée Fox's research (1964) was crucial to medical reform in that country likewise demanded that she not "let go" of the project. This is merely to point out, as documented in numerous other studies (e.g., Daniels, 1967; Madan, 1967), that the field researcher inevitably establishes multifaceted relationships with those studied which not only make it difficult to define the exact nature of those relationships but which also complicate the imperative to leave.

If getting in and getting out are processes, then we should look for phased entries and departures. A great deal has been written on the entry aspect of the overall research process, including discussions of problems of access, coding, cultivating key informants, data collection, role management, moral obligations, and publishing research results (Becker, 1970; Bogdan and Taylor, 1975; Habenstein, 1970; Junker, 1960; Lofland, 1971; Schatzman and Strauss, 1973; Wax, 1971), but nothing of any substance regarding the leaving phase. In examining dozens of methodological accounts of ethnographic research, we found that not one research description has recounted the elements involved in exiting from the field. Among the more than a dozen field methods texts we examined, however, there was some comment regarding leaving but little substantive analysis. Denzin (1970: 192–193), for instance, briefly discusses role disengagement in terms of how data are reported; Junker (1960: 11) points to "getting in," "staying in," and "easing out" as phases of the researcher "accommodating himself to that [participant observer] role"; and Wax (1971: 16) mentions the "post-field stage." The most illuminating discussion we found is provided by anthropologist Thomas Rhys Williams (1967).

While his analysis is far from extensive, he does indicate certain problems of leaving the field and offers several suggestions on how to leave. He notes, for instance, that long-term field research creates "an atmosphere of permanency," and so, "when it becomes known that plans are being made for concluding research and leaving, there is likely to be a time of considerable upset in relations with informants" (Williams, 1967: 54). He also notes that there are often "patterned ways for dealing with severing of personal relationships" in a culture (p. 55) and that the special rituals and forms of leaving which are part of the culture should be employed. Moreover, leaving can also create special problems for the group studied, especially informants. "The village headman was unhappy for weeks because we no longer would give him increased status as our mentor, protector, and close friend" (p. 56). Finally, the detail devoted to leaving is important because field researchers never know exactly what the group members think of them. "It may come as a great surprise to hear you have been on a drunken orgy for a year, running about naked, or have been poisoning rivers and streams, promoting atheism, or cheating your informants of their family heirlooms" (p. 58).

What Williams is trying to point out, of course, is that leaving the field can be problematic and that it involves more than the mere physical act of leaving. Even though researchers often do terminate their data collection simply by not returning to the field site, it is clear that there are varied and multiple contingencies involved in the process and that these warrant investigation.

THEORETICAL CONSIDERATIONS

In some sense, the field research is like Simmel's stranger: ". . . he is not the wanderer who comes today and goes tomorrow, but rather he is the man who comes today and stays tomorrow" (Levine, 1971: 143).[3] It is that "staying" and the methodological imperative to form meaningful and to some extent enduring social relationships that we contend lies at the heart of the structuring process which gives rise to different forms of leaving. It is a process not unlike the one described by Becker (1960) in his analysis of commitment. Becker's concern was in transcending the individualistic assumptions of previous analyses of commitment by attempting to lodge them in the social organizational processes surrounding personal action. In this respect, commitments were seen to limit alternatives currently available to the person because "he has staked something of value to him, something originally unrelated to his present line of actions, on being consistent in his present line of behavior" (Becker, 1960: 35). In this sense, leaving cannot be seen as an isolated act. Rather, it is a process whose essential character is conditioned by the manner in which researchers enter the field, the nature of the social relationships they form while conducting the research, the bargains they make, and the kinds of persons they become to their subjects. All phases of field research become important for leaving, then, simply because field researchers know that so long as they remain researchers, they must and eventually will face the fact of leaving. Gerson's (1976) analysis is especially helpful in explaining this process insofar as he provides a way of viewing commitments as processes involving the relationships between situations. Seen this way, patterns of participation are always presupposed by other patterns of participation. Thus, one's investment in a given line of action not only sets the context for subsequent lines of action but is also conditioned by previous activity as well as the action of others.

A substantial body of research findings forms the basis of the conceptual approach. Becker and Carper's (1956) work on occupational commitment, Geer's (1968) research on teaching, Faulkner's (1971) investigation of studio musicians, Glazer's (1972) study of contractors, Hearn and Stoll's (1976) study of cocktail waitresses, and Gerson's (1976) investigation of quality of life all lend support to the viability and applicability of the approach. This research supports a view of structural process in which commitments impose boundaries on action without totally determining it. One generic result of this is an ongoing process of negotiation between the structuring effects of others' actions and the creative capacities of individuals to influence their futures. Which one emerges as the more influential is an empirical question answerable only in terms of the characteristics of particular settings. Certainly it can be said, however, that the distribution, clusterings, and nature of commitments create a multivariate matrix within which voluntaristic action takes place.

This conceptual orientation, then, informs our analysis of the relation of field entrance and the social relationships established during the research to field exiting. Besides attempting to show that particular connection, we also hope to reflect on the phasing of entrance and exiting processes mentioned earlier. Some of the same types of social relationships may appear in both phases (e.g., "lingering contacts"), and while entering and leaving are generally differentiated by the allocation of time and resources, it often is difficult to specify when one is "in" or "out." The writing up of results phase isn't even a diagnostic test for indicating when one has departed, since the recording of conclusions, hypotheses, and theoretical statements is a continuing process (Lofland, 1971; Schatzman and Strauss, 1973; Wax, 1971). Thus, we are dealing here with what Goffman calls "main involvements" rather than exclusive involvements. In reflecting on these kinds of issues, we report on three ethnographic studies—one conducted by each author—in which leaving the field is described.[4] They include a study of postdoctoral students, one of professional wrestlers, and one of an Orthodox Jewish community. Our procedure will be to describe how the researchers got into the study and how the process of entering affected the leaving phase.

THREE CASES OF LEAVING THE FIELD

Study One: Postdoctoral Students

This study concerned the careers and identities of postdoctoral students and was carried out at the University of Minnesota between 1971 and 1973. The field site was selected because my wife, who had received her Ph.D. in 1970, had accepted a postdoctoral appointment in the

university's pharmacology department, and disjunctive career requirements could easily be combined.

Except for support from a predoctoral fellowship, the study was
unsponsored, and since the university didn't keep records on their
postdoctorals, finding them became a problem. Initially I hung around
my wife's laboratory, where I simply became "Dr.—'s husband," but the
personnel there and eventually others in the department came to understand that I was doing a doctoral thesis on postdoctoral students. In this
initial phase, my wife was a tremendous source of information. I kept
detailed notes on her experiences, changing perceptions, attitudes, and
problems. In fact, I kept a diary on my wife for more than a year, which
constituted an exceedingly detailed case study of the "becoming" of one
postdoctoral student. As we became friends with other postdoctorals,
technicians, and faculty members in the department, I had an ongoing
source of information throughout the study concerning that one department. In general I maintained the "husband who was studying postdoctorals" identity, and only once formally interviewed other postdoctoral students in the department. The rest of the time was devoted to
conversational interviewing and observing.

I had to collect data in other departments, however, and the only way
to do that was to go to each department and ask whether any postdoctoral
students were working there. In presenting a rationale to secretaries,
departmental chairpersons, or graduate student advisors, I responded that
I was doing a doctoral thesis on the work routines of postdoctoral
students. While this was generally true, I was specifically interested in
identity transformations and responses to structured ambiguity. However,
since the study was an inquiry into the social organization of work and
issues of identity were seen in terms of work, the account was thought to
be sufficiently accurate.

Since I had been rebuffed earlier by a dean for being an outsider (I
was working on the degree of another university), I left implicit the idea
that I was a degree candidate at Minnesota. As a result, fewer questions
about my legitimacy were raised. By foraging around the campus,
department by department, I eventually came up with a list of postdoctorals and the laboratories in which they worked. I selected more than forty
postdoctorals for intensive interviews. In those interviews, I again had to
state that I was a doctoral candidate studying postdoctoral work routines,
but I correctly identified myself as a degree candidate at the University of
Missouri because it allowed me to utilize certain stronger interviewing
tactics.

I had no major problems of access concerning my research identity.
Except for minor details, I was candid and straightforward. I soon
discovered that my choice of research had one advantage: The people I

was studying had themselves just finished doctoral theses or, in the case of faculty members, were involved in their supervision. Although I realized this in advance of the study, I had no idea that it would be helpful. Occasionally, for example, someone would express sympathy for "what I was going through." The important point, though, is that everyone I met knew about doctoral theses, academic research, and the graduate student role. It was only with the deans that I had problems of legitimacy, and that was because they were sensitive to issues of student rights and privacy. For the most part, those I was studying made the same kinds of legitimating assumptions that I made. These assumptions constituted rules truly taken for granted, as we all shared the same general universe of discourse and rhetoric.

My interviews ended in a way that allowed me to visit the respondents again, and for theoretical reasons I reinterviewed certain postdoctorals. I also saw on a fairly regular basis those whose laboratories were housed in the same building complex as the pharmocology department. For those postdoctorals in other buildings, however, I left the field when I finished interviewing and observing. No questions were asked, and the issue of my leaving never arose. For those near the pharmacology department (the physiology department, for instance, is on the floor directly above, and everyone uses the same exit door), I became a familiar face, but except for a few, not an everyday interactant. For these postdoctorals, I left when I had enough data but lingered on as someone they would see from time to time. Except for those with whom I became more friendly, no one asked me about my study or what I was doing. I account for this, again, in terms of the shared experience of having done a thesis and regarding it essentially in instrumental terms. By this time, however (it was well into 1972), many of those interviewed had left Minnesota to take faculty positions elsewhere; thus, rather than my having left them, they left me. This is important because postdoctoral students are a highly transitory population (their appointments are usually only for two years, and they almost never take a faculty position in the postdoctoral department) who are highly work and career oriented. Moreover, like academic personnel in general, they are accustomed to the regular influx and outflow of people each year. Thus, my "disappearing" was of little concern to them. My reason for being there, in both form and purpose, was well suited to their assumptions about academic social worlds and networks.

In late summer 1972, I was awarded a NIMH postdoctoral fellowship to study a different aspect of postdoctoral life. I finished the thesis in January 1973 and then was faced with reacquainting myself with some of the postdoctorals. The study design called for case histories of the fifteen first-year postdoctorals previously interviewed. I felt that some of them would think I was using them if I simply showed up again one year later. But I did just that—merely showed up one day—and was quite surprised to find that they weren't disturbed at my having neglected them. I told them that I had finished the dissertation and received a postdoctoral fellowship to study a related aspect of postdoctoral work. That turned out to be a satisfactory explanation. In fact, they took it all in stride, and some commented that it was nice to be able to follow up on a thesis project; others suggested that I must have really learned from my thesis because of my ability in obtaining the fellowship.

This very congenial and unproblematic reacquaintance process eventuated because I was studying "my own kind." They understood, had little to hide, and cooperated most generously. I was frequently asked to "come to the lab and see for yourself," which I did. This phase of my study of postdoctorals continued until August 1973, when my wife and I left Minneapolis for New York. It was a good career move for us, and when I mentioned it to those postdoctorals who asked what I would be doing the next year, they responded approvingly. "Leaving the field" when studying postdoctorals, therefore, presents few if any difficulties because the researcher and the subjects are involved in the same kinds of processes relating to career stage, mobility, goals, and family orientations.

Study Two: Professional Wrestlers

I had hoped that my initial foray into the world of professional wrestling would consist of presenting myself as a sociologist, making the necessary research bargains with the promotional office, and beginning the task of data collection. Unfortunately, this was not the case.

As a result of the wrestling community's strong information control, I soon realized that I would be unable to gain any formal or informal access as a sociologist. I discovered that the wrestling community's open hostility toward anyone seeking information is a consequence of what wrestlers and promoters refer to as "bad press"—exposés of wrestling as fakery, of wrestlers as morons, of audiences as dupes, and of promoters as racketeers.

The wrestling community's anxieties about information leaks to outsiders prevented me from being candid about my research intentions. Since a complete participant role was not possible, I made arrangements to become a reporter for a wrestling magazine. Thus, entry was accomplished through the appropriation of an organizational identity. Had it not been appropriated, a participant observer strategy would have been extremely difficult, if not impossible. As a wrestling reporter, I was required to write articles for the magazine in an effort to maintain credibility with both the journal and the wrestling community.

For the first eight months of the research project, I was identified as a reporter, which raised the moral question of misrepresentation, and while providing access to the everyday life of wrestlers, the reporter identity locked me into types of relationships that did not yield the range of information needed for the study. As a reporter, there were certain questions I should not have asked and certain statements which I could not make. Yet as a sociologist, there were certain things that I needed to know. Thus, it became necessary to alter the wrestling office's understanding of my interest in its activities, and my friendship with the promoter provided the circumstances for realigning my identity. I informed him that I was engaged in research on wrestling for a master's thesis at McGill University. He expressed initial disbelief that a prestigious university would have any academic interest in his occupation. Assured, however, that my interests were as much sociological as they were journalistic, he regularly introduced me to visitors as a graduate student who was writing a book about wrestling. This realignment, then, resulted in even greater involvement with the wrestlers, and the interpenetration between my personal and professional lives assumed a moral career of its own.

As they participate in a staged event, members of the wrestling world are commited to the task of information control. Public awareness about their world would be detrimental to the welfare and livelihood of the entire wrestling community. As a member in good standing of that world, I adopted their "official line." When their version of their activity was called into question by wrestling fans, I often found myself explaining and defending that version. I began experiencing the feeling of going native and was participating in the staging of events at the promotional office in support of wrestling as authentic sport rather than drama.

My personal involvement in the research was further enhanced by the meaningful friendships which developed during the course of the study. For example, I regularly joined some of the wrestlers for meals after their evening performance, attended a birthday party organized by the wrestling champion for his son, and met socially with a number of the wrestlers and their families. During an evening meal, the wrestling promoter confessed that he had come to view me as a son. In short, I began to share in the everyday life experiences of the community. I became involved as an active public relations assistant to the promotional office and soon recognized that these work tasks were becoming routinized and taken for granted by the promoter and his assistants.

It was in this context of involvement that I realized that simply leaving after accumulating sufficient data to complete the thesis was not possible. I was confronted by a moral dilemma, knowing that those in the wrestling community had come to depend on me in certain areas of activity. As I recognized that my departure from that world was inevitable,

I perceived my exit in terms of a strategy of gradual withdrawal. I slowly relinquished some of my reporter responsibilities and began systematically to withdraw from my circle of key sponsors, informants, and friends. This strategy was neither well understood nor appreciated by the promotional office. Involved in a set of multiple roles in the wrestling community—those of sociologist, reporter, and friend—I was identified as someone who would never leave. Though my life as a researcher had come to an end, their lives as members living and working in that community were ongoing, and they implicitly insisted that my life continue to mesh with theirs.

In the early phases of the disengagement process, I received mail and telephone calls from the promoter's office on a weekly basis. I tried to be evasive by stalling in my response, but feeling guilt pangs, I visited the promotional office and continued my nonresearch tasks as usual. Such involvement continued for about two months. Finally, it was only after I openly stated that my research writing had priority that my relationship with people in the wrestling office became better understood. They reluctantly accepted my decision to no longer appear with the same regularity.

I initially suspected that both the promoter and the wrestlers might be critical of my departure from their occupational community because of the knowledge which they knew I possessed about the dynamics of staging contests. My suspicions were unfounded. For the promoter and the wrestlers my departure marked the end of a warm friendship, and it was to this concern that they addressed themselves.

Study Three: An Orthodox Jewish Community

My interests in studying the Chasidic community in Montreal brought to my attention the existence of a community of Chasidic Jews, once residents of Montreal, who judged the secular influences of the city as too threatening and relocated to a rural community to the north of it. Although, at the outset, my information—provided by non-Chasidic Jews—about this community was almost exclusively hearsay, after one visit I concluded that my analysis of Chasidic life in Montreal would be more complete if it included data about the organization of this particular group.

On the basis of previous data gathering in other Chasidic communities, I could anticipate this group's response to my request to collect information about their community organization and way of life. As I would be identified as an outsider, I reasoned that they would wish to be insulated from any sustained contact with anyone not of "their own kind" and would therefore not sanction the research. Such reasoning did not result from the usual trepidations experienced by researchers as they enter new settings but was based on advice from individuals familiar with the community and on my own experiences with other Chasidic communities. Accordingly, at the beginning I neither sought nor received formal permission to begin collecting data.

My biggest problem was to devise some means whereby I could be present in the community on a regular basis without arousing strong suspicions as to my actual intentions. The community's distance from the city, in addition to its isolated geographical location, would prevent me from saying that I was in the area and dropped in, or that the community's synagogue was the most convenient for my purposes. Though such justifications might be proffered occasionally, they would not be acceptable to sustain any regular presence.

I believed that this difficulty would be overcome when one of the rabbis informed that he would soon be searching for a part-time instructor for secular studies. My hopes were raised when I was invited to be interviewed for the position but dashed when I was informed that I would probably be bored by teaching students whose interests in secular studies were minimal. When I assured the rabbi to the contrary, I was told, "Actually, you wouldn't be suitable because of your dress and appearance. It just wouldn't work out." Very simply, the person sought to fill the position was one whose life style would not adversely affect the student body. Thus, an Orthodox Jew or a Gentile would be preferable to someone like myself, a Jewish male, whose affiliation with Orthodox Judaism was judged far too minimal. This incident underscored my impression that the community would not knowingly cooperate with an outsider like myself, who did not have the acquaintance of anyone who might serve as a sponsor and whose interest in the community was to conduct research.

A chance encounter some months later with a non-Chasidic ex-employee of the community helped me to secure the position of typist and letter writer there. When asked during the interview why I was interested in the position, I explained that I was searching for part-time work and that, as a Jew, I was interested in understanding the Chasidic life style. I was offered the job by one of the individuals who believed I was unsuitable for the teaching position.

Based on my suspicion that the members of the community would not sanction any sociological investigation of it, I did not inform them that I was collecting data. I did tell those who were interested, however, that I was a graduate student at a local university and was studying sociology. I successfully used my interest in sociology to add legitimacy to the kinds of questions I often asked about the community. When people occasionally expressed surprise as to my interest in certain community affairs, I would claim that my inquisitiveness was linked to my academic background. This explanation proved acceptable and even provided some members of the community with a reason to volunteer certain information that was assumed to be of interest to someone studying at the university.

Though my status as a graduate student was common knowledge, it was one that few people in the community could clearly comprehend. This particular Chasidic group's insulation from the larger society meant that only a handful of its members were familiar with the academic world. Instead, these Chasidim conferred upon me a status which they could comprehend and with which they could easily identify: that I was concerned about becoming an Orthodox Jew and wished to begin observing many of its precepts. I neither discouraged nor objected to this recognition of me and probably, both actively and passively, contributed to its reinforcement. Thus, for instance, I listened attentively to the explanations that were provided for the observance of various Jewish laws, participated in prayer services when called upon, and expressed enthusiasm for wishing to enhance my knowledge and understanding of Orthodox Judaism.

Whereas my position as an office worker and typist helped me gain access to considerable information about the community's organization, in the final analysis my role as a secret observer severely constrained the range of data that I could collect. My position entitled me to read through many of the community's files, especially those concerning financial matters and relations with outsiders who were regularly called upon to assist the community in various ways. Regrettably, however, my position also locked me into a series of activities outside of which I was not expected to become involved. Thus, for instance, I was expected to discuss matters with certain individuals whose information would facilitate the performance of my duties, but at the same time I was discouraged from conversing on topics unrelated to my work. Specifically, male students who wished to talk to me were informed by the rabbi that their conversations interrupted the completion of very important tasks. I, however, was continually reminded that these students' responsibilities did not permit them to engage in conversations with me. Analysis of my field notes revealed important gaps in the data relating to what I judged were important themes for investigations, and I was unable to imagine how such data would eventually become available.

While working in this Chasidic community during the day, my evenings were spent conducting interviews and participant observation research among members of a different Chasidic group. I soon realized that my full-time position among the Chasidim would have to be reduced if I were to meet my deadline for completing the master's thesis. Accordingly, I met with the two persons with whom I worked most closely, explained that I was required to begin writing a master's thesis, and requested that I be permitted to work only half days. When asked, I claimed that the thesis would deal with pool halls. At this point, one of the persons described to the other his image and impression of a pool hall, and both quickly agreed that I ought to be dissuaded from pursuing this research. They suggested that, instead, I consider writing a thesis about their community. One said, "Look, you know us. Why don't you write about us and we could help you?" We agreed to meet the next day to further discuss the suggestion.

By the following day, both individuals no longer considered their suggestion worthy of pursuit. One maintained that he didn't want his name to appear in print, while the other claimed that Gentiles would read about the Chasidim and conclude that "the Jews are funny." This individual also believed that since my knowledge of Orthodox Judaism was so limited, I would not know the significant questions worth asking. He suggested that, instead, an excellent thesis topic would deal with "good government in Canada" and promised to provide me with his ideas on this matter. At the same time, I was informed that the community was unable to continue paying a salary for my work.

My attempts to have these individuals reconsider their decision were unsuccessful. My departure from the field, though immediate, was nonetheless amicable. I was assured that I would be a welcomed guest whenever I visited and that the community would attempt to secure part-time employment for me elsewhere. While an offer for other employment was not forthcoming, I was always favorably received during visits to the community. My contact with members of the community continues to this day, approximately ten years since the completion of the master's thesis, though I have never disclosed to anyone in the community that I once conducted covert research among them.

Analytic Significance of the Three Cases

A key dimension in the case of the postdoctoral students was that the social organization of postdoctoral work and careers overlapped considerable with those of the researcher, which led to a smooth process of leaving the field. The two important elements were that (1) the researcher was not committed to a false research identity which he had to account for later and (2) the norms of leaving which guided the subjects were the same as those which guided the researcher. In the study of professional wrestlers, the key features were the appropriation of the reporter role, the concealment of the research identity, and the consequent kinds of information unavailable to the researcher. The leaving process explicitly required the use of withdrawal tactics because the researcher found himself committed to a set of moral relationships which limited how they were to be terminated. Dropping the reporter role and giving the impression of waning interest were utilized to lessen involvement. In the third case, the researcher accurately anticipated a lack of ccoperation on the part of the Chasidic community and decided not to raise the topic of research at all. The typist position allowed him to collect some data, but as in the professional wrestler study, it also denied him access to other data. With no research identity, therefore, his only relationship to the community was an organic one. Thus, when his salary ended, so did his research. There was no "easing out" of the field, as the very processes which kept him in were those which, when removed, forced him out. This is one of the ways in which the covert researcher is covertly "kicked out."

DISCUSSION

We have proposed that the process of leaving the field in ethnographic research is at least partly a function of the commitment structures formed during the research process. To illustrate, we described the committing and leaving processes of three field studies. In general, we conclude that the problems, concerns, and ease of field exiting are not uniformly distributed across research settings. Rather, the leaving process is an aspect of the ongoing interplay between field circumstances and the ways in which the researcher negotiates social relationships and a workable identity. We therefore contend that leaving the field is not merely a benign and passive phase of the research but often plays a dramatic part.

Field research requires researchers to form committed social relationships with those being studied. Not to do so or not to be *able* to do so proves to be devastating. Donald Roy (1965), who was faced with a situation in which mill workers thought he might be a spy for management, was forced to terminate his study even before it got underway;[5] and Carpenter (1965), in his research among Eskimos, informs us that until he developed relationships with some individuals and families, he felt clumsy, stupid, mentally defective, and somehow less than human. Thus, on the one hand, there is the imperative to form social bonds; on the other hand, these very bonds can lead to problematic situations. Wax (1971: 44) points out that often it is at the point of leaving that researchers find they do not want to go and realize their degree of emersion in the field. One's attitude toward leaving, then, is a measure of involvement and may be reflected in the researcher's approach to writing up the data.

. . . every time I have been in the field and become truly involved I have had to struggle with an impulse to stay longer than I should have stayed. By this I mean that I felt an almost irresistible urge to gather more data rather than face the grim task of organizing and reporting on the data I had (Wax, 1971: 45).

Staying too long, therefore, can create the practical problem of not allowing enough time for writing up results.

This issue of emersion in the field has many direct implications for leaving. For one thing, this notion involves not only establishing research contacts but making friends. Daniels (1967: 290) vividly and candidly describes how such friends can be disturbed by published results, and Whyte (1943) found himself condemned by a local social worker for "turning his back on his friends." This issue raises the question, What does the researcher owe the subjects once the project is completed? Another issue pertains to legal matters. Polsky (1967) notes that if one gets too involved in the field study of criminal behavior, it may be impossible to leave. Researchers must walk a fine line. They must become involved enough to gather the proper kind of data—observations "on the hoof," as Everett Hughes has called them—but not so involved as to actually commit a crime. Thus, the researcher must act so as to avoid being labeled a dangerous outsider and at the same time gain maximum access to strategic data. An error in the former can result in an aborted study; an error in the latter can land the researcher in jail. Maintaining that balance between detachment and involvement, then, is not only problematic (Glazer, 1972; Wax, 1971) but can also have direct consequences for conducting research and leaving the field.

One advantage of research methods other than participant observation is that they distance the researcher from the subjects. In survey research, for example, the questionnaire or interview schedule is typically regarded as an instrument which mediates and even neutralizes the researcher-subject relationship. In ethnographic research, however, there is always a tension between being overly personalized and overly detached. We suspect that this very tension, and the necessary accommodations and negotiations which result from it, is one reason fieldworkers tend to neglect problems and issues of leaving the field. As Johnson (1975: 145) points out, they tend to hide their feelings behind an imagery of instrumentality. Further, we contend, they define themselves as someone who drops by, stays a while, and leaves. Prudence Rains has reminded us that many research subjects are probably willing and eager to adopt the same definition. We fully agree, but we also agree with Millman, who writes that "sociologists . . . have to be constantly mindful that they come for a while in order to watch, and not to stay" (1976: 16). Thus, leaving is a methodological imperative. We do not refer to leaving merely in the physical sense. That may be done by relocating or simply not going back.

Rather, we refer to the more fundamentally sociological sense of leaving—a change in social relationships in which fewer, more widely spaced field encounters reflect transformations in meaning. From this perspective, it matters little whether or not there is a correspondence between the researcher's definition of self and the perception of the subjects. The leaving process merely looks different.

This brings us to another issue—namely, that researchers may leave for many reasons. The summer ends, research funds run out, the thesis deadline is near, the setting changes, one gets a divorce or gets tired of the research. These factors can shape or mobilize the leaving process. Therefore, it is in our interest to attempt to delineate some of the dimensions of leaving. The following discussion is not complete; it merely suggests the kinds of issues that might be considered.

One important dimension is *temporality*. Is the exit quick and sharpely defined, or is it gradual and drawn out? Rosalie Wax illustrates the former type, and as she shows, it may take on many of the elements of a status passage.

> The Jumping Bulls ("Charging Bears" in my book) gave a grand farewell party for us, to which they invited members of all the districts on the reservation, and Cecelia Jumping Bull gave us many fine parting gifts.[6]

Rains' (1971) study of unwed mothers likewise demonstrates the quick exit, but with the added element of permanence.

> With unwed mothers in one of the places I studied it was fairly clear that we all ended our contact with one another once out the doors of the place.[7]

Anselm Strauss' studies of dying (Glaser and Strauss, 1968), on the other hand, illustrates a more gradual process—"drifting off," as he calls it.

> But leaving, I think, was simply a matter of our own knowing we would be going on to another ward—and often we were studying two or three at a time. Essentially, I suppose, we drifted off the ward without formal goodbyes, and knowing sometimes we would be back to talk. Also sometimes we did not observe consecutive days, but intermittently so the staff would not look for us each day but re-see us all over again when we appeared.[8]

It should be pointed out here that the gradual exit also fits nicely with certain interviewing styles. Schatzman and Strauss (1973: 74), for instance, speak of interviews as being "suspended" rather than "terminated." The researcher should always leave room to drift back and resume or add on to the interview at a later date.

Closely related to the dimension of temporality is that of *sequencing*. The following statement by Donald Roy, who for years has been studying Southern labor organizing campaigns (Roy, 1970), shows how leaving can be a recurring phenomenon.

> Yes, I leave given campaign locales, after the election is held, win or lose. Workers expect me to leave, when a given battle is over. The organizers leave, too; but they may come back for a second campaign and I may return too. At any rate, I meet the same organizers at other campaign sites, and meet new ones there.[9]

This raises the important issues of coordinating research schedules with the schedules of the subjects. In one home for unwed mothers, Rains remained with the group of girls through their entire stay, and when they left she left. This is a matter of timing, and in this case it worked rather well. Roy, however, shows that sometimes it is the *researcher* who gets left; in fact, if he stays around along enough, he can become a central figure representing continuity.

> There has always been turnover in organizers in my area of investigation, and lately there has been a great expansion, lots of new faces. This is because the IUD and ACTWU [have] been expanding organizing staff to cover more . . . campaigns. So I meet new people more rapidly than before and must establish good relationships in each instance. But I have the old-timer core; so the problem has not been serious. And, speaking of "old-timers," the realization struck me that I am now on my second generation of southern organizers and officials. A whole generation has retired and/or died and otherwise left the organizing scene. They leave or die one at a time, and not *en masse*; so the transition from one generation to the next is not difficult. This matter of turnover is interesting. Four years after I had left a factory research scene, where I had spent a previous four years, I returned for one day to look up the workers and management people that I had known so well. With the exception of the Personnel Manager, management had moved on (dead, retired, fired, transferred, quit). And the work force had also turned over almost completely. I found one worker that I knew from the "old days." It was weird. It gave me the creeps. Like a four-year period in a university. The freshmen had graduated. A few years later the plant was torn down and production moved elsewhere. If a longitudinal study carries on too long it runs out of original personnel. The fact that I stayed in the field, thus easing the transition between one generation of respondents and the next, saves me from such ghastly "where in the hell has everybody gone" shocks.[10]

A third dimension is that of *desirability*. Does the researcher want to leave or stay? This issue, mentioned earlier, pertains to the value dimension of leaving. Howard Becker notes that the researcher can, in effect, get saturated with an area of study and will leave the field in order to move on intellectually. In reference to the research on *Boys in White*, Becker observes:

> It's also partly true that we had had there, as I have always had in every field study I've done, the feeling that is commonly reported of "not finding out anything new." I guess what that means is that you keep getting the same answers to your questions—the same modal observations and the same variations—*and* don't think of any more new questions. That's odd, isn't it, because we always describe fieldwork as a process in which you are always thinking up new questions. And you always could think up some new ones, but at some point you stop—either can't or more likely won't allow yourself to think up anymore. You get tired—but that's not an explanation, just a placeholder for one. I think maybe it has something to do with something referred to above, namely, that you begin to feel trapped in not just the study but the world of people and interests to which the study is connected—not the people in the field but the ones outside, the other people doing studies of similar stuff, the fundgivers, the "experts," etc. That's quite a strong feeling for me since I really believe that it's important at least for me to keep moving and not get too embedded in any of those worlds, that I will do sociology better by being very comparative, both in my experiences and analysis.[11]

Attachments, though, can become exceedingly strong, as Wax indicates.

> Being by that time experienced fieldworkers, Murray and I had planned to stay six months in the field and spend six months writing our report. But rough as life was, I had become so attached to some of my Indian friends that I talked Murray into staying an extra month— even at temperatures of 30 below zero. I did not want to leave but I had to.[12]

And, for quite different reasons, the researcher might wish to remain in the field but be forced out by external circumstances. Recalling the manner in which she left the Japanese relocation project, Wax writes:

> In the middle of May, Dr. Thomas telephoned me and ordered me to leave Tule Lake immediately without letting anyone know that I was departing. I packed my few belongings and got out that night, assisted by one of the few staff members I could trust, a minister.

Arriving in Berkeley the next morning I learned that a Washington official of the WRA had called on Dr. Thomas and insisted that I be removed from the center. He backed up this demand with a list of impressive accusations: I had consorted with pro-Japanese agitators and attended ceremonies devoted to the worship of the Japanese emperor. I had had immoral (sex) relations with a number of Japanese-Americans. I had made disrespectful remarks about the project director. I had been a general troublemaker and had tried to subvert WRA policies. . . . So far as I can remember (for I took no notes), Dr. Thomas did not pay much heed to these accusations. Her attitude was that if she made any fuss about my expulsion it might create a scandal and jeopardize the research project and the reception of the eventual publications that would issue from it. Therefore, the best thing for me to do was to get out of Tule Lake and keep my mouth shut (1971: 169).

Other external reasons can also facilitate the leaving process. With reference to his research for *The Levittowners*, Herbert Gans writes:

I left there after two years of fieldwork, as I had wanted to do originally, but there was also an external reason; my marriage broke up. This made it easier to leave, because in those days (1960) the idea of a single person living in suburbia was still unusual; moreover, it provided an explanation to my neighbors who in a fairly transient area, did not like to see any "old resident" leave.[13]

The dimensions of temporality, sequencing, and desirability are only three of many analytical properties in the process of leaving the field. Others might include whether the study is an *individual or group* project (and whether field exiting is collective or single), *funded or unfunded*; whether the setting is *relatively closed or open, transient or residentially stable*; and whether there are *regularized rituals or methods of leaving* observed by the participants. Theoretically, these various properties might combine in patterned or perhaps even predictable ways. They might cluster in combinations which could result in differing modal types or styles of leaving. But that is an empirical question which we cannot answer at this time. What we can say is that the settings that prove most difficult to leave are probably those in which persons are not acquainted with the conventions of research—who, in other words, first accepted the researcher as a person and not as a fieldworker. In the course of work, the researcher may be primarily identified as a friend and confidant. The ensuing social relationships are organized around a theme of personal friendship, thus complicating the researcher's termination of work and departure from the setting.

To briefly sum up, then, our purposes in this selection were (1) to show that variations exist in field exit processes; (2) to suggest that these processes are partially a function of the commitments the researcher makes while conducting the research; and (3) to raise questions concerning the neglected topic of leaving the field. We maintain that although considerable negotiation occurs in field research, certain prior conditions and field circumstances come together in often fateful ways. Ongoing and appropriated identities having practical value in the field can later force researchers to make certain choices. This applies directly to how researchers leave the field, the decisions they make with regard to it, and the situations in which they find themselves.

Notes

1. This is an expanded and revised version of a paper presented at the 72nd Annual Meeting of the American Sociological Association, Chicago, 1977. We gratefully acknowledge the helpful comments of Howard Becker, Rosalie Wax, Herbert Gans, Norman Denzin, Anselm Struass, Robert Habenstein, Prudence Rains, Malcolm Spector, and Donald Roy.

2. One need only glance at the sociology literature to get a hint of the significance of this dimension. It is either explicitly or implicitly dealt with in studies of occupational mobility, migration, marriage and divorce, educational attainment, professionalization, life cycle processes, political realignment, social change, and death and dying, as well as those focusing on face-to-face encounters. All have in common the process of movement from one sphere of life to another.

3. For an incisive account of the ethnologist as a stranger, see Nash (1963).

4. These three cases were written separately by each author with the aid of a general topical guide. Hopefully, our use of the first person singular will not distract the reader. "I" refers to only one of the authors at a time, not collectively.

5. Roy eloquently makes our point for us: "I tried to play the role, but they would not play appropriate roles with me; there was no social system to back up my performance. In retrospect, the whole thing looks ridiculous, like trying to play Romeo without Juliet and the rest of the Montagues and Capulets, highly frustrating for Romeo unless he chances to be schizophrenic" (1965: 263).

6. Personal correspondence with the senior author, December 12, 1977.

7. Personal correspondence with the authors, n.d.

8. Personal correspondence with the senior author, December 10, 1977.

9. Personal correspondence with the senior author, December 14, 1977.

10. Personal correspondence with the senior author, January 22, 1978.

11. Personal correspondence with the senior author, December 27, 1977.

12. Personal correspondence with the senior author, December 12, 1977.

13. Personal correspondence with the senior author, December 13, 1977.

References

BECKER, H.S. "Notes on the Concept of Commitment." *American Journal of Sociology*, 66 (1960), 32–40.

280   DAVID R. MAINES ET AL.

BECKER, H.S. *Sociological Work: Method and Substance.* Chicago: Aldine, 1970.

BECKER, H., and J. CARPER. "The Elements of Identification with an Occupation." *American Sociological Review,* 21 (1956), 341–348.

BOGDAN, R., and S. TAYLOR. *Introduction to Qualitative Research Methods: A Phenomenological Approach to the Social Sciences.* New York: Wiley, 1975.

CARPENTER, E. "Comment on Research Among Eskimos." *Current Anthropology,* 1 (1965), 55–60.

DANIELS, A.K. "The Low-Caste Stranger in Social Research." In G. Sjobert, ed. *Ethics, Politics, and Social Research.* Cambridge, Mass.: Schenkman, 1967, pp. 267–296.

DENZIN, N. *The Research Act.* Chicago: Aldine, 1970.

FAULKNER, R. *Hollywood Studio Musicians.* Chicago, Aldine: 1971.

FOX, R. "An American Sociologist in the Land of Belgian Medical Research." In P. Hammond, ed. *Sociologists at Work.* New York: Basic Books, 1964, pp. 345–391.

GEER, B. "Occupational Commitment and the Teaching Profession." In H. Becker et al., eds., *Institutions and the Person.* Chicago: Aldine, 1968, pp. 221–235.

GEER, B. "Studying a College." In R. Habenstein, ed., *Pathways to Data.* Chicago: Aldine, 1970, pp. 81–98.

GERSON, E. "On 'Quality of Life.'" *American Sociological Review,* 41 (1976), 793–806.

GLASER, B., and A. STRAUSS. *Time for Dying.* Chicago: Aldine, 1968.

GLAZER, M. *The Research Adventure: Promise and Problems of Fieldwork.* New York: Random House, 1972.

HABENSTEIN, R. (ed.). *Pathways to Data.* Chicago: Aldine, 1970.

HEARN, H.L., and P. STOLL. "Continuance Commitment in Low-status Occupations: The Cocktail Waitress." *Sociological Quarterly,* 16 (1976), 105–114.

JOHNSON, J.M. *Doing Field Research.* New York: Free Press, 1975.

JUNKER, B.H. *Field Work: An Introduction to the Social Sciences.* Chicago: University of Chicago Press, 1960.

LEVINE, D. (ed.). *Georg Simmel on Individuality and Social Forms.* Chicago: University of Chicago Press, 1971.

LOFLAND, J. *Analyzing Social Settings: A Guide to Qualitative Observation and Analysis.* Belmond, Calif.: Wadsworth, 1971.

MADAN, T.N. "Political Pressures and Ethical Constraints Upon Indian Sociologists." In G. Sjoberg, ed., *Ethnics, Politics, and Social Research.* Cambridge, Mass.: Schenkman, 1967, pp. 162–179.

MILLMAN, M. *The Unkindest Cut.* New York: Morrow, 1976.

NASH, D. "The Ethnologist as Stranger: An Essay in the Sociology of Knowledge." *Southwestern Journal of Anthropology,* 19 (1963), 159–167.

POLSKY, N. *Hustlers, Beats, and Others.* New York: Doubleday, 1969.

RAINS, P. *Becoming an Unwed Mother.* Chicago: Aldine, 1971.

ROY, D. "The Role of the Researcher in the Study of Social Conflict: A Theory of Protective Distortion of Response." *Human Organization,* 24 (1965), 262–271.

ROY, D. "The Study of Southern Labor Union Organizing Campaigns." In Habenstein, ed. *Pathways to Data.* Chicago: Aldine, 1970, 216–244.

SCHATZMAN, L., and A. STRAUSS. *Field Research: Strategies for a Natural Sociology*. Englewood Cliffs, N.J.: Prentice-Hall, 1973.

VIDICH, A., and J. BENSMAN. *Small Town in Mass Society*. Princeton, N.J.: Princeton University Press, 1968.

WAX, R. *Doing Field Work: Warnings and Advice*. Chicago: University of Chicago Press, 1971.

WHYTE, W.F. *Street Corner Society*. Chicago: University of Chicago Press, 1943.

WILLIAMS, T.R. *Field Methods in the Study of Culture*. New York: Holt, Rinehart and Winston, 1967.

Breaking Relationships with Research Subjects: Some Problems and Suggestions

ALLAN ROADBURG *Dalhousie University*

By its nature, participant observation research includes field techniques that are both unique to each research situation and potentially problematic. In order to prepare for contingencies before entering the field, one can consult the literature which deals with these problems and seek advice from researchers who have had field experience.[1] These sources can be useful in discussing how a number of research-related problems have been sidestepped or solved. However, no matter how well prepared one may be, and irrespective of past experience in participant observation research, one can never predict or plan for all problems that might be encountered. This selection deals with a group of problems that tend to be overlooked in the literature! breaking relationships with research subjects.[2]

Participant observation research includes a unique form of interaction between the researcher(s) and subject(s). It is unique insofar as neither party has any control over the fact that the termination of the relationship coincides with the termination of the research. If individuals wish to continue a relationship after the research has concluded, it will no longer be a researcher-subject relationship but will be based on different criteria. Since problems of breaking relationships differ from situation to situation, this selection should be viewed as a summary of those problems encountered personally by the author.

The problems to be discussed were experienced while collecting data in Scotland for a study on the meanings of work and leisure.[3] The research was based on the premise that it is the context of the activity, rather than the activity itself, which is defined as work or leisure. As such, it included subjects who defined a certain activity as work and others who defined that same activity—but in a different context—as leisure. Individual definitions were ascertained through a questionnaire. The fieldwork included five months of participant observation with a full-time professional soccer club (hereafter to be referred to as the Pros),[4] six months with two amateur clubs (hereafter to be referred to as Amateur 1 and Amateur 2),[5] and a questionnaire to remunerated and nonremunerated gardeners. Before elaborating on the problems I encountered when breaking relationships with research subjects, it is necessary to outline a number of conditions which precipitated them.

CONDITIONS WHICH PRECIPITATE PROBLEMS

Breaking relationships with research subjects can present problems based on (1) the degree of interpersonal friendship or closeness between researcher and subjects; (2) the degree to which the researcher has suppressed personal ego with respect to the role of the scientist; (3) the degree to which the subjects have confided in the researcher; (4) the types of experiences shared by the researcher and subjects; (5) the conditions of the agreement established before the research began, and (6) whether the research was carried out alone or with colleagues.

It is likely that the more involved with subjects the researcher becomes, the greater the difficulty of breaking relationships. This can be explained on the basis of two elements: the length of time spent with subjects and the degree to which relationships develop between the researcher and each subject. For example, in my research with the Pros, I spent five months training, eating, and socializing with the players on a daily basis. I even bathed with them every day after training in a large tub which held up to twenty people. We spent a great deal of time together, and it would have been difficult not to become closely involved with them. Had I remained detached from personal relationships—if, for example, my research had involved observation alone—it is probable that I would have been excluded from certain after-training social activities. Consequently, I would have been unable to develop close rapport with my subjects. Alternatively, participation with the amateur football subjects was not as intense as with the Pros, simply because I did not spend as much time with them. Our time together was limited to one evening per week for training and the Saturday afternoon game. Since I decided to include two amateur teams in one season, and since I could not be in the company of both simultaneously, contacts were limited in time and intensity. Hence, terminating relationships with the amateurs caused fewer problems than with the Pros.

The second condition involves the dual roles of the participant observer. Indeed, the scientist must remain objective,[6] but at the same time, the scientist is a social being with an ego, sensitivities, needs, and failings. Conflict between these roles can be a problem in a participant observation situation, and the degree to which one has managed to separate them will have an affect on breaking relationships with subjects.

Because I spent a great deal of time with the Pros, on occasion I found myself struggling to reconcile my dual roles. On the one hand, I wanted to feel accepted by the players; on the other hand, I did not want to influence the research situation. My need for acceptance stemmed from the fact that I found myself becoming friendly with certain players. I was invited to their homes and drank with them in pubs; we went to the bookmakers (betting shop) after training and played cards together. On one occasion, a player asked my advice on a business venture he had in mind. The researcher's need for acceptance by the subjects can thus increase the likelihood of problems in breaking relationships.

Conflict between personal ego and scientific behavior can work in a different direction. For example, training invariably included some form of competitive race. These involved team efforts, such as relay races, and individual efforts, in which two players would sprint against each other. In the early stages of my research on the Pros, I accepted the fact that I would inevitably lose a sprint. However, as my physical condition improved, I found myself wanting to win. My ego asserted itself, I exerted myself, and I won a race. Immediately the scientist in me realized that I had erred. I was congratulated by a number of players, but the person I beat (I shall call him Steve) felt badly. Winning races was important to the Pros, and to be beat by an academic was embarrassing. Subsequently I indicated to Steve that I had "given it everything I had," and as a result my legs hurt. Steve then complained that he had pulled a muscle in last Saturday's game and his leg also hurt. When it came time for the next race, someone asked Steve to run against him. Steve replied, "I'm running against Alan." Steve easily redressed the situation by beating me soundly.

The third condition—the degree to which stubjects have confided in the researcher—reflects the level of confidence or trust between researcher and subjects. For example, my field notes with the Pros recorded at least a dozen players who commented, "I hope you don't write about this in your book." On each occasion, I was sharing an activity with the players that they preferred to keep from the manager or the media. These so-called secrets included what may be termed "unprofessional" behavior—that is, evenings in a pub or disco, or playing cards. The behavior in question was problematic only to professional athletes. It would have been perfectly acceptable to most amateur players or to most males in the Scottish culture.

As a further example of the Pros taking me into their confidence, I attended a discussion involving the signing of the players' contract for the following season. Many players were unhappy with the amount of money offered by the club, and an ad hoc meeting took place one afternoon after training. During this meeting, one player spoke of strike action while others drew up a number of contract demands. The important point is that the players allowed me to be present at the meeting. This followed, I believe, from the degree of confidence and trust which had been built up between us.

In the amateur football situations, none of the players were concerned about my joining them in their social life or in grievance sessions. They were not worried because they had nothing to hide and no one to hide it from. I joined Amateur 2 on one occasion in the pub following a game which ended in defeat. This was their third consecutive defeat, and the players returned to the pub to complain to each other and to argue over who was at fault for the current losing streak. The consequences of this discussion cannot be compared to those of the Pros' wage discussion or to the possible consequences to the Pros if the manager or the media learned about their evenings out. Yet, in spite of the fact that the Pros had more to lose than the amateurs, the Pros took me into their confidence on a number of occasions.

With respect to the fourth condition, the types of experiences I shared with the Pros differed from those I shared with the amateur football subjects. In effect, I shared a major segment of the Pros' lives. I did not share fully because I did not play in regular league games. Nevertheless, I played in training games and took part in the club's Christmas party and in a number of celebrations, such as players' twenty-first birthday parties, stag nights, and disco evenings. I even shared criticisms from the coach and manager for not trying hard enough at training. I experienced exercises players complained about, in the cold and the rain, and exercises they enjoyed. Although I also shared a segment of the amateur footballers' lives, the involvement here was minor.

The nature of the agreement established before the research began is the fifth condition that might influence the types of problems one might encounter in breaking relationships. This condition generally applies more to the person who gave permission to carry out the research. In the case of the Pros, I was given permission by the team manager; Amateur 1 by a committee member; and Amateur 2 by the captain.

The final condition has to do with whether the research was carried out alone or with colleagues. If carried out with others, the researcher has an ally within the research situation. This individual can act as a personal refuge for support when problems are encountered. Although sympathy and understanding can come from colleagues away from the field, it is not quite the same as having a co-worker who shares the actual fieldwork. In this respect, problems of leaving the field can be reduced somewhat if one shares the research load with others. My research on the Scottish soccer players was conducted alone.

TYPES OF PROBLEMS

In the context of this discussion, it is necessary to distinguish between what can be termed "pure" and "quasi" research subjects. The former includes individuals who define themselves or accept the fact that they are subjects of research. The latter includes individuals who do not necessarily consider themselves subjects. Pure subjects know they are the focus of the researcher's attention and do not expect to influence the direction of the project. Alternatively, quasi-subjects generally include those who gave the researcher permission to carry out the project. This difference relates to varying expectations and thus to different problems of breaking relationships.

As noted above, I received permission from the team manager to study the Pros. This individual held a formally appointed position of authority and power and apparently did not consider himself to be a subject (even though I considered him as such). He took me aside on a number of occasions to ask how I was progressing, what my findings were, and whether he could be of any further assistance. In the amateur soccer situations, the individuals who gave me permission held elected positions with little power, and both conceived of themselves as players first (in spite of the fact that the committee member rarely played) and organizers second. Accordingly, they considered themselves as pure rather than quasi-subjects, compared with the manager of the Pros, who was not a player and did not consider himself to be a research subject.

Moreover, it is necessary to distinguish between tactical and psychological problems. The former include the mechanics of breaking relationships, while the latter include personal feelings and definitions. Thus, in discussing problems of breaking relationships with research subjects I shall describe four types. These appear as four cells in Figure 1.

TACTICAL PROBLEMS: PURE SUBJECTS

The main tactical problems to be overcome, both prior to and during the process of breaking relationships, was to determine when and how to inform the pure subjects. This was not a problem with the Pros because

Figure 1.   Typology of Problems

Problem

		TACTICAL	PSYCHOLOGICAL
	PURE	1	3
Subject	QUASI	2	4

my research ended with the soccer season. In fact, my last day with the Pros was a ceremonious one. I entered the dressing room after training, and a player asked me for the time. I told him I was not wearing my watch. Suddenly, I was surrounded by a group of players who picked me up and carried me to the bathtub. On the count of three, they threw me fully clothed (in a track suit and running shoes), into the tub. Later I was told that this was a club tradition on the player's last day.

The situation was similar with Amateur 2. At the end of their season, most members of the team went on tour to play different amateur teams in Germany and Holland. I was invited to accompany them; when I declined, it was apparent that my research had concluded. With respect to Amateur 1, I informed both a committee member and a key player that I would be leaving on a specific date to do research on another soccer club (Amateur 2).

TACTICAL PROBLEMS: QUASI-SUBJECTS

The only quasi-subject to be discussed is the manager of the Pros. I experienced problems in breaking relations with him that did not occur with the pure subjects. At the outset, I told him that I would probably be with the club for a "couple of months." He agreed to this. However, as time went by, I found myself faced with the problem of deciding when to terminate my research. I was in a unique research situation (I do not know of any other case where participant observation research has been carried out on a British professional soccer club by a social scientist), and I wanted to be certain that I would gather sufficient data. Consequently, after several months with the Pros, the manager asked how much longer I planned to stay. When I indicated the end of the season—a total of five months—he agreed.

PSYCHOLOGICAL PROBLEMS: PURE SUBJECTS

The tactical problems of when and how to break relationships with subjects contrast sharply to the psychological problems which could result later on. In my case, I experienced feelings of guilt and alienation— that is, isolation—as well as a degree of melancholy after completing my research on the Pros. I will discuss these feelings in turn.

The problems of alienation and guilt arose some time after I left the Pros. I left at the end of the season, and because I had to wait until the following season to pay a friendly visit, I found that the longer I stayed away, the more difficult the visit became. Since so much time had elapsed, I kept putting off a return visit. On the one hand, I felt I should visit the players in their usual pub after a game. On the other hand, I felt I no longer "belonged"; I did not deserve to share their after-game drink because I was an outsider. I felt isolated from the players.

I did return to the stadium on a number of occasions, but it was difficult to catch the players together. During the period when we trained, we were together all the time. On a return visit, however, I either had to find them early in the morning before training, in the dressing room after training, or in the dining room eating lunch. On those occasions when I met a few players, I felt somewhat embarrassed and detached. I saw new faces, and it was as though the players had carried on without me. I felt that I had somehow let my friends down. I shared part of their lives and then just left. When I returned, I was no longer part of them. The players acknowledged me in a friendly manner, but the rapport was missing. Although my purpose in joining had been different from the players', I felt as though I had paid a return visit to friends I had previously rejected. To appreciate how I felt, the reader can recall or imagine a visit to a former place of employment. It was as though I had left them for a better life while they were forced to remain behind.

Describing my feelings of alienation and guilt after breaking relationships with the Pros is not easy. Furthermore, they reflect my definition of the situation. Perhaps these subjects did not share my feelings. Perhaps they were so involved in their own lives that they had little concern for my presence, even when I was among them. I realize that I may have projected my feelings onto these subjects, yet from my perspective, my feelings were real in their consequences.

It did not seem necessary to pay a return visit to the amateur soccer players; I did not feel close to them and had not shared a major portion of their lives in terms of experiences or time. Compared with the Pros, with whom I spent at least twenty-five hours each week for five months, I was with each amateur team for only a few hours a week for three months. Had I paid the amateur subjects a postresearch visit, it is probably that I would have felt no more detached than I did during the research. Consequently, feelings of guilt and alienation did not occur after breaking relationships with these subjects.

In addition to feelings of alienation and guilt, I also experienced a degree of melancholy and disruption after breaking relationships with the Pros. Although these feelings did not persist, I felt sad when the research ended. I had invested a great deal of time and energy in these relationships, and due to my reason for being among them, I began to understand their thoughts, feelings, and attitudes. When my research began, I was alone among thirty-two strangers. I was overweight, unfit, and unable to complete most of the exercises. As time elapsed, and as I began to develop friendships with as well as sympathy and understanding for these individuals, I came to feel that I belonged. I was never totally one of them because I maintained my role as a scientist and, as mentioned, did not participate in league games—a major point of distinction. Nevertheless, upon terminating my research, I had lost fifteen pounds, could complete most of the exercises—and, most important of all, felt at home with and accepted by the players. For this reason, I felt sad when the research was over.

Feelings of disruption pertained not only to breaking relationships with the Pros but also to terminating a daily routine. Five days a week for five months, I had arrived at the stadium around 9 A.M., went through a daily training schedule, and ate lunch with the players. Sometimes I met players after lunch to visit a pub or the bookies, or to play cards at the stadium. Each afternoon I laboriously completed my daily field notes. Subsequently, I was obliged to reorient myself after the research ended. In contrast, I experienced neither melancholy nor disruption after completing my research on the amateur subjects because this stage of my research did not include a daily routine.

PSYCHOLOGICAL PROBLEMS: QUASI-SUBJECTS

After terminating my relationship with the Pros' manager, I encountered a feeling of guilt. Unlike my feelings in regard to the pure subjects, this was based on an unfulfilled promise made before the research began. When I first approached the manager about my research, he agreed to let me join his club and requested a copy of my research report. I was involved in a commitment. I had contracted to produce a document of my observation, while the manager contracted to let me join his club and have a free hand in my fieldwork. After I left the field, and due to the fact that my written report included research the following season on two amatuer clubs (as well as data from thirty-seven gardener respondents), the promised document took some time to produce. I therefore felt a sense of guilt whenever I met the Pros' manager following my fieldwork. My guilt was based on a personal feeling (perhaps ill-founded) that because the report was unfinished, the manager felt that my five months with the club were a waste of time.

Almost a year elapsed before I presented the manager with a copy of my findings. In the interim, I published an article based on one segment of my research with the Pros.[7] When I indicated to the manager that this article had been published, his response was, "Why didn't you let me see it before you had it published?" Although this was not made explicit at the outset, when we discussed publication of my findings, the manager's primary concern was anonymity. I explained that the article was in an academic journal and would not be read by the general public. I also emphasized that I had not mentioned the club or the players' names. Nevertheless, the feeling of guilt persisted.

This feeling was not experienced with the amateur subjects, since I did not promise either team a copy of my final report. I did not promise a report because they did not ask for one. In general, it appears that guilt feelings depend upon the researcher's sense of obligation to the person who permitted the research. In the Pros' soccer situation, the manager was doing me a big favor in the sense of time spent with the players (including club-provided lunches) and letting me in on the inner workings of the club. Furthermore, a professional soccer club has more to hide than an amateur club. For example, when I asked all subjects in the interview if they felt that certain secrets should be kept from the public, all the Pros and 31 percent of the amateur subjects answered in the affirmative. Types of secrets mentioned by the Pros included wages (65 percent), players' private social life (32 percent), internal disputes (29 percent), and injuries (10 percent). One player for example, said:

> Certainly certain things are best kept secret. X's drinking habits, just to mention one. What players do after training and the night before a game, it would be best keeping most of that secret. Certain of the carryon's which occur when players are traveling together as a party. I think it would take some of the aura away from the players if all of their misdemeanors were reported. They would look a bit childish at times.

Since the amateur subjects had less to hide, it was not difficult to gain permission for my research. Moreover, although these subjects were interested, they neither expected nor were promised a copy of the findings.

For this reason, I did not feel guilt toward the permission givers on the amateur soccer teams.

When I presented the Pros' manager with my report, my feeling of guilt was alleviated. Since I had fulfilled my part of the contract, his attitude toward me seemed to have changed. During my fieldwork, I felt that he was doing me a favor—that I was taking rather than giving. But after giving him the findings, I felt I had redressed the balance. I found, for example, that he was more open in discussing his feelings about his role in professional soccer (the manager had changed teams in the interim).

OVERCOMING PROBLEMS

Before my research began, the possibility of having to overcome problems in breaking relationships with subjects simply did not occur to me. Consequently, took no steps to alleviate these problems. In retrospect, however, I can suggest the following.

It is important to make clear at the outset how long one intends to remain in the research situation. I did not specify how long I planned to remain with either amateur soccer club, and I was wrong in my estimation of timing with the Pros. If this had been made clear, the Pros' manager would not have had to wonder how much longer I would be with the club. It is also important to make clear at the outset how long the final report will take, assuming one is expected. It might well be that the greater the favor given by the permission giver(s) in allowing the researcher to work, the greater the likelihood that a final report is expected. By making it clear at the outset how long the report will take, false expectations will be eliminated.

To allay the psychological problems of leaving the field, instead of simply saying goodbye and then worrying about paying a visit months later (which I was forced to do with the Pros), it would be preferable for the researcher to return periodically to the research scene before paying a final visit. This way, new relationships based on visits of diminishing frequency could replace former relationships based on daily personal contact. In my case, I could have joined the Pros in their postgame drink at the beginning of the following season.

In conclusion, my research experiences suggest a positive relationship between closeness to one's subjects and the likelihood of experiencing feelings of alienation, guilt, and melancholy when these relationships are broken. The difficulty, of course, lies in the fact that if the researcher remains aloof, significant data may be bypassed. Alternatively, if the researcher becomes too close to the subjects, problems in reporting certain personal information, problems of objectivity, and problems of breaking relationships with these subjects can be encountered. Participant observation research is, by its very nature highly susceptible to these problems.

Although I have focused on my research and highlighted my feelings, the reader should not be left with the impression that I experienced serious problems after breaking relationships with my subjects. Furthermore, it must be reemphasized that the feelings described reflect my personal definition of the situation. I was conducting research on a unique group of individuals. British professional football players tend to lead a cloistered, ethnocentric existence and to be wary of outsiders. It is possible that my feelings of alienation and guilt are specific to this type of research situation.

Notes

1. For additional literature on participant observation research, see, for example: Robert Bogdan and Steven J. Taylor, *Introduction to Qualitative Research Methods* (New York: Wiley, 1975): Norman K. Denzin, ed., *Sociological Methods: A Sourcebook* (Chicago: Aldine, 1965): William J. Filstead, ed., *Qualitative Methodology* (Chicago: Markham, 1970): John Lofland, *Doing Social Life* (New York: Wiley, 1976): and George J. McCall and J. L. Simmons, eds., *Issues in Participant Observation* (Reading, Mass.: Addison-Wesley, 1969).

2. I would like to express my appreciation to John Pooley and John McCabe for their comments and suggestions.

3. This paper is based on research carried out for my Ph.D. at the University of Edinburgh.

4. Twenty-seven subjects defined their professional football situation as work, three defined it as both work and leisure, and two defined it as leisure.

5. Thirty subjects defined their amateur football situation as leisure and one defined it as work.

6. This is not the place to enter the debate on the objectivity of participant observation research or of social research in general. For a discussion on this point, see Severyn T. Bruyn, *The Human Perspective in Sociology* (Englewood Cliffs, N.J.: Prentice-Hall, 1966), pp. 219-33.

7. Alan Roadburg, "Is Professional Football a Profession?" *International Review of Sport Sociology*, 3 (1976), 27-37.

8. See note 6 above. The point here is if the researcher becomes too close to the subjects, the recording and interpretation of data may be further biased.

Crime as Work: Leaving the Field

PETER LETKEMANN *University of Lethbridge*

INTRODUCTION

This research project began almost imperceptibly, developed and took form slowly over a period of two years, then formally ended after several months of intensive interviewing and a flurry of "winding-up" activities. Research of this type is not usually characterized by a clearly defined beginning or completion, but my imminent departure for employment elsewhere required that the data collecting be concluded. That was ten years ago, and although the data have long since been analyzed and published, there are social ties which endure and research implications which continue.

How one leaves the field depends a great deal on how one entered it. If the data one seeks is accessible through observation and minimal or disguised participation, exiting may be fairly simple. A friend obtained all her data by serving as a secretary in a lawyer's office; leaving the field was a matter of terminating employment. On the other hand, research that depends on trust and friendship between researcher and respondent may be difficult to end in a way that is acceptable to both. The ease with which one leaves the field may also depend on the degree of care and sophistication with which one begins. The experienced and knowledge-able researcher will anticipate social relationships and, knowing his or her own capacity for making and maintaining friendships, will govern the social activities accordingly.

Not all research begins in such a deliberate manner, however. To study criminal behavior is to study activities which are largely hidden from public view, and even the most carefully designed research will come to nothing if the researcher is unable to gain the confidence of those who can provide access to such data. It is not surprising, therefore, that much of the research on criminal behavior is the result of fortuitous circumstances rather than deliberate plan. This is not to suggest that one simply "falls into" such research, nor, as I shall show, can one simply "fall out" of it. Field research on criminal behavior often grows out of existing friendships, work contacts, and chance opportunities which provide access to usually inaccessible data.

My own avenue to the data on crime as work originated in a small government study which I did partly to help out an overworked professor. I was asked to study and make recommendations about Habitual Offender and Dangerous Sexual Offender legislation, which brought me into contact with criminals both in and out of prison, defense lawyers, prosecutors, and parole and prison officials. Gradually, over a six-month period, relationships with some parolees developed into friendships and mutual trust. Many hours were spent in casual conversation while eating, driving, fishing, and other leisure-time activities.

It is difficult, in retrospect, to place this initial socialization within the framework of a formal research design, since at that time no further research was intended. My research was beginning, as it were, well before its formal inception. As a result of friendship, curiosity, and opportunity, and with the encouragement and help of these friends, a new and specific study developed. I interviewed forty-five experienced criminals, some in prison and some outside, as a result of referrals from persons I had come to trust. Some of the associations were entirely research-related and ended with the completion of the study; others continue, based on friendship and mutual interests. One can avoid bad feelings when leaving the field if the distinction between these associations is consciously maintained, permitting some relationships to flourish and others to end without misunderstandings. The researcher cannot usually be a friend to all, or to none.

It is ironic that the circumstances which make the research possible also put restrictions on it, and may, in fact, make it almost impossible. Given the existing relationships out of which the research is likely to have come, the researcher will not be entirely free in the choice of additional friends and respondents; all must be acceptable to the "charter members." Some respondents will expect friendship in exchange for their help. Some will expect to be more than mere respondents because they are "friends of friends." Existing friendships may be strained when the researcher begins taking notes during their conversations and thereby transforms a friend into a respondent.

Anyone who is contemplating a field study would do well to ask, in advance, How would I like this experience to end? Do I wish to cultivate ongoing associations, or should all relationships be research-dependent? The clearer the expectations, the more likely it is that the research will end in good will.

Dimensions of Reciprocity

To avoid misunderstanding and to provide criteria whereby both researcher and respondent can later determine whether the "research bargain" was a good one, it is important that researchers explain at the outset what benefits, if any, respondents may reasonably expect in exchange for cooperation. The actual fieldwork will involve an ongoing and subtle process of negotiation. Researchers may want additional data and wider access; respondents who do not understand fully what was agreed to at the outset may want to renegotiate for more recognition or tangible help in exchange. Researchers operate under financial, moral, and professional restraints, and although they need to be flexible, they must guard against succumbing to extortion.

As a result of the habitual criminal study, I began the research on crime as work with some of my key informants feeling indebted to me for submitting a report which brought their major grievances to the attention of the government. These respondents expected nothing else in return for their continued cooperation. In fact, some felt that I was the one being cheated, since they could see little value in the information they were giving me.

In all my interviews, I explicitly stated that the benefits of the research would not be mutual. I said that I expected to learn from them; they, in turn, should not expect me to do anything for them, for I had no connections which might assist their chances of parole, employment, or whatever.

Once the research was underway, expectations become more specific, sometimes leading me into situations of serious role conflict. I might ask for an additional interview and the respondent, in turn, might ask that I contact his parole officer on his behalf. Such negotiating was seldom explicit but rather flowed from the understanding and sense of fairness that were generated by the interview itself. Within this context, the expectations appear eminently reasonable, and it may not be until later that the researcher realizes the implications of the bargain. The researcher needs to be mentally and emotionally prepared for situations in which the research role may come into serious conflict with one's responsibilities as a human being. On a few occasions, for reasons of friendship or compassion, I knowingly jeopardized my access to prisons by interceding on behalf of some inmates.

In summary, some respondents cooperated because of personal

friendship, others because they were friends of friends, and some felt indebted because of my earlier study. There was, however, another dimension which should not be overlooked—namely, the respondents' own curiosity and interest in the study.

As mèthodologists have emphasized, one of the payoffs for the person being interviewed is the satisfaction of the interview itself. Since I avoided questions which I knew they disliked ("Why did you do it?") and concentrated on their skills as a criminal ("How did you do it?"), respondents appeared to derive considerable satisfaction from the interview itself. I was one of those rare outsiders who had not come to analyze their deficiencies. They received a great deal of satisfaction from discussing their much discredited skills with someone genuinely interested. Those persons not imprisoned were able to take an ongoing interest in the project, resulting in many discussions and unstructured interviews.

I will never know how many cooperated in order to gain favor with their superiors, or conversely, because of the fear of reprisals should they refuse. Although I gave strong verbal assurance prior to each interview that failure to cooperate would not be reported to anyone, one must recognize that prisoners are not free agents. Whatever the reason for their initial cooperation, respondents' candor and continued help will be dependent on a number of subtle, yet critical, considerations.

To begin with, as Polsky[1] has emphasized, it is important that the researcher have a clear identity. It should be understood that he or she cannot be persuaded to become "one of them," and that what is learned will not be reported to the police.

Secondly, researchers are not exempt from everyday social obligations. They may rightfully balk at being ombudsmen, but it is reasonable to expect them to be punctual, considerate, willing to use their car for the convenience of subjects, and surely to be as generous with their time as the respondents are with theirs.

A third consideration, and one that applies particularly to the study of deviance, is the interviewer's ability to manage the discrediting, and possibly incriminating, information received. To begin with, the vulnerable respondent needs to be assured that the researcher is legitimate, not an undercover police officer or a psychologist doing an assessment. Such assurance must come from those whom they already trust; hence the importance of researchers being known within the circles to which they have access. The respondent can quickly assess whether you are legitimate and whether you can be trusted not to go to the police, but it takes longer to know whether the researcher is self-disciplined and alert enough in everyday social settings to manage the information provided. This trust is a prerequisite should the researcher require participation in the respondent's social world, and earning it is not easy. Criminals expected that I would not reveal their status to others. While I interviewed a bank robber in his home, he advised me that we would need to change the topic each time his children entered the room. A fishing partner and former safe-cracker would advise me, prior to each outing, whether the other persons accompanying us knew of his status. If they didn't know, the entire fishing trip would need to pass without my saying anything that could discredit him. When phoning such respondents, one must ask whether they are alone before asking any questions related to the research. Secrets will not be told to those judged unable to keep them.

There is another, more subtle aspect to confidentiality—namely, a respect for things said by the respondent which he would not want the researcher to repeat and preferably not even to remember. These consist of gossipy items, criticism of other respondents, partners, and friends, revelations about their personal habits, and so on. It is ironic that the best data may be revealed when the researcher is perceived as a friend rather than a researcher. Fred Davis has described this very well:

> There then follows for many a fieldworker the unsettling recognition that, within very broad limits, it is precisely when his subjects palpably relate to him in his "out-of-research role" self . . . that the raison d'etre for his "in-role" self is most nearly realized; they are more themselves, they tell and "give away" more, they supply connections and insights which he would otherwise have never grasped. . . . It is in large measure due to this ineluctable transmuta-tion of role postures in field situations that, when he later reports, the sociologist often experiences a certain guilt, a sense of having be-trayed. . . . [2]

Just how comfortable one feels about the exploitation of friendships, whether in research or elsewhere, will depend upon personal values and sensitivity, but the sense of having betrayed can be minimized, even if never entirely eliminated. What is said in confidence can be kept confiden-tial, however much it might have added to the final report. Such informa-tion, even when not reported, retains much of its value, allowing the researcher to better understand those activities and attitudes that can be reported freely. Unless one chooses to leave the field and run, regardless of the repercussions of one's research upon the respondents, some compro-mise between research demands and the obligations of friendship is inescapable.

Researchers who deal with confidential data may be torn between the need for confidentiality and the need to give recognition to the subjects. Many of my subjects considered it important to read my final report when completed. I assured them that it would be available. Copies of the resulting Ph.D. dissertation were given to some informants for comments.

It became clear that my assurances of anonymity were not greeted with enthusiasm by everyone; some wished to be identified, some may have been hurt because they were quoted less frequently than others, and some found pleasure in identifying persons who had been quoted. These issues became even more critical when the study was published, as I shall discuss later.

The promise to provide a copy of the final report to subjects is a recognition of their contributions, but it may also be useful to the researcher. It is a strong incentive to finish the task. Some of my respondents would have felt betrayed had I not completed the study, and they put more pressure on me to get it done than did my graduate school!

LEAVING THE FIELD

Because of the social relationships which are necessarily developed during research of this type, it is best to terminate interviews, relationships, and the research itself on the basis of impersonal and external factors. The expiration of a research grant, termination of a visa, or, as in my case, the need to move are factors which allow the research and many of its social obligations to end without embarrassment or offense.

I thought it best, for example, to terminate individual prison interviews in keeping with the demands of prison routine. To have dismissed a respondent prior to 10:55 or 3:55 (at which time *all* inmates were called to their cells) might have implied that the respondent was not as productive or helpful as others, who were kept as long as possible.

When the respondents are part of a closed community, the permission to interview, given by administrators, may include a research termination date. Although prison administrators did not specify a date, it was clear that they did not expect my research to continue indefinitely. Prison respondents understood and accepted the fact that my association with them would be very limited.

It was more difficult in regard to those whom I interviewed and associated with outside of prison. Prior to my move, it had already become obvious that I would not have time to complete the research if I continued extensive social activity with so many of my respondents. I began, slowly and deliberately, to limit my nonresearch association to two respondents whom I found most congenial and compatible. This shift in association is precarious, and researchers should follow some important guidelines in order to avoid accusations of insincerity and exploitation. They should recognize, before beginning the research, that the success of the project is not likely to require them to become close personal friends of all or many respondents. This would not only tax the objectivity of the researchers but might make it impossible to complete the study as well as keep up social obligations. It would be difficult later to "cool out" friendships without appearing to have been insincere. It is possible to be a friendly researcher without becoming a friend. Depending on the nature of the research and the type of community being studied, it would seem best to keep relationships at a casual level, with personal friendships limited by one's ability to meet the obligations involved.

My geographic move served to sever direct social contact with all but the two respondents whose friendship I wished to maintain. More about this later.

PUBLICATION

Several years after leaving the field, I had the opportunity to publish my results in book form. Since the proposed book was to be only half the length of the original report, I was faced with the decision of what to include and what to exclude. It was at this time that I became most conscious of the way in which factors external to the research may influence the analysis and reporting of data.

There was the matter of objectivity. Knowing that respondents expect to read the final report may influence the selection of material, especially when respondents have become casual or personal friends. I was conscious of the fact that my respondents would recognize their own contributions, especially through direct quotations. I knew that I could not give each of them equal space and still handle the data responsibly. Would some be offended if they were quoted less often, or not at all? Could I be objective in my interpretation without offending someone? Could I be misinterpreted? I was nervous about this, since I had made a blunder in my dissertation copy. A respondent had called to indicate that he was offended by my reference to him as a "key informer"; of course, I had meant "key informant." A small mistake, and duly corrected, but of considerable importance to someone who had been a "solid" criminal and not a "rat" or "informer."

There were questions of self-interest. Perhaps I would someday wish to do prison research again; should I therefore be less critical of prisons in this report, so that I might again have the cooperation of the prison administrators? There were questions regarding the interests of prisoners. Some had been specifically critical of persons in power. Could these prisoners be identified and punished, or worse still, could someone be mistakenly identified and punished? And then there were prison employees who, in being helpful to me, may have overstepped their mandate. There was also the question of civic responsibility; could the material be used for illegal purposes? I considered this to be unlikely; besides, the details of criminal procedures were essential to my analysis.

Publication was important to me for professional/academic reasons. However, it was more than that; it allowed me to pay a debt to my respondents as a group. The book does not resemble a penal reform tract, but it does have implications of that sort. In addition, I was able, on the basis of the data, to present a picture of the career criminal as someone whose behavior can be explained without reference to psychopathology. The publication also provided external confirmation of the value of the respondents' contribution and my ability to do justice to it.

I sent complimentary copies to my two key informants, and they, in turn, distributed these to others whom they could contact. The response was gratifying and actually widened my circle of contacts. I received letters from offenders both in and out of prison from across Canada and the United States, as well as from corrections personnel and, of course, academics. I received much good advice, all of it filed for a possible second edition.

The effects of publication were not all pleasant. During the investigation of a riot and hostage-taking incident, guards found *Crime as Work* in a prison cell. Noting that it contained descriptions of safe blowing and robbery, they confiscated the book, indicating that they would use it as evidence in the investigation to the effect that their correctional efforts were being undermined by prison programs. By this they were referring to the fact that *Crime as Work* had entered the prison as recommended reading for an English course for inmates being taught by a university professor. The guards wanted the book declared contraband. The professor vigorously defended his right to choose his texts freely and solicited expert opinions to the effect that the book was academically sound. Furthermore, he argued, much of the information had originally come from inmates; they could get it on their cell block without the trouble of reading a book. The professor made his point so well in the local paper that the matter was dropped. I was relieved at the time to remember that my graduate school had insisted that lawyers review and approve the material before accepting my dissertation.

This issue highlighted the general concern researchers have for the possible use, misuse, or nonuse of their findings. The findings of the habitual offender study, referred to earlier, were not at all reflected in the official recommendations of the sponsoring agency. I am dismayed and embarrassed that my name is indirectly associated with these recommendations. *Crime as Work* has potential for misuse in the same way, ironically, that a book on "how to protect yourself from theft" provides helpful clues to the would-be thief. On the other hand, bank managers have found the text helpful in assessing bank security. While guards wanted to have it declared contraband, the International Association of Chiefs of Police were using it as a text in burglary prevention courses. The researcher must live with these incongruities.

KEEPING IN TOUCH

Although I was 800 miles away and involved in setting up a new home, my research respondents were initially never far from my thoughts. Newscasts and newspapers took on special meaning. I checked crime items eagerly, hoping that I would not find a respondent back "in trouble." Ten years later, I still try to keep informed about their welfare, although I have lost track of most of them. While attending a Corrections Conference in Vancouver, I was informed by a prison warden that one of my respondents had had his parole revoked and was back in prison; he arranged special visiting privileges for me. The prisoner had his parole reinstated shortly thereafter, and he credits me (mistakenly, I suspect) with facilitating his release. Since completing the research, I have corresponded with several parole officers, who have asked me for assessments of persons I had come to know through the research. I have also written letters of reference at the request, and on behalf, of some respondents. With the research completed, this helping relationship has not involved the role conflict experienced earlier.

My continuing contact is mainly with my two key informants, who, in turn, tell me about those persons of mutual acquaintance. This contact is via correspondence, phone calls, and annual visits. In addition to the personal pleasure my family and I derive from this contact, it also keeps me in touch with what is happening in the criminal world. I look forward each year to a guided tour through Vancouver's skid row, to see how the patterns of crime, and the participants, change from year to year. These friends also serve as valuable advisors on potential research and on questions of obligation. For example, I sought their advice when asked to lecture on burglary to police recruits. They did not think my respondents would consider this a betrayal of their trust.

I have earlier discussed the dilemma of the researcher who discovers that the best research takes place when in the role of friend. It was with some relief, therefore, when the research was completed and published to return to the respondents in the role of friend alone. Only then, did I feel, could I prove that my earlier friendship was sincere. I am surprised to find that my friends are not relieved, or as pleased with my new role, as I expected; they are repeatedly providing me with new research ideas and encouraging me to write another book. I do not doubt their sincerity but have come to realize that the respondents' friendship is not necessarily any purer than the researcher's.

Researchers would do well to calculate, in advance, the potential of a research project for ongoing social and moral obligations. A colleague who had been willing to lend his respondents some money during his research found that such requests continued after the research was completed. Since he could not move away, he was able to extricate himself from those obligations only by alienating those who had made his research possible. Research projects have a way of identifying researchers with particular causes. I became identified with prison reform and received numerous letters from prisoners in both the United States and Canada. Personal interest, much of it generated by the research, has prompted letters to the Canadian Law Reform Commission and involvement in volunteer work on behalf of prison reform. There are no rules to indicate when the obligations stemming from research are laid to rest; researchers must be prepared to deal with these issues on a personal basis.

If one of the payoffs of an interview is the pleasure of the social interaction, then one of the rewards of field research is the possibility of continued contact with respondents. Broadly defined as continued learning on a specific topic, the research on crime as work is not yet ended. The research field consists essentially of human beings who can continue to enrich the researcher's life long after the original data is forgotten.

Notes

1. Ned Polsky, *Hustlers, Beats and Others* (Chicago: Aldine, 1967), pp. 117–149.
2. Fred Davis, "Comment on 'Initial Interaction of Newcomers in Alcoholics Anonymous'," *Social Problems*, 8 (Spring 1961), 365.

Leaving the Newsroom

DAVID L. ALTHEIDE   *Arizona State University*

My studies of TV news have raised a number of questions about the research process, including how a researcher comes to know certain things about a setting, as well as the way one realizes that certain features of the insider's perspective have been grasped. My experience in a variety of news settings became more intelligible once I left the field and became reintegrated with other outsiders. In the following selection, I will discuss how my exitings were accomplished and how they provided additional substantive material.

I studied a network affiliate between October 1971 and September 1972 (Altheide, 1974). Other news settings in which I have spent less time, both during and after the affiliate study, include other affiliates in three states (Altheide and Rasmussen, 1976), various aspects of all news operations at the national political conventions in 1972, and a network owned and operated station (Altheide, 1976). In addition to reading and conversing with the authors of some two dozen studies about news operations throughout the United States, Canada, and Europe, I have pursued informal as well as more structured interviews with journalists during the last six years. And each time a study is read, an author conversed with, or a journalist interviewed, I must reflect on the original year spent at the network affiliate. Such recollection and comparison usually elicit details I did not previously think important, or forges connections which had heretofore slipped through my analytical scheme. Thus, even though I left that particular research scene some six years ago, I am still going back to it, at least through recollection. This experience, common to many researchers I have talked with, suggests that leaving a setting is not unidimensional and cut-and-dried, but instead involves an interaction among the researcher, subjects, and varieties of data.

My physical detachment from the network affiliate differed in important ways from the other news settings I encountered, as well as several non-news involvements. First, in the other settings, I knew my stay would be limited, perhaps as little as one day, or only as long as a particular event lasted. An example of the latter was the national political conventions in 1972. While I arrived several days before each conclave began, I knew at the outset that I would return home—as the journalists would—within a day or so after the respective candidates were nominated. And my more recent investigations of sports reporters are scheduled according to season, and in some cases, particular athletic contests. Even though the research time usually exceeds the sports event time there is nevertheless a parallel.

My study of the network affiliate was much different. First, it was a general study of the news process, although my original point for entry was to study the station's treatment of a national political convention which was scheduled to occur, but was then withdrawn to another city. In that sense, my original plans were somewhat event bound, but even in this case, there was much preconvention planning to observe. Thus, I had a bit of leeway as far as the management was concerned. But staying in the setting was a problem throughout this study. On one occasion, when the news director, who had little admiration for me or my study, wondered why I was still around since the convention had departed, I explained that the convention was only *one* thing I wanted to observe. I was mainly interested in the news process in general, and originally felt that the convention would be a good event on which to focus. More importantly, I was able to use his invitation to leave the setting as a way to obtain further legitimation by establishing a seven-month timetable which included spending time with several other departments (e.g., editorial), and several newsworkers who had been able to avoid my scrutiny. Also, I was able to arrange to interview the news director officially, an original oversight on my part, which may have given the newsroom boss the impression that I felt he was not important. Thus, the threat to throw me out was itself turned into an important research strategy. But it also provided some insights into the news director's perspective regarding his place in the operation. Finally, this confrontation enabled me to further define myself as a researcher and, in the process, gain further time-based legitimation.

Implicit in the above comments is the realization that researchers are often unaware of how the members regard them until they are either about to leave or are actually out the door. This poses certain validity problems, since investigators would like some assurance that the previously collected data were not blatantly devised to cool them out, minimize contact, or simple get rid of them. For these reasons, then, it is useful to have some inside knowledge about the members' sense of the researcher before the study is terminated. In my case, this was an ongoing concern, although I felt quite confident that I knew the people I could trust, as well as those who often intentionally avoided me. Nevertheless, I sought other verification of my perceptions of these people and situations, although I did not really know how to obtain it. Part of my problem was solved by the aid of an inside informant who was instrumental in paving my initial entry into the newsroom. Not only did this person provide much technical understanding and introductions to personnel, but he was also able to verify a number of my impressions and observations, as well as let me know what some people were saying about me when I was absent.

The insider's attentiveness was especially helpful to me on three occasions when I had left the newsroom for extended periods. My first leave-taking occurred as I was making final preparations for my oral Ph.D. examination. The three weeks I was gone—from the end of May to June 20—gave some members the impression I was gone for good, despite my prior explanations. For example, one cameraman scornfully said he thought I'd gone south with a book he had loaned me. During this time, my informant learned several things about some members' overall assessment of me and my research. Fortunately for me, little of this private information entailed major changes on my part, though it was possible.

The other two times I left the setting were to attend the national political conventions. On July 3, just three days prior to my leaving for the Democratic Convention, the news director questioned me about the use of a tape recorder. One cameraman was unaware that my recorder was on while I talked with him and a reporter. I was told in no uncertain terms by the news director that this should not happen again. It was at that time that he requested the timetable for the remainder of my study which I referred to above. I returned from the Democratic Convention and reenetered the newsroom on July 27, only to have my inside informant tell me that the news director had boasted to him about "bringing me down" several notches. This information served to validate a number of prior impressions I had of the news director's perceived role as the absolute ruler of the newsroom. Most importantly, this comment may not have been forthcoming if I had not left the newsroom for a period of time.

My final prolonged absence from the newsroom occurred when I left for the Republican Convention on August 16. I returned via the American Sociological Association Convention in New Orleans, finally reentering the newsroom on September 6. As with my prior return from the Democratic conclave, I was greeted as though I were a returning staff member; there was no fanfare, and only a few members expressed curiosity about my convention experience. And as before, the members' definitions of me were clarified even if they still appeared to be ambiguous. For one thing, throughout the entire study few members remembered that I was doing research; several felt that I was looking for a job, and at least one suspicious insider believed I was spying on them. My closest friends in the setting simply took my presence for granted and accepted me, even to the point of informing me about sexual involvements which only a select few would ever know about. While this acceptance obviously had tremendous research payoffs—I did not have to keep justifying my existence—it did pose some problems since the members often expected me to know some things that, as a researcher, I wanted to confirm. But I discovered several times that I could not just keep asking them to delineate certain procedures and assessments; they felt that any competent insider should know these things already, including me. My periodic leave-taking, however, did serve to remind some of the members that I was a visitor, and that certain renewed greetings were in order, including fresh inquiries about what I was doing and trying to find out. When these situations arose, I would take every opportunity to ask them what they were doing, what they felt was important, and most pertinent, what had been going on while I had been gone. This was a useful strategy—using my temporary leaves not only to obtain further information about their activities but also to provide me with a comparative, time-based assessment of what the members felt a researcher was and would be interested in, as well as what they felt a researcher could tell them. In short, leave-taking served to generate comments and observations worthy of constructing a reflexive assessment of who and what a researcher is, as well as to clarify further whether I was regarded as an enigma who would be missed and hotly discussed as soon as he disappeared. I did not get the impression that this was the case. This, in turn, leads me to tentatively conclude that *I was to them as I perceived myself to be to them*: an outsider who gradually became a quasi-insider who some people liked and others did not. This was of the utmost significance in laying to rest any fears I may have had—and actually lost sleep over—as to my place in the research setting. While for me it was a mixture of a research and work setting, for them I was merely in their work setting as someone who wanted to learn and to help in the news process.

My use of the partial or temporary leaves of absence from the newsroom to further document important information about the workers' definitions of me, the research, and my status as a member-researcher also prepared me for the time when I would permanently leave the newsroom. The decision to leave was informed by practical considerations, such as proceeding with the data analysis and writing phase of my dissertation, but equally important as a clue that I was ready to leave was the realization that many situations were being repeated, and that I was learning little that was new. My reading of a variety of classical and contemporary research reports indicated that a year seemed to be optimal. I realized that most people—including colleagues and professors—would regard this as a reasonable observation period, especially since I had also attended the national political conventions and had visited several other news settings. Further, I was nearing the end of the scheduled time I had proposed to the news director. While this was never mentioned, I was aware of it, and worried about not overextending a stay that was, frankly, often traumatic for me. So, in a sense I was ready to leave.

The subjects were also ready to see me go, but in a very friendly way. Throughout the study, and especially after I had temporarily withdrawn to prepare for my examinations or attend the conventions, I would be asked about my forthcoming "exposé" and when it would be completed. Indeed, one informant—a good friend during my research—had even gone so far as to suggest that I could get it done sooner if I were not so lazy!

Still another reason for deciding to leave was that I was simply getting bored. Much of the novelty had worn off, and I was anxious to complete the study in order to move on to other projects. (I have since discovered that this is a pitfall of my long-term involvements with projects, a fate a number of my colleagues appear to share.) Related to this realization that few new insights were coming my way, although more would appear in the months after I left, was the belief that certain crucial questions and more forthright research strategies could not be proposed until I had made the decision to leave. In other words, partly because of my concern about not stepping on toes, or saying the wrong thing lest the news director terminate the study, I had avoided more direct assaults on certain topics, and with particular individuals, until I was ready to leave. If the information I sought was not forthcoming and I was thrown out, then little would be lost since I already had most of what was needed. That was a point I had to build up to in regard to the nature and types of data, as well as an awareness that I had reached the point where my analytical emotional categories had been saturated.

One example of the harder push linked to the decision to leave was my direct questioning of certain workers about the station's involvement in local politics. I knew this was a taboo topic; whenever I tired to get subjects to discuss it, they would only allude to it, lest it should come back to haunt them in the form of loss of overtime, bad assignments, or in the extreme case, being fired. I believed then, and still believe, that many of their fears were a bit overdrawn, but nevertheless, several workers perceived the situation as such. Editorials were the most direct form of station involvement in local politics. My previous requests to the news director to attend editorial meetings were met with a cold rebuff and a strong refusal. Indeed, he later boasted to my major professor at a cocktail party how he had prevented me from attending these meetings. Of course, he had good reason to be concerned since it was he who dictated the topic and the station's position. All news workers felt that these practices violated a distinction between news and editorials. The editorial researcher would then do the "dirty work" of getting together the "respectable facts" following a meeting with the news director and the station manager, a powerful member of the state Republican party. The news director was especially partial to the mayor, whom he took some credit for getting elected, and boasted to his friends in the newsroom that he would help propel him into even higher office. For these reasons, I wanted to find out more about the editorial process. And for these same reasons, I was hesitant to pursue it until I knew the research was about finished.

When I made the decision to speak to the editorial researcher about the entire process during my final week or so at the station, he was willing to help. One reason was that I had been quite friendly and supportive of his attempts to gain the respect of the exploitive news director as well as the remainder of the staff. He agreed to get me copies of all station editorials during the last year and to discuss certain facets of specific cases. As we talked, it became apparent that he was having some difficulty in obtaining full information about how the TV audience was receiving a brief morning newscast with which he was involved. He had just received negative feedback from the news director but suspected that some positive letters and comments were not getting through to him. Since this was consistent with my experience and personal assessment of the news director, I agreed to have several of my friends write letters about the newscast to the news director, who would tell me whether he received them. In return, I would get help in learning about the editorial process. Thus, a bargain produced a natural experiment. He never got the letters, but I did get the editorial materials I desired, plus further verification about the news director's tactics in running the newsroom.

Another distinct change when I was preparing to leave the newsroom permanently was my willingness to comment more openly and answer questions put to me by news workers. As an advanced graduate student, I was frequently asked by reporters and camera operators about my political views and how I felt a certain point in a story should or should not be emphasized. I was occasionally asked to editorialize on particular editoral positions and station policy in general. And even though I usually agreed with the workers when they felt the wrath of the news director, I tried to contain my feelings and, when possible, defuse or neutralize my own involvement. This was especially relevant to the station's avowed as well as actual policy regarding local politicians, community service, and minority group coverage. All this was apparent to me as well, but it was only during my final month or so that I began to more realistically—and even enthusiastically—follow up on invitations to express my point of view on, for example, the station's public service commitment and how well—or poorly—it was being fulfilled. I told one reporter without hesitation that it could do a lot better. And in another case, I explained to a reporter how a statistical assessment of violence in high school prepared by the school board was irremediably biased due to major sampling errors and offered to provide a distinguished professor who would be very critical of the report. When the reporter asked why I had not said something earlier, I sheepishly replied that I did not realize the error at that time.

On another occasion, I pursued a top investigative reporter with probing questions about the station's involvement in local politics that was promoting the interests of selected officials. He made it clear that he felt the station had been the handmaiden of the power structure, but he couldn't really prove it since he did not have time and the station would not fund a depth probe. I want to emphasize that I considered more direct assaults on staff members to be quite risky, and it was only when I was prepared to exit that the path to these data was symbolically cleared.

There were a number of other less tangible but still important examples of my altered demeanor in the newsroom. While I was usually quite at ease with certain workers, I found myself becoming more daring as my terminal date approached. I would openly laugh, spar, and goof off with the veterans regardless of the news director's presence. While this was still not as natural for me as for some of the workers, it was markedly different from the caution I generally used when moving through the newsroom, always wary of the news director's foreboding request to "come into my office, young man." The payoff in this more direct involvement with news operations such as answering telephones, writing news stories, and giving advice and counsel to callers was that I became more like the other members, and was less concerned about being singled out for special treatment by the news director, even though I knew it could happen at any time.

On my last day at the station, I said a very casual good-bye to several of the workers, noting that I would be seeing them before long. In most cases this was true, since during the next six months I saw them on stories at the university where I was writing my dissertation or, as in one case, encountered a news crew on the city streets filming an unsuccessful armed robbery. In another case, I chatted with a reporter while sitting around a condominium swimming pool with a friend who had recently moved in. One trusted informant was sought out while he visited his recently divorced wife, who lived in the same student housing complex I did.

One reason I did not engage in a long and formal farewell was that I doubted it would be final. Also, however, I did not want to define a situation in which the news director could again demand that drafts of all written work be submitted to him for approval. He had insisted at one point during the study that he had veto rights over any report that came out of the research, even though we had never agreed to this unreasonable and unsatisfactory condition at the outset. So, in a manner of speaking, I had to slip out of the setting, noticed by several friends, but not in an eventful way that would have called forth the news director's wrath. At least, that was my interpretation at the time.

Although I had left the newsroom, my work did not stop. I continued to view news reports and take notes on format changes, topics covered, and technical features. I also kept in close contact with my inside informant, who continued to let me know what was going on, as well as verify, confirm, or explain certain issues. I also attempted to learn how a competing station used social scientists to survey viewers in order to hype its own newscast.

I continued to code the field data and further develop my analytical perspective in order to begin writing the dissertation, but I still felt an attachment to the newsroom. Not only was the routine different now that all I had to do was teach several classes off campus, perform my duties as a graduate student, spend time with my family, and of course, finish the dissertation, but I both missed and dreaded the news scene I had left. I missed it because I liked most of the people, who had been very helpful;

they were refreshing options to the competitiveness of some fellow graduate students and the uncooperativeness of certain faculty members who were determined to make life miserable for several of my friends and, if they could, for me as well. Of course, I tended to remember the good times, like having lunch on a breaker-lined beach filled with beautiful women and joking about how the assignment editor who had sent us to the story had not succeeded in ruining our day after all. That was easy to miss, but at the same time, I dreaded the thought of the news director either calling me or, worse, stopping by the office to find out what I was doing and asking when he would be able to preview my report. I dreamed of this more than I care to remember. And the concern persisted even after this man lost his job because of a shakeup to improve the ratings; the irony was that he accepted a position in public relations at a local university. At the bottom of it all, of course, was my belief that I could not be safe from his potential troublemaking capacity until my dissertation was completed and accepted. And it was only when I accepted a position several hundred miles away at another university, and then finished my dissertation some six months later, that I felt safe from the fear and dread induced by this man.

There were still the good times and the good friends, who I realized would not be part of my life in the future. Ironically, it was my concern with their well-being, and my commitment not to betray their trust or hurt them in any way, that created certain ethical problems for me in regard to informing them about the results of my study. For one thing, it was clear that the members would recognize the various individuals referred to, even though anonymity was respected throughout. In some instances the anonymity may have worked too well, since at least three journalists who worked for news operations in other cities have claimed that my study was obviously about their station! Nevertheless, the weak subjects in my report would stand out to their co-workers, and I did not want them to be ridiculed by their fellows or, for that matter, confront them with the absurdity, albeit the integrity, of many of their activities. And I did not want some of the members to read what their "anonymous" co-workers had said about them. These concerns led me to avoid giving a copy of my dissertation to the news director, although I did send certain members abstracts which indicated where they could obtain a copy. I pursued much the same strategy when some portions of the dissertation were combined with new materials to form the basis for my book on the news perspective (Altheide, 1976). I felt that this fulfilled my responsibility to make them aware of the material without forcing it on them. And most importantly, this decision enabled me symbolically to leave the newsroom just as I had left it physically several years earlier.

CONCLUSION

My experience with leaving my research setting was not clear-cut, but was instead more of a process involving myself, the subjects I studied, and varieties of data that often appeared only after I had left. By engaging in repeated leaves of absence, I was able to gain more detail and a fuller perspective on my place in the newsroom and the members' definitions of me. Each time this was done, more insight was gained, especially a capacity to reflect on my role in the data-generating and collecting aspect of the study. In this sense, these leave-takings made important substantive contributions.

My decision to leave the newsroom was partly made for me by the recurrence of familiar situations and the feeling that little worthwhile was being revealed. I would have to take a more active role, which held the potential of stepping on toes and raising the news director's ire. However, after some reflection, including an awareness that nearly a year had passed since the study began, I felt that more direct steps could be chanced since the end was in sight. My altered activities, along with the new data acquired, opened up new possibilities for analysis of what I had been taking in for all those months, but it also symbolically closed off the research site. There was little left to wonder about in regard to the members' perspectives and activities; the new challenge was to make sense of it all, and that would be done in the final phases of writing and analysis. But it is still quite clear that the departing process was an important part of the research experience.

References

ALTHEIDE, D.L. "The News Scene." Ph.D. dissertation. San Diego: Dept. of Sociology, University of California, 1974.

ALTHEIDE, D.L. *Creating Reality: How TV News Distorts Events.* Beverly Hills, Calif. Sage Publications, 1976.

ALTHEIDE, D.L., and P.K. RASMUSSEN. "Becoming News: A Study of Two Newsrooms." *Sociology of Work and Occupations,* 3 (1976), 223–246.

Bibliography

ALTHEIDE, D.L. *The News Scene*. Ph.D. dissertation, San Diego: Dept. of Sociology, University of California, 1974.

ALTHEIDE, D.L. *Creating Reality: How TV News Distorts Events*. Beverly Hills, Calif.: Sage Publications, 1976.

ALTHEIDE, D.L., and P.K. RASMUSSEN. "Becoming News: A Study of Two Newsrooms." *Sociology of Work and Occupations*, 3 (1976), 223-246.

BALTZELL, E.D. *The Protestant Establishment*. New York: Random House, 1964.

BARNES, J.A. "Some Ethical Problems in Modern Field Work. *British Journal of Sociology*, 14 (1963), 118-134.

BECKER, H.S. "Problems of Inference and Proof in Participant Observation." *American Sociological Review*, 23 (1958), 652-660.

BECKER, H.S. "Notes on the Concept of Commitment," *American Journal of Sociology*, 66 (1960), 32-40.

BECKER, H.S. "Problems in the Publication of Field Studies." In A.J. Vidich, J. Bensman, eds., and M.R. Stein, *Reflections on Community Studies*. pp. 267-284. New York: Wiley, 1964.

BECKER, H.S. "Review of *Sociologists at work*, ed. P.E. Hammond." *American Sociological Review*, 30 (1965), 602-603.

BECKER, H.S. *Sociological Work: Method and substance*. Chicago: Aldine, 1970a.

BECKER, H.S. "Practitioners of Vice and Crime." In R. Habenstein, ed., *Pathways to Data*. Chicago: Aldine, 1970b, pp. 30-49.

BECKER, H.S. "Field Work Evidence." In H.S. Becker, *Sociological Work: Method and Substance*. Chicago: Aldine, 1970c.

BECKER, H.S. "Interviewing Medical Students." In W.J. Filstead, ed., *Qualitative Methodology*. Chicago: Markham, 1970d.

BECKER, H.S. "Whose Side Are We On?" In W.J. Filstead, ed., *Qualitative Methodology*. Chicago: Markham, 1970e.

BECKER, H.S. *Sociological Work: Method and Substance*. Chicago: Aldine, 1971.

BECKER, H.S. "Art as Collective Action." *American Sociological Review*, 39 (1974), 767-776.

BECKER, H.S. "Arts and Crafts." *American Journal of Sociology*, 83 (1978), 862–889.

BECKER, H.S., and J. CARPER. "The Elements of Identification with an Occupation." *American Sociological Review*, 21 (1956), 341–348.

BECKER, H.S., and B. GEER. "Participant Observation and Interviewing: A Comparison." *Human Organization*, 16 (1957), 28–32.

BECKER, H.S., B. GEER, E.C. HUGHES, and A.L. STRAUSS. *Boys in White*. Chicago: University of Chicago Press, 1961.

BELL, C., and H. NEWBY, eds. *Doing Sociological Research*. London: Allen & Unwin, 1977.

BERARDO, F.M. "Social Adaptation to Widowhood among Rural-Urban Aged Population." Washington State College of Agriculture, *Experimental Station Bulletin 689*, 1967.

BERARDO, F.M. "Survivorship and Social Isolation: A Case of the Aged Widower." *The Family Coordinator*, 1 (1970), 11–25.

BERGER, P.L. *Invitation to Sociology: A Humanistic Perspective*. Garden City, N.Y.: Doubleday, 1963.

BERK, R. "Re: Qualitative Methodology." Unpublished manuscript. Evanston, Ill.: Northwestern University.

BERK, R.A., and J. ADAMS. "Establishing Rapport with Deviant Groups." *Social Problems*, 18 (1970), 102–117.

BLUMER, H. *Symbolic Interactionism*. Englewood Cliffs, N.J.: Prentice-Hall, 1969.

BOGDAN, R., and S.J. TAYLOR. *Introduction to Qualitative Research Methods: A Phenomenological Approach to the Social Sciences*. New York: Wiley, 1975.

BOGDAN, R., and S.J. TAYLOR. "The Judged Not the Judges: Insiders' Views of Mental Retardation." *The American Psychologist*, 31 (1976), 47–52.

BOWEN, ELENORE. *Return to Laughter*. Garden City, N.Y.: Doubleday, 1964.

BRIGGS, J.L. *Never in Anger*. Cambridge, Mass. Harvard University Press, 1970.

BROMLEY, D.G., and A.D. SHUPE, JR. "Just a Few Years Seem Like a Lifetime: A Role Theory Approach to Participation in Religious Movements." In L. Kriesberg, ed., *Research in Social Movements, Conflict*, Greenwich, Conn.: JAI Press, 1979a.

BROMLEY, D.G., A.D. SHUPE, Jr., and J.C. VENTIMIGLIA. "The Role of Anecdotal Attrocities in the Social Construction of Evil." In James T. Richardson, ed. *The Deprogramming Controversy: Sociological, Psychological, Legal and Historical Perspectives*. New Brunswick, N.J. Transaction Books, forthcoming.

BRUYN, S. *The Humanistic Perspective in Sociology: The Methodology of Participant Observation*. Englewood Cliffs, N.J.: Prentice-Hall, 1966.

BURNHAM, S. *The Art Crowd*. New York: David McKay, 1973.

CAMERON, M.O. *The Booster and the Snitch*. Toronto: Collier-Macmillan, 1964.

CARRIER, J. "Cultural Factors Affecting Urban Mexican Male Homosexual Behavior." *Archives of Sexual Behavior*, 5 (1976), 103–124.

CARPENTER, E. "Comment on Research among Eskimos." *Current Anthropology*, 1 (1965), 55–60.

CHRISTOPHERSON, R. "Making Art with Machines: Photography's Institutional Inadequacies." *Urban Life and Culture*, 3 (1974), 3–34.

CICOUREL, A.V. *Method and Measurement in Sociology.* New York: Free Press, 1964.

COLVARD, R. "Interaction and Identification in Reporting Field Research: A Critical Reconsideration of Protective Procedures." In G. Sjoberg, ed., *Ethics, Politics and Social Research.* Cambridge, Mass.: Schenkman, 1967, pp. 319-358.

CORK, M. *The Forgotten Children.* Don Mills, Ontario: General Publishing, 1969.

DALTON, M. *Men Who Manage.* New York: Wiley, 1959.

DANIELS, A.K. "The Low-Caste Stranger in Social Research." In G. Sjoberg, ed., *Ethics, Politics, and Social Research.* Cambridge, Mass.: Schenkman, 1967.

DAVIS, F. "Comment in Initial Interaction of Newcomers in Alcoholics Anonymous." *Social Problems,* 8 (1961), 364-365.

DAVIS, F. "Stories and Sociology." *Urban Life and Culture,* 3 (1974), 310-316.

DENZIN, N.K. *Sociological Methods: A Sourcebook.* Chicago: Aldine, 1970.

DENZIN, N.K. *The Research Act.* Chicago: Aldine., 1970.

DEUTSCHER, I. "Word and Deeds: Social Science and Social Policy." *Social Problems,* 13 (1965), 233-254.

DOMHOFF, G.W. *The Higher Circles.* Toronto: Random House, 1971.

DOUGLAS, J.D. *Investigative Social Research: Individual and Team Field Research.* Beverly Hills, Calif.: Sage Publications, 1976.

ERIKSON, K.T. "A Comment on Disguised Observation in Sociology." *Social Problems,* 14 (1965), 366-373.

FAULKNER, R. *Hollywood Studio Musicians.* Chicago: Aldine, 1971.

FEINBLOOM, D., M. FLEMING, V. KIJEWSKI, and M. SCHULTER. "Lesbian/Feminist Orientation among Male-to-Female Transsexuals." *Journal of Homosexuality,* 2 (1976), 59-71.

FILSTEAD, W.J. *Qualitative Methodology: Firsthand Involvement with the Social World.* Chicago: Markham, 1970.

FINE, G.A., and B. GLASSNER. "Participant Observation With Children: Promise and Problems." *Urban Life,* 8 (1979), 153-174.

FOX, R. "An American Sociologist in the Land of Belgian Medical Research." In P. Hammond, ed., *Sociologists at Work.* New York: Basic Books, 1964, pp. 345-391.

FREIDSON, E. *The Profession of Medicine.* New York: Dodd Mead, 1970.

FREILICH, M., ed. *Marginal Natives: Anthropologists at Work.* New York: Harper & Row, 1970.

GAFFIELD, G., and W.G. WEST. "Introduction." In H. Berkeley, C. Gaffield, and W.G. West, eds., *Children's Rights in Canada: Educational and Legal Issues.* Toronto: OISE Publications, 1978.

GALLAGHER, A., JR. "Plainville: The Twice Studied Town." In A.J. Vidich, J. Bensman, and M.R. Stein, eds. *Reflections on Community Studies.* New York: Harper & Row, 1964.

GANS, H. "The Participant Observer as a Human Being: Observations on the Personal Aspects of Field Work." In H.S. Becker, B. Geer, D. Riesman, and R. Weiss, eds., *Institutions and the Person.* Chicago: Aldine, 1968, pp. 300-317.

GARFINKEL, H. *Studies in Ethnomethodology.* Englewood Cliffs, N.J.: Prentice-Hall, 1967.

GEER, B. "First Days in the Field." In P. Hammond, ed., *Sociologists at Work*. New York: Basic Books, 1964, pp. 322–344.

GEER, B. "Occupational Commitment and the Teaching Profession." In H.S. Becker, B. Geer, D. Riesman, and R. Weiss, eds., *Institutions and the Person*. Chicago: Aldine, 1968, pp. 221–235.

GEER, B. "Studying a College." In R. Habenstein, ed., *Pathways to Data*. Chicago: Aldine, 1970, pp. 81–98.

GEER, B., J. HAAS, C. VIVONA, S.J. MILLER, C. WOODS, and H.S. BECKER. "Learning the Ropes: Situational Learning in Four Occupational Training Programs." In I. Deutscher and E. Thompson, eds., *Among the People: Encounters with the Poor*. New York: Basic Books, 1968, pp. 209–233.

GERSON, E. "On 'Quality of Life.'" *American Sociological Review*, 41 (1976), 793–806.

GLASER, B., and A. STRAUSS. "Awareness Contexts and Social Interaction." *American Sociological Review*, 29 (1964), 669–679.

GLASER, B., and A. STRAUSS. *The Discovery of Grounded Theory*. Chicago: Aldine, 1967.

GLASER, B., and A. STRAUSS. *Time for Dying*. Chicago: Aldine, 1968.

GLASER, B., and A. STRAUSS. "The Discovery of Substantive Theory." In W. Filstead, ed., *Qualitative Methodology*. Chicago: Markham, 1970, pp. 288–304.

GLASSNER, B. "Kid Society." *Urban Education*, 11 (1976), 5–22.

GLAZER, M. *The Research Adventure: Promise and Problems of Fieldwork*. New York: Random House, 1972.

GLICK, I., R. WEISS, and C.M. PARKES. *First Years of Bereavement*. New York: Wiley, 1974.

GOFFMAN, E. *The Presentation of Self in Everyday Life*. New York: Doubleday, 1959.

GOFFMAN, E. *Encounters*. Indianapolis: Bobbs-Merrill, 1961.

GOFFMAN, E. *Behavior in Public Places*. Glencoe, Ill.: Free Press, 1963.

GOLD, R.L. "Roles in Sociological Field Observations." *Social Forces*, 36 (1958), 217–223.

GOLDE, P., ed. *Women in the Field: Anthropological Experiences*. Chicago: Aldine, 1970.

GOODMAN, P. *Growing Up Absurd*. New York: Random House, 1960.

GORER, G. *Death, Grief and Mourning*. Garden City, N.Y.: Doubleday, 1967.

GRUEN, J. *The Party's Over Now*. New York: Viking, 1972.

HAAS, J. "Binging: Educational Control among High-Steel Iron Workers." *American Behavioral Scientist*, 16 (1972), 27–34.

HAAS, J., and W. SHAFFIR. "The Professionalization of Medical Students: Developing Competence and a Cloak of Competence." *Symbolic Interaction*, 1 (1977), 71–88.

HAAS, J., and W. SHAFFIR. "Do New Ways of Professional Socialization Make a Difference? A Study of Professional Socialization." Paper presented at the Ninth World Congress of Sociology. Uppsala, Sweden, August 1978.

HABENSTEIN, R., ed. *Pathways to data: Field Methods for Studying Ongoing Social Organizations*. Chicago: Aldine, 1970.

HADDEN, J.K. *The Gathering Storm in the Churches.* Garden City, N.Y.: Doubleday, 1969.

HAMMOND, P.G., ed. *Sociologists at Work: Essays on the Craft of Social Research.* New York: Basic Books, 1964.

HANNERZ, U. *Soulside.* New York: Columbia University Press, 1969.

HEARN, H.L., and P. STOLL. "Continuance Commitment in Low-Status Occupations: The Cocktail Waitress." *Sociological Quarterly,* 16 (1976), 105–114.

HEINEMANN, G. "Methodology." In H.Z. Lopata, ed., *Support Systems Involving Widows in a Metropolitan Area of the United States,* Appendix A3. Washington, D.C.: U.S. Government Printing Office, Social Security Administration, 1977.

HENSLIN, J.M. "Trust and the Cab Driver." In M. Truzzi, ed., *Sociology and Everyday Life.* Englewood Cliffs, N.J.: Prentice-Hall, 1968.

HUGHES, E.C. "Mistakes at Work." *Canadian Journal of Economics and Political Science,* 17 (1951), 320–327.

HUGHES, E.C. "Introduction: The Place of Field Work and Social Science." In B. Junker, *Field Work: An Introduction to the Social Sciences.* Chicago: University fo Chicago Press, 1960, pp. iii–xiii.

HUGHES, E.C. *The Sociological Eye.* Chicago: Aldine, 1971a.

HUGHES, E.C. "The Place of Work in Social Science." In E.C. Hughes, ed., *The Sociological Eye.* Chicago: Aldine, 1971b, pp. 496–506.

HUGHES, E.C. "Dilemmas and Contradictions of Status." In E.C. Hughes, ed. *The Sociological Eye.* Chicago: Aldine, 1971c, pp. 141–150.

HUMPHREYS, L. *Tearoom Trade: Impersonal Sex in Public Places,* enlarged ed. Chicago: Aldine, 1975. (Orig. 1970.)

IRWIN, J. "Participant Observation of Criminals." In J.D. Douglas, ed., *Research on Deviance.* New York: Random House, 1972, pp. 117–137.

JACOBS, J.B. "Participant Observation in Prison." *Urban Life and Culture,* 3 (1974), 221–240.

JANES, ROBERT W. "A Note on Phases of the Community Role of the Participant Observer." *American Sociological Review,* 26 (1961), 446–450.

JETTE, P.R., and F. MONTANINO. "Face to Face Interaction in the Criminal Justice System." *Criminology,* 16 (1978), 67–86.

JOHNSON, J.M. *Doing Field Research.* New York: Free Press, 1975.

JUNKER, B.H. *Field Work: An Introduction to the Social Sciences.* Chicago: University of Chicago Press, 1960.

KARP, D., G. STONE, and W. YOELS. *Being Urban: A Social Psychological View of City Life.* Lexington, Mass.: D.C. Heath, 1977.

KLEINMAN, S., and G.A. FINE. "Rhetorics and Action in Moral Organizations: Social Control of Little Leaguers and Ministry Students." *Urban Life,* forthcoming.

KLOCKARS, C.B. *The Professional Fence.* New York: Macmillan, 1974.

KOTARBA, J.A. "American Acupuncturists: The New Entrepreneurs of Hope." *Urban Life,* 4 (1975), 149–177.

KOTARBA, J.A. "The Chronic Pain Experience." In J.D. Douglas and J.M. Johnson, eds., *Existential Sociology.* New York: Cambridge University Press, 1977, pp. 257–272.

KOTARBA, J.A. "Alcohol Use and the Interstitial Management of Chronic Pain." Paper presented at the annual meeting of the Society for the Study of Symbolic Interactionism. San Francisco: September 1978.

KUHN, M.H. "The Interview and the Professional Relationship." In A.M. Rose, ed., *Human Behavior and Social Processes*. Boston: Houghton Mifflin, 1962, pp. 193-206.

LARSON, M.S. *The Rise of Professionalism: A Sociological Analysis*. Berkeley: University of California Press, 1977.

LEVINE, D., ed. *Georg Simmel on Individuality and Social Forms*. Chicago: University of Chicago Press, 1971.

LEVINE, E.M. "Chicago's Art World: The Influence of Status Interests on Its Social and Distribution Systems. *Urban Life and Culture*, 1 (1972), 293-323.

LIGHT, M. "Some Automotive Play Activities of Suburban Teenagers," *New York Folklore Quarterly*, 30 (1974), 44-65.

LIEBOW, E. *Tally's Corner*. Boston: Little, Brown, 1967.

LINDEMANN, E. "Symptomatology and Management of Acute Grief." *American Journal of Psychiatry*, 101 (1944), 141-148.

LIPMAN-BLUMEN, J. "The Vicarious Achievement Ethic in Non-Traditional Roles for Women." Paper presented at the annual meeting of the Eastern Sociological Society, 1973.

LIVINGSTON, J. *Compulsive Gamblers*. New York: Harper & Row, 1974.

LOFLAND, J.A. *Analyzing Social Settings: A Guide to Qualitative Observation and Analysis*. Belmont, Calif.: Wadsworth, 1971.

LOFLAND, J.A. *Doing Social Life: The Qualitative Study of Human Interaction in Natural Settings*. New York: Wiley, 1976.

LOFLAND, J.A. "Reply to Davis' Comment on Initial Interaction." *Social Problems*, 8 (1961), 365-375.

LOFLAND, J.A., and R.A. LEJEUNE. "Initial Interaction of Newcomers in Alcoholics Anonymous: A Field Experiment in Class Symbols and Socialization." *Social Problems*, 8 (1960), 102-111.

LOPATA, H.Z. *Occupation: Housewife*. New York: Oxford University Press, 1971.

LOPATA, H.Z. *Widowhood in an American City*. Cambridge, Mass.: Schenkman, 1973.

LOPATA, H.Z. *Women as Widows: Support Systems*. New York: Elsevier, 1979.

LYMAN, S., and M. SCOTT. *Sociology of the Absurd*. New York: Appleton-Century-Crofts, 1970.

LYON, E. "Behind the Scenes: The Organization of Theatrical Production." Ph.D. dissertation, Evanston: Northwestern University, 1975.

MADAN, T.N. "Political Pressures and Ethical Constraints upon Indian Sociologists." In G. Sjoberg, ed., *Ethics, Politics, and Social Research*. Cambridge, Mass.: Schenkman, 1967, pp. 162-179.

MAINES, D.R. "A Topical Consideration of Observational Data Pertaining to Behavior in the Subway." Mimeo.

MAINES, D.R. "Tactile Relationships in the Subway as Affected by Racial, Sexual and Crowded Seating Situations." *Environmental Psychology and Nonverbal Behavior*, 2 (1977), 100-108.

MAINES, D.R. "Ecological and Negotiation Processes in New York Subways." *Journal of Social Psychology*, 108 (1979), 29-36.

MANN, F.C. "Human Relations Skills in Social Research." In W.J. Filstead, ed., *Qualitative Methodology*. Chicago: Markham, 1970.

MARRIS, P. *Widows and their Families*. London: Routledge & Kegan Paul, 1958.

MARTIN, W.B. *The Negotiated Order of the School*. Toronto: Macmillan of Canada Ltd., 1976.

MATZA, D. *Delinquency and Drift*. New York: Wiley, 1964.

MATZA, D. *Becoming Deviant*. Englewood Cliffs, N.J.: Prentice-Hall, 1969.

McCALL, G.J. "The Social Organization of Relationships." In G.J. McCall, M.M. McCall, N.K. Denzin, G.D. Suttles, and S.B. Kurth, eds., *Social Relationships*. Chicago: Aldine, 1970, pp. 3-34.

McCALL, G.J. *Observing the Law*. Rockville, Md.: National Institutes of Mental Health, Crime and Delinquency Issues, 1975.

McCALL, G.J., and J.L. SIMMONS, eds. *Issues in Participant Observation*. Reading, Mass.: Addison-Wesley, 1969.

McCALL, M.M. "Boundary Rules and Relationships in Encounters." In G.J. McCall, M.M. McCall, N.K. Denzin, G.D. Suttles, and S.B. Kurth, eds., *Social Relationships*. Chicago: Aldine, 1970, pp. 35-61.

McCALL, M.M. "The Sociology of Female Artists: A Study of Female Painters, Sculptors, and Printmakers in St. Louis." Ph.D. dissertation, Urbana: University of Illinois, 1975.

McCALL, M.M. "Art Without a Market: Creating Artistic Value in a Provincial Art World." *Symbolic Interaction*, 1 (1977), 32-43.

MEAD, G.H. *The Philosophy of the Present*. Chicago: Open Court Press, 1932.

MERTON, R.K., G.G. READER, and P.L. KENDALL, eds. *The Student Physician*. Cambridge, Mass.: Harvard University Press, 1957.

MERTON, R.K. "Forward" In Bernard Barber, *Science and the Social Order*. Rev. ed. New York: Collier Books, 1962.

MILGRAM, S. "The Experience of Living in Cities." *Science*, 167 (1970), 1461-1468.

MILLER, B. "Adult Sexual Resocialization: Adjustments Toward a Stigmatized Identity." *Alternative Lifestyles*, 1 (1978a), 207-234.

MILLER, B. "Stigma Contamination: Attitudes and Adjustments of Women Married to Gay Men." Paper presented at the meeting of the Canadian Psychological Association. Ottawa, Canada: June 1978b.

MILLER, B., and L. HUMPHREYS. "Life Style as a Neglected Variable in Criminal Victimization." Paper presented at the meetings of the Sociology of Lifestyles Conference. Los Angeles: September 1978.

MILLER, B. "Gay Fathers and Their Children." *Family Coordinator* 28 (1979).

MILLER, S.M. "The Participant Observer and 'Over-Rapport,'" *American Sociological Review*, 17 (1952), 97-99.

MILLMAN, M. *The Unkindest Cut*. New York: Morrow, 1976.

MILNER, R., and C. MILNER. *Black Players: The Secret World of Black Pimps*. Boston: Little, Brown, 1972.

MORGAN, M. *The Total Woman*. Old Tappan, N.J.: Revell, 1973.

MORTON, M.E., and W.G. WEST. *An Evaluation of the Frontenac Juvenile Diversion Program.* Ottawa: Ministry of the Solicitor General, 1978.

NASH, D. "The Ethnologist as Stranger: An Essay on the Sociology of Knowledge." *Southwestern Journal of Anthropology,* 19 (1963), 159–167.

NEJELSKI, P., and K. FINSTERBUSCH. "The Prosecutor and the Researcher: Present Prospective Variation in the Supreme Court's *Bransburg* Decision." *Social Problems,* 21 (1973), 3–21.

NEWBY, H. "In the Field: Reflections on the Study of Suffolk Farm Workers." In C. Bell and H. Newby, eds., *Doing Sociological Research.* London: Allen & Unwin, 1977, pp. 108–129.

NEWELL, W.W. *Games and Songs of American Children.* New York: Dover, 1963. (Orig. 1883.)

NEWTON, ESTER. *Mothercamp: Female Impersonators in America.* Englewood Cliffs, N.J.: Prentice-Hall, 1972.

NYE, I.F., and F.M. BERARDO. *The Family.* New York: Macmillan, 1973.

OLESEN, V.L., and E.W. WHITTAKER. *The Silent Dialogue.* San Francisco: Jossey-Bass, 1968.

OPIE, I., and P. OPIE. *Lore and Lanaguage of School Children.* London: Oxford University Press, 1959.

ORNE, M.T. "On the Social Psychology of the Psychological Experiment." *American Psychologist,* 17 (1962), 776–783.

PAUL, B. "Interview Techniques and Field Relationships." In A.L. Kroeber, ed., *Anthropology Today.* Chicago: University of Chicago Press, 1953, pp. 430–451.

POLSKY, N. *Hustlers, Beats, and Others.* Garden City, N.Y.: Doubleday, 1969.

POWDERMAKER, H. *Strangers and Friends: The Way of an Anthropologist.* New York: Norton, 1966.

POWDERMAKER, H. "Field Work." In D.L. Sills, ed., *International Encyclopedia of the Social Sciences,* Vol. 5. New York: Macmillan, 1968, pp. 418–424.

PRUS, R., and C.R.D. SHARPER. *Road Hustler: Career Contingencies of Professional Card and Dice Hustlers.* Lexington, Mass.: Lexington Books, 1977.

PRUS, R., and S. VASSILAKOPOULOUS. "Desk Clerks and Hookers: Hustling in a 'Shady' Hotel." Paper presented at the Canadian Sociology and Anthropology Meetings. Fredericton, New Brunswick: 1977.

RAINS, P. *Becoming an Unwed Mother.* Chicago: Aldine, 1971.

RAINWATER, L., and D.J. PITTMAN. "Ethical Problems in Studying a Politically Sensitive and Deviant Community." *Social Problems,* 14 (1967), 357–366.

ROADBURG, A. "Is Professional Football a Profession?" *International Review of Sport Sociology,* 3 (1976), 27–37.

ROBINSON, W.S. "A Logical Structure of Analytic Induction." *American Sociological Review,* 16 (1951), 812–818.

ROSENTHAL, R. "Interpersonal Expectations." In R. Rosenthal and R. Rosnow, eds., *Sources of Artifact in Social Research.* New York: Academic Press, 1970, pp. 181–277.

ROSENTHAL, R., and R. ROSNOW, eds. *Sources of Artifact in Social Research.* New York: Academic Press, 1970.

Rosow, I. *The Social Integration of the Aged.* New York: Free Press, 1967.
Ross, A. "Philanthropic Activity and the Business Career." *Social Forces,* 32 (1954), 257-280.
Roszak, T. *The Making of a Counter Culture.* New York: Doubleday, 1969.
Roth, J. "Comments on Secret Observation." *Social Problems,* 9 (1960), 283-284.
Roth, J. "Management Bias in Social Science Study of Medical Treatment." *Human Organization,* 21 (1962), 47-50.
Roth, J. *Timetables.* Indianapolis: Bobbs-Merrill, 1963.
Roth, J. "Hired Hand Research." *American Sociologist,* 1 (1966), 190-196.
Roy, D. "The Role of the Researcher in the Study of Social Conflict: A Theory of Protective Distortion of Response." *Human Organization,* 24 (1965), 262-271.
Roy, D. "The Study of Southern Labor Union Organizing Campaigns." In R. Habenstein, ed., *Pathways to Data.* Chicago: Aldine, 1970.
Rynkiewich, M.A., and J.F. Spradley. "The Nacerima: A Neglected Culture." In J.F. Spradley and M.A. Rynkiewich, eds., *The Nacerima.* Boston: Little, Brown, 1975.
Sagarin, E. "The Research Setting and the Right Not to Be Researched." *Social Problems,* 21 (1973), 52-65.
Sanders, C.R. "Psyching out the Crowd: Folk Performers and Their Audiences." *Urban Life and Culture,* 3 (1974), 264-282.
Sanders, C.R. "Caught in the Con-game: The Young, White Drug User's Contact with the Legal System." *Law and Society Review,* 9 (1975), 197-217.
Sanders, C.R., and E. Lyon. "The Humanistic Professional: The Reorientation of Artistic Production." In J.E. Gerstl and G. Jacobs, eds., *Professions for the People: The Politics of Skill.* Cambridge, Mass.: Schenkman, 1976.
Schaps, E., and C. Sanders. "Purposes, Patterns and Protection in a Campus Drug Using Community." *Journal of Health and Social Behavior,* 11 (1970), 135-145.
Schatzman, L., and A. Strauss. *Field Research: Strategies for a Natural Sociology.* Englewood Cliffs, N.J.: Prentice-Hall, 1973.
Schwartz, Morris S., and Charlotte Green Schwartz. "Problems in Participant Observation." *American Journal of Sociology,* 60 (1955), 343-353.
Shaffir, W. *Life in a Religious Community.* Toronto: Holt, Rinehart and Winston of Canada, 1974.
Shaffir, W., V. Marshall, and J. Haas. "Competing Commitments: Unanticipated Problems of Field Research." *Qualitative Sociology,* 1979.
Sherif, M., and C.W. Sherif. *Groups in Harmony and Tension.* New York: Harper & Row, 1953.
Sherif, M., O.J. Harvey, B.J. White, W.R. Hood, and C.W. Sherif. *Intergroup Conflicts and Cooperation: The Robbers Cave Experiment.* Norman, Okla.: University of Oklahoma Book Exchange, 1961.
Sherman, S.R. "Demand Curves in an Experiment on Attitude Change." *Sociometry,* 30 (1967), 246-261.
Shipman, M., ed. *The Organization and Impact of Social Research.* London: Routledge & Kegan Paul, 1976.
Shupe, A.D., Jr., J.C. Ventimiglia, D.G. Bromley, and S. Stigall. "Political

Control of Radically Innovative Religions." Paper presented at the annual meeting of the Association for the Scientific Study of Religion: Southwest, 1977.

SHUPE, A.D., JR., R. SPIELMANN, and S. STIGALL. "Deprogramming: The New Exorcism." *American Behavioral Scientist*, 20 (1977a), 941–956.

SHUPE, A.D., JR., R. SPIELMANN, and S. STIGALL. "Deprogramming and the Emerging American Anti-Cult Movement." Paper presented at the annual meeting of the Society for the Scientific Study of Religion, 1977b.

SIMMEL, G. "The Triad." In K.H. Wolff, ed., *The Sociology of George Simmel.* New York: Free Press, 1950, pp. 145–169.

SIMMEL, G. "The Secret." In K.H. Wolff, ed., *The Sociology of George Simmel.* New York: Free Press, 1950, pp. 307–376.

SNIDER, L., and W.G. WEST. "Crime and Conflict in Canada." In R.J. Ossenberg, ed., *Canadian Society: Conflict and Change.* Toronto: McClelland and Stewart, 1979.

SPECTOR, M. "Legitimizing Homosexuality." *Society* (July/August 1977), 52–56.

SPECTOR, M., and J.I. KITSUSE. *Constructing Social Problems.* Menlo Park, Calif.: Cummings, 1977.

SPEIER, M. *How to Observe Face-to-face Communication.* Pacific Palisades, Calif.: Goodyear, 1973.

STEBBINS, R.A. "The Unstructured Research Interview as an Incipient Interpersonal Relationship." *Sociology and Social Research*, 56 (1972), 164–172.

STEBBINS, R.A. "Putting People On: Deception of Our Fellow Man in Everyday Life." *Sociology and Social Research*, 59 (1975), 189–200.

STRAUS, R. "The Nature and Status of Medical Sociology." *American Sociological Review*, 22 (1957), 203–213.

STRAUSS, A., L. SCHATZMAN, R. BUCHER, D. EHRLICH, and M. SABSHIN. *Psychiatric Ideologies and Institutions.* New York: Free Press, 1964.

SUTHERLAND, E., and C. CONWELL. *Professional Thief.* Chicago: University of Chicago Press, 1967.

SUTTLES, G. *The Social Order of the Slum.* Chicago: University of Chicago Press, 1967.

SZASZ, T. *Ideology and Insanity.* Garden City, N.Y.: Anchor Books, 1970

TORNABENE, L. *I Passed as a Teenager.* New York: Simon & Schuster, 1967.

TOWNSEND, P. *The Family Life of Old People.* London: Routledge & Kegan Paul, 1957.

TRAVISANO, R.V. "Alternation and Conversion as Qualitatively Different Transformations." In G.P. Stone and H.A. Farberman, eds., *Social Psychology Through Symbolic Interaction.* Waltham, Mass.: Ginn, 1970.

TREAS. J.K., and L.A. MORGAN. "Widowhood Stigma: Pitfall to Intervening and Advocacy." Paper presented at the Widowhood and Middle-age session of the Eleventh International Congress on Gerontology. Tokyo, Japan: August 1978.

TROLL, L., J. ISRAEL, and K. ISRAEL, eds. *Looking Ahead: A Woman's Guide to the Problems and Joys of Growing Older.* Englewood Cliffs, N.J.: Prentice-Hall, 1977.

TUNSTALL, J. *Old and Alone.* London: Routledge & Kegan Paul, 1966.

TURNER, R.H. "The Quest for Universals in Sociological Research." *American Sociological Review*, 18 (1953), 604–611.

TUROWETZ, ALLAN. "An Ethnography of Professional Wrestling: Elements of a Staged Contest." Unpublished M.A. thesis, McGill University, 1974.

VALENTINE, C. *Culture and Poverty*. Chicago: University of Chicago Press, 1968.

VIDICH, A. "Participant Observation and the Collection and Interpretation of Data." *American Journal of Sociology*, 60 (1955), 354–360.

VIDICH, A., and J. BENSMAN. "The Springdale Case: Academic Bureaucrats and Sensitive Townspeople." In A. Vidich, J. Bensman, and M.R. Stein, eds., *Reflections on Community Studies*. New York: Harper & Row, 1964, pp. 313–349.

VIDICH, A., and J. BENSMAN. *Small Town in Mass Society*. Princeton, N.J.: Princeton University Press, 1968.

VIDICH, A., J. BENSMAN, and M.R. STEIN, eds. *Reflections on Community Studies*. New York: Harper & Row, 1964.

WALLIS, R. "The Moral Career of a Research Project." In C. Bell and H. Newby, eds., *Doing Sociological Research*. London: Allen & Unwin, 1977a, pp. 149–167.

WALLIS, R. *The Road to Total Freedom: A Sociological Analysis of Scientology*. New York: Columbia University Press, 1977b.

WAX, R. *Doing Field Work: Warnings and Advice*. Chicago: University of Chicago Press, 1971.

WEBB, E.J., D.T. CAMPBELL, R.D. SCHWARTZ, and L. SECHREST. *Unobtrusive Measures: Nonreactive Measures in the Social Sciences*. Chicago: Rand-McNally, 1966.

WEINBERG, M.S., and C.J. WILLIAMS. "Fieldwork Among Deviants: Social Relations with Subjects and Others." In J. Douglas, ed., *Research on Deviance*. New York: Random House, 1972, pp. 165–186.

WERTHMAN, C. Delinquency and moral character. In D. Cressey and D. Ward, eds., *Delinquency, Crime, and Social Process*. New York: Harper & Row, 1969, pp. 613–632.

WEST, W.G. "Drifting Clusters: A Study of Non-Gang Delinquency." B.A. thesis. Toronto: Dept. of Sociology, York University, 1968.

WEST, W.G. "Adolescent Perspectives: On being a Greaser, Freak or Straight." Paper presented at the annual meetings of the Canadian Sociology and Anthropology Association. Edmonton, Canada, 1971.

WEST, W.G. "Serious Thieves: Lower-class Adolescent Males in a Short-term Deviant Occupation." Ph.D. dissertation, Evanston: Northwestern University, Dept. of Sociology, 1974.

WEST, W.G. "Participant Observation Research on the Social Construction of Everyday Classroom Order." *Interchange*, 6 (1975), 35–43.

WEST, W.G. "Adolescent Perspectives and Delinquency: A Corroboration of Control Theory." Kingston, Ontario: Dept. of Sociology, Queens University, 1977a.

WEST, W.G. "Adolescent Territoriality." Kingston, Ontario: Dept. of Sociology, Queen's University, 1977b.

WEST, W.G. "Participant Observation in Canadian Classrooms: The Need,

Rationale, Technique and Development Implications. *Canadian Journal of Education*, 2 (1977c), 55–74.

WEST, W.G. "The Short-term Careers of Serious Thieves. *Canadian Journal of Criminology*, 20 (1978a), 169–90.

WEST, W.G. "Serious Theft as an Occupation." Paper presented to the annual meetings of the Society for the Study of Social Problems. San Francisco, 1978b.

WEST, W.G. Serious Thieves: Lower-class Adolescent Males in a Short-term Deviant Occupation." In E. Vaz and N.A. Lodhi, eds., *Crime and Delinquency: The Canadian Case*. Toronto: Prentice-Hall, 1978c, pp. 247–268.

WEST, W.G. "Adolescent Perspectives and Identity Changes." *Adolescence*, Forthcoming.

WHITE, H., and C. WHITE. *Canvases and Careers*. New York: Wiley, 1965.

Who's Who in American Art. New York: Jacques Cattell Press, 1973.

WHYTE, W.F. *Street Corner Society*. Chicago: University of Chicago Press, 1955. (Orig. 1943.)

WILLIAMS, T.R. *Field Methods in the Study of Culture*. New York: Holt, Rinehart and Winston, 1967.

WISEMAN, J. *Stations of the Lost: The Treatment of Skid Row Alcoholics*. Englewood Cliffs, N.J.: Prentice-Hall, 1970.

WISEMAN, J. "The Research Web." *Urban Life and Culture*, 3 (1974), 317–328.

YABLONSKY, L. "Experiences with the Criminal Community." In A. Gouldner and S.M. Miller, eds., *Applied Sociology*. New York: Free Press, 1965, pp. 55–73.

ZELDITCH, M., JR. "Some Methodological Problems of Field Studies." *American Journal of Sociology*, 67 (1962), 566–576.

ZNANIECKI, F. *The Method of Sociology*. New York: Farrar and Rinehart, 1934.

Index